Essential Skills for Management Research

Essential Skills for Management Research

Edited by David Partington

SAGE Publications
London • Thousand Oaks • New Delhi

Editorial selection © David Partington 2002
Chapter 1 © Robert Chia 2002
Chapter 2 © Nada Korac-Kakabadse, Andrew Kakabadse and
Alexander Kouzmin 2002
Chapter 3 © David A. Whetten 2002
Chapter 4 © Anne Sigismund Huff 2002
Chapter 5 © Kim James and Susan Vinnicombe 2002
Chapter 6 © Phyl Johnson and Don Harris 2002
Chapter 7 © Val Singh and John Dickson 2002
Chapter 8 © David Partington 2002
Chapter 9 © Alan Harrison 2002
Chapter 10 © Mark Jenkins 2002
Chapter 11 © Keith Goffin 2002
Chapter 12 © Susan Baker 2002
Chapter 13 © Colin Eden and Chris Huxham 2002

First published 2002

SAGE Publications Ltd
6 Bonhill Street
London EC2A 4PU

SAGE Publications Inc
2455 Teller Road
Thousand Oaks, California 91320

SAGE Publications India Pvt Ltd
32, M-Block Market
Greater Kailash – I
New Delhi 110 048

British Library Cataloguing in Publication data

A catalogue record for this book is
available from the British Library

ISBN 0–7619–7007–X
ISBN 0–7619–7008–8 (pbk)

Library of Congress Control Number: 2001132942

Typeset by M Rules
Printed in Great Britain by The Cromwell Press Ltd,
Trowbridge, Wiltshire

Contents

7 Ethnographic Approaches to the Study of Organizations 117

Val Singh and John Dickson

8 Grounded Theory 136

David Partington

9 Case Study Research 158

Alan Harrison

Contributors

Susan Baker lectures in marketing at Cranfield School of Management. Prior to academia, Susan pursued a ten-year career in services marketing in leisure retailing from which she gained experience on both client and agency sides of the business. She worked at senior management level in the UK and also in Germany. At Cranfield, Susan specializes in bringing learning from consumer marketing to organizations across all sectors. Her particular focus is on understanding consumer markets and she is co-director of the New Marketing Research Group which aims to understand the impact on marketing of the postmodern consumer. She firmly believes in the notion that a picture paints a thousand words, hence the appeal of laddering and mapping, and she has employed a means–end approach to understanding buyer behaviour across various product categories, among adults and young consumers.

Robert Chia is Professor of Strategy and Organization at the School of Business and Economics, University of Exeter. He is the author of three books and a significant number of journal articles on organization theory and management and has presented numerous conference papers at the US Academy of Management, the British Academy of Management and other international conferences in management and organization studies. Robert holds a Masters degree (with distinction) in organizational analysis and behaviour and a PhD in organization studies. He is a Fellow of the Royal Society of Arts and has consulted with a number of international organizations and institutions including the International Federation of the Red Cross (Geneva), British Airways, BNFL, British Aerospace, Ciba–Geigy and Cathay Pacific Airlines.

Prior to entering academia, he worked for 16 years in aircraft maintenance engineering, manufacturing management and human resource management and was group human resource manager of Metal Box Asia Pacific based in Singapore before he left to pursue an academic career. Since then he has remained actively engaged with the practitioner world of management, particularly through consultancy work and executive training and education. His main research interests revolve around the issues of world-views, modes of thought and their implications for strategic vision and foresight; complexity and creativity; contrasting East–West metaphysical attitudes; critical cultural studies and postmodernism.

John Dickson is an independent management consultant, who undertook his doctorate at Cranfield School of Management. John's ethnographic study of enterprise in Papua New Guinea identified a new model for doing business in a rural community. His consulting work in strategy development, organizational change and marketing assists companies to become more effective by incorporating 'soft' issues such as culture with more traditional 'hard' issues of task and budget. John has consulted for international agencies such as UNICEF and UNHCR on the design and delivery of their business development programmes. He also has wide experience of the problems faced by growing businesses. As well as his work with local enterprise agencies in the UK, John frequently lectures on small business and entrepreneurship at the micro level.

Colin Eden is Director of the University of Strathclyde Graduate School of Business, and is Professor of Management Science. He has written over 200 articles published in management, operational research and strategy journals. He has published seven books in the field of management science, managerial and organizational cognition, group decision support and strategy-making. His most recent book, with Fran Ackermann and entitled *Making Strategy: The Journey of Strategic Management*, introduces an attention to the strategy-making process and the role of qualitative modelling to a strategic management audience. Recently he has been a consultant to the senior management teams of, for example, Scottish Natural Heritage, Bombardier Inc., the Northern Ireland Office, Elsevier Science and the Royal Ulster Constabulary. As well as a continuing interest in strategic problem-solving and strategy-making, he is currently conducting research into strategic risk and the behaviour of disrupted and delayed complex projects.

Keith Goffin is Professor of Innovation Management at Stuttgart Institute of Management and Technology (SIMT) in Germany and a visiting professor at Cranfield School of Management. He graduated with a first class honours degree in Physics in 1977 and subsequently obtained an MSc in Medical Physics. For 14 years he worked for the Medical Products Group of Hewlett-Packard, in a number of management roles in marketing and product support. Parallel to his management responsibilities, Keith researched the management of customer support and received his PhD in 1992. From 1995–2001 he was full-time member of the faculty at Cranfield, where he taught on both MBA and Executive Programmes. His main research interest is innovation management and he has published one book and over 80 reports, papers and articles. He has extensive experience of using repertory grid technique in, for example, studies of customer support, supplier management and new product development.

Don Harris is Senior Research Fellow in Human Factors Engineering in the Human Factors Group at Cranfield School of Management. His principal teaching and research interests lie in the design and evaluation of flight deck control and display systems, accident investigation and analysis, and system safety. Until recently he was also an aircraft accident investigator (specializing in human factors) on call to the British Army Division of Army Aviation. Don has also worked in the safety assessment of helicopter operations for North Sea oil exploration and exploitation. Don is a professional member of the Ergonomics Society and the International Association of Applied Psychologists. He is Chairman of the International Conference Series on Engineering Psychology and Cognitive Ergonomics. Don sits on the editorial boards of the *International Journal of Cognitive Ergonomics*, the *International Journal of Cognition, Technology and Work* and is also co-editor in chief of the academic journal *Human Factors and Aerospace Safety*.

Alan Harrison is Professor of Operations and Logistics at Cranfield School of Management. After graduating in chemistry at Oxford University, he followed a career in manufacturing industry with Procter & Gamble, BL and GEC. Having been converted to academic life, he joined Warwick Business School in 1986 as a senior research fellow studying the application of Japanese manufacturing methods to UK manufacturing. He completed his doctorate in enablers and inhibitors to material flow at Cranfield School of Management, which he joined in 1996. He is author of *Just in Time Manufacturing in Perspective* (Prentice Hall, 1992), joint author of *Operations Management* (2nd edition, Pitman, 1998) and author of *Logistics Management and Strategy* (Pearson Education, 2002).

Alan has undertaken extensive research into supply chains in several sectors, including automotive, aerospace and grocery. He has extended his research base from applications of just in time to limitations of this approach, and his recent work has been concerned with developing capabilities for enhanced customer responsiveness. This has resulted in such publications as *Creating the Agile Supply Chain* (Institute of Logistics and Transport, 1999) and the establishment of the Agile Supply Chain Research Club at Cranfield, which has attracted some £850k in funds.

Anne Sigismund Huff is a Professor in Strategic Management at the University of Colorado, Boulder who also holds a professorial appointment at Cranfield School of Management. She received an MA in Sociology and a PhD in Management from Northwestern University, and has been on the faculty at UCLA and the University of Illinois. Her research interests focus on strategic change, both as a dynamic process of interaction among firms and as a cognitive process affected by the interaction of individuals over time. She is the strategy editor for the book series *Foundations in Organization Science* (Sage Publications) and serves on the editorial boards of the *Strategic Management Journal*, the *Journal of Management Studies*, the *British Journal of Management*, *Management Learning* and the electronic journal, *M@n@gement*. In 1998–99 she was President of the Academy of Management, an international organization of over 11,000 scholars interested in management issues.

Chris Huxham is Professor of Management and Director of Research in the University of Strathclyde Graduate School of Business. She has led an action research programme spanning more than 12 years that is concerned with the development of practice-oriented theory into the management of collaborative ventures. This involves her in working extensively with practitioners involved in partnerships and alliances. She takes a variety of roles in these interventions, including facilitator, awareness raiser, sounding board, policy adviser and participant. She has published extensively both on collaboration and on action research as a research methodology. She is editor of *Creating Collaborative Advantage* (Sage, 1996) and an Editorial Board member of *Public Management Review*. Chris graduated from the University of Sussex with a BSc in Mathematics, an MSc and DPhil in Operational Research.

Kim James is a Chartered Psychologist. She obtained her PhD for research into the career development needs of senior executives. She has worked as a consultant in a wide range of organizations, including automotive, aerospace, pharmaceutical, insurance, banking and distributive companies, police, local authorities, the health service and utilities.

Kim works with clients to assist their capacity for organization learning and change at both personal and organization levels; understanding organization dynamics can help organizations in transition and transformation in a very practical way. Her current interests include managing people through transition, personal development for leadership, women managers' development, organizational stress management, coaching and team consulting for strategic learning.

At Cranfield School of Management, Kim has directed many public and in-house management development programmes as well as postgraduate teaching and supervision. She is the Director of the Research Methodology Course for PhD students researching at the School of Management. She is currently on the editorial boards of *Management Learning* and the *Journal of Management Development*.

Mark Jenkins is Professor of Competitive Strategy and Director of the DBA programme at Cranfield School of Management. Prior to joining Cranfield he worked for the Lex Service Group and Massey Ferguson Tractors Ltd. His teaching focuses on the areas of competitive strategy, knowledge management and innovation. His consulting activities reflect these specializations where he has worked throughout Europe, the USA and in parts of the Far East and Middle East. In addition to his work at Cranfield he has been a visiting Professor in Strategic Management at the University of Colorado and has contributed to the MBA programme at Warwick Business School. He is currently researching the role of knowledge and innovation in the development of Formula One motorsport. He has published and presented a wide range of work in the areas of strategy and marketing. He is a founding editor of the *Journal of Marketing Practice*, a member of the editorial review board for the *European Journal of Marketing* and is author of *The Customer Centred Strategy* (Pitman, 1997).

Phyl Johnson is a lecturer in Organisational Behaviour at the University of Strathclyde Graduate School of Business. She gained her PhD in shared thinking in top management teams during strategy development from Cranfield School of Management. She is a Chartered Psychologist and is currently training part-time as a psychotherapist and sees clients who are serving personnel or their families, on behalf of HM Naval Base Clyde.

She has presented her work on managerial and organizational cognition at international conferences and contributed chapters to several key research texts in the field. Her areas of research interest are managerial cognition, interaction in top management teams, the role of women directors and emotional life in the boardroom. She acts as a reviewer for the *British Journal of Management*, *Journal of Management Studies* and *Journal of Occupational and Organizational Psychology*.

Andrew Kakabadse is Professor of International Management Development and Deputy Director of Cranfield School of Management. He is also Head of the Human Resources Group. Andrew has published 21 books, over 120 articles, 14 monographs and made over 70 conference presentations. He is Editor of the *Journal of Management Development* and has been Founding Editor of the *Journal of Managerial Psychology* and the *Leadership and Organisational Development Journal*.

He has lectured widely in Europe, the USA, Russia, South East Asia, Japan and China. He is consultant to numerous organizations and to various governments. He is also a non-executive chairman and non-executive director for a number of companies.

Nada Korac-Kakabadse is a Senior Research Fellow at Cranfield School of Management. She has a BSc in Mathematics and Computing, a Graduate Diploma in Management Sciences and a Masters Degree in Public Administration at the University of Canberra (Australia), and has earned her PhD in Management at the University of Western Sydney – Nepean (Australia). Her PhD thesis was concerned with 'Leadership Philosophies and Organizational Adoption of a New Information Technology'.

Nada has co-authored five books (with Andrew Kakabadse), *Leadership in Government: A Comparative Benchmark Analysis* (Ashgate, 1998), *Essence of Leadership* (International Thomson Business Press, 1999), *Creating Futures: Innovative Applications of IS/IT* (Ashgate, 2000), *The Geopolitics of Governance* (Palgrave, 2001) and *Smart Sourcing* (Palgrave, 2002). She has contributed 28 chapters to international volumes and has published 56 scholarly and review articles. She is co-editor of the *Journal of Management Development* and European Editor of the *International Journal of Corporate Governance*.

Alexander Kouzmin holds the Chair in Organizational Behaviour at the Cranfield School of Management. He has published eight volumes of commissioned work. Among these are his edited *Public Sector Administration: New Perspectives* (Longman Cheshire, 1983); his co-edited (with N. Scott) *Dynamics in Australian Public Management: Selected Essays* (Macmillan, 1990); (with L. Still and P. Clarke) *New Directions in Management* (McGraw Hill, 1994); (with J. Garnett) *Handbook of Administrative Communication* (Marcel Dekker, 1997); and (with A. Hayne) *Essays in Economic Globalization, Trans-national Policies and Vulnerability* (IOP Press, 1999). He has contributed 60 chapters to many national and international volumes and has published some 220 papers, including scholarly and review articles in more than 65 leading international refereed journals. He is on the editorial boards of 11 international journals and is a founding co-editor of the international *Journal of Contingencies and Crisis Management,* published quarterly since 1993.

David Partington lectures in project management and research methods at Cranfield School of Management. He has published several journal articles and book chapters on organization theory and research methods, and has presented a number of papers at conferences, including the British Academy of Management and the US Academy of Management. He is director of the Cranfield programme of management research workshops, which form the basis of this book. Before entering the academic world in 1988 he had more than 17 years' experience as an engineer and manager in the international construction sector, working on major projects in South America, the Middle East and the United Kingdom. He graduated from UMIST with a BSc in engineering, and has an MSc in project management and a PhD in organizational behaviour, both from Cranfield. Working with a number of global organizations, David's research interests include knowledge management and the implementation of programmes of strategic change.

Val Singh is Senior Research Fellow in organizational behaviour, working in the Centre for Developing Women Business Leaders at Cranfield School of Management, where she undertook her doctorate into gender and managerial meanings of 'commitment' in engineering companies in the UK and Sweden. Her current research focuses on three areas: women directors on FTSE 100 company boards; the business case for gender diversity; and impression management strategies for enhanced personal reputation and visibility. She is also interested in career barriers and facilitators for women managers, especially mentoring. Val lectures on the Cranfield Research Methodology Course, taking sessions on Ethnography, Evaluating Research Reports, Introduction to Research Process, and the use of QSR NVivo and NUD.IST qualitative data analysis packages. She has published a number of journal articles, book chapters and conference papers, as well as occasional practitioner and newspaper articles.

Susan Vinnicombe is Professor of Organizational Behaviour and Diversity Management, Director of Graduate Research, and Director of the Cranfield Centre for Developing Women Business Leaders at Cranfield School of Management.

As Director of the Centre for Developing Women Business Leaders Susan designed and directed in-company Women's Management Development Programmes for British Telecom and National Power; both programmes have won prestigious Opportunity 2000 awards. Susan's particular research interests are women's leadership styles and the issues involved in women developing their managerial careers. Increasingly the focus of her work is on the issues facing women operating at, or striving to reach, the highest levels of management.

David A. Whetten is the Jack Wheatley Professor of Organizational Behavior and Director of the Faculty Center at Brigham Young University. Prior to joining the Marriott School of Management in 1994 he was on the faculty at the University of Illinois for 20 years, where he served as Associate Dean of the College of Commerce, Harry Gray Professor of Business Administration, and Director of the Office of Organizational Research.

He currently serves as the Editor of the *Foundations for Organizational Science* series, and he is a former Editor of the *Academy of Management Review*. He has published over 50 articles and books. He received the Outstanding Educator Award from the Organizational Behavior Teaching Society in 1992 for his pioneering work in management skills education.

He has been an active member of the Academy of Management. In 1994 he received the Academy's Distinguished Service Award, he was elected an Academy Fellow in 1991, and in 1996 he was elected to a five-year term as an officer, culminating with his presidency in 2000.

Preface

This book has grown out of a programme of themed management research workshops hosted by Cranfield School of Management. The workshops, which were based on Cranfield's doctoral research methods programme, were attended by research students, professional researchers and teachers of management research from a wide variety of academic institutions. Many of the book's authors have been associated with these programmes, and with wider research agendas at Cranfield and elsewhere. Our collective experiences of an evolving demand among management researchers to understand and apply particular research tools, approaches and intellectual traditions drive and inform the book's content.

Arising from these experiences the book has two distinctive features. First, there is an emphasis on the practical concerns of management researchers. We focus on the details of developing and applying a particular set of research skills, not just on historical overviews and inward debate. Techniques and frameworks are illustrated by examples of their successful application by the authors and their students, as well as in well-known published exemplars.

Second, the book acknowledges increasingly vocal concerns in European and American management and academic communities that much published management research fails to address practical concerns of managers. Today many students are under pressure to deliver research that makes a practical contribution to solving a particular management problem or usefully enlightening a particular issue in an organization or sector, in addition to making a contribution to knowledge. The book therefore has a strong bias towards research designs which tend towards the interpretive and action-oriented end of the methodological spectrum.

STRUCTURE

The book is divided into three parts. Part 1 is concerned with the crucial links between philosophy and research. Part 2 deals with three important but often neglected general issues relating to the process of conducting and disseminating management research. Part 3 consists of eight chapters each offering its authors' unique insights into specific management research approaches and techniques.

Part 1

Chapter 1: Robert Chia offers a unique view of the *philosophy* of management research. He argues that the wide range of theoretical perspectives – including positivism, hermeneutics, critical theory and realism – are all amalgams of two basic opposing strategies for knowledge creation, characterized as ontologies of *being* and *becoming*. The chapter concludes that only postmodernism presents a radical challenge to traditional approaches, bringing us closer to the realities and pragmatic concerns of the practitioner world.

Chapter 2: Nada Korac-Kakabadse, Andrew Kakabadse and Alexander Kouzmin deal with the branch of philosophy known as *ethics*. They focus on a range of issues of ethical conduct which are particularly important in practically oriented management research. The authors offer a reflexive framework for resolving the range of personal ethical dilemmas that researchers may encounter.

Part 2

Chapter 3: David Whetten provides structured insight into the *theory-development* process. He argues that only good theories are likely to have a practical use, and that producing good theory is a skill which can be taught. By means of an orderly, easy-to-use methodology David explains how to develop theories that meet the twin criteria of being complete and systematic.

Chapter 4: Anne Huff is an established authority on *writing for scholarly publication*. In this chapter she bases her arguments on the premise that scholarship is a community activity, and offers a wealth of hard-won practical advice to management scholars seeking to publish their work.

Chapter 5: Kim James and Sue Vinnicombe encourage researchers to *acknowledge their individuality*, and to take account of their background, personal values, orientations and preferences in the design and conduct of their research. They discuss the importance of self-awareness and reflexive behaviour, and offer a model for understanding natural preferences.

Part 3

Chapter 6: Phyl Johnson and Don Harris compare and contrast *quantitative and qualitative research designs*, and discuss the range of key issues which are likely to concern researchers adopting either – or both – of these broadly categorized approaches in a management setting.

Chapter 7: Val Singh and John Dixon provide an overview of *ethnography* in management research, giving advice on ethnographic processes of observation, interpretation and description. Val and John focus on practical concerns, including gaining access to research settings, collecting and analysing data.

Chapter 8: David Partington describes how the research approach known as *grounded theory* has developed from its sociological origins to become one of the most widely applied strategies for building theories of management action from qualitative data. David offers a practical step-by-step procedure for grounded theory-building.

Chapter 9: Alan Harrison dispels common myths and misconceptions surrounding *case study research*, and presents an insightful guide to this approach. The chapter provides a highly practical, yet rigorous guide to ensuring that the case study methodology delivers useful research results of high quality.

Chapter 10: Mark Jenkins introduces the technique known as *cognitive mapping* as the basis for conducting management research. Mark discusses the foundations of the approach in cognitive psychology, and describes its role in offering insights into managerial and organizational behaviour.

Chapter 11: Keith Goffin offers a detailed description of the theory and conduct of *repertory grid technique*, another strategy that can be used in a wide variety of management situations to help respondents articulate their views on complex topics whilst reducing researcher bias.

Chapter 12: Susan Baker introduces the powerful, structured approach to in-depth interviewing and analysis known as *laddering*. The laddering technique is used to understand meaning, linking relatively concrete meanings at an attribute level with abstract meanings of more pervasive existential importance.

Chapter 13: Colin Eden and Chris Huxham describe their approach to *action research*, an interventionist research strategy used where there is intent to bring about change in organizations. The chapter enumerates the essential characteristics of rigorous, action-oriented research.

Acknowledgements

Every effort has been made to trace all the copyright holders, but if any have been inadvertently overlooked the publishers will be pleased to make the necessary arrangement at the first opportunity.

Figure 3.1: D.A. Whetten and K.S. Cameron, *Developing Management Skills, fifth edition*, Figure 5, p. 329, 2002. Upper Saddle River, NJ: Prentice Hall.

Figure 9.1: W.L. Wallace, *The Logic of Science*, p. 18, 1971. Reprinted by permission of Aldine de Gruyter, a division of Walter de Gruyter, Inc.

Figure 9.2: J. Meredith, 'Theory Building through Conceptual Models', *International Journal of Operations & Production Management*, 13 (5): 3, 1993. Reprinted by permission of MCB University Press.

Figure 9.3: J.R. Meredith et al., 'Alternative Research Paradigms in Operations', *Journal of Operations Management*, 8 (4): 309, 1989. Reprinted by permission of Elsevier Science.

Figure 9.4: B.B. Flynn et al., 'Empirical Research Methods in Operations Management', *Journal of Operations Management*, 9 (2): 254, 1990. Reprinted by permission of Elsevier Science.

Table 9.1: C.C. Ragin, *The Comparative Method: Moving Beyond Qualitative and Quantitative*, Table 1, 1987. Reprinted by permission of the University of California Press.

Table 9.2: K.M. Eisenhardt, 'Building Theories from Case Study Research', *Academy of Management Review*, 14 (4): 533, 1989. Reprinted by permission of the Academy of Management.

Figure 10.1: C.D. Wickens, 'A Basic Information-Processing Framework for the Analysis of Human Cognition' in C.D. Wickens and J. Hollands, *Engineering Psychology and Human Performance, third edition*, p.11, 1999. Upper Saddle River, NJ: Prentice Hall.

Figure 10.2: M. Jenkins, 'The Theory and Practice of Comparing Causal Maps' in C. Eden and J.C. Spender (eds), *Managerial and Organizational Cognition: Theory, Methods and Research*, pp. 231–49, 1998. Reprinted by permission of Sage Publications Ltd.

Figure 10.3: J.F. Porac, H. Thomas and C. Baden-Fuller, 'Competitive Groups as Cognitive Communities: The Case of Scottish Knitwear Manufacturers', *Journal of Management Studies*, 26 (4): 407, July 1989. Reprinted by permission of Blackwell Publishers Ltd.

Figure 10.5: M. Jenkins and G. Johnson, 'Entrepreneurial Intentions and Outcomes: A Comparative Causal Mapping Study', *Journal of Management Studies*, 34 (6): 911, November 1997. Reprinted by permission of Blackwell Publishers Ltd.

Figure 10.6: P.S. Barr, J.L. Stimpert and A.S. Huff, 'Cognitive Change, Strategic Action and Organizational Renewal', *Strategic Management Journal*, 13 (Summer Special Issue): 26, 1992. Reprinted by permission of John Wiley & Sons.

Figure 10.7: M. Jenkins, 'Theory and Practice in Comparing Causal Maps' in C. Eden and J.C. Spender (eds), *Managerial and Organizational Cognition*, p. 233, 1998. Reprinted by permission of Sage Publications Ltd.

Chapter 13: C. Eden and C. Huxham, 'Action Research for the Study of Organizations' in S. Clegg, C. Hardy and W. Nord, *Handbook of Organization Studies*, 1996. Reprinted by permission of Sage Publications Ltd.

PART 1

Philosophy and Research

1

The Production of Management Knowledge: Philosophical Underpinnings of Research Design

Robert Chia

OVERVIEW

Management research deals fundamentally with the production and legitimation of the various forms of knowledge associated with the practices of management. Most traditional approaches to management research and knowledge creation involve a varied combination of the key processes of observation, reflection, theoretical conjecturing and the testing of theories and models developed to capture the essence of management realities. A seemingly wide panoply of theoretical perspectives has been proffered in recent times in the social sciences and in management research in particular, including positivism, hermeneutics, phenomenology, critical theory and realism. Despite this apparent diversity of philosophical approaches, this chapter will show that they basically represent various amalgams of two opposing epistemological impulses driving research and knowledge creation in the Western world. Only the more recent rise of postmodernism poses a radical ontological challenge to the metaphysical premises of modern research.

This chapter traces the philosophical roots of modern Western thought and identifies the key philosophical traditions and assumptions shaping perceptions of knowledge and knowledge creation in general and in management research in particular. I begin by examining the crucial link between philosophy and research in order to show how the former informs the latter in the academic production of management knowledge. This is followed by a systematic tracing of the intellectual origins of Western thought and the identification of the key metaphysical foundations of modern knowledge. This, in turn, leads to a discussion and comparison of the two basic strategies of knowledge creation associated with these foundations. The relationships between each of the various theoretical derivatives commonly used and the two basic forms of philosophic thinking are then carefully examined and explained.

PHILOSOPHY AND MANAGEMENT RESEARCH

What is the nature of reality? Are the patterns and regularities we seemingly find around us products of our own imagination or are they embedded in an external objective reality? What attitude of enquiry should we adopt in order to establish with the greatest possible certainty our knowledge of reality? What forms of reasoning should we deploy to help us gain a better understanding of phenomena around us? What is the status of what we believe we know and how do we ascertain if what we believe we know is actually true or false? How do we justify our beliefs to others? Is there any difference between knowledge acquired from learning a theory and knowledge acquired through observation? How do new knowledge discoveries affect the status of what we believe we know? The substantive field of enquiry that examines these and many other related questions is called *philosophy*. Philosophy is primarily concerned with rigorously establishing, regulating and improving the methods of knowledge-creation in all fields of intellectual endeavour, including the field of management research. Many people assume that philosophy deals only with very general and seemingly esoteric questions about nature and reality that have very little to do with everyday life and especially with the applied field of management research. However, this is a rather prejudiced view that bears little resemblance to what philosophy throughout the ages has always been about. Philosophy, in fact, is more a rigorous and enquiring attitude of mind than an academic discipline. In philosophical enquiry, the facts, the theory, the alternatives and the ideals are brought together and weighed against each other in the creation of knowledge. Philosophical thinking revolves around the four pillars of *metaphysics, logic, epistemology* and *ethics*.

Metaphysics is concerned with questions of being and knowing. Is absolute reality permanent and unchanging or is it continuously in flux and transformation? Should we characterize reality as comprising discrete, atomistic entities or should we think of it in terms of fluid and dynamic ebbs and flows? In metaphysical enquiries, therefore, questions of *ontology* – the nature of reality – are central. *Logic*, on the other hand, deals with the methods of reasoning that we employ in apprehending reality in order to extract from it certain useful universal generalizations about how things work. The study of logic enables us to establish how certain knowledge claims are arrived at and legitimated, and hence the validity and reliability of such knowledge claims. *Epistemology* deals with questions about how and what it is possible to know. In epistemological investigations we attempt to reflect on the methods and standards through which reliable and verifiable knowledge is produced.

Epistemological claims are always founded on certain metaphysical assumptions and on the use of particular methods of reasoning. They have to be constantly defended against criticisms levied by others who either do not share the same metaphysical assumptions or who do not find the logic employed coherent and plausible. *Ethics*, which deals with moral evaluation and judgement, is the subject of Chapter 2. For the purposes of this chapter, I shall concentrate primarily on the first three aspects of philosophy and explore their implications for management research.

Knowledge, interpretation and action

Philosophical attitudes shape and orient us towards particular strategies for knowledge production and action. Such attitudes are often inherited from our cultural settings. As the mathematician-turned-philosopher Alfred North Whitehead noted some time ago, observational discrimination is not dictated by impartial facts. Instead, 'We inherit an observational order, namely the types of things which we do in fact discriminate; and we inherit a conceptual order, namely a rough system of ideas in terms of which we do in fact interpret' (Whitehead, 1933/48: 183). These constitute the 'unconscious metaphysics' shaping our modes of thought and our methods of sense-making. They influence our focus of attention, what we consider to be significant or insignificant, and ultimately our methods of conceptualization. Research orientations are, therefore, inextricably linked to philosophical preferences which are, in turn, influenced, though not necessarily determined, by the embedded collective histories and cultural traditions within which our own individual identities have emerged. Certain forms of knowledge are, hence, privileged over others in each historical epoch and cultural tradition and this has multiple consequences for what we construe as legitimate and reliable knowledge and how such knowledge informs action. For instance, within certain cultures *aural* knowledge rather than *written* knowledge constitutes the primary basis for action and decision-making. In other instances, the tacit and the 'unspoken' are privileged over the explicit and expressed. In these cases, what is not said or is merely alluded to is just as meaningful or even more so than what is expressed. This means that the modern researcher whose primary task it is to convert what is said and observed into a documentary written form may actually be very partial and selective, albeit unconsciously, in the process of recording. Selective abstraction and interpretation are, thus, inevitable facts of the process of knowledge-creation.

Moreover, it must not be assumed that the researcher and the practitioner, even within a particular cultural context, hold similar attitudes and definitions of what constitutes knowledge. Whereas the management researcher seeks primarily to *understand* and *explain* an observed organizational phenomenon by developing a theory around it, the practitioner is often more concerned with the *consequences* and instrumental *effects* of a particular set of management insights, policies and actions. Justification, for the practitioner, does not come by way of empirical verification or conceptual rigour, but by way of desired outcomes – the ends often justify the means. Whereas the researcher is governed by a code of practice established by a community of scholars because of its inevitably truth-seeking orientation, the practitioner is essentially a pragmatist – what *works* is more important than what is *true*. It is therefore important to bear in mind that the form of knowledge privileged by the world of academia and research does not necessarily correspond directly with the priorities and preoccupations of the practitioner world, even if it *does* indirectly inform the latter. In both cases, there is an implicit set of philosophical assumptions that justifies their different individual orientations. These deeply embedded differences in priorities imply that the process of creating and legitimizing knowledge is fraught with epistemological pitfalls and minefields. It is therefore important for any aspiring researcher to become fully aware of the complexities attending the research process.

Understanding the process of knowledge creation

Essentially, the process of knowledge creation may be likened to any other manufacturing process. In the manufacture of aluminium beer cans, for instance, a thin aluminium sheet-coil is fed through a number of stages of stamping presses where cans are successively cut and drawn until they become the familiar cylindrical shape and height. They are then printed externally with the necessary design and coated on the inside with a lacquer to prevent corrosion. In each operation tight specifications are set to ensure the desired outcome of a quality product.

This is likewise the case for the production of management knowledge. In this process, the 'raw material' is no longer an aluminium coil but the unfolding 'coil' of our human life experiences – our 'stream of consciousness', as the American philosopher William James puts it. For James our initial life-world is an undifferentiated flux of fleeting sense-impressions, and it is out of this brute, aboriginal flux of lived experience that attention focuses upon and carves out concepts which conception then names:

> . . . in the sky 'constellations', on earth 'beach', 'sea', 'cliff', 'bushes', 'grass'. Out of time we cut 'days' and 'nights', 'summers' and 'winters'. We say *what* each part of the sensible continuum is, and all these abstract *whats* are concepts. (James, 1911/96: 50; emphasis in original)

Like the stamping presses, we actively cut, draw out and construct social reality from an initially undifferentiated flux of interactions and sense impressions. These isolated parts of social reality are then identified, labelled and causally linked to other parts of our experiences in order to form a coherent system of explanation. It is, thus, through this process of differentiating, cutting out, naming, labelling, classifying and relating that modern knowledge is systematically constructed. Knowledge is therefore produced through this process of selective abstraction, identification and recombination. This implies that researchers must be circumspect about their findings and the limits and limitations of any truth-claims made. The viability of such claims is dependent upon a deeply embedded set of metaphysical assumptions underpinning Western thought.

The metaphysical roots of Western thought

Western modes of thought remain circumscribed by two opposing and enduring metaphysical traditions. Heraclitus, a native of Ephesus in ancient Greece, emphasized the primacy of a fluxing, changeable and emergent world, whilst Parmenides, his successor, insisted upon the permanent and unchangeable nature of reality. One viewed reality as inclusively processual; the other privileged a homeostatic and entitative conception of reality. This seemingly intractable opposition between a Heraclitean ontology of *becoming* and a Parmenidean ontology of *being* provides us with the key for understanding contemporary debates in the philosophy of the social sciences and their implications for management research. Although there is clear evidence of a resurgence of interest in Heraclitean-type thinking in recent years, it is the Parmenidean-inspired mindset which has decisively prevailed in the West. According to this neo-Parmenidean world-view, reality is made up of atomistic and clearly formed entities with identifiable properties and characteristics. Accordingly, form, order, individuality, identity and presence are privileged over formlessness, chaos, relationality, interpenetration and absence. Such a dominant metaphysical mindset presupposes the existence of universal patterns of order underlying the presentation of reality. Thus, clear-cut, definite things are deemed to occupy clear-cut, definite places in space and time. It is this atomistic assumption of matter which allowed Newton to formulate his now famous laws of motion by assuming that the state of 'rest' is natural whilst movement, flux and change are regarded as secondary phenomena of these basically stable entities. It also enabled the associated notion of *causality* to become, therefore, an invaluable concept for re-linking these (initially assumed) isolated entities so that their observed behaviours and tendencies can be adequately accounted for in a coherent system of explanation.

This privileging of an entitative conception of reality generates an attitude that assumes the possibility and desirability of symbolically representing the diverse aspects of our phenomenal experiences using an established and atemporal repository of terms and conceptual categories for the purposes of classification and description. For it is only when portions of reality are assumed to be stable – and hence fixable in space–time – that they can be adequately represented by symbols, words and concepts. A *representationalist* epistemology thus ensues, in which signs and linguistic terms are taken to be accurately representing an external world of discrete and identifiable objects and phenomena. Such a representationalist epistemology inevitably orients our thinking towards *outcomes* and *end-states* rather than on the processes of change themselves. It is this basic epistemological orientation which provides the inspiration for the scientific obsession with precision, accuracy and parsimony in representing and explaining social and material phenomena, including the practices of management and organization (Pfeffer, 1993). Social phenomena are frequently regarded as relatively stable, concrete and objective entities. The consequences of this orientation for the direction that management research and theorizing has taken must not be underestimated. Indeed, it has instilled a set of instinctive 'readinesses' (Vickers, 1965: 67) amongst management academics to construe theories as being 'about' an externally existing and pre-ordered reality. This predisposition remains endemic in management research.

TWO BASIC EPISTEMOLOGICAL STRATEGIES: A MULTIPLICITY OF PERSPECTIVES

Commitment to a representationalist epistemology within the Western tradition precipitated two basic habits of knowledge creation which William James (1909/96) identified as *empiricism* and *rationalism*. Empiricism, in its broadest sense, is the habit of explaining universalities from the particulars of experience. Rationalism is the tendency to explain particulars in terms of universalistic and idealized categories. In both cases, reality is assumed to be atomistic and relatively unchanging. Knowledge is thus created either by extrapolating from concrete experience or derived from the logical verification of immutable laws and principles. The romantic Coleridge is often quoted as saying that everyone is born either a Platonist or an Aristotelian. By Aristotelian he meant the empiricist tendency to rely on personal experience and observation whilst the Platonist is a rationalist who relies on logic and reason to arrive at truth. Rationalists are concerned with abstract principles, whereas empiricists privilege facts. Yet such a stark distinction is only useful as a starting point since Aristotelian empiricism, which provides the basis for modern science, remains very much indebted to Platonic rationalism.

For Aristotle, as for much of modern classical science, 'to know a thing is to name it, and to name it is to attach one or usually more universal predicates to it' (Carter, 1990: 26). Accordingly, knowledge is predicational judgement precisely because the world is logical, and lends itself to the grasp of language. To know is to say what a thing 'is' or what it 'is not'. All knowledge is, thus, of the form such that the subject of a judgement is subsumed by the wider, predicate term. Hence 'red' and 'wine' are not individual 'thises', but universal classifications pointing to the original intuition of the individually observed thing. The Aristotelian method of knowing therefore entails the *breaking down*, *fixing*, *locating* and *naming* of all experienced phenomena so much so that only the *fixed* within the *flow* of lived experience and the *universal* in the *particular* are accorded legitimate knowledge status.

Aristotle's attempts to combine Platonic rationalism with his own emphasis on empirical observation provides one of the most integrated and influential systems of thought, much of which remains present in the modern scientific method. However, despite his overwhelming influence, rationalism and empiricism remain distinctly different in terms of their intellectual traditions and theoretical emphases. It is not uncommon, therefore, to find in the philosophic literature a clear distinction being made between Cartesian rationalism, a form of rigorous abstract and logical thinking associated with continental philosophy, and the more concrete empiricist tradition inspired by Locke, Berkeley and Hume which is often called 'British empiricism'. Rational thought is thought dominated by logic and reason and displays an overwhelming concern with abstract symbols, concepts and idealized objects. It is, hence, unable to penetrate the thickness and depth of our empirical experiences. Empiricists, on the other hand, rely primarily on particular observations to formulate and justify their views and hence repeatedly fail to provide an adequate and robust account of the perceived regularities of nature. Conventional empiricism fails because it either denies or underplays the significance of hidden universal causes and is therefore unable to account for why things appear as ordered as they do. Because of the perceived weaknesses and inadequacies of both these habits of thought, a number of alternative theoretical perspectives have emerged over the last century. These have attempted to combine in one way or another the strengths of these two vastly different epistemological strategies that are united only by their common commitment to a *being* ontology.

Logical positivism as rationalized empiricism

Logical positivism or logical empiricism, which is also occasionally referred to as commonsense realism (Lawson and Appignanesi, 1989) represents one of the more recent influential attempts at synthesizing rationalism and empiricism. It provides the most widely held epistemological position within the natural and social sciences and draws substantially from the Aristotelian approach by combining logic and rationality with empirical observation. The term 'positivism' was first invented in the nineteenth century by the French social philosopher Auguste Comte who chose the term because of its felicitous connotations. Comte saw knowledge as developing from a theological to a metaphysical and, finally, to a positivist stage in which non-observable entities and abstract principles were rejected in favour of the primacy of raw observation as the starting point of knowledge. Nowadays, however, when reference is made to the 'positivists', it is usually associated with the group of logical positivists who met regularly in Vienna in the 1920s and 1930s and developed a research doctrine which drew heavily on the philosophies of Ernst Mach and Bertrand Russell. This 'Vienna Circle' championed a version of logical empiricism in which knowledge claims and universal generalizations are considered acceptable only if they can be verified by hard facts acquired through careful observation.

In its most basic form, positivism assumes that the researcher is a sort of 'spectator' of the object of enquiry. Reality is assumed to be unproblematically existing 'out there' independent of the perceptions, beliefs and biases of the researcher. For positivists, therefore, good research consists of the undistorted recording of observations obtained through efficiency-driven methods of investigation and the use of precise terminologies and classifications in the documentary process. Observational rigour on the part of the researcher using systems of cross-referencing provides the necessary form of 'quality assurance' in this process of knowledge production. It thus follows that good researchers must diligently rid themselves of all subjective tendencies by adopting a dispassionate attitude in the enquiry process and by using well-established data-recording methods in a rigorous manner in order to ensure the reliability and validity of the data collected. Explanations regarding the observed pattern of regularities connecting one set of phenomena with another can then be systematically developed and empirically verified.

What positivism does is to subsume the empirical under the imperative of the rational. Reason and logic are critical to theory-building even if the truth-claims generated must, in the final analysis, be empirically justified. So although empirical observation is given a key role, it is rational analysis that rules in the positivist camp. Moreover, all observations are guided by the use of established terminologies, concepts and theories which provide a common basis for unifying the research enterprise. As such, positivists do not consider the effects our language and concepts have in shaping our perceptions of reality. Instead, language is thought of merely as an instrument of communication. This naivety regarding the impact of language on perception and thought has provided the basis of criticism by those who advocate a more radical form of empiricism that begins with the immediacy of brute lived experience.

Phenomenology as radicalized empiricism

The unique combination of empirical and rationalistic tendencies to produce positivism represents only one among a range of other epistemological possibilities. Such a positivistic method of adjusting for the inadequacies of empiricism, however, has been criticized for bringing in unnecessary and unaccountable factors which only further detach us from the primacy of our lived experiences. Positivism is, in fact, a kind of 'false empiricism' because it is a priori 'contaminated' by rationalist terms, concepts and categories. As such observations made are always 'guided' observations and hence not truly empirical. It is the rejection of this rationalistic imperative in positivism that defines the task of phenomenology. Phenomenologists argue that instead of adopting a rationally modified empiricism because of the apparent inadequacies of empiricism, it may be better to revise the rationalist critique by assuming that the flux of experience itself contains an *immanent* logic and rationality that has hitherto been overlooked. This turn *towards* experience and *away* from abstract representations marks a genuine alternative to both rationalism and positivism. It is an uncompromising insistence on a return to the purity and primacy of lived experience, our 'life-world', as the starting point of consciousness and knowledge. Such a broad existential emphasis has precipitated a number of distinct but related perspectives, including especially the 'radical empiricism' of William James (1912/96), the 'intuitionism' of Henri Bergson (1903/49) and the 'phenomenology' of Edmund Husserl (1964) and Maurice Merleau-Ponty (1962).

Phenomenology, intuitionism or radical empiricism therefore, despite some crucial differences, which will become clearer later in this section, share a common epistemological orientation that is predicated upon the idea of a pure and unmediated experience of phenomena as its necessary starting point. For phenomenologists, to know, in its most rich and basic sense, therefore, is to experience – directly, immediately and purely. Such an intuitive knowing must not be confused with intellectualized knowledge that we acquire of things. It is a knowing prior to the creation of the subject/object distinction. In this pristine state, there is no separation of knower and known. Separation of knower and known only occurs when a given 'bit' is abstracted from the flow of experience and retrospectively considered in the context of other categories. This form of radicalized empiricism is vastly different from the orthodox empiricism previously discussed. It provides us with an alternative metaphysical foundation or *Weltanschauung* for grounding knowledge and knowledge creation. It is also a world-view that intuitively resonates with Eastern forms of thought (Chang, 1968; Nishida, 1911/90).

A genuine empiricism must not admit into its construction 'any element that is not directly experienced', nor exclude 'any element that is directly experienced' (James, 1912/96: 42). It is that which attempts 'to search deeply into its life, and . . . to feel the throbbing of its soul' (Bergson, 1903/49: 36). Such an empiricism does not proceed by relying on ready-made ideas and concepts and combining them uncritically to produce knowledge. Instead, it takes raw pristine experience as its necessary starting point. This insistence on extracting knowledge from the immediacy of lived experience is what conjoins the epistemological projects of James and Bergson with the phenomenological approach of Husserl who was their contemporary and with Merleau-Ponty who studied under Bergson.

Like James and Bergson, Husserl viewed the way classical science produces knowledge as concealing crucial aspects of our human experiences because of its over-reliance on abstract and idealized concepts and terminologies. For Husserl ultimate knowledge is to be directly intuited from an original field of pure experience. In this regard, *intentionality* plays a central role in focusing our consciousness and in the selective creation of knowledge. Any form of consciousness is thus consciousness *of* and there is no such thing as an independent object existing prior to our consciousness of it. Like James and Bergson, therefore, Husserl sought to apprehend that pure phenomenon of experience which manifests itself immediately in consciousness and which is pre-reflexive and hence pre-judgemental. This same concern was echoed by Maurice Merleau-Ponty, another influential phenomenologist who studied under Bergson.

For Merleau-Ponty, scientific thinking promotes a kind of disembodied form of knowing which constructs 'man and history on the basis of a few abstract indices' (Merleau-Ponty, 1962: 161). Such a detached form of knowing is inadequate for an intimate understanding of our 'being-in-the-world', our lived experiential existence. As conscious humans we are inextricably enmeshed in a natural-cultural-historical milieu of which we inevitably participate in an ongoing and open-ended way. This means that all forms of knowing take place within the horizons opened up by our acts of perception. Moreover, these primordial structures of perception pervade the entire range of reflective experience so that ideas can never be absolutely pure thought. Instead, they are cultural objects whose primordial source is the phenomenal body itself. Knowing, therefore, cannot be dispassionate and impartial. Instead we must start with our immediate situation and attempt to illuminate it from within.

Despite distinct differences in emphases, James, Bergson, Husserl and Merleau-Ponty are clearly united in the belief that in order truly to appreciate the human condition we must return to that corporeal site: 'the soil of the sensible opened world such as is in our life and our body' (Merleau-Ponty, 1962: 161). Although we can acknowledge that there is a whole culturally constructed world that constitutes a realm of abstraction above and beyond our perceptual experiences, we must not forget that it is these initial acts of perception which provide us with the fundamental basis for knowledge creation. Phenomenology's primary concern therefore is with the exploration of that pre-reflective realm which provides the background for all conscious perception and knowledge.

From this overly brief treatment we can see that phenomenology is really a radicalized form of empiricism that seeks a kind of *immanent* rationality rather than the *transcendent* rationality associated with Platonism. Unlike rationalism, which begins by relying on abstract universal and immutable principles or positivism which uncritically relies on conceptualized observations, phenomenology insists on returning to the immediacy of a pre-linguistic lived experience as the necessary starting point for knowledge. Yet, whilst clearly advocating an epistemological approach vastly different from positivism, phenomenology does not sufficiently deal explicitly with the ontological status of reality. Although it wholeheartedly champions the primacy of lived experience, it tends to treat such experiences as discrete, atomistic and isolatable. In other words, it remains committed to a *being* ontology. This is where phenomenology seemingly parts company with the radical empiricism of William James or with the intuitionism of Henri Bergson, both of whom may be regarded as the precursors of what is now called postmodernism. This phenomenological turn towards raw experience is, however, in some measure countered by the more recent *realist* turn towards abstract rationalism.

Realism as modified positivism

A first approximation of the epistemologically realist position would begin with the assertion that the picture that science portrays of the world is a true one, accurate and faithful in all its details. For the realist researcher, objects of investigation such as 'an organization', its 'structure', 'culture' and 'strategy' exist and act, for the most part, quite independently of their observers or indeed the individual actors themselves. Hence, they are considered quite amenable to systematic analysis and comparison in the same way as natural phenomena. Knowledge is thus advanced through the process of 'theory-building' in which new 'discoveries' of the nature of reality are cumulatively added to what is already known. Unlike positivism, however, realism takes seriously the view that there are different 'levels' of reality which can be systematically revealed through the rigorous application of the methods of science. Reality, for the realists, comprises things, structures, events and underlying 'generative mechanisms' which, regardless of whether they are observable, are none the less 'real' (Bhaskar, 1978). The task of enquiry, therefore, is to seek to explain observable facts in terms of 'more fundamental structures, and in the process, it may reveal some of these "facts", such as the observable motion of the sun across the sky, to be, in part, illusions'

(Outhwaite, 1987: 9). Conversely, it may also reveal the real existence of hypothetical entities that cannot be immediately observed. The discovery of the virus is a good example of the realist claim that unobservable entities may yet be subsequently proved to exist through the development of more adequate instruments of observation such as the microscope (Keat and Urry, 1975).

Realists are critical of the positivist reliance on the Humean notion of causality to justify its claims. Hume famously maintained that the constant conjunction of two events occurring provides a legitimate basis for explaining cause and effect. Accordingly, if it is observed, for example, that a match lights up because it is struck, one can simply conclude that striking a match is the *cause* for it lighting up. However, for the realist, to say that a match 'lit' because it was 'struck' is a misapplication of the concept of causality. A true causal explanation should be capable of answering the question why the match lit in terms of generative mechanisms such as the chemical properties of the match head, the roughness of the surface it was struck against and the force applied. Such generative mechanisms may not be immediately detected or visible to the eye yet for the realist they none the less exist just like physically observable entities. Theory, therefore, for the realist becomes the means for 'describing the relations between the unobservable causal mechanisms (or structures) and their (observable) effects' (Layder, 1990: 13). This emphasis on real but unobservable generative mechanisms, including immutable laws and universal principles is very much inspired by a rationalist reworking of positivism.

For realists, reality exists and acts independently of our observations. Moreover, whether it is in material form or as unobservable structures or mechanisms, reality creates effects that can only be understood through the postulation and acceptance of theoretical entities. Thus, atoms, genes, viruses and gravity exist as concrete, stable entities or generative forces even though they may not be ever directly observable. Accordingly, established theories are mirror images of the world and reflect how it is actually ordered. The more accurately our theories correspond with reality, the more true they are held to be (Rorty, 1980).

What realism proposes, therefore, is the acceptance of a dualism, not just between mind and matter, but also between our theories about reality and reality itself. In other words, theories do not serve to construct an arbitrary picture of reality. Rather they seek to accurately mirror in a discursive form an externally existing reality that is itself taken to be relatively stable and enduring. This means that we are realists, in so far as we believe that what our theory is about is essentially independent of the theory itself. Realism is fundamentally a philosophical position concerning the word–world connection and, hence, at root assumes this distinction to be a legitimate one. It is a position that elevates rationalism over empiricism and is, hence, diametrically opposed to that of the radicalized empiricism that phenomenology represents.

Hermeneutics as empiricized rationalism

Hermeneutics can be loosely defined as the theory or method for aiding the art of interpretation. It was initially developed and applied to the understanding of biblical texts and subsequently extended to the field of the human sciences. The realization that human intentions and expressions are deeply personal and meaningful and as such not always immediately apparent has given rise to the problem of interpretation: 'How do we render accounts of subjectively intended meanings more objective in the face of the fact that they are necessarily mediated by the interpreter's own subjectivity?' This is the central problem that traditional hermeneutics seeks to resolve. Hermeneutics is less an epistemology than a methodological approach for resolving an essentially intractable epistemological problem. This is the problem of meaning and intention that is purportedly captured or represented by the signs and symbols used by an actor or author or alternatively the artefacts produced in a creative act. Unlike positivism, which emphasizes the centrality of conceptualized observation, or phenomenology, which privileges the raw experiences of our 'life-worlds', or even realism, which places greater epistemological value on abstract immutable laws and universal principles, traditional hermeneutics locates itself at the level of the visible signs, symbols and representations which purportedly contain the conscious actions and intentions of authors. The artefacts of human expression are the starting point from which an attempt is made to trace authorial meanings and intentions. The outcome of such authorial intentions may be a text, a painting, a performance or any other observable outcomes and representations. What is sought is an authentic account of the actor's or author's meanings and intentions lying beneath the layers of symbolic expressions. It is this art of deciphering meaning that constitutes the central task of traditional hermeneutic enquiry. Traditional hermeneutics is thus not altogether incompatible with rationalism or even realism[1] in that it seeks to go beyond visible empirical appearances to an ultimate truth or 'correct' interpretation – in this case the meanings and intentions of authors and actors.

In the course of its historical development, hermeneutics has emerged as a powerful theory of interpretation whenever it became necessary to translate authoritative texts or authorial accounts under conditions where the original meaning of a text was either disputed or remained hidden and hence necessitated rendering it more transparent. Traditional hermeneutics has, therefore, sought to recover the 'correct' meanings of texts, human actions and institutions. Contemporary hermeneutics, however, has moved some way away from this original formulation. Currently, there are two dominant strains in hermeneutic theory. One reflects the search for a more 'contextualist' account of the meaning of texts and performances as separated from authorial/actorial intentions (Gadamer, 1975). The other, associated more with Marx, Nietzsche and Freud, reflects a more critical 'hermeneutics of suspicion' (Thompson, 1981: 46–7). In the former case, interpretation is motivated by an act of faith and by a willingness to listen and to passively contemplate the contemporary relevance of what has been previously said, written or done. It is acknowledged that all accounts are constructed within the context of a particular social-historical or cultural setting such that it is often difficult or even impossible to fully appreciate the original intentions and meanings of an author/actor. What is therefore sought is not so much the original intention of an actor or author but a 'fusion of horizons' in which the reader/researcher achieves a level of coherence and comprehension in their own system of understanding. Here it is explicitly acknowledged that given the reader/researcher's own necessary situatedness in a particular historical epoch and cultural context the original intent and meaning of what was written or said may never be, in principle recoverable. Hermeneutics then becomes, not in the traditional sense, the way of recovering the original meaning, but of making historical texts and actions *meaningful* to us within the contemporary context of our *own* horizons of understanding. This is a significant departure from the form of traditional hermeneutics proposed by writers such as Schleiermacher (1977) and Dilthey (1976). It is a perspective inspired by Gadamer's (1975) more contemporary rendering of the hermeneutic project.

The 'hermeneutics of suspicion', on the other hand, pursues a different ideological agenda. It is animated by a suspicious attitude or scepticism towards the given and is characterized by a rejection of that respect for the purported authenticity of reported accounts. Such a perspective treats the immediate contents of consciousness as being in some sense inevitably superficial, false or self-deluding. Hence, the true import of actions must be deciphered in a way that reveals the hidden, repressed or generative, and oftentimes unconscious motivations underlying that set of actions. This is where the hermeneutic enterprise turns towards the tradition of critical theory for its necessary complement. Critical theory is an intellectual tradition inspired by a particular reading of Marx initiated by the Frankfurt school in the early 1930s and 1940s and is currently championed by its leading contemporary exponent Jürgen Habermas (1972, 1984). It shifts attention and analysis away from individual actors'/authors' meanings and intentions to the manner in which the prevailing cultural, ideological and political 'superstructures' inevitably shape and influence behaviours and outcomes. For critical theorists, actors/authors are often caught up in an ideological milieu that they themselves are unaware of. This means that a truly critical hermeneutic understanding must seek to reach beneath the everyday presentation of things and the seeming obviousness of human situations.

In a similar manner to critical theory, Freudian psychoanalysis may be understood as another version of this 'hermeneutics of suspicion', since a critical interpretation of intentionality, especially the elevation of the role of the 'unconscious', forms a central feature in the diagnosis of an analysand's malaise. Finally, this critical dimension of interpretation has been ingeniously incorporated into a revised 'critical realism' championed by Bhaskar (1978, 1989) that is increasingly attracting a large and influential following in the social sciences (Archer, 1995; Archer et al., 1998; Collier, 1994; Outhwaite, 1983, 1987).

Whilst contemporary 'contextualist' hermeneutics may be understood as a revised attempt to validate knowledge at the level of lived experience on the part of the reader/researcher, 'critical' hermeneutics nods towards a more transcendental and rationalist account of human action and intention. In the former case, subjectivity, meaning and intention more than objectivity, fact and observable behaviour provide the basis for grounding meaning. Putting it more plainly, contextualist hermeneutics seeks knowledge by grounding it in subjective reading[2] experiences. Thus, knowledge is to be gleaned not from transcendental and immutable laws and principles, but from a sensitive reading of the subjective acts and intentions of actors negotiating their way through the vagaries of life. In this regard it aligns itself more with an empiricist epistemology. On the other hand, critical hermeneutics rejects the authentic claims of lived experience in favour of a transcendental and universalized explanation. It aligns itself with a certain claim of objectivity and rationality that is compatible with a realism not found in contextualist hermeneutics. We can, therefore, see that contemporary hermeneutics remains divided by the central issues of rationalism and empiricism previously identified.

A REVISED *BECOMING* ONTOLOGY: POSTMODERNISM AND SOCIAL CONSTRUCTION

The previous four perspectives of positivism, phenomenology, realism and hermeneutics are, as I have tried to show, underpinned by the ongoing tensions between rationalism and empiricism. I have further noted that, despite their vast epistemological distances, all these, implicitly or explicitly, continue to subscribe to a *being* ontology – the idea that absolute reality, whether experienced or transcendental, is assumed to be relatively stable, discrete and unchanging. Notwithstanding their obvious differences, these four perspectives do not explicitly countenance reality in terms of an interminable and formless flux and transformation. The alternative *becoming* ontology is that which takes seriously the Heraclitean axiom: 'everything flows and nothing abides . . .'. It is the manifest plausibility of this alternative world-view which informs the project of postmodernism. Postmodernism, as such, may be viewed as an ontological extension of phenomenology and a revival of the kind of radical empiricism and intuitionism championed by William James and Henri Bergson.

The term 'postmodernism' made its first appearance in the title of a book – *Postmodernism and Other Essays* written by Bernard Iddings Bell – as early as 1926. Since then it has rapidly shifted from awkward neologism to populist cliché without apparently ever having attained the dignified status of an established concept. Increasingly loosely employed in much of the academic literature in art, science, literary criticism, philosophy, sociology, politics and now even in management and organization studies, its use none the less evokes vastly contrasting reactions. On the one hand, postmodernism is frequently dismissed as an extremely simplistic and cynical tendency towards nihilism within contemporary culture; on the other it is regarded as an extremely subtle and complex philosophical attempt at reworking the metaphysical bases of modern knowledge. The word 'postmodern' is therefore characterized from its very inception by an essential ambiguity – a certain *'semantic* instability' (Hassan, 1985: 121) – that prevents clear consensus about its meaning and effects.

For our purposes, and within the context of this treatment of philosophy and research, the term postmodernism may be invoked to describe an alternative *style of thought* which attempts to adequately comprehend the almost inexorable 'logic of world-making' underpinning the modernist project. Modern rationality, and hence representationalism, is thus viewed as a method of social construction which creates legitimate objects of knowledge for a knowing subject. The perceived routines and regularities that make up our social world are, therefore, arbitrarily socially constructed rather than the result of immutable laws and universal principles. In this process, significant portions of our tacit and embodied forms of knowing are denied legitimacy in the modernist scheme of things. The postmodern, then, is centrally concerned with giving voice and legitimacy to those tacit and oftentimes unpresentable forms of knowledge that the modern epistemologies of both conventional empiricism and rationalism inevitably depend upon yet conveniently overlook or gloss over in the process of knowledge creation. This is the real project of the postmodern critique.

Four intellectual axioms and imperatives are detectable in the postmodern approach to research and analysis. First, in place of the modernist emphasis on the ontological primacy of substance, stability, identity, order, regularity and form, postmodern analyses seek to emphasize the Heraclitean primacy accorded to process, indeterminacy, flux, interpenetration, formlessness and incessant change. Such a processual orientation must not be equated with the commonsense idea of the process that a system is deemed to undergo in transition. Rather it is a metaphysical orientation that emphasizes an ontological primacy in the *becoming* of things; that sees things as always already momentary outcomes or effects of historical processes. It rejects what Rescher (1996) calls the *process reducibility thesis*, whereby processes are often assumed to be processes *of* primary 'things'. Instead, it insists that 'things', social entities, generative mechanisms etc., are no more than 'stability waves in a sea of process' (Rescher, 1996: 53). This process ontology promotes a decentred and dispersive view of reality as a heterogeneous concatenation of atomic event-occurrences that cannot be adequately captured by static symbols and representations. For process ontology the basic unit of reality is not an atom or thing but an 'event-cluster'.

Second, from this commitment to a *becoming* ontology, it follows that language, and in particular the activities of *naming* and *symbolic representation*, provides the first ordering impulse for the systematic structuring of our human life-worlds. Postmodernists argue that it is the structured nature of language that creates the impression that reality itself is stable, pre-organized and law-like in character. They insist that without the social acts of differentiating, identifying, naming, classifying and the creation of a subject–predicate structure through language, lived reality is but a 'shapeless and indistinct mass' (Saussure, 1966: 111). Postmodernists therefore reject the kind of representationalist epistemology championed by modern science but widely held implicitly even amongst the theoretical alternatives previously discussed. For postmodernists, theories are viewed more pragmatically as selective and useful devices that help us to negotiate our way through the world even if they do not necessarily tell us how the world really is. In other words, theories may be *workable*, but may not be timelessly *true*. Moreover, because all theories are manifestly incomplete, there are always parts of reality that are ignored or not accounted for in our scheme of things. This leads to a third preoccupation with tacit and unconscious forms of knowing.

Third, postmodernism seeks to modify the conceptual asymmetry created between conscious action and *unconscious* forces. The elevation of rationality, intentionality and choice in the modernist explanatory schema surreptitiously overlooks the role of unconscious nomadic forces in shaping planned action and outcomes. Postmodern analysis emphasizes the heterogeneous, multiple and *alinear* character of real-world happenings. It draws attention to the fact that events in the real world, as we experience it, do not unfold in a conscious, homogeneous, linear and predictable manner. Instead they 'leak in insensibly' (James, 1909/1996: 399). Human action and motives must, therefore, not be simply understood in terms of actors' intentions or even the result of underlying generative mechanisms, but rather in terms of embedded contextual experiences, accumulated memories and cultural traditions that create and define the very possibilities for interpretation and action. Surprise, chance and the unexpected are the real order of things. Postmodernism thus advocates a more tentative and modest attitude towards the status of our current forms of knowledge.

Finally, instead of thinking in terms of tightly coupled causal explanations that attempt to link observed phenomena with underlying tendencies, postmodernism elevates the roles of resonance, recursion and resemblance as more adequate terms for explaining the 'loosely coupled' and heterogeneous nature of real-world happenings. It is argued that thinking in this more allusive and elliptical manner enables us to better appreciate how social phenomena such as 'individuals' and 'organizations' can be viewed as coincidental and temporarily stabilized event-clusters rather than as deliberately engineered concrete systems and entities. It is the stubbornly held idea that reality is invariably 'systemic', and hence mechanistic and predictable, which postmodern analyses seek to disabuse us.

These four theoretical emphases in the postmodern approach provide a fertile alternative basis for reframing research in organization and management. It is one which elevates the role of creativity, chance and novelty in our explanatory schemas. According to this postmodern manifesto change does not take place in a linear manner or even propagate in a tree-like manner. Instead, real change is quintessentially 'rhizomic' in character, taking place through 'variations, restless expansion, opportunistic conquests, sudden captures and offshoots' (Chia, 1999: 222). It is this alternative, more 'unwieldy' image of the real goings-on in organizational life that postmodernist management research emphasizes.

Conclusion

Management research is a knowledge-creating activity which may be compared to any manufacturing process where the type of technology employed (philosophical orientation) and the method of production adopted (research method), as well as the raw material used (experience and established knowledge) together with the operator's capabilities (researcher's competence), ultimately determine the quality and reliability of the product itself. What constitutes legitimate and acceptable knowledge is very much determined by the philosophical attitude adopted by a community of scholars which itself may change from period to period. Knowledge creation and legitimation is never a static thing. It is always renewing itself. Thus, within the field of management research, although there remains an established tradition centred around positivistic research, acceptance of the alternative theoretical perspectives discussed in this chapter is growing. Phenomenological, hermeneutic and realist approaches have begun to establish a foothold in the field of management studies. Postmodernism radicalizes these alternatives by replacing a *being* orientation, implicit in all the alternatives, with a *becoming* orientation in our theoretical formulations. Thus, whilst positivism, phenomenology, realism and hermeneutics represent viable epistemological alternatives, postmodernism offers a radical ontological revision of our dominant modes of thought.

Such a radicalized ontological revision ironically brings the world of academia closer to the world of practice. Postmodernism alludes to the impossibility of systemically capturing the goings-on of real-world happenings because of the inherent limitations of our methods of conceptualization. By demonstrating the constructed and, hence, arbitrary nature of social reality, postmodernism brings us closer to the realities and pragmatic concerns of a practitioner world that intuitively recognizes the limits of a truth-seeking form of knowledge. It is a way of thinking which readily embraces the existence of a realm of tacit and unspeakable – as well as often unconscious – knowing as the unshakable foundation of management action and decision-making. In other words, postmodernism seeks to bring practitioner realism back into our theorizing and a level of intellectual modesty into our knowledge claims.

Study questions

1 How does the adoption of a particular philosophical perspective affect the kind of knowledge produced?
2 Why does commitment to a *being* ontology result in a representationalist epistemology?
3 In what way is postmodernism fundamentally different from the other theoretical alternatives to positivism?

Recommended further reading

Bergson, H. (1903/49) *An Introduction to Metaphysics*. Englewood Cliffs, NJ: Prentice Hall. (A short and very readable critique of representationalism)

Bhaskar, R. (1978) *A Realist Theory of Science*. Hassock: Harvester Press. (The most definitive statement on what is now called 'critical realism')

Gadamer, H-G. (1975) *Truth and Method*. London: Sheed & Ward. (Gadamer's *magnum opus*, which reworks hermeneutics into its more current 'contextualist' form)

Lawson, H. and Appignanesi, L. (1989) *Dismantling Truth: Reality in the Post-Modern World*. London: Weidenfeld and Nicolson. (A very readable text which introduces the problems of commonsense realism and points the way towards a postmodern world-view)

Outhwaite, W. (1987) *New Philosophies of Social Science: Realism, Hermeneutics and Critical Theory*. Basingstoke: Macmillan. (A very useful and comprehensive discussion of the differences between realism, hermeneutics and critical theory)

Rescher, N. (1996) *Process Metaphysics: An Introduction to Process Philosophy*. New York: State University of New York Press. (An exceptionally clear working out of the implications of process philosophy)

Vickers, G. (1965) *The Art of Judgement: A Study of Policy Making*. London: Chapman and Hall. (A rich and insightful account of how decision-making takes place in reality)

Whitehead, A.N. (1933/48) *Adventures of Ideas*. Harmondsworth: Penguin Books. (Without doubt, one of the most compelling arguments for adopting a philosophical outlook in business and management research)

Notes

1 Indeed, it is the combining of the Marxist-inspired critical theory as a 'hermeneutics of suspicion' with realism which has spawned a new and increasingly influential movement called critical realism, which takes after the work of Roy Bhaskar. For a more detailed exposition of this perspective see Archer, Bhaskar, Collier, Lawson and Norrie (1998).

2 Reading here refers to both the reading of texts and the 'reading' of the actions and intentions of actors in a research situation.

References

Archer, M. (1995) *Realist Social Theory: The Morphogenetic Approach*. Cambridge: Cambridge University Press.

Archer, M., Bhaskar, R., Collier, A., Lawson, T. and Norrie, A. (1998) *Critical Realism: Essential Readings*. London and New York: Routledge.

Bell, B.I. (1926) *Postmodernism and Other Essays*. Milwaukee: Morehouse Publishing.

Bergson, H. (1903/49) *An Introduction to Metaphysics*. Englewood Cliffs, NJ: Prentice Hall.

Bhaskar, R. (1978) *A Realist Theory of Science*. Hassock: Harvester Press.

Bhaskar, R. (1989) *Reclaiming Reality*. London: Verso.

Carter, R. (1990) *The Nothingness Beyond God*. New York: Paragon House.

Chang, C-Y. (1968) *Creativity and Taoism*. New York: Harper & Row.

Chia, R. (1999) 'A Rhizomic Model of Organizational Change: Perspectives from a Metaphysics of Change', *British Journal of Management*, 10 (3), pp. 209–27.

Collier, A. (1994) *Critical Realism*. London and New York: Verso.

Dilthey, W. (1976) *Selected Writings* (translated and edited by H.P. Rickman). Cambridge: Cambridge University Press.

Gadamer, H-G. (1975) *Truth and Method*. London: Sheed & Ward.

Habermas, J. (1972) *Knowledge and Human Interests*. London: Heinemann.

Habermas, J. (1984) *The Theory of Communicative Action*, Vol. 1: *Reason and the Rationalization of Society*. London: Heinemann.

Hassan, I. (1985) 'The Culture of Postmodernism', *Theory, Culture & Society*, 2 (3), pp. 119–31.

Husserl, E. (1964) *Cartesian Meditations: An Introduction to Phenomenology*. Atlantic Highlands, NJ: Humanities Press.

James, W. (1909/96) *A Pluralistic Universe*. Lincoln, NB and London: University of Nebraska Press.

James, W. (1911/96) *Some Problems of Philosophy*. Lincoln, NB and London: University of Nebraska Press.

James, W. (1912/96) *Essays in Radical Empiricism*. Lincoln, NB and London: University of Nebraska Press.

Keat, R. and Urry, J. (1975) *Social Theory as Science*. London: Routledge and Kegan Paul.

Lawson, H. and Appignanesi, L. (1989) *Dismantling Truth: Reality in the Post-Modern World*. London: Weidenfeld & Nicolson.

Layder, D. (1990) *The Realist Image in Social Science*. Basingstoke: Macmillan.

Merleau-Ponty, M. (1962) *Phenomenology of Perception*. London: Routledge & Kegan Paul.

Nishida, K. (1911/90) *An Inquiry into the Good* (trans. M. Abe and C. Ives). New Haven, CT: Yale University Press.

Outhwaite, W. (1983) 'Towards a Realist Perspective', in G. Morgan (ed.), *Beyond Method*. Newbury Park, CA: Sage.

Outhwaite, W. (1987) *New Philosophies of Social Science: Realism, Hermeneutics and Critical Theory*. Basingstoke: Macmillan.

Pfeffer, J. (1993) 'Barriers to the Advance of Organizational Science: Paradigm Development as a Dependent Variable', *Academy of Management Review*, 18 (4): 599–620.

Rescher, N. (1996) *Process Metaphysics: An Introduction to Process Philosophy*. New York: State University of New York Press.

Rorty, R. (1980) *Philosophy and the Mirror of Nature*. Oxford: Blackwell.

Saussure, F. de (1966) *Course in General Linguistics*. London: Fontana/Collins.

Schleiermacher, F.D. (1977) *Hermeneutics: The Handwritten Manuscripts* (edited by H. Kimmerle, translated by J. Duke and J. Forstman). Missoula, Mont.: Scholars Press.

Thompson, J. (1981) *Critical Hermeneutics: A Study in the Thought of Paul Ricoeur and Jürgen Habermas*. Cambridge: Cambridge University Press.

Vickers, G. (1965) *The Art of Judgement: A Study of Policy Making*. London: Chapman and Hall.

Whitehead, A.N. (1933/48) *Adventures of Ideas*. Harmondsworth: Penguin Books.

2

Ethical Considerations in Management Research: A 'Truth' Seeker's Guide

Nada Korac-Kakabadse, Andrew Kakabadse and Alexander Kouzmin

> Will not knowledge of the good, then, have a great influence on life?
> Shall we not, like archers who have a mark to aim at, be more likely to
> hit upon what is right? (Aristotle, 1962: 17)

OVERVIEW

Every art and every enquiry, and similarly every action and pursuit, is
thought to aim at some good; and for this reason the good has rightly been
declared to be that at which all things aim (Aristotle, 1962). A basic motivation
for research is the desire for new and better insights – for new knowledge.
From a 'purist' research perspective, knowledge is an end in itself. From an
organizational and management perspective, knowledge also has a practical
side. Organizational and management research advances and shapes organizational objectives, culture, individuals and societies as it provides new
insights that inform premises upon which decisions and judgements are
based. Moreover, management research may uncover undesirable circumstances and contribute to the identification of alternative courses of action and
their likely consequences. Management research can also contribute to important critical correctives by shedding light on situations of undesirable
organizational outcomes. As such, the demand on the research community is,
primarily, focused on knowledge and insight, where the most important obligation of research is to seek new insight. On the other hand, social researchers
can never guarantee that they have arrived at a 'true' statement. Most conclusions in management and social research remain provisional as researchers
rarely reach results due to human values choices, norms and institutions,
work and traditions, language, thought and communication – all contextual.
Empathy and interpretation are necessary elements of the management
research process. Notwithstanding the uncertainty attaching to research, it
does not relieve researchers of the obligation to dismiss arbitrary views and

to seek validity and clarity in their argumentation. Irrespective of the methodological choice, management research is inevitably influenced by the researcher's ontological positioning or views of social reality. Researchers need to guard against their own biases, often to the benefit of their research. This subjective influence of the researcher's own values over the research process requires the researcher to consider and examine how their own attitudes might influence research choices and the weighing of possible interpretations of findings. The methodological demand of the research community for the highest standards of research modes, demonstration of research verifiability and respectful criticism assists researchers at reaching a consensus – a legitimacy that prevents research from being marked by prejudices or values of which no account is given.

Management research requires that researchers explicitly understand their own values, examine and clarify traditions, perspectives, social processes, values and attitudes of self and others. Hence, a call for ethical conduct in research. For example, research into organizational culture reveals and helps researchers to assess the values underlying prominent, contemporary modes of thought and traditions in management thinking. Research that undertakes a critical examination of the organizational heritage and of social processes also helps review and shape the values, institutions and attitudes which organizations hand down to succeeding generations. Hence, ethics, or a theory of values, represents a third pillar of research philosophy that guides researcher conduct during the research process – from the beginning of defining one's ontological positioning to the justifying of epistemological positioning.

The objective of this chapter is threefold. First, it is to raise researcher awareness of ethics in management research by reviewing a range of ethical issues that researchers may encounter during the life of a research project. Second, it is to assist researchers to appreciate the source and depth of ethical and moral thinking, views and attitudes, enabling them to reach well-founded decisions. Third, it is to provide guidance and a pathway to resolving ethical dilemmas that researchers may encounter during research.

The first part of the chapter provides an overview of a philosophy of ethics, with emphasis on ethical theories and related perspectives that may underpin a researcher's ethical reasoning. It provides a framework for an individual understanding of one's own ethical positioning and a basis of one's own value system. The second part of the chapter provides a framework for understanding causes of ethical dilemmas in the context of management research and provides some strategies for a way forward through dilemmas. This framework builds on value-clarification theory originally developed by Raths et al. (1966) and later re-conceptualized by others (Kinnier, 1995; Kirschenbaum, 1977; Raths et al., 1978). At the end of the chapter, three sets of exercises pertinent to research ethics are set out in order to provide 'hands-on' experience and familiarization with the framework.

Concept of ethics

The troublesome, and impossible to escape, question posed by Socrates, 'What ought one do?' (Plato, 1984) projects the same multitude of ethical dilemmas onto decision-makers of today as it may have done to philosophers in ancient times. For Socrates, the force of his original question lies in the fact that it demands some sort of account from actors as to why they choose one 'good' over another. In fact, at its deeper level, Socrates' question requires actors to articulate some sort of founding vision of what they consider to be 'good'.

Ethical concerns permeate every aspect of the management research process; in some manner, they permeate all human actions and interactions. Ethical concerns arise in connection with core values the researcher holds, as in the case of honesty or justice. Ethical concerns are also potentially at issue whenever action or decisions affect other people, although they can also arise when other people's rights and interest are not directly at stake. Whenever there is a choice to be made between values, or several ways of doing something, or an issue is deemed to be good, an ethical judgement is involved. In this broad sense, in management research, most judgements, choices and decisions about goals, standards, quality, priorities and knowledge are ethical issues. Moreover, describing someone/something as ethical does not imply that it is ethically correct (McIntyre, 1981). Being ethical is not breaking any laws or code of agreements. Being ethically correct calls on judgement in evaluating someone's action, decision or intention.

Socrates, Plato, Aristotle and Kant promoted a virtue-based approach which emphasized the will, intentions and character of the individual. The virtuous actor behaves according to inner conviction and strength, irrespective of the consequences of the action and its impact on any relationship – whether it be based on kinship, professional or friendship ties. This focus on the individual as the pillar of ethics has the advantage that the onus is clearly allocated; but it has the disadvantage of being rigid and presuming, wrongly, that all that is needed to achieve an ethical society is for its members to act according to subjective notions of virtue.

Ethics is a philosophical term derived from the Greek word *Ethos*, meaning character or custom. It connotes a community or social code conveying moral integrity and consistent values in service to the public. More formally defined, ethical behaviour represents that which is morally accepted as 'good' and 'right' as opposed to 'bad' and 'wrong' in a particular context (Simms, 1992). The challenge of what constitutes ethical behaviour lies in a 'grey zone', where clear-cut right versus wrong and good versus bad dichotomies may not always exist. Ethics is concerned not only with distinguishing between the dichotomies but, also, with the commitment to do what is right or what is good. As such, the concept of ethics is inextricably linked to that of values; enduring beliefs that influence the choices actors make from available means and ends. While some values (wealth, success) have relatively little direct connection with ethics, others (fairness, honesty) are, in essence, concerned with what is right or good and can be described as ethical values (Kernaghan and Langford, 1990). The critical link between ethics and values is that ethical standards and principles can be applied to the resolution of value conflicts *or* dilemmas. Ethics is conceived by some as a system of moral values; a moral philosophy, the rules or standards governing the conduct of a person in both personal and business activities.

Hence, an idea or a deed is ethical when it conforms to the values expressed by this moral philosophy. Normative ethics is defined as basic moral principles, criteria or standards used when deciding what action to take, what is right or wrong about an action and what one's rights are regarding the action (Frankena, 1973).

Meaning of ethical values

A key characteristic of human perception and knowledge, values, requires careful examination, as the values with which one sees the world, exemplified by assumptions about change, freedom and creativity, allow the researcher both to see and to limit possible understanding. Although most people assume that they know what values are, the concept has been difficult to define precisely (Patterson, 1989). A statement of values that seems to capture the main components in the literature defines values as 'concepts or beliefs, about desirable end-states or behaviours, that transcend specific situations, guide selection or evaluation of behaviour and events and are ordered by relative importance' (Schwartz and Bilsky, 1987: 551). Hence, values is a term that may refer to utility, meaning or functionality and, as such, may be found, experienced and enjoyed but cannot be reduced to only one of these terms (Moore, 1988).

Values can assume many forms, depending upon an individual's needs and enjoyment, leading to controversy about definitional boundaries between values and related concepts such as needs, interests and attitudes (Super, 1987). However, these values are always relative. Ethical values refer to that which an individual affirms as moral in human behaviour or in products of spirit (Xiaohe, 2000). As such, ethical values have three dimensions; they can meet an individual's needs for moral life, they are willed or practised by an individual and they are appreciated or enjoyed with moral satisfaction and with a lofty sense (Xiaohe, 2000). For example, ethical values, such as honesty, loyalty, benevolence, justice and good, represent some categories of ethics. In a manner of all other spiritual values, but not economic values, ethical values usually are 'carried by' human behaviour or spiritual products. However, unlike other spiritual values, ethical values have a unique normative function (Xiaohe, 2000). Moreover, ethical values are embedded in the complex 'push and pull' of everyday life surrounding research (Raths et al., 1978: 26) and, as such, are not self-sustaining but appear to be individual, 'resting on some carrier or values object' (Frondizi, 1977: 276).

Research values, for example, can be either with or without ethical values. Therefore, to speak of research values with ethical values does not deny research values, rather it stresses and affirms their interdependence. Ethical values can be affirmed as having research and public utility. However, an ethical value meets an individual's moral need and is affirmed because it has research or public utility value. This notwithstanding, the relation between research and ethical values is not dichotomous, such as 'means–end'. Both need to be pursued and affirmed by researchers who do not draw an 'end–means' distinction. If one makes the acceptance of an ethical value contingent upon whether it promotes research value, then even cheating

TABLE 2.1 *Ethical/moral positions of reasoning*

Philosophical positioning	Criteria for action	Focus of ethical reasoning
Teleological		
• Egoism	• Well-being of moral actor	• Consequences of alternative actions
• Utilitarianism: act and rule	• Aggregate of common good – greatest good for the greatest number	
Deontological		
• Duty-based	• Duties of behaviour (fidelity, justice, humility)	• Relevant duty in the situation
• Right-based	• Rights of individuals (freedom, dignity, liberty)	• Relevant rights of individual affected by actions
Relativism	• Practice and norms accepted by a social group at a specific place and time	• Conventions of own social grouping

will be beyond reproach if it generates tangible ends (Howard, 1985; Pedersen, 1991).

Nor are those researchers correct who think that making ethical values into end-values will solve all problems. Research activities connect to and overlap with many other activities. As such, research values are the primary ones for meeting research central needs. The real issue is not whether ethical or research values are 'end-values' but whether the various values are harmonious and capable of realization (Xiaohe, 2000). Without the support of related ethical values, research values cannot stand their ground. Nor are ethical values the basis of research values. Both values are based on the human need for harmony and, as such, represent two sides of the same coin. The two values cooperate with each other, with neither being subordinate to the other. Research values and ethical values have always maintained a strong connection that cannot and should not be severed.

Notwithstanding that a number of ethical theories have been developed – exemplified by utilitarianism, justice, rights, cultural relativism (see Table 2.1) – much contemporary work on ethics is built on two major philosophical perspectives – teleology and deontology (Cavanagh et al., 1981; Tsalikis and Fritzsche, 1989). These two philosophies have been pivotal in the development of numerous theories, leading to other theories aimed at their synthesis – all of which can give rise to moralities (so understood).

The teleological philosophy has its origins in ancient Greece and centres on the final causes of human action (Fulton, 1967). The teleological philosophy of ethics links the moral worth of human actions with their consequences, thus giving rise to consequential or teleological theories (utilitarianism, egoism) (Pettit, 1993). Hence, behaviour itself has no moral status: moral worth attaches with the consequences. Conversely, the deontological philosophy maintains that the concept of duty is logically independent of the concept of good and that actions are not justified by the consequences of the actors; insisting on the importance of motives and character of the actor rather than the consequences actually produced by the actor – sparking the non-consequential theories of ethics (Beauchamp and Bowie, 1983).

Ethical theories contrasted

The teleological perspective and consequential theories

The two most influential consequential theories to date have been born out of the very nature of the teleological perspective: whether the consequences focus on the outcome of the individual or collective behaviour – egoism and utilitarianism. Egoism focuses on the individual's long-term interests (Reidenbach and Robin, 1990). Philosophers supporting egoism contend that acting against one's own interest is actually contrary to reason. Egoism, as a means to the common good, a view shared by Adam Smith (1976), maintains that under some conditions the best way of promoting the common good is to promote individual good and well-being. Rational egoism centres around the idea that it is always rational and always right to aim at one's own greater good. Ethical egoism, derived from accepting the premise that what is ethical must be rational and that since acting out of self-interest is rational and, therefore, also ethical, holds that conventional morality is tinged with irrational sentiments and indefensible constraints on the individual (Beauchamp and Bowie, 1983). Hobbes (1962) implied this to both rational and ethical rationalism. Egoism has no way of solving conflicts of egoistic interests and, thus, does not satisfy the goals of ethical philosophy: the development and maintenance of conditions that allow actors in a society to pursue a stable and happy life (Reidenbach and Robin, 1990). Ethical egoism is criticized on the basis that it ignores what most actors would agree are blatant wrongs (Reidenbach and Robin, 1990).

Utilitarianism, like egoism, is teleological in structure, with the main difference between the two schools of thought being the subject of the decision. Utilitarianism focuses on a society's long-term interests and is concerned with the consequences of corporate decisions to society at large, in economic or non-economic terms, that may be applicable to any stockholders and measured by net costs and benefits (Boal and Perry, 1985; Frederick et al., 1988). It is rooted in the thesis that an action is right if it leads to the greatest good for the greatest number or to the least possible balance of bad consequences (Beauchamp and Bowie, 1983); its telos (purpose or objective) is popularly characterized as the greatest good for the greatest number (Shaw and Post, 1993). Utilitarian theory proposes that the actor should evaluate all outcomes of an action or inaction and weigh one against another to determine what is best for society in terms of its social consequences (Reidenbach and Robin, 1990). The utilitarian standpoint is most famously associated with Jeremy Bentham (1789/1988) and John Stewart Mill (1969), who argued that businesses operating in their own self interest would produce the greatest economic good for society through an invisible hand metaphor. Fascination with this theory is prominent amongst economic rationalists (Kouzmin et al.,

1997) and those interested in cost/benefit analysis – both dogmas rapidly having been accepted by management in recent years.

Act utilitarianism focuses on how right an act is in terms of its producing the greatest ratio of good to evil for all concerned; *rule utilitarianism* advocates that the actor should try to formulate a set of rules for ethical conduct and that those rules should be evaluated according to the ratio of good versus evil which is produced for all concerned, whether the rule is obeyed or disobeyed. This teleological doctrine differs according to how the conception of good is specified (Aristotle, 1962; Neitzsche, 1976). If good is taken as the realization of human excellence in the various forms of culture, it is perceived as perfectionism. If a good is defined as pleasure, it is perceived as hedonism, if as happiness, eudaimonism, and so on; or, in utilitarian terms, the satisfaction of (rational) desire (Rawls, 1971: 25).

The deontological perspective and non-consequential theories

From a deontological perspective, there is no need to justify duties by showing that they are productive of good; the philosophy focuses on universal statements of right and wrong. However, where exceptions exist, philosophers have suggested that *prima facie* universals allow these exceptions in certain situations (Robin, 1980). The principle is always to act so that everyone, faced with the same situation, should take the same actions. From the deontological (or duty-bound) philosophical perspective, the moral system of thinking is based on the view that particular types of action and/or behaviour are intrinsically ethical or unethical, within rights and justice principles (Scheler, 1963). For example, cheating is always dishonest and, hence, always unethical; the behaviour or action being wrong is not mitigated by how good either the motive behind it or the consequences flowing from it are.

Deontological (non-consequential duty justice, Kantian theory) ethics have been criticized for being overly reliant on over-riding moral principles dictated by reason (Abelson and Nielson, 1967); hence its weakness in explaining away exceptions to universal truths (Tsalikis and Fritzsche, 1989). Criticism of Kant's theory (1901, 1909) from a consequentialist perspective contends that if consequences are disregarded, the actor ends up with a blind acceptance of duty regardless of any consequence. Problems in the management arena may centre around conflicting duties and loyalties, as well as the disobedience of duty to overt, unpleasant consequences (whistle blowing being an example) (Dancy, 1994; Pence, 1994). Accordingly, the 'fundamental moral rule' (Kant, 1909) has a limited capacity for dealing with clashes of duties and rights; providing little assistance in situations where the fundamental rules are in conflict or the rights of two different groups, or actors, cannot both be met by any of the actions or rules that might apply. The rights may both be legitimate according to deontological ethics. However, the ethics do not aid conflict resolution between them – increasing the right of some actors, through the *Freedom of Information Act*, to have access to information held by government agencies may decrease the rights to privacy of other actors, groups and corporations.

Theoretical synthesis

Both teleological and deontological perspectives and, thus, consequential and non-consequential theories, have been equally accused of 'ethical absolutism': the belief that there is one true ethical code or guide for behaviour (Tsalikis and Fritzsche, 1989), leading to the emergence of a hybrid of the two former perspectives attempting to achieve a theoretical synthesis (Ross' *prima facie* duties, Rawls' maximum principle of justice, Garrett's principle of proportionality, ethical relativism). Garrett (1966), for example, tries to synthesize consequentialism and non-consequentialism. He proposes the principle of proportionality, postulating that moral decisions have three elements: intention, means and ends.

In a similar manner, Ross (1930) attempts to join aspects of utilitarianism and Kantianism in his theory of *prima facie* duties. Ross (1930) contended that there are duties and obligations (fidelity, gratitude, justice, beneficence, self-improvement and non-injury) which bind actors morally and in making an ethical decision an actor should weigh up all the duties involved and their options – determining from there which duty is most obligatory or *prima facie*.

Rawls' (1971) justice-based theory of ethics attempts to use a classic 'multi-method' approach to ethical theory: using the strengths of consequentialist and non-consequentialist philosophies whilst avoiding their weaknesses. Rawlsian (1971) social justice (Rawlsian utilitarianism) is based on the view that actions which produce the greatest good for the greatest number are ethical and are so because the objective measure of good is more reliable than other approaches, as it is based on realism to ensure an ethical society. He proposes two principles: the equal liberty (impartial and equitable administration of rules which defines a practice) and the justice principle. For Rawls (1971), a just society is one in which inequalities can be justified. Rawls (1971) specified under what conditions the equal liberty principle can be violated.

Ethical relativism maintains that decisions concerning what is ethical are a function of a culture or individual and, therefore, no universal rules exist that apply to everyone (Reidenbach and Robin, 1990). The relativist perspective has its roots in the great thinkers of ancient Greece; Protagoras, in the fifth century BC, held that moral principles cannot be shown to be valid for everyone and that people ought to follow the conventions of their own grouping. Cultural relativism posits that moral standards cannot be universally valid, because of value differences in culture. Hence, moral norms are culture-specific, where each culture and society has its own norms – morality is a matter of conforming to the standards and rules acceptable in one's own culture (Brandt, 1959; Hansen, 1992). Moral views are simply based on how an actor feels or how a culture accommodates the desires of its actors, not on some deeper set of objectively justifiable principles (Beauchamp and Bowie, 1983). From a relativist perspective, a moral standard is simply a historical product sanctioned by custom (Beauchamp and Bowie, 1983; Hansen, 1992). Hence, an actor's initial position is bound to be the dialectical situation which the actor experiences in the temporal period in which the actor resides – the problems of the actor reflect the truths and virtues the community generally accepts, excluding societal deviants (Dewey, 1930).

Extreme relativism (Robin, 1980) asserts that since there are two sides to every moral dilemma and since every individual is entitled to their own system of values, neither side is more correct than the other. The relativist weakness is the assumption that, deep down, there is no real difference between moral beliefs; that if analysis probes deeply enough into the decision-making processes, one would reach a point where the basic rationales were the same: Not a satisfying ethical philosophy (Reidenbach and Robin, 1990).

UNDERSTANDING CAUSES OF ETHICAL DILEMMAS IN RESEARCH

There are many influences on ethical decision-making and researcher behaviour that can add to ethical dilemmas. These factors can be loosely grouped into four broad categories; personality-based, organizational-based, issue-related and society-related factors, where the personality-based category includes cognitive development, personal experiences as well as an innate biological tendency or personal orientation to react more intensely to lower levels of stress than others and to take longer to recover (Kernberg, 1995; Linehan, 1993). Personality-based factors are shaped through family, education, religious upbringing/training, gender, work position and role, *locus* of control and culture (Trevino and Youngblood, 1990).

Organizational-based factors highlight the effect of significant others within the organizational setting, exemplified by top management's actions, corporate policies, behaviour of peers, reward systems, organizational climate and professional codes of ethics (Jones, 1991; Victor and Cullen, 1988). Issue-based factors that influence ethical decisions and behaviour include rewards associated with unethical action, the magnitude of consequence, temporal immediacy, proximity, probability of effect, concentration of effect, social consensus and the nature of relationships (Heimer, 1992). A variety of societal factors have been identified as influential on ethical decision-making and behaviour, such as society's political ethics and climate, moral climate, legislation and governmental regulations, as well as media coverage and disclosure (Brenner and Molander, 1977).

There are three broad categories of causes of dilemmas, namely conflict of values within an individual's value system, conflict of values between two value systems and the dilemma due to personal orientation. Each of those categories can provide the basis of personal dilemmas during the research process. To violate any of the deeply held claims defining conscience would be de-humanizing and create moral discord for the individual. Often, the ethical issues surrounding modern research in organizations challenge traditional ethical thinking and the professional's conscience becomes the key to discord. Indeed, one can argue that if the researcher does not encounter conflict with his/her values or within two sets of values, such a situation would be exceptional. Conflict of values in management research can be taken as the norm. Most people encounter a struggle with unclear or conflicting values during their research and need to work through these dilemmas. Honest self-examination and open-minded search can be achieved through clarification of

TABLE 2.2 *Examples of ethical dilemmas due to clash of researcher's values*

Objectivity	*versus*	Subjectivity
Personal gain	*versus*	Stakeholders' benefits
Respect of personal comfort zone	*versus*	Respect of stakeholders' comfort zone

one's priorities or one's positions on values in a given context. The processes of critically thinking about and discussing aspects of an individual's particular value conflict often can help those individuals resolve such conflict (Kirschenbaum, 1977; Kohlberg, 1981; Raths et al., 1978; Rest, 1983).

Decisional conflict of ethical values in research can occur when there are simultaneous opposing tendencies within the individual to accept and reject a given course of action (Janis and Mann, 1977: 42). This can lead to intra- and inter-personal values conflict, where two or more values are in opposition within an individual or within an individual value system and others' values. An ethical values conflict may be conceptualized as a decisional conflict that transcends a specific situation (Rokeach, 1973). For example, the decision as to whether or not to ask research participants potentially embarrassing questions may or may not involve a value conflict and such a decision could be simply a one-off choice. Ethical values conflict, such as presenting organizationally sensitive research findings openly versus withholding some research results, may lead to moral dilemmas such as job security versus research integrity. Conflict of values can relate to both the subject matter of research and to the conduct of the research. Moreover, it involves both personal and professional elements.

Conflict between values within an individual's own value system

Conflict in aspects of life being valued by an individual creates an ethical dilemma. For example, Actor X was a passionate advocate of information-sharing within organizations and was instrumental in drafting a code of conduct for e-mail use. During her research on the effects of e-mail communication on individual performance, she discovered that a number of employees were misusing this channel of communication. In addition, the main offender of the organizational code of conduct was Actor X's brother-in-law. She had the dilemma as to whether to share this information with management sponsoring her research (duty) or withhold this information (protection of the family member). Examples of ethical dilemmas that researchers may encounter during research are provided in Table 2.2.

Conflict between two sets of values: clash of value systems

Different sets of values between individuals (pacifism, abolition of experiments with animals) and organizational or professional codes provide fertile ground for conflict. For example, Hanna was facing a classic dilemma of a

TABLE 2.3 *Examples of ethical dilemmas due to clash of value systems*

Professional code	*versus*	Organizational code
Research community values	*versus*	Professional values
Individual values	*versus*	Host organization values

person in transition. Hanna spent the first 35 years of her life in a kibbutz, where she was a practising psychologist. Her role for many years was one of caring for clients and the community. When Hanna undertook her PhD research, at the leading firm in the area of market segmentation, she found that her family and professional values, such as 'compassionate caring', seemed to be in conflict with organizational values such as 'survival', 'profit maximization' and 'influencing customers'. Hanna needed to re-frame the problem as one of clarifying values. She tried to understand her own values more fully and then develop a way of making decisions when those values appeared to conflict. She prioritized compassionate caring with other values such as honesty, fairness and respectfulness, to name just a few. At the end of the process, she decided to change her research and research site. Her new site was the high school and her research topic was affirmation of self-identity of school lives through 'mirroring'. Examples of ethical dilemmas due to a clash of value systems that the researcher may encounter are provided in Table 2.3.

Personal orientation as a source of ethical dilemma

Some scholars theorize that individuals are born with an innate biological tendency or personal orientation to react more intensely to lower levels of stress than others and to take longer to recover (Kernberg, 1995; Linehan, 1993). They argue that these individuals peak 'higher' emotionally on less provocation and take longer 'coming down', whilst the psychodynamic theory of developmental psychology argues that personal orientation is learned and developed. Development comes through the insight into, awareness of, the 'coming to terms with' and integration of the unconscious part of one's psyche (Back and Gergen, 1968; Erikson, 1959; Freud, 1938; Jung, 1945/1981). Whether individuals are born with certain predispositions or whether individuals experience environments in which their beliefs about themselves are continually devalued or invalidated (Kernberg, 1995), or a combination of these factors, these individuals develop personal orientations that portray an uncertainty of the truth of their own feelings and are confronted by three paradoxes that need to be resolved:

- vulnerability versus invalidation;
- active passivity (tendency to be passive when confronted with a problem and actively seek a rescuer) versus apparent competence (appearing to be capable when in reality internally things are falling apart); and
- unremitting crises versus inhibited grief.

Such individuals lack 'emotional skin' (Linehan, 1993). They feel agony at the slightest emotional demand – exemplified by choice of one good over another – and perpetually experience ethical dilemmas or experience moral anxiety (Freud, 1988; Nunberg, 1955). The emotional burns may be caused by shattered early trust in people close to them, over-criticism or rejection, thus engendering a feeling of 'needing' someone else to survive – dependency, need for affection and reassurance, rejection of authority and influence and a sensitivity to criticism. Some individuals develop an unusually high degree of interpersonal sensitivity, insight and empathy. An individual's level of development, including cognitive moral development, strongly influences the person's decisions regarding what is right or wrong – the rights, duties and obligations involved in a particular ethical dilemma (Kohlberg, 1981: 602; Lickona, 1991; Trevino, 1986). The individual's reactions to dilemmas are deeply seated, largely unconscious and intimately connected to the development of identity – they have emotional content (Kernberg, 1995). An individual who is confused or unclear about his/her values tends to behave in immature, over-conforming or over-dissenting ways (Raths et al., 1978). In part, the extent of dilemmas faced by researchers in organizational and management research are congruent with the researcher's own attitudes towards such dilemmas, his/her behaviours when confronted by issues and the researcher's own ability to work through these dilemmas and, in part, to the presence or absence of the organization and/or professional guidelines in place. Owing to personal orientation, some individuals have dilemmas due to their sense of empathy; ambivalence to values and utility of influence; over-defiance or compliance to authority; lack of trust and poor self-image.

In research, empathy needs to balance respect for the individual *and* for the task at hand. However, some individuals experience on-going dilemmas due to empathy for the individual research subject and task at hand versus research objectivity. The typical dilemma a researcher may experience is between being overly involved with the research subject, losing objectivity of research or being over-focused on research and not doing enough to help research subjects. Actor Y, for example, spent most of her time changing her methodology. When questioned why, she admitted that all methodologies were too restrictive for the study of office harassment. At the same time, she admitted that she had lost her objectivity and that she was on a witch-hunt of harassers.

Having empathy can be beneficial in research. It empowers stakeholders to take risks and provides researchers with confidential information which, if not handled correctly, can cause discomfort and even a job loss (Goffee and Jones, 2000). Empathy facilitates communication and authenticity, the precondition for effective research. For example, research stakeholders will be more likely to show their true selves in front of empathetic researchers, instead of playing roles during interview (Goffee and Jones, 2000). This allows for the research of sensitive aspects of organizations. However, there is also a need for balancing empathy with research goals and methodology. Examples of ethical dilemmas that some researchers may encounter due to personal orientations are provided in Table 2.4. Many people feel a deep ambivalence about the utility and value of influence, in general. Psychologists argue that

TABLE 2.4 *Examples of dilemmas due to researcher's personal orientation*

Information/knowledge sharing	*versus*	Information/knowledge control
Trusting	*versus*	Mistrusting
Taking feedback	*versus*	Defensiveness

these feelings often stem from unconscious fear of one's capacity for destructiveness (Waldroop and Butler, 2000). In the research community, many guard against influence in order to preserve impartiality. Typical dilemmas researchers face are influencing others in order to achieve desired outcomes for organization or personal gain. For example, during his three years of research, Actor Z changed the title of his research nine times. When questioned why, he declared that he is trying to compensate for overly influencing his research subjects. Researchers whose personal orientation is ambivalent to influence need to examine the real motives driving their research. They have to recognize when and how influence should be used in order to gain support or access for research in an ethical manner. Exercising influence is necessary in management research in order to secure access to funding and access to, often, very sensitive information. Influence should not be exercised for personal gain (Kakabadse, 1991).

Some individuals face authority-based dilemmas. Depending on their orientation to authority, some defy perceived authority in every possible instance and in every possible way, whilst others are overly deferential. Such individuals may reject advice from others (supervisors) or may become overly dependent on others. They usually experience a directiveness-dependency dilemma such as, are my research stakeholders (supervisors, boss) overly directive in research or am I too dependent on my stakeholders (supervisors or colleagues)?

Nature of research dilemmas

An unlimited number of value conflicts can exist as any combination of two or more opposing value positions within a research issue can arise during the research process, either in relation to research conduct or in relation to communication of research results. Two broad categories of research dilemmas can be defined; namely, dilemmas based on the researcher's conduct during the research process and dilemmas based on research epistemology, exemplified by communication of research results. Dilemmas based on the researcher's conduct are of a contingent nature and can appear at any time during the research process. For example, at the very beginning of the research process researchers may have a dilemma such as the desire to follow individual interests in research versus following research that would provide benefit to the host organization. Because of its contingent nature, it is often difficult to foresee dilemmas in advance, although researchers need to think of the unthinkable and be prepared to deal with dilemmas as they arise. Examples of conduct-based dilemmas are provided in Table 2.5.

TABLE 2.5   *Examples of conduct-based dilemmas*

Negotiation for access	*versus*	Expectation of delivery
Consistency of application	*versus*	Individual comfort zone
Universalistic principles	*versus*	Contextual considerations

TABLE 2.6   *Examples of epistemologically based dilemmas*

Information/knowledge sharing	*versus*	Information/knowledge withholding
Information/knowledge distribution	*versus*	Selective sharing
Transparency	*versus*	Falsification

Epistemologically based dilemmas are foreseeable during the life of research as they occur at particular, critical parts of research – such as the time of arriving at new knowledge or its communication to research stakeholders. They can appear at the time when the researcher needs to give sensitive feedback to research participants. Researchers may question how much to reveal without causing discomfort (emotional and physical) to other stakeholders. Epistemologically based dilemmas often come in clusters and are predictable; thus, researchers can, to some extent, plan in advance strategies as to how to handle them. Researchers may have dilemmas owing to the organizational code of ethics for privacy versus research code of ethics for authenticity. Examples of epistemologically based dilemmas are provided in Table 2.6.

CODE OF ETHICS

The field of organizational and management research ethics can afford to be no less vigilant than other disciplines in the pursuit of knowledge concerning the implications of multicultural similarities and differences for successful international professional practice. Particularly critical is the need to test the assumptions that ethical standards for organizational and management research conduct are transportable to other research sites. Globalization of technology, in its broader context, often lays the groundwork for the transfer of respective values, goals, needs, skills, abilities and praxis – IT technology is not culture-free (Korac-Boisvert, 1992; White and Rhodeback, 1992: 664). Although written ethical rules, in general, and codes of ethics, in particular, are important elements in building an ethical society, they are not sufficient means for conducting ethical research. Notwithstanding, there have been a number of attempts to provide a universal code of ethics for the research community – exemplified by Glass (1966), Cournand and Meyer (1976) and the Academy of Management (*Academy of Management Journal*, 1992).

Glass' (1966) code of ethics governing the behaviour of the researcher consists of:

- cherish complete truthfulness;
- avoid self-aggrandizement at the expense of one's fellow researcher;
- defend the freedom of scientific enquiry and opinion; and
- fully communicate one's findings through primary publication, synthesis and instructions.

Cournand and Meyer's (1976) five-point code of ethics governing the behaviour of the researcher consists of objectivity, honesty, tolerance, doubt of certitude and self-lessons.

The Academy of Management credo states codes that should guide member behaviour in relation to students, advancement of managerial knowledge, the larger professional environment, the practice of management and the world community (*Academy of Management Journal*, 1992).

The models of codes being adopted by research institutions and researchers themselves vary in form and context; from a Ten Commandment approach covering a small number of general precepts, expressed in broad terms, but with no provision for the code's administration, to a Justinian Code approach, by providing a comprehensive coverage of ethical rules with guidelines for their implementation. While research codes of ethics have their usefulness in providing guidance to researchers, they have been also criticized on many accounts: being too specific or too general, unworkable, unused, unknown or, simply, that statements of rules are not the ideal medium for answering complicated ethical dilemmas faced by researchers. First, they are incomplete as codes are focused on the pursuit of knowledge in isolation from a research context. Furthermore, they are dependent upon the relative values which one places on knowledge, as compared with other social values. In addition, they do not provide explicit or implicit guidance on how researchers should conduct themselves with respect to the application of scientific knowledge to particular affairs. Organizational and management research is a social activity which must take account of other social values where research may also have other roles. For example, a researcher may also be a mentor, a therapist and adviser, an employee and a citizen who cannot always separate science from human beings.

Some research codes of ethics in particular organizational contexts can lead to an ethical paradox. For example, a researcher in organizations with a code of ethics that upholds privacy and a research code that upholds freedom of information may lead a researcher to such an ethical paradox. Codes of conduct, however, remain important mechanisms for ethical standards, even in societies that have reduced the rules and regulation approach to research.

Because of the incongruency between promoted/desired values by the research organization or researcher and the contextual realities of the host organization or professional affiliation, researchers are likely to encounter a paradoxical dilemma. They face the paradox of what one *should* do (work within the desired values?) and what one *ought* to do (what is needed in the particular context?). Some of the paradoxes that researchers have to contend with are summarized in Table 2.7.

TABLE 2.7   *Example of ethical paradoxes in the research context*

Values		Values
Free market economy (Utilitarian)	*versus*	Accountability (Deontological)
Freedom of information (Deontological)	*versus*	Privacy (Deontological)
Information sharing (Utilitarian)	*versus*	Confidentiality (Deontological)
Public sector codes (Deontological)	*versus*	Ministerial discretion (Utilitarian)
Public servant (Deontological)	*versus*	Political servant (Utilitarian or Egoist)
Organizational codes with focus on shareholder values (Deontological)	*versus*	Research codes such as self-lessons (Deontological)
Universalistic (Deontological)	*versus*	Particularistic (Act utilitarian)

A REFLEXIVE FRAMEWORK FOR ETHICAL WAYS FORWARD

Opportunities for misunderstanding in management research are ample, starting from initiation, through execution of research to dissemination of results. Management research is a social activity that must take account of other social values within research and the broader social context. Moreover, within the research context, researchers may have many roles. In addition, increasingly, organizations are becoming multicultural communities.

Management research lends itself to qualitative research, with particular attention to the focus group and cooperative methods allowing for the understanding of phenomena. However, appreciation of cultural differences and the recognition of common versus specific cultural characteristics need to be respected. Culturally informed and sensitive researchers need to tailor their information-gathering efforts to match the client's cultural expectations. Researchers also need to be aware of possible value conflicts and ethnic differences with respect to specific norms, attitudes and cultural expectations. Perhaps nowhere does values conflict play out more dramatically than in the workplace – where rights and needs of various stakeholders must be continuously negotiated and harmonized.

The concept of values clarification was originally developed by Raths et al. (1978), both as a theory and an intervention. The theory was built on the work of humanistic scholars (Dewey, 1930; Maslow, 1959; Rogers, 1969). Maslow (1959) and Rogers (1969) contended that individuals are responsible for discovering their own values through the processes of honest self-examination and open-minded search for truths about life. Dewey (1930: 65) held that 'valuing occurs when the head and heart . . . unite in the direction of action' and that the experience of valuing involves the interdependent processes of reasoning, emoting and behaving. Some earlier writers argued that human beings, if they are to complete their development and reach their potential, must be prepared to re-evaluate their values (Barrett, 1958; Rogers, 1969).

To find a way forward in ethical dilemmas individuals can utilize strategies based on two conceptual methods, which considerably overlap, for clarifying one's values, rational intuitive methods (Agor, 1986; Clarke and Greenberg, 1986; Harren, 1979; Heppner, 1989; Kohlberg, 1981; Levy, 1977; MacPhail-Wilcox and Bryant, 1988; Simon, 1957; Simon et al., 1972) and a psychological awareness strategy in order to improve psychological awareness of oneself (Back and Gergen, 1968; Erikson, 1959; Jung, 1945/1981). The rational model consists of logical decision-making procedures which include information-gathering and the systematic comparison and elimination of alternatives (Clarke and Greenberg, 1986). The intuition-enhancing model consists of techniques designed to de-structure thinking and allow the often unconscious 'wisdom of the organism' to emerge (Clarke and Greenberg, 1986: 11; Greenberg and Higgins, 1980). The psychological awareness strategy is based on the idea that the development, or realization, of individual self-identity continues over the course of one's entire lifetime (Back and Gergen, 1968; Erikson, 1959; Jung, 1945/1981). The psychological awareness strategy is based on selection of various intervention models (Back and Gergen, 1968).

A framework of rational and intuition-enhancing-based strategies, as well as psychological awareness strategies, that can assist individuals to resolve ethical dilemmas in research are presented below. Each of these strategies can be adapted for idiosyncratic values conflicts. These strategies can focus individual attention on research and bring to one's mind, for evaluation, one's own attitudes, feelings, activities, goals, aspirations, interests, beliefs and conflicts and can highlight some of the confusing issues of research, such as relationships, hope, power, generosity, justice and the rest (Raths et al., 1978: 150). Secondly, strategies can help individuals deal with research dilemmas more skilfully and more comprehensively, as they give individual practice in choosing freely, seeking alternatives, anticipating consequences and recognizing what one prizes and cherishes, by verbalizing and affirming what one cares about – acting on one's own choices and doing so with some consistency (Raths et al., 1978: 150). The proposed framework of strategies offers a process for individuals to compare alternative actions, consider consequences and make choices. However, the framework does not prevent an individual from choosing or from accepting other codes and/or authority as the final 'truth', be it the Bible, the Talmud, the Koran or their equivalents. An individual may decide to embrace any particular dogma or code of ethics as true or can hold that some values positions are inherently morally superior to others.

Rational strategies

First identify your ethical dilemma and then ask yourself the following questions:

- What is my intention in making this decision? How does this intention compare with the probable results?
- Have I:
  - Obtained sufficient information to make an informed decision in this situation? What are the known facts of the situation? Have I defined the event accurately? Do I have the ability to understand the world from the perspective of my stakeholders?
  - Defined research boundaries clearly?
  - Involved others who have a right to have an input and/or be involved in making this decision? Who are the key stakeholders and what do they value and what are their desired outcomes? Have I compared alternatives and considered consequences logically. Have I eliminated alternatives systematically?
  - Anticipated and attempted to accommodate the consequences that this decision may have on those who are significantly affected by it? To whom could my decision/action cause discomfort? How can I prevent discomfort to stakeholders? What are the underlying drivers causing discomfort?
- In priority order, rank the top five or so ethical values that you hold in the context of your research, then ask:
  - Does this decision/action plan uphold my enduring values relevant to this situation?
  - In priority order, what operating values do I think I should uphold in this situation? Will this be as valid over a long period of time?
  - Am I over-influenced by my context?
  - Do I apply universal principles or attain the greatest good for the greatest number?
  - Is my ego driving what I do? If honest, am I pursuing what is best for my immediate circle?
  - Where does my loyalty lie as a member of the research community and the organization that provides context for my research? Under what conditions would I allow exceptions to my position?

Intuition-enhancing strategies

- With emotional focusing, ask yourself the following questions:
  - How would I feel if I was one of the stakeholders in this situation? Would I perceive this decision/action to be essentially fair, given all of the circumstances?
  - Are hearts and minds won through published words or constancy of behaviour?
  - Could I disclose, without qualm, my decision or action to others (working associates, the board of directors, my family, society as a whole)?

- Brainstorm all your conflict resolution ideas/free association.
- Review your research and/or life goals.
- Use guided imagery into hypothetical futures.
- Use incubation (meditation, 'sleeping on it').
- Exercise self-confrontation, such as adopting dialectical debate or devil's advocate roles, which confront your own morality by involving both rational discourse and a focus on affective reactions. The dialectic method calls for structuring a self-debate between conflicting views regardless of a member's personal feeling (Cosier and Schwenk, 1990). The benefits of the dialectic method are in the presentation and debate of the assumptions underlying proposed courses of action (Benson, 1977; Brown, 1978). False or misleading summations become apparent and can head off unethical decisions based on poor assumptions (Korac-Kakabadse et al., 1999, 2000; Simms, 1992).

Psychological awareness strategies

Some individuals may benefit from improving psychological awareness through use of an intervention model (Back and Gergen, 1968). Improving psychological awareness can help individuals come to an understanding of their own self-identity, what is important to them and how to deal with the complexities in life. It can help them move from being other-directed in determining their behaviour to looking within themselves for what are the most authentic expressions of who they are – both in their personal and professional lives as researchers.

Moreover, it can help researchers in organizations and management have the courage to come to terms with, and deal effectively and appropriately with, the dilemmas stemming from the reality of their own and other people's lives, rather than spending energy on how they imagine research should be. In other words, it can help people 'break the bubble' of illusion, which often leads to a lack of action, inappropriate action, un-authentic action and subsequent dissatisfaction with their personal and professional lives (Back and Gergen, 1968).

External interventions in the form of coaching, mentoring or counselling can provide a fresh perspective and approach when trying to work through ethical dilemmas due to personal orientation. Such interventions can certainly assist individual learning and development. These interventions can utilize a variety of 'leading edge' models and techniques in order to develop and/or raise psychological awareness. Some of the more commonly used interventions can include:

- Psychodynamic models (Jungian, cognitive, psychoanalysis, bio-energetics).
- Mirroring, a process of confirmation of, or reflection about, the appropriateness of identity as it is and which provides an emotional basis for an identity sought to be developed (Schwartz-Salant, 1982).
- Drama workshops, which explore psychological themes such as influence, selfishness and authority.
- Body/mind therapies, such as meditation and relaxation techniques.
- Feedback, analysis, goal-setting models and techniques.

Irrespective of the strategy one utilizes, researchers need to be vigilant about maladaptive affects regarding conflict resolution such as excessive worry, post-decisional regret, irrational beliefs and attempts to use cognitive restructuring, emotional inoculation or stress-reduction techniques to counter maladaptive affects. Moreover, as research dilemmas and individuals' situations change over time, new intra- and inter-personal values conflict permutations are likely to emerge. Consequently, resolving values conflicts in research is an on-going process and, for some, a life-long activity. Becoming clearer about one's research beliefs, values and priorities, although not a sufficient condition, may, at least, be a necessary one for the pursuit of ethical research and for psychological health and peace of mind. In addition, research codes of ethics, research stakeholders, the research community and society at large, act as a buffer against bias and personal gains in research whilst simultaneously providing context for new dilemmas and ethical paradoxes.

Part of the management research role is to re-define established social patterns and, thus, one can expect contradictions to arise. Management research should be seen as a dialectical interplay of individuals whose roles change from objectivity to subjectivity, interpretation and creation, one part of the system to another, and who remain open to dialogue and discussion in the continuing concern for new knowledge. Researchers need to 'work through', 'engage in dialogue' and 'critically discuss' the dilemmas and psychodynamics they encounter.

Study questions

1 In the course of everyday work, researchers are faced with a myriad of ethical dilemmas, all of which involve moral judgements, standards, rules of conduct and perceptions regarding right or wrong. Identify the most difficult ethical problems that came up in your research. Reflect on these ethical dilemmas you have encountered in your research to date and how you have resolved them.

2 Clarify your enduring research values and construct an action plan for dealing with potential conflicts:

- In priority order, rank the five or so ethical values you hold in the context of research.
- Identify which of those values you will be willing to negotiate and under which circumstances.
- Consider any ethical values that might be prized by stakeholders of your research. For example, consider expectations of your founders, colleagues and research community.
- Rank in priority order five ethical values for each stakeholder group.
- Identify any potential clashes between your values and your stakeholders' values.
- Devise action plans as to how to overcome identified conflicts.

3 Compose a personal code of ethics for your research. In order to guard against criticism by those who consider codes of ethics vacuous because

they are only a list of ethical values and, as such, do not clarify values by associating examples of behaviour, attempt to associate with each at least two example behaviours that reflect that value. Examples of two ethical values, 'integrity in research' and 'communication with others' are provided below to illustrate this exercise.

Integrity in research is defined as a willingness to communicate openly, directly and honestly and exhibit high standards of personal behaviour, acting in line with the research spirit, even when difficult to do so, thus engendering trustworthiness and loyalty to the research community and research stakeholders. Behaviour that communicates 'integrity in research' is considered as one that:

- Demonstrates courage of convictions, accepts responsibility for research conduct and results.
- Is open with stakeholders and builds trust.
- Keeps commitments, states intentions and carries them out.
- Admits mistakes and limitations of research.
- Recognizes own personal biases that influence research.
- Demonstrates respect for all research stakeholders.
- Shows loyalty to people and ideas.
- Deals with all equitably, is consistent in treatment of others and research standards worked with.
- Constitutes a role model for others.

Communication with others is defined as the ability to build sound relationships with a research community and other stakeholders and using appropriate communication methods. Behaviours that demonstrate 'communication with others' include:

- Listens and questions in a way that encourages open dialogue and enhances understanding.
- Can interpret collected information and make it meaningful to other stakeholders.
- Uses different methods of communication as appropriate.
- States cases, gives information clearly and logically, in user-friendly manner.
- Keeps stakeholders informed and actively listens to others' views.
- Values the opinion of other stakeholders and actively seeks their views.
- Creates good relationship with stakeholders built on trust and respect.

Recommended further reading

Fukuyama, F. (1995) *Trust: The Social Virtues and the Creation of Prosperity*. London: Hamish Hamilton. (A controversial treatise on social values and collaboration)

Kakabadse, A. (1991) 'Politics and Ethics in Action Research', in C. Smith and P. Dainty (eds), *The Management Research Handbook*. London: Routledge, pp. 289–99. (Ethics in practical research and interventions)

Kakabadse, A. and Kakabadse, N. (1999) 'Working Through Ethical Dilemmas', in *Essence of Leadership*. London: International Thomson Business Press, pp. 372–416. (A practical guide for resolving ethical issues)

Kimmel, A.J. (1988) *Ethics and Values in Applied Social Research*. Applied Social Research Methods Series: Volume 12. London: Sage. (A basic primer for researchers)

Morley, D. (1978) *The Sensitive Scientist*. Report of a British Association Study Group. London: SCM Press. (A popularized statement of accepted codes and practices)

References

Abelson, R. and Nielson, K. (1967) 'The History of Ethics', in P. Edwards (ed.), *Encyclopaedia of Ethics*. New York: Macmillan, pp. 81–116.

Academy of Management (1992) 'The Academy of Management Code of Ethical Conduct', *Academy of Management Journal*, 35 (5), pp. 1135–42.

Agor, W.H. (1986) *The Logic of Intuitive Decision Making*. New York: Quorum Books.

Aristotle (1962) *Nicomachean Ethics*. New York: Macmillan and Library of Liberal Arts.

Back, K.W. and Gergen, K.J. (1968) 'The Self Through the Latter Span of Life', in K.W. Back and K.J. Gergen (eds), *The Self in Social Interaction*. New York: Wiley, pp. 241–50.

Barrett, W. (1958) *Irrational Man: A Study in Existential Philosophy*. New York: Doubleday Anchor Books.

Beauchamp, T.L. and Bowie, N.E. (1983) *Ethical Theory and Business*, 2nd edn. Englewood Cliffs, NJ: Prentice Hall.

Benson, J.K. (1977) 'Organizations: A Dialectical View', *Administrative Science Quarterly*, 22 (1), pp. 1–21.

Bentham, J. (1789/1988) *Introduction to the Principles of Morals and Legislation*. New York: Hafner.

Boal, K.B. and Perry, N. (1985) 'The Cognitive Structure of Corporate Social Responsibility', *Journal of Management*, 11 (3), pp. 71–82.

Brandt, R. (1959) *Ethical Theory*. Englewood Cliffs, NJ: Prentice Hall.

Brenner, S.N. and Molander, E.A. (1977) 'Is the Ethics for Business Changing?', *Harvard Business Review*, 55 (1), pp. 57–71.

Brown, R.H. (1978) 'Bureaucracy as Praxis: Towards a Political Phenomenology of Formal Organizations', *Administrative Science Quarterly*, 23 (3), pp. 365–8.

Cavanagh, G.F., Moberg, J.D. and Velasquez, M. (1981) 'The Ethics of Organizational Politics', *Academy of Management Review*, 6 (3), pp. 363–74.

Clarke, K.M. and Greenberg, L.S. (1986) 'Differential Effects of the Gestalt Two-Chair Intervention and Problem Solving in Resolving Decisional Conflict', *Journal of Counselling Psychology*, 33 (1), pp. 11–15.

Cosier, R.A. and Schwenk, C.R. (1990) 'Agreement and Thinking Alike: Ingredients for Poor Decisions', *Academy of Management Executive*, 4 (1), pp. 69–74.

Cournand, A. and Meyer, M. (1976) 'The Scientist's Code', *New Scientist*, 14 (1), pp. 79–96.

Dancy, J. (1994) 'An Ethic of Prima Facie Duties', in P. Singer (ed.), *A Companion to Ethics*. Oxford: Blackwell, pp. 219–29.

Dewey, J. (1930) 'From Absolutism to Experimentalism', in R.J. Bernstein (ed.), *John Dewey on Experience, Nature and Freedom*. New York: The Library of the Liberal Arts, pp. 17–31.

Erikson, E.H. (1959) *Identity and the Life Cycle*. New York: W.W. Norton.

Frankena, W. (1973) *Ethics*. Englewood Cliffs, NJ: Prentice Hall.

Frederick, W.C., Davis, C.K. and Post, J.E. (1988) *Business and Society*, 6th edition. New York: McGraw-Hill.

Freud, S. (1938) *The Basic Writings of Sigmund Freud*. New York: The Modern Library.

Freud, S. (1988) *New Introductory Lectures on Psychoanalysis*. London: Pelican Freud Library.

Frondizi, R. (1977) 'Basic Problems in Axiology', in M. Smith (ed.), *A Practical Guide to Values Clarification*. La Jolla, CA: University Associates, pp. 268–78.

Fulton, W. (1967), 'Teleology', in P. Edwards (ed.), *Encyclopaedia of Philosophy*, Volume 12. New York: Macmillan and The Free Press, pp. 215–16.

Garrett, T. (1966) *Business Ethics*. Englewood Cliffs, NJ: Prentice Hall.

Glass, B. (1966) *Science and Ethical Values*. Oxford: Oxford University Press.

Goffee, R. and Jones, G. (2000) 'Why Should Anyone be Led by You?' *Harvard Business Review*, 78 (5), pp. 63–70.

Greenberg, L.S. and Higgins, H.M. (1980) 'Effects of Two-Chair Dialogue on Conflict Resolution', *Journal of Counselling Psychology*, 27 (2), pp. 221–4.

Hansen, R.S. (1992) 'A Multi-Dimensional Scale for Measuring Business Ethics: A Purification and Refinement', *Journal of Business Ethics*, 11 (7), pp. 523–34.

Harren, V.A. (1979) 'A Model of Career Decision Making for College Students', *Journal of Vocational Behaviour*, 14 (1), pp. 119–33.

Heimer, C.A. (1992) 'Doing Your Job and Helping Your Friends: Universalistic Norms About Obligations to Particular Others in Networks', in N. Nogria and R.G. Eccless (eds), *Networks and Organizations*. Boston, MA: Harvard University Press, pp. 143–64.

Heppner, P.P. (1989) 'Identifying the Complexities Within Clients' Thinking and Decision Making', *Journal of Counselling Psychology*, 36 (2), pp. 257–9.

Hobbes, T. (1962) *Leviathan* (edited and abridged by J.P. Plamenatz), London: Collins.

Howard, G.S. (1985) 'The Role of Values in the Science of Psychology', *American Psychologist*, 40 (2), pp. 255–65.

Janis, J.L. and Mann, L. (1977) *Decision-making: A Psychological Analysis of Conflict, Choice and Commitment*. New York: The Free Press.

Jones, T.M. (1991) 'Ethical Decision-Making by Individuals in Organizations: An Issues-Contingent Model', *Academy of Management Review*, 16 (3), pp. 366–95.

Jung, C.G. (1945/1981) *The Structure and Dynamics of the Psyche*, Volume 8 of The Collected Works of C.G. Jung. Princeton, NJ: Princeton University Press.

Kakabadse, A. (1991) *The Wealth Creators: Top People, Top Teams and Executive Best Practice*. London: Kogan Page.

Kant, I. (1901) *Critique of Pure Reason*, rev. edn, translated by J.M.D. Meiklejohn. London: Wiley.

Kant, I. (1909) 'Preface to the Metaphysical Elements of Ethics', in T.K. Abbott (trans.), *Kant's Critique of Practical Reason and Other Works on the Theory of Ethics*, sixth edition. London: Longmans, Green and Company, pp. 45–80.

Kernaghan, K. and Langford, J. (1990) *The Responsible Public Servant*. Institute of Public Administration of Canada, Halifax and Institute for Research of Public Policy, Toronto.

Kernberg, O. (1995) *Object Relations Theory and Clinical Psychoanalysis*. New York: Jason Aronson.

Kinnier, R. (1995) 'A Reconceptualization of Values Clarification: Values Conflict Resolution', *Journal of Counselling and Development*, 74 (1), pp. 18–28.

Kirschenbaum, H. (1977) *Advanced Values Clarification*. La Jolla, CA: University Associates.

Kohlberg, L. (1981) *Philosophy of Moral Development*. San Francisco: Harper and Row.

Korac-Boisvert, N. (1992) 'Developing Economies and Information Technology: A Meta-Policy Review', paper presented at the Australian and New Zealand Academy of Management (ANZAM), Annual Conference on Re-discovering Australasian Management Competence in a Global Context, Sydney, December, pp. 1–34.

Korac-Kakabadse, N., Kakabadse, A. and Kouzmin, A. (1999) 'Dysfunctionality in Citizenship Behaviour in Decentralised Organizations: A Research Note', *Journal of Managerial Psychology* (Special Issue on Living with Change), 14 (7–8), pp. 526–44.

Korac-Kakabadse, N., Kouzmin, A., Knyght, P.R. and Kakabadse, A. (2000) 'The Impact of Information Technology on the Ethics of Public Sector Management in the Third Millennium', *Global Virtue Ethics Review*, September, 2 (1), pp. 74–124.

Kouzmin, A., Leivesley, R. and Korac-Kakabadse, N. (1997) 'From Managerialism and Economic Rationalism: Towards "Re-Inventing" Economic Ideology and Administrative Diversity', *Administrative Theory and Praxis*, 19 (1), pp. 19–42.

Levy, J. (1977) 'The Mammalian Brain and the Adaptive Advantage of Cerebral Asymmetry', *Annals of the New York Academy of Science*, 299 (2), pp. 264–72.

Lickona, T. (1991) *Educating for Character*. New York: Bantam.

Linehan, M.M. (1993) *Cognitive-Behavioural Treatment of Borderline Personality Disorder*. New York: Guilford Press.

MacPhail-Wilcox, B. and Bryant, B.H.D. (1988) 'A Descriptive Model of Decision Making: Review of Idiographic Influences', *Journal of Research and Development in Education*, 22 (1), pp. 7–22.

Maslow, A.H. (1959) *New Knowledge in Human Values*. New York: Harper & Brothers.

McIntyre, A. (1981) *After Virtue: A Study in Moral Theory*. New York: Gerald Duckworth and Company.

Mill, J.S. (1969) 'Utilitarianism', in J.M. Robson, F.E.L. Priestley and D.P. Dryer (eds), *Essays on Ethics, Religion and Society*. Toronto: University of Toronto Press, pp. 201–60.

Moore, G.E. (1988) *Principia Ethica (Great Books in Philosophy)*. New York: Prometheus Books.

Nietzsche, F. (1976) *The Will to Power*. New York: Vintage.

Nunberg, N. (1955) *Principles of Psychoanalysis*. New York: International University.

Patterson, C.H. (1989) 'Values in Counselling and Psychotherapy', *Counselling and Values*, 33 (1), pp. 164–76.

Pedersen, P.B. (ed.) (1991) 'Multiculturalism as a fourth force in counselling', *Journal of Counselling and Development*, Special Issue, 70 (1), pp. 1–4.

Pence, G. (1994) 'Virtual Theory', in P. Singer (ed.), *A Companion to Ethics*. Oxford: Blackwell, pp. 249–58.

Pettit, P. (1993) 'Consequentialism', in P. Singer (ed.), *A Companion to Ethics*. Oxford: Blackwell, pp. 230–40.

Plato (1984) *The Dialogues of Plato*, Volume 1. New Haven, CT: Yale University Press.

Raths, L., Harmin, M. and Simon, S. (1966) *Values and Teaching: Working with Values in the Classroom*. Columbus, OH: Charles E. Merrill.

Raths, L., Harmin, M. and Simon, S. (1978) *Values and Teaching: Working with Values in the Classroom*, 2nd edition. Columbus, OH: Charles E. Merrill.

Rawls, J. (1971) *A Theory of Justice*. Cambridge, MA: Harvard University Press.

Reidenbach, R. and Robin, D. (1990) 'Toward the Development of a Multidimensional Scale for Improving Evaluations of Business Ethics', *Journal of Business Ethics*, 9 (8), pp. 639–53.

Rest, J.R. (1983) 'Morality', in J. Flavell and E. Markman (eds), *Manual of Child Psychology: Cognitive Development*, Volume 4. New York: Wiley, pp. 214–23.

Robin, P.D. (1980) 'Value Issues in Marketing', in W.C. Lamb and M.P. Dunne (eds), *Theoretical Developments in Marketing*. American Marketing Association, Proceeding Series.

Rogers, C. (1969) *Freedom to Learn*. Columbus, OH: C.E. Merrill.

Rokeach, M. (1973) *The Nature of Human Values*. New York: The Free Press.

Ross, W.D. (1930) *The Right and the Good*. Oxford: Clarendon Press.

Scheler, M. (1963) *Formalism in Ethics and the Material Ethics of Value*. Oxford: Clarendon Press.

Schwartz, S.H. and Bilsky, W. (1987) 'Towards a Universal Psychological Structure of Human Values', *Journal of Personality and Social Psychology*, 53, pp. 550–62.

Schwartz-Salant, N. (1982) *Narcissism and Character Transformation*. Toronto: Inner City Books.

Shaw, B. and Post, F.R. (1993) 'Amoral Basis for Corporate Philanthropy', *Journal of Business Ethics*, 12 (10), pp. 745–51.

Simms, R.R. (1992) 'Linking Groupthink to Unethical Behavior in Organizations', *Journal of Business Ethics*, 11 (9), pp. 651–62.

Simon, H. (1957) *Administrative Behavior*. New York: The Free Press.

Simon, S.B., Howe, L.W. and Kirschenbaum, H. (1972) *Values Clarification: A Handbook of Practical Strategies for Teachers and Students*. New York: Hart.

Smith, A. (1976) *An Inquiry Into the Nature and Causes of the Wealth of Nations*, sixth edition. London: Methuen.

Super, D.E. (1987) 'Needs, Values, Interests and Attitudes: Constructs and Measures Needing Clarification', paper presented at the Annual Convention of the American Psychological Association, New York, August.

Trevino, L.K. (1986) 'Ethical Decision Making in Organizations: A Person-Situation Interactions Model', *Academy of Management Review*, 11 (3), pp. 601–17.

Trevino, L.K. and Youngblood, S.A. (1990) 'Bad Apples in Bad Barrels; A Causal Analysis of Ethical Decision-Making Behavior', *Journal of Applied Psychology*, 75 (3), pp. 378–85.

Tsalikis, J. and Fritzsche, D.J. (1989) 'Business Ethics: A Literature Review with a Focus on Marketing Ethics', *Journal of Business Ethics*, 8 (5), pp. 695–743.

Victor, B. and Cullen, J.B. (1988) 'The Organizational Bases of Ethical Work Climate', *Administrative Science Quarterly*, 33 (1), pp. 101–5.

Waldroop, J. and Butler, T. (2000) 'Managing Away Bad Habits', *Harvard Business Review*, 78 (5), pp. 89–98.

White, L.P. and Rhodeback, M.J. (1992) 'Ethical Dilemmas in Organization Development: A Cross-Cultural Analysis', *Journal of Business Ethics*, 11 (9), pp. 663–70.

Xiaohe, L. (2000) 'On Economic and Ethical Values', *The Online Journal of Ethics*, 2 (1), pp. 37–42.

PART 2

Research Processes

3

Modelling-as-Theorizing: A Systematic Methodology for Theory Development

David A. Whetten

OVERVIEW

> Organizational researchers are primarily trained in data collection techniques and the latest analytical tools, not the nuances of theory building. Our doctoral programs tend to skip over theory building perhaps because it is not a step-by-step process that can be taught like LISREL or event-history analysis. Reading major theorists and writing literature review papers is often passed off as training in theory building, even though such assignments really don't teach one how to craft conceptual arguments. (Sutton and Staw, 1995: 380)

I second Sutton and Staw's sobering assessment regarding the paucity of theory-development training in the field of organizational studies. Furthermore, I strongly endorse Weick's (1989: 516) observation, 'Theory cannot be improved until we improve the theorizing process, and we cannot improve the theorizing process until we describe it more efficiently, [and] operate [it] more self-consciously . . .'

Reflecting the link between this edited volume and a series of workshops for doctoral students sponsored by Cranfield School of Management, what follows has a strong pedagogical purpose and flavour. Given the 'critical path' function of theorizing in the development of scholarly knowledge, our field is not well served by the myth that theory development is high art, known and knowable only to a rare, elite cadre of organizational theorists, and beyond the grasp of less insightful scholars who, by default, are relegated to the less difficult (because it is codified) task of theory testing. I believe that theory development, like theory testing, is a competence that can and must be taught, practised and improved.

Kurt Lewin's (1945) oft-quoted endorsement of theory, 'there is nothing quite so practical as a good theory', contains two key claims: theory is *practical* – it is useful in guiding practice – and, only *good* theory is practical – bad theory is often dysfunctional, and even harmful. As reflected in my October 1989 *Academy of Management Review* essay 'What constitutes a theoretical contribution?', my abiding interest is in making the case for developing *good* theory. Furthermore, because I believe the quality of the organizational theories generally available to both scholars and managers for guiding their respective forms of practice is closely linked to the quality of the theory-development tools commonly practised, I welcome this opportunity to encourage the use of better theory-development practices.

Above all else, effective theory development practices produce theories that lend themselves to further development. I will argue in this chapter that this requirement necessarily requires scholars to make their implicit theoretical notions explicit. I will further argue that systematic theoretical conceptions are superior to unsystematic ones, and that systematic conceptions are more likely to arise from systematic conceptual processes. The core of the chapter describes a formal methodology for codifying theoretical assumptions and claims, thus making them more amenable to improvement through ongoing logical, empirical and practical assessment.

ASSUMPTIONS ABOUT THEORY AND THEORY DEVELOPMENT

I need to set the stage by specifying several key assumptions and assertions. First, I subscribe to the widely held notion that, at its core, theory is best conceived of as the answer to questions of *why* (Kaplan, 1964; Mohr, 1982). As Sutton and Staw observed, 'Theory is about the connections among phenomena, a story about why acts, events, structure and thoughts occur' (1995: 378). This conception of theory allows us to distinguish between scholarly *description* (one that is informed by theory but is limited to insights regarding *what* is happening) and scholarly *explanation*. Descriptions, regardless of how detailed or insightful they are, may be considered conceptual contrbutions, but without an explanation for what is observed, they do not qualify as theoretical contrbutions.

Second, I believe that the most promising arena for theory development in our field is the incremental improvement of middle-range theories (Whetten, 1989). Although most scholars dream of creating a wholly new, full-blown, broad-gauged theoretical perspective, few realize this dream. Instead, theory development mostly focuses on improving extant explanations for what is readily observable, via a process of incremental change informed by logical, empirical or practical tests. My point is that although our field is perpetually anticipating radical new conceptualizations of motivation, leadership, group dynamics, or strategy, this form of theorizing should not be thought of as the primary (and certainly not as the exclusive) domain of the scholarly craft known as theory development.

Third, I support the position that efforts to improve theory development should be guided by the supposition that better theory is desirable because it is more useful. Given the applied nature of our field, we cannot afford the luxury of viewing the scholarly exercise of improving theory as an end in itself. Hence, I agree with Campbell (1990: 66): 'It is difficult to imagine that very useful theory could be created by someone who only knew the general laws of theory development and had never spent time in an organization, never tried or intended to collect data, and knew nothing of measurement and other methodological issues.'

Fourth, having agreed with Campbell's argument that discussions of theory development must not become preoccupied with elegant formalism at the expense of considerations of sound substance, I strongly resist the implication that knowledge of good form contributes little to one's ability to generate good theory. In fact, to suggest that there is no merit in method-ological discussions of how to develop good theory makes no more sense than the reciprocal argument that empirical tests of theory should be con-ducted and evaluated without regard for accepted methodological conventions and standards. Although there is undoubtedly a spark of cre-ative inspiration at the core of all noteworthy theory-development initiatives, it is not at all obvious that inspiration and insight are unique to theory build-ing (surely they are at least as evident in creative tests of theory), nor am I aware of any evidence that the use of a structured approach to theory build-ing extinguishes the generative flame of insight. On the contrary, it has been my experience that many seemingly interesting and creative insights never make it to the pages of our journals because they are so ill-formed that they are judged to be ill-conceived. Hence, while the medium should never be thought of as the message, our choice of medium for conceptualizing has a profound effect on the quality and type of conceptualization we are able to craft.

Fifth, the objective of theory-development training should be the articula-tion of theories that are closer and closer approximations of the requirements of *strong theory* (Weick, 1995). It has been widely observed that theorizing is not unique to the scholarly enterprise. Instead, it arises from a universal human need to order and explain personal experience (Dubin, 1978). Given that seemingly 'everyone has theories about everything', then science's claim of distinction must be supported by an obvious qualitative difference between *ordinary explanations* and *scholarly explanations*. This qualitative difference is often referred to as the power, or strength, of a theory. (See Campbell, 1990: 65 for an excellent working definition.)

For purposes of assessing how well our theory development efforts approximate this ideal, I suggest a simplified benchmark. In his classic trea-tise on scientific knowledge, Kant (1998) argued that a body of scholarship should be both *complete* and *systematic*. That is, what scholars have to say about a subject should represent a complete, or satisfactory, accounting of the matter, in the sense that it shouldn't contain obvious, gaping holes. In addition, the body of knowledge should be organized, coherent and self-consistent.

In retrospect, my 1989 *AMR* article focused primarily on developing complete theories – those containing certain essential elements. During the past decade, my interest has expanded to include theory-development tools, or processes, that encourage the development of scholarly knowledge that is systematic, in other words, structured and orderly. The development of theories that are both complete and systematic, by means of an orderly, easy-to-use methodology is the objective of this chapter. But before wading into the details of this presentation I need to introduce an important distinction.

CONTRIBUTIONS OF THEORY VERSUS CONTRIBUTIONS TO THEORY

Treatises on theory development need to distinguish between contributions *of* theory and contributions *to* theory (Whetten, 1989). The former use theory to improve enquiry; the latter use enquiry to improve theory. For my present purposes, this distinction reminds us that how we use our theories (what we consider to be a contribution *of* theory) affects the level of attention we devote to improving our theories (the value we place on making contributions *to* theory).

In making this distinction, I have a particular concern in mind. The common practice in our field (especially 'macro' organizational studies) of using theoretical frameworks as if they are competing theoretical perspectives, or lenses (for example, how does what I see through the lens of institutional theory compare with what I see through the lens of resource control theory?) tends to shift our focus away from the permanent need to continuously improve the quality of each and every theoretical lens. The practice of using theories as perspectives tends to produce paradigmatic boundaries around our theories, which in turn fosters winner-take-all, *between-theory* scholarly debates (Pfeffer, 1993). Taken to the logical extreme, advocates of a particular theoretical perspective become so focused on advancing the merits of their point of view that their impassioned advocacy actually deflects attention away from the underlying theory-development question 'Is this the best we can do?' (Greenwald et al., 1986). Although so-called 'paradigm wars' often have theoretical merit (McKinley and Mone, 1998), we should not overlook the theory development opportunity costs associated with between-theory debates – namely, they can, and often do, direct attention away from much needed *within-theory* improvement.

Let me briefly illustrate this proposition. In 1997, Anjali Sastry published a paper in *Administrative Science Quarterly* in which she critically examined punctuated equilibrium theory, which had been introduced in our field by Mike Tushman and Elaine Romanelli during the mid-1980s (Tushman and Romanelli, 1985). What I find striking about the literature review in Sastry's paper is that it contains numerous references to applications of punctuated equilibrium as a theoretical perspective, but there is not a single reference to systematic critiques of, or claimed improvements in, the theory.

It is particularly instructive to examine Sastry's theory development methodology. She begins by systematically identifying the theory's constitutive elements, including four core constructs and several key relationships between those constructs. After deconstructing the punctuated equilibrium theoretical lens into a set of focal elements, Sastry proceeds to systematically test the theory's core assertions using simulation data. Based on these results she proposes several non-trivial improvements in this well-worn theoretical perspective.

This exemplary piece of theory-development scholarship illustrates the necessary change in focus required of those who wish to make contributions *to* theory, from uncritically looking through a theoretical lens, to regularly and assiduously looking at the lens.

DEVELOPING COMPLETE AND SYSTEMATIC THEORIES

The title of Weick's (1989) classic article, 'Theory construction as disciplined imagination' sets the tone for what follows. I am sure that graduate students who have worked with me will find it ironic that I am making a case for disciplining one's imagination. Because I am by nature a divergent thinker, I easily succumb to theoretical rapture, a state of supernal intellectual bliss in which I can envision connections between anything and everything that can be imagined. However, I have experienced enough frustration trying to test, let alone express, conceptualizations that are overly complex and hopelessly convoluted, that I have grudgingly developed an appreciation for theories that are both complete *and* systematic.

It seems that young scholars are particularly susceptible to the allure of needlessly complex conceptualizations. Given the amount of information doctoral students are required to master during a highly compressed period of learning, coupled with an associated bias against uninformed (read, naïve) explanations underlying all scientific discourse, it is not surprising that aspiring scholars are inclined to construct unwieldy conceptual maps. Although the impulse to add value by adding variables may be justified on the grounds that it will produce a more complete conception, failure to discipline this impulse typically yields a hodge-podge conceptualization that is not practical for any purpose. What many of us need is a proven antidote for this learned mental affliction.

The notion that the enterprise of scholarship is devoted to instilling not just scholarly knowledge, but also scholarly 'habits of mind' (Fine, 1995), is at the heart of the 'critical thinking' movement in education circles, as reflected in the following observation.

> Everyone thinks; it is our nature to do so. But much of our thinking, left to itself, is biased, distorted, partial, uninformed or down-right prejudiced. Yet the quality of our life and that of what we produce, make, or build depends precisely on the quality of our thought. Shoddy thinking is costly, both in money and in quality of life. Excellence in thought, however, must be systematically cultivated.

Critical thinking is that mode of thinking – about any subject, content, or problem – in which the thinker improves the quality of his or her thinking by *skillfully taking charge of the structures inherent in thinking and imposing intellectual standards upon them*. (Paul and Elder, 2001: xx; emphasis added)

Several years ago, at a conference on the subject of conducting research that is both scholarly and practical, I was reminded of the practical value of disciplining our scholarly imagination by subjecting it to intellectual standards and conventions. During this meeting, two senior, highly distinguished organizational scholars, independently said something like the following: 'I am an experimental social psychologist by training. Recently, my scholarly interests have shifted from testing theories about organizing to solving problems in organizations. Therefore, I don't plan to conduct any more laboratory experiments. However, I'm glad that I've spent several years designing lab studies because the experimental design logic cultivates rigorous thinking.'

The language and logic of experimental design are one of the many intellectual standards that can be used to discipline our imagination. Because of my sociological background I am more comfortable with modelling, with a strong preference for graphical models. When students want to discuss a new research idea with me, I instinctively start drawing diagrams, figures and models.

One of the nice features of graphical models is their versatility, as tools of scholarship. For example, modeling techniques can be used to organize ethnographic field notes and to make sense out of a large body of scholarly knowledge. As these applications suggest, most formalized decision support aids and cognitive mapping tools rely on some form of graphical modeling (Huff and Jenkins, 2002). Models are equally useful as instruments of effective discourse. Audiences, consisting of students, executives or colleagues, always seem to be most attentive to the graphical elements in a written or oral presentation.

The simplest, most compelling justification for using graphical models to guide the theorizing process is that the features of the tool of choice for constituting and representing theories should exemplify the qualities of the ideal theory. Graphical modeling naturally lends itself to developing conceptualizations that are both complete and systematic. In addition, modeling is equally useful as a theory development tool for constructing emergent explanations of 'new' phenomena (Eisenhardt, 1989) and for improving long standing explanations (Bachrach, 1989).

Let me hasten to agree with Sutton and Staw (1995): a diagram, by itself, is not a theory. If we think of a theory as a story about 'why', then a model is properly viewed as a visual aid that helps storytellers highlight the main features of their explanations. In other words, when models-as-visual aids are used by scholars-as-theorists, it is easier to understand authors' arguments and to evaluate the merits of their claims. Sutton and Staw (1995: 376) said it well: 'For researchers who are not good writers, a set of diagrams can provide structure to otherwise rambling or amorphous arguments. For those researchers who are talented writers, having a concrete model may prevent obfuscation of specious or inconsistent arguments.'

Modelling-as-theorizing

What follows is a rudimentary theory-development methodology, using basic graphical modelling logic and conventions. Those who are interested in learning more about modelling as a theory-development tool are referred to Asher (1976), Dubin (1976), Jacobsen et al. (1990), Abell (1971) and Guetzkow (1962). For related examples of the use of graphical models as analytical tools in our field see Huff and Jenkins (2002), Morecraft and Sterman (1994), Cossette and Audet (1992), Porac and Thomas (1990).

The proposed modelling methodology contains four steps, corresponding to the four elements of a good theory described in my 1989 *AMR* article: What, How, Why, When/Where/Who. This step-by-step approach provides a systematic framework for codifying the constitutive elements of an extant theoretical perspective or for espousing an emergent theoretical perspective. To enhance the usability of this methodology, the description of each step contains guidelines for practice.[1]

I will not take time to review the terminology introduced in my 1989 article (What, How, Why, etc.), but my usage is similar to the following: '[A theory] is a collection of assertions, both verbal and symbolic, that identifies WHAT variables are important for what reasons, specifies HOW they are interrelated and WHY, and identifies the CONDITIONS under which they should be related or not related' (Campbell, 1990: 65; emphasis added).

Step 1: 'Whats'-as-constructs

A few years ago I taught a course with Bonner Ritchie, a legendary teacher at Brigham Young University. During one of the class periods he articulated a compelling theory of moral choice. After class a student asked him how he had come up with such a clear and clearly thoughtful understanding of a highly abstract and complex subject. Later, his intriguing reply, 'I developed this model in a motel room in Laramie, Wyoming', was expanded into the following story. 'Driving from Michigan to Utah I encountered a severe snow storm in Wyoming. Hearing that the interstate was closed in the middle of the state, I stopped in Laramie and found a motel room. Before settling in for the night I went to a grocery store and purchased a long strip of butcher paper and some large markers. I had been thinking about moral decision making while I was driving and I wanted to use this time to clarify and organize my thoughts. Back in my room, I taped the butcher paper on the wall and began drawing circles, each one representing a key concept in my emerging framework.'

I'm confident that motel owners and campus janitors are grateful that academics now have a viable substitute for butcher paper and indelible marker pens: 'Post-it® Notes' (PIN). As illustrated by Bonner's story, the question guiding this initial phase of the model building process is, 'What are the elements of my conceptualization?' Equipped with a packet of PINs, consider the following guidelines as you begin to explore this question.

1   Treat each PIN as a circle, or box, in a graphical model. Each PIN should contain the name of a single construct, written as a noun or noun phrase.[2]

Start with your core construct – the target of your theorizing; the focal point of the puzzle or question you are trying to understand. Then, expand your focus by adding more and more related constructs, including those that might represent causes, effects and correlates. At this point I suggest you err on the side of inclusion rather than on the side of parsimony, because subsequent steps in the process will help you be more selective.

As you list your constructs, keep in mind that it is generally preferable to think in terms of *variables*, not values (variable levels). That is, in most cases, theoretical explanations that account for the full range of a construct (high to low, top to bottom, good to bad etc.) are preferable to theories of only one level, form or degree. Given the applied nature of our field, it is not surprising that most of our theories of leadership, or effectiveness, or quality, actually only cover one end of the implied continuum – good leaders, high effectiveness, good quality. This practice encourages incomplete conceptualizations and inaccurate characterizations. There are numerous examples in our literature where the explanations for the opposite ends, or values, of a commonly used construct are not simply mirror images, for example, organizational effectiveness versus ineffectiveness (Cameron, 1984) and growth versus decline (Whetten, 1980). So, unless you have a compelling reason for focusing only on part of the range of your constructs, go through your list and scratch out any qualifiers (for example, motivation, ability, performance).

2 After creating a list of constructs (a stack of PINs) assess them as a set, especially their complementarity, or compatibility. As a starting point, use the characteristics of your focal construct as a benchmark for evaluating the suitability of the other constructs (given how I'm conceptualizing X, how complementary are the other elements in my set?) We will consider two criteria for guiding this assessment: the scope and the coherence of the construct set.

(a) *The scope of the concepts.* Scope, or extension, generally refers to the breadth of the behaviour or activity covered, the class of things to which it applies, or the totality of the objects that it identifies (Osigweh, 1989: 584). For example, the meaning of a commonly used term like 'employee participation' can range from 'all efforts to broaden a worker's control and involvement in organizational affairs', to 'a subordinate's involvement in the decision-making process with guidance from superiors' (Osigweh, 1989: 583).

There is no absolute standard that we can invoke in the assessment of scope. Instead, the scope of a theoretical framework needs to be appropriate for its intended use, for example, as a general explanation, or as a guide for contextualised research. Here is the rub: There is a demonstrated preference in our field for broad theoretical perspectives (McKinley et al., 1999), but these are often difficult to translate into realistic research designs, for several reasons.

First, broad theoretical conceptions tend to rely on 'theoretical concepts' (in contrast to empirical, or observable concepts) whose 'systemic meaning' is derived solely from their part in a theoretical conception (Abell, 1971; Osigweh, 1989). Examples include synergy, adaptability, decentralization, formalization, reputation, image, identity and stress. Given that the meaning of these constructs is derived from their specific, and often imprecise, theoretical usage, there is a high risk that the theorist espousing a theory and the empiricist testing a theory will have difficulty agreeing on the validity of a theoretical conception because they're not sure if they are talking about the same thing.

Second, broad gauged theoretical models necessarily leave out critical elements of the naturally occurring phenomenon. This results in an under-specified model, in which critical components of the logical argument are left unspecified.[3] For example, arguing that the presence or absence of a written code of conduct, or an ethical organizational climate, affects organizational performance, or that participation in decision-making leads to greater employee commitment, raises questions about the implied intermediate causal links and unspecified conditions. The obvious problem with using an incomplete theoretical explanation to guide research is that it is difficult to derive testable propositions.

Third, the data collection requirements necessary to test very broad conceptualizations are often unrealistic. One way to assess the feasibility of constructing a research design suitable for your construct set is to group your constructs according to their associated data collection requirements, for example, tally the number of different types of data (employee attitudes, company performance), the number of sources of data (employees, company records, industry statistics) and the number of data collection cycles (employee data from multiple companies, observations at three points in time).

(b) *The coherence of the constructs.* It is important to keep in mind that a model is a visual aid for telling a story, and that the story needs to be coherent. An argument is coherent to the extent that it 'hangs together'. The standard of coherence requires us to grant the criterion of *systematic* trumping rights over the criterion of *complete*. A common source of hard-to-follow, difficult-to-understand explanations is unnecessary complexity, resulting from the inclusion of bits and pieces of knowledge that are legitimately related to the subject but that are not germane to the author's particular interest in the subject (or that exceed the author's capacity to do justice to the subject).

For example, the literature on organizational identity contains references to a number of related constructs, including image, reputation, legitimacy, identification and multiple identity management strategies (Whetten and Godfrey, 1998). But just because these concepts are related to organizational identity doesn't mean they must be included in a particular theoretical treatment of identity.

As a general rule, the larger the number of constructs used to formulate an explanation, the greater the risk that the composite explanation will not make sense. But there is an even greater threat to coherence, namely, the use of concepts that differ in kind. Space allows me only to draw attention to a single example: concepts that don't share a common level (conceptual/organizational) of analysis.

Theories of 'organizational behaviour' can focus on *contextual properties* (for example, industry performance, availability of human or financial capital), that are external to the target of investigation, *global properties* (for example, size, age, function) that are observable, and originate, at the work unit or organizational level, *shared properties* (for example, organizational climate, group norms), that are common to group members, or *individual properties* (for example, personal demographics, job performance, satisfaction level), that are unique to each person.

Although there are some excellent, recent examples of theorizing across multiple organizational levels (Aldrich, 1999; Arrow et al., 2000), as well as some important conceptual advancements in our understanding of the phenomenon of cross-level effects in organizations (Goodman, 2000; Klein and Kozlowski, 2000; Waldman and Yammarino, 1999), this continues to be treacherous conceptual terrain.

The literature on multi-level approaches to theory development presents the following conundrum. On the one hand, given that most constructs of interest to organizational scholars are embedded in a complex, multi-level set of interdependent processes, all single-level explanations of these constructs are, by definition, seriously underspecified. On the other hand, given the quantum increase in conceptual complexity associated with multi-level theorizing, it is inappropriate to include concepts from multiple organizational levels in a theoretical conception without clearly identifying the specific type of cross-level effect proposed (Waldman and Yammarino, 1999, list four different types), and the cross-level process that accounts for the effects, principally, emergence or embeddedness.

Emergence has to do with the processes by which individual properties, including attitudes and behaviours, are shaped through interaction and are manifest as higher level, collective phenomena. For example, Kozlowski and Klein (2000) identify two broad emergent processes, *compilation* (team performance) and *composition* (group climate), with three sub-types for each.[4] In contrast, *embeddedness* refers to the processes whereby lower level phenomena are brought into alignment with higher level phenomena. For example, Rousseau (1978) has argued that work-unit technology and structure exercise cross-level effects on individuals because they constrain the characteristics of jobs. In contrast, organizational size, strategy or structure are less likely to exhibit similar individual-level effects, because the causal cross-level connections are less direct, or proximal.

In general, the challenges posed by multi-level theorizing are so nettlesome that the prudent path, especially for novice scholars is to '. . . act as if the phenomena occur at only one level of theory and analysis. In this way, a theorist temporarily restricts his or her focus, putting off consideration of multilevel processes for a period' (Kozlowski and Klein, 2000: 13).

Step 2: 'Hows'-as-relationships

This is a critical step in the theory-development process, because the specification of relationships between constructs is the key difference between a theory and a list of reasons or examples. Lists of best practices for leaders, or of enabling conditions for organizational change, may be useful conceptual heuristics for teaching or consulting, but they do not qualify as explanations, and they provide inadequate direction for research. Basically, a list is an incomplete theory – it contains 'whats', but no 'hows', which means it can't inform questions of why.

It is important to keep in mind that the distinction between variance and process theories described in Mohr's (1982) highly acclaimed treatise on theory development is not the same as the distinction between the 'what' and the 'how' elements of a theory. Although the focus and form of process and variance theories are extremely different, they are constructed using similar materials and in a similar manner (that is, they both contain whats, hows etc.). Ironically, many process-oriented conceptualizations are incomplete theories because they gloss over the 'how' components. Here's how Mohr sees it. 'Process oriented ideas in organizational behavior, and in social science more broadly, tend to be of the stage naming variety. They are incomplete from the standpoint of theory in that they simply rehearse a series of steps; they lack the lines of action – either causal or probabilistic – that must be present to convey a sense of explanation' (1982: 53).

Although the basic 'how' questions must be addressed in all theoretical frameworks, the level of detail you need to provide regarding the relationships in your model will vary based on whether you intend to make a 'what' versus a 'how' theoretical contribution. For example, if your theoretical assertion is that a new moderating variable needs to be added to an existing conceptualization, then your accompanying justification will naturally be heavily content-oriented. In contrast, if the point of your theoretical argument is that the nature, or form, of a relationship has been mis-specified, or that the indirect or recursive effects of a particular construct in a complex model have been under-specified, then your focus will be centred on a detailed specification of these relationships.

An in-depth treatment of the myriad conventions used for specifying the precise nature of relationships in a model is beyond the scope of this chapter, so a couple of pointers will have to suffice. First, be aware that there is no consensus regarding the language of 'how'. For example, the cognitive mapping literature refers to 'relationships of influence' (Cossette and Lapointe, 1997), the sociology theory-development literature uses the term 'laws of interaction' (Dubin, 1978), and the systems-dynamics literature focuses on the specification of 'causal links' (Sterman, 2000). Second, keep in mind that many of the more detailed and technical discussions of relationship types or forms have a strong methodological orientation. Therefore, unless the focus of your conceptualization is on an unusual type of relationship, it is reasonable to postpone consideration of detailed relationship questions until you've completed your first pass through this theory-development cycle. Third, all organizational scholars need to come to terms with the nettlesome issue of causality in social science research. To that end, here are some thoughts to consider.

With few exceptions (Mohr, 1982, is a good example), debates regarding the implied or explicit use of 'causal links' in our conceptualizations tend to have more symbolic than substantive merit. Because causation is inferred, not observed, scholars' expressed views about the legitimate use of causation in scholarship seldom inform the question of how the proposition that A is related to B should be tested (Dubin, 1978). For this reason, I resonate with Dubin's (1978) advice to avoid the subject of causation in our theorizing, altogether. In its place he suggests invoking specific, acausal, 'laws of interaction' – two of which are particularly appropriate for theory development in our field.

The first is called *categoric*, meaning that two constructs are associated, for example, 'When A, then B'. Think of this type of relationship as a suitable default option. That is, use it unless you have sound justification to specify a more complicated form of interaction. (You are in good company – most canonized social science is based on categoric relationship claims.) The other commonly used law of interaction is called *sequential* because it invokes a temporal dimension, for example, 'A precedes B', or 'B follows A'. If you choose to utilize the sequential law in your theorizing you should be prepared to discuss the various forms that sequential relationships might take. For example, are you invoking a natural law argument (X logically follows Y), an historical argument (X generally precedes Y) or a developmental argument (Y emerges from X)?

With this general information about relationships between constructs as a backdrop, we now turn our attention to specific suggestions for completing this step of the theorizing methodology. The goal of these guidelines is to help you avoid creating models that 'more closely resemble a complex wiring diagram than a comprehensible theory' (Sutton and Staw, 1995: 376).

1   Determine the role of your core construct in your explanation – does it play the role of an *explanatory* construct or an *explained* construct (Abell, 1971)? To help you answer this question, place your core construct in the centre of a page and then arrange the remaining constructs horizontally on the page (to the left or right of your starting point). The distinction between a 'contribution to' versus a 'contribution of' introduced earlier suggests a simple way of determining whether your constructs should be placed to the left or to the right of the core construct. Specifically, what is on the left side can be thought of as a 'contribution to' your explanation of the core construct, whereas what is on the right can be thought of as a 'contribution of' the core construct to the explanation of your outcome of choice.

Another way of thinking about the left versus right distinction is that your left side constructs will be used to explain your core construct (why it is), whereas what is on the right side serves as a justification for the core construct (why it is worthy of study, for example, because it is a significant predictor of organizational performance). This is similar to the distinction made by Cossette and Audet (1992: 342) between 'cause–effect' and 'means–end' relationships. The former concerns the 'why' of the effect, and suggests that the discussion of a cause-as-an-explanation begins with the word 'because'. The second type of relationship constitutes a reason for the means and suggests a justification beginning with 'in order to'. (Cossette and Audet's example: Mr Brown could delegate *because* his firm is growing, or *in order to* have more time for himself.) In the first case, the initial variable controls the final variable, much like a stimulus in classical conditioning. In the second case, it is the final variable that determines the initial variable, analogous to the role of reinforcement in operant conditioning.

In suggesting that you arrange your constructs to the left or to the right of your core construct I am not implying that your goal should be a symmetrical distribution. Indeed, there are relatively few published theoretical models and even fewer published empirical studies that use the core construct as both an explanatory and an explained variable. Therefore, a symmetrical model is best suited for a comprehensive representation of a body of knowledge, rather than as a guide for a specific research project.

2   After you have grouped your constructs to the left and to the right of your core construct, select the ones you wish to use in constructing your *core sequence*. These should be arranged from left to right, forming the horizontal axis of your model. These contructs constitute the primary elements of your theory. For example, in the illustrative model shown in Figure 3.1[5] the core, or primary sequence contains four constructs: Effort (motivation), Performance, Outcomes and Satisfaction. The intermediate constructs in this sequence (Performance and Outcomes) are referred to as *mediators*, in the sense that they mediate the relationship between the constructs on either side. According to this model, the Outcomes (rewards and discipline) given to workers are based on their Performance, not their Effort. Hence, the relationship between Effort and Outcomes is said to be mediated by Performance. (In other words, the link between motivation and outcomes goes *through* performance.) Assuming the horizontal axis in your model contains more than two constructs, make sure that the intervening linkages satisfy the definition of a mediating relationship (Baron and Kenny, 1986).

3   Now, begin fleshing out the vertical dimension of your model by arranging the remainder of your constructs above and below your horizontal axis, locating them left to right in reference to one or more of the constructs in your core sequence. Constructs that are located above and below the horizontal axis generally serve as *moderators*. A moderating construct is one that changes the relationship between two other constructs when it is present (Baron and Kenny, 1986). For example, in Figure 3.1, Ability is included as a moderating construct between Effort and Performance. This means that in order to fully understand the relationship between motivation and performance we must take into consideration a person's ability.

4   Now that you have logically arranged your constructs, in a horizontal and vertical fashion, the next step is to make explicit the theoretically relevant relationships in your conceptualization. The ability to portray specific relationships, as well as an overall pattern of relationships, is one of the strengths of graphic modelling. 'Arrows' are the convention most commonly used for this purpose. In addition, postulated feedback loops

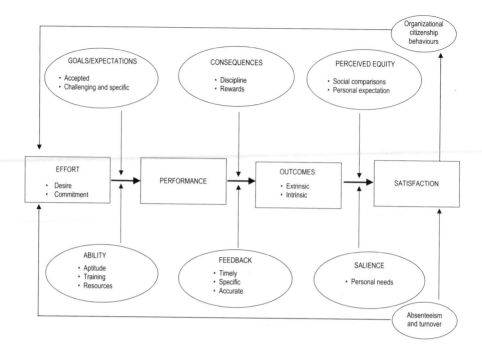

FIGURE 3.1   *A comprehensive model of individual performance and satisfaction (adapted from Whetten and Cameron, 2001)*

and/or reciprocal causality can be signified using various types of 'double arrows'. Kerlinger (1973: 34) even suggests the practice of signifying the strength of a proposed relationship using a solid line to represent a well-established, empirically verified, relationship versus a dotted line to represent a postulated relationship, requiring further examination. Finally, in some theoretical conceptions, especially those based on cybernetic logic, the 'sign' of a given relationship as well as the total number of positive and negative relationships in the model are key visual referents for important theoretical arguments.[6]

Step 3: 'Whys'-as-conceptual assumptions

Whereas the first two steps in the methodology focused on constructing a graphical representation of a theory, these final two steps require us to specify the context, or boundary conditions, of our theory. In other words, this marks a transition from focusing on the composition of a model to focusing on the context of the model. To formalize this distinction, you might find it useful to draw a box around your model and write 'conceptual assumptions' (step 3) above the model and 'contextual assumptions' (step 4) below the model.

The conceptual assumptions underlying a theory can be thought of as 'second order explanations' – the implicit whys underlying an explicit answer to a specific why question. Conceptual assumptions come in various forms. Nagle (1961) identified a number of broad explanatory principles that are commonly invoked in science, for example, deductive, functional, probabilistic, teleological and genetic. Closer to home, Van de Ven and Poole (1995) posited four explanatory principles, referred to as 'motors of change', that undergird various scientific conceptions of change, namely evolution processes, dialectic processes, life cycle processes and teleological processes.

In our field, conceptual assumptions are often articulated using the language of foundational theories, for example, rational choice theory, need theory, personality theory, learning theory, acculturation theory, identity theory, etc. Alternatively, they might be expressed in terms of fundamental organizing modalities embedded in organizational patterns and processes, such as power and influence relations, communication links and content, leader–follower interacts, resource control needs, goal accomplishment, etc. In retrospect, when my graduate adviser asked me to articulate my theory of organizing before specifying my theory of interorganizational relations, I now recognize that he was encouraging me to align my explanations of observable phenomena with my assumptions regarding why one would expect to observe certain patterns and not others.

The evolution of organizational scholarship reflects a pattern of 'making changes at the boundaries' of our theories, in the sense of modifying accepted scholarly explanations by relaxing their assumptions. This practice is especially common at the interface between disciplinary perspectives, for example, Williamson's (1985) conception of an organization as a modified form of a market, or Simon's (1955) notion of bounded rationality, or the recent 'cognitive turn' in institutional theory (Scott, 2001).

Consider the following guidelines for guiding the process of making your conceptual assumptions explicit.

1 Think of this as a side bar conversation between you and your readers, something like, 'The sensibility of this explanation is predicated upon the following assumptions about human behaviour.' For example, a theory of ethical leadership might be based on the assumption of enlightened self-interest, a theory of decision-making would likely be predicated on some form of rational choice, and a theory of conflict resolution might assume a particular set of values regarding the utility of conflict.

2 To stimulate your thinking, consider reviewing various typologies in our field, including those classifying epistemological assumptions held by scholars (Astley and Van de Ven, 1983; Miles and Snow, 1978; Morgan, 1986) and those classifying cultural assumptions held by organizational members (Bolman and Deal, 1997; Cameron and Quinn, 1999).

3 Earlier, we introduced the criterion of coherence as a tool for evaluating the suitability of a construct set. Specifically, we argued that it was difficult to craft a coherent explanation using explanatory concepts that differ in kind, for example, individual level explanations of organizational outcomes. As you systematically flesh out the conceptual assumptions underlying your theoretical model, it is a good idea to consider how the

number and variety of your conceptual assumptions can pose a similar threat to coherence.

Let me offer an illustration from my own work. Several years ago I was asked to facilitate several focus group discussions involving faculty members from a wide range of departments on my campus. Our university was contemplating some important changes and the administration wanted to sound out faculty members' preferences. In the course of those conversations, I became intrigued by the diversity of administrative practices and structures across academic disciplines. For example, it appeared that science departments tended to be governed by strong, long-term, department heads, coupled with relatively weak faculty advisory committees. In contrast, humanities faculty seemed to prefer a more participative form of governance, including rotating department chairs and strong faculty committees.

At that time, the prevailing theoretical explanation in our literature for differences in departmental organizing preferences was contrasting levels of paradigm development across disiplines (Beyer, 1982). In pursuit of a broader understanding of what I had observed, I attempted to formulate a comprehensive explanation of faculty members' satisfaction with their department's administrative structure (Whetten and Bettenhausen, 1987).

A retrospective examination of this study illustrates why the search for a more complete explanation often results in a much less coherent explanation. I can now see how unlikely it was that an article-length, coherent explanation could be crafted using constructs drawn from a wide range of foundational theories pertaining to personal political values, institutional ideology, work design, career ladders, resource dependence and professional status. This example underscores the importance of identifying the theoretical taproots of our constructs at this stage of the model building process, especially when our intent is to use the emergent conceptualization as a guide for research.

Step 4: 'When/where/who'-as-contextual assumptions

This final step involves specifying the contextual boundaries, or conditions, that circumscribe a set of theoretical propositions (Bacharach, 1989; Dubin, 1976; Rousseau and Fried, 2001). Unfortunately, theory-development treatises in our field rarely explore the subject of contextual constraints, or conditions. This oversight reduces their 'power' as explanations. Sutton and Staw (1995: 376) put it this way: 'One indication that a strong theory has been proposed is that it is possible to discern conditions in which the major proposition or hypothesis is most and least likely to hold.' In his discussion of a 'contextualist theory of knowledge', McGuire (1983) reinforces this sentiment by arguing that empirical tests of a hypothesized theoretical relationship should not focus on whether the hypothesis is true or false, but rather on the conditions under which the hypothesis holds. Supporting this argument, negative research results can often be more informative than positive ones, if they suggest important limiting conditions that should be examined more closely. This conception of scholarship is analogous to Roethlisberger's notion of a 'knowledge enterprise'. Recognizing the challenge organizational schol-ars face in our quest to comprehend what he called the 'elusive phenomena' of human behaviour, Fritz Roethlisberger (1977) proposed a highly interac-tive, continuous interplay between 'contexualized clinical' knowledge and 'generalized analytical' knowledge.

There is another justification for specifying the contextual limitations of our theories that is particularly salient for scholars in an 'applied discipline', like organizational studies. In the introduction, I referenced Lewin's obser-vation that only good theories are practical. In Lewin's writing, he leaves little doubt that good theories must be sensitive to context. Reflecting a highly pragmatic view of knowledge (Dewey, 1929), Lewin's aphorism is an affir-mation of the belief that the validity of an argument depends on the consequences of acting upon it. This is consistent with what another pioneer in our field, Mary Parker Follett (1924), referred to as 'the law of the situation', meaning that the value of a theoretical conception as a tool for guiding prac-tice is subject to the circumstances of any given situation. The implication of the 'law of the situation' is that the failure to understand how contextual constraints temper general claims significantly undermines the utility, and hence, the credibility, of scholarly explanations.

The tension, inherent in an applied disipline, between the twin require-ments of producing generalizable explanations and contexualized explanations can either be viewed as an insurmountable obstacle to effective theory development or as a generative prod to continuously improve our extant views. The latter perspective is illustrated by the evolution of schol-arly thought on the subject of job enrichment. The initial blanket claim that job enrichment would increase the satisfaction of workers was subsequently challenged by the empirical observation that this relationship did not hold for a substantial portion of the workforce, for example, blue-collar workers who do not closely identify with their work (Hackman and Oldham, 1980). Subsequent analysis of this anomaly led to the addition of 'high growth need strength' as a key moderating construct in the job design model (if individuals have high growth need strength, then enriching their jobs will produce positive psychological outcomes). This example illustrates a common theory-improvement path: efforts to assess the adequacy of a theory uncover previously unspecified contextual constraints, which in turn lead to the addition of a new moderating variable within the theory (Baron and Kenny, 1986).

Although it is impractical to assume that scholars can a priori identify all of the potential contextual limitations pertaining to a proposed conceptual-ization, the literature on related subjects often provides helpful clues. For example, much of the recent discussion in our field about the need to make our theoretical contextual assumptions explicit has been stimulated by the results from cross-cultural studies. Scholarship in this area has identified important contextual limitations on the generalizability of Western theories of managing and organizing (Cheng, 1994). These include differences in cul-tural values (Erez and Earley, 1993), personal attribution tendencies (Choi et al., 1999), institutional environments (Child, 2000) and social networks (Heimer, 1992).

THE VALUE OF MODELS IN THEORY ASSESSMENT

One of the guiding principles of this chapter is that we should give preference to theory-development methodologies yielding theoretical conceptions that lend themselves to further development. One of the espoused benefits of a structured, systematic approach to theory articulation is that the theories represented in this manner can be readily subjected to logical, empirical and practical tests (Bacharach, 1989).

Although a detailed discussion of the connection between articulating theories and testing theories is beyond the scope of this chapter, it is important to point out some of the benefits of using formal models as a rhetorical bridge, spanning conversations about theory articulation and theory testing.

First, it makes it easier to apply logical tests to theoretical conceptions. The graphical modelling methodology proposed herein is analogous to diagramming a sentence, in that it deconstructs a rhetorical statement, thereby making it easier to apply certain rules or standards. One such standard is the logical test of necessary and sufficient conditions (Bacharach, 1989; Mohr, 1982). The relationship between X and Y is logically necessary if every time we see a Y we also see an X (without X, Y cannot be). The relationship between X and Y is logically sufficient if every time we see an X we also see a Y (X, by itself, always produces Y).

Of course, these are extreme tests, which we can seldom satisfy in social science. However, they are useful heuristics for testing the logical adequacy of our theoretical arguments. The necessity test invokes the criteria of parsimony. To conduct this logical test, begin from the left side of your model and consider whether each of the antecedent constructs is necessary for what follows. If you think of your model as a story, can you tell your story without this plot element? The sufficiency test invokes the criteria of completeness.[7] To conduct this logical test, begin with the constructs on the right side of your model and work backwards, asking yourself how confident you are that a given outcome can be adequately explained using the antecedent constructs. What you are looking for in this exercise are problematic gaps in your explanation. The sufficiency test is particularly relevant for models that use some type of global performance measure to justify the core construct. The risk associated with using a global construct like performance as the end that justifies our favourite means (core construct) is that means-end models can easily be construed as cause-effect models (Cossette and Audet, 1992: 342), in which case what was intended as a single means (to the end of performance) can be viewed as a single cause (explanation) – implying a grossly underspecified model of performance.[8]

The second benefit of using models to bridge theory articulation and theory assessment is that they make it easier to empirically test specific theoretical propositions. Several years ago, during a panel discussion on the subject of theory development, Jeff Pfeffer proposed that one of the most important actions we could take to improve the quality of our theories would be to insist that anyone proposing a new theory must also test that theory. In keeping with Pfeffer's sentiment that responsible theorizing entails theorists taking responsibility for testing their theories, authors of theory papers need to give more than token attention to the question of how their arguments could be tested.

To that end, one of the benefits of presenting a model version of a theoretical argument is that it focuses the attention of authors and readers on the specific propositions that constitute the theory's unique claims (Asher, 1976). As we observed in the example of Sastry's test of specific propositions derived from punctuated equilibrium theory, the first step in that process was transforming a general perspective into a formal model, with an associated set of propositions.

I am often asked in workshops how many propositions are appropriate and which relationships should be formalized as propositions. Although the number of propositions will vary according to the complexity of the model, a reasonable default guideline is to formulate one proposition for each theoretically significant 'path' in your model. Using the language of our modelling exercise, this suggests that you begin writing propositions (literally, explanations) for each of your outcomes (explained constructs) on your main horizontal axis, beginning with the first explained variable on the left side of the model. Using Figure 3.1 as an example, this suggests that the first proposition would focus on an explanation for 'performance', using the elements of the model located to its left.

The third benefit of using models to guide the assessment of theory is that this practice facilitates a critical step in the ongoing process of theory development – using the results of theory-guided inquiry to improve current theory. It is common practice for scholars writing 'theory papers' to draw upon a broad base of evidence, culled from research reports, to support proposed changes in current theoretical conceptions. Given that we have few conventional standards for writing conceptual papers, the process of evaluating contributions *to* theory is inherently ambiguous.

In my 1989 *AMR* editorial essay I addressed this concern by suggesting that prospective authors focus on three rhetorical questions: (1) What's new? What specific change is being proposed and what specific deficiency in current thinking is being targeted? (2) Why so? What is the justification for the proposed change, for example, is the current theory incomplete or logically flawed? (3) So what? What difference would the proposed change make? That is, if experts on this subject agree that the proposed change is warranted, how much of a substantive difference would it make in the way they designed their next empirical study?

My current thinking on this subject has been heavily influenced by Anne Huff's workshops on writing (described in Chapter 4 of this volume). She suggests that writing for publication is like joining a conversation, in the sense that we must first understand what is currently being discussed and then identify what we might add to enrich the conversation. To make this metaphor more tangible, she proposes that writers make copies of three or four articles that represent the existing conversation they wish to join, and use them as points of reference throughout the writing process. This convention lends itself to side-by-side comparisons between 'what is' and 'what is proposed' as a significant addition or correction.

The fact that this type of comparison is very natural and straightforward if the theoretical conception under scrutiny has been formally specified as a model, constitutes one of the most compelling justifications for the theorizing-as-modelling methodology presented in this chapter. As I noted at the beginning, "Above all else, effective theory development practices produce theories that lend themselves to further development."

CONCLUSION

I began this chapter by making the case for devoting more collective attention to theory development in our field. A claim of distinction shared by scholars in general is that their work is theoretical, in the sense that scholarly enquiry builds or tests theory, and that theory guides scholarly enquiry. In our field this distinction is reflected in a common concern expressed by organizational scholars regarding many of the recommendations for practice made by organizational consultants or management practitioners, namely, they are not informed by the relevant theoretical perspectives and frameworks from our discipline. By extension, one can argue that the distinctive intellectual capital associated with the field of organizational scholarship is our theoretical knowledge. This supposition is reflected in the design of most doctoral education programmes: we often send our graduate students to other departments to take their research methods classes, but we insist they take their core content courses from us. It follows that, as a field, we need to place a high priority on continuously upgrading and improving our theoretical/conceptual knowledge base. This means that all extant theoretical conceptions should be subjected to constant assessment, with an eye towards continuously upgrading the power of our theoretical lenses.

To guide this process I proposed a systematic theory-development process, or methodology, that draws heavily on graphical modelling techniques. I have argued that this approach to theorizing has a number of commendable features.

First, modelling provides a structured process for making explicit the elements of a theoretical argument or perspective. Earlier, I compared the difference between making a contribution *of* theory versus making a contribution *to* theory to the actions of looking through a lens versus looking at the lens. This shift in focus is unlikely absent a detailed set of design specifications. As demonstrated in the Sastry example, until and unless a theoretical perspective is deconstructed into its constitutive elements, it is unlikely that theory application will stimulate theory development. In reference to the key constructs in Figure 3.1, I recall debates conducted in our scholarly journals during the early days of my career over questions like the following: Is the relationship between ability and motivation, as predictors of performance, additive or multiplicative? Does satisfaction explain performance, or does performance explain satisfaction? How are motivation, performance and satisfaction related? Arguably, much of the progress we've made as a field in answering these foundational questions can be attributed to the clarity in these debates regarding the constructs and relationships in question.

Second, modeling allows the theory-development process to be guided by accepted standards of scholarly knowledge, such as Kant's dual criteria of complete and systematic. One of the benefits of modeling, especially for inexperienced scholars, is that it disciplines the impulse to formulate more and more complete explanations that are less and less systematic. As usual, Weick had it right: effective theory development requires *disciplined* imagination.

Third, the language of modeling provides a standard vocabulary that can be applied to a) a wide range of subjects, spanning micro and macro concepts, b) a broad spectrum of processes and logics, including developmental sequences, logical arguments, event histories, causal relations, and c) a variety of theoretical conceptions, including variance and process theories. Thus, modelling, like network analysis and other related analytical tools, provides a robust framework that facilitates scholarly discourse across a wide variety of conceptual and empirical domains.

The fourth, and most straightforward, positive feature of modeling is that it creates models, which serve as useful guides for designing theory-based research projects. Using Figure 3.1 as an example, if someone is interested in studying the antecedents of job performance, this model identifies the set of variables that should be included **in** the study. It also suggests a number of specific propositions regarding the relationships among those variables that could be incorporated into the study.

Fifth, and finally, modelling democratizes the theory-development craft by making the tools for building good theory widely accessible. Given the premise that the future of our field is tied to the quality of our intellectual assets, it is imperative that all scholars who are inclined to improve our theoretical knowledge are able to do so, easily and effectively.

Study questions

Following are several theory-development exercises, based on the methodology described in the chapter. What insights do you gain into the theory-development process from each exercise? What opportunities for developing theory emerge from each exercise?

1 *Codifying gestalts*: Following the Sastry example cited in the chapter, use this modeling methodology to codify a broad theoretical perspective in our field, specifying its constructs, relationships, propositions, and so on.
2 *Explicating assumptions*: Select a well-known theoretical framework in your specific area of study and make a list of its key propositions. Next, draw a box around these propositions and then make a list of the conceptual and/or contextual conditions that are assumed but not stated by the authors. Then, brainstorm a list of conditions that might alter or even falsify these propositions.
3 *Community theory-building*: Identify a construct that has not attracted

much attention in our field, for example compassion or identity. Place it on a large Post-it® Note (PIN) in the centre of a bulletin board in your department commons area and invite colleagues (faculty and students) over a period of time to add other constructs (PINs), arrange the existing constructs, specify limiting conceptual and/or contextual conditions for the emerging conception, etc. (Try using different colors of PINs for different elements of the model.) When the nascent model is starting to take shape, schedule a brown bag discussion and engage in a group sense-making exercise.

4 *Doctoral course exercise*: Identify the key propositions (implied or explicitly stated) in the literature assigned for each major course topic, for example, leadership, motivation, power etc. Using these propositions, 'reverse engineer' a model, that is, try to construct a sensible model that contains all of the key propositions, specified as relationships among constructs.

5 *Doctoral preliminary exam question*: Select a well-established theoretical perspective on a given topic. Present it as a model and then propose improvements, in the following manner. First, create a figure featuring a side-by-by comparison between the current and the proposed models. Second, use this figure as a reference in explaining and justifying your proposal. Be sure to address the following questions: (1) What's new? What specific change is being proposed and what specific deficiency in current thinking is being targeted? (2) Why so? What is the justification for the proposed change, for example, is the current theory incomplete or logically flawed? (3) So what? What difference would the proposed change make? That is, if experts on this subject agree that the proposed change is warranted, how much of a substantive difference would it make in the way they designed their next empirical study?

Recommended further reading

Bacharach, S.B. (1989) 'Organizational Theories: Some Criteria for Evaluation', *Academy of Management Review*, 14 (4), pp. 496–515.

Campbell, J.P. (1990) 'The Role of Theory in Industrial and Organizational Psychology', in M.D. Dunnette and L.M. Hough (eds), *Handbook of Industrial and Organizational Psychology*. Palo Alto: Consulting Psychologists Press, pp. 39–73.

Dubin, R. (1976) 'Theory Building in Applied Areas', in M.D. Dunnette (ed.), *Handbook of Industrial and Organizational Psychology*. Chicago: Rand–McNally, pp. 17–39.

Sastry, M.A. (1997) 'Problems and Paradoxes in a Model of Punctuated Organizational Change', *Administrative Science Quarterly*, 42, pp. 237–75.

Sutton, R.I. and Staw, B.M. (1995) 'What Theory Is Not', *Administrative Science Quarterly*, 40, pp. 371–84.

Weick, K.E. (1989) 'Theory Construction as Disciplined Imagination', *Academy of Management Review*, 14, pp. 516–31.

Whetten, D.A. (1989) 'What Constitutes a Theoretical Contribution?', *Academy of Management Review*, 14, pp. 490–5.

Notes

I would like to thank the following colleagues for their comments on earlier drafts: Chris Early, Art Brief, Blake Ashforth, Terry Mitchell and John Wagner.

1 If you are planning to use this methodology as a decision support aid for formulating a specific research project, I encourage you to write down a carefully crafted research question or problem statement before proceeding. The presence of an orienting problem statement or research question provides an extra measure of discipline that is often necessary to insure that what we articulate as a theoretical conception can actually be assessed. Keep in mind the following 'prime directive' from the systems dynamics literature: 'The most important step in modeling is problem articulation . . . beware the analyst who proposes to model an entire business or social system rather than a problem' (Sterman, 2000: 89).

2 In my 1989 article I briefly discussed the difference between constructs and variables and the corollary difference between propositions and hypotheses. See Kaplan (1964) and Abell (1971) for a broader discussion of these terms.

3 Campbell (1990) refers to this as the problem of the loose derivation chain, and Guttman (1971) calls it the problem of the incomplete mapping sentence.

4 To illustrate the importance of specifying one's theory of emergence Kozlowski and Klein, (2000) argue that the use of group means as measures of group characteristics is appropriate for compositional concepts, but not for compilational concepts.

5 This model was developed for the purpose of summarizing a body of knowledge. Hence, it has some characteristics that are at variance with the format recommended for theory-development models. I've elected to use it because most readers will be familiar with these constructs, and because the history of how the current conceptualization of this subject matter emerged is particularly illustrative.

6 For an easy-to-understand discussion of 'link polarity' (the assigning of positive and negative signs to links) and 'loop polarity' (the determination of whether a feedback loop is *reinforcing* or *balancing*), see Sterman (2000). Also, for a discussion of assessing the relative significance, or importance, of the variables in a model, by examining the frequency of links between variables, assessing the 'intensity of the influence' of one variable on another, etc., see Cossette and Lapointe (1997).

7 The common test of the completeness of our predictive models is explained variance – the implication being that unless all of the reliable variance is explained we are doing bad science. However, because it is generally difficult to isolate the sources of error in our predictive studies, explained variance is an unreliable test of the sufficiency of a theoretical explanation (Campbell, 1990). It is, therefore, advisable to couple this empirical test with a complementary conceptual assessment, comparing the completeness of our model with the relevant scholarly literature. If nothing else, this gives us an opportunity to inform readers that we understand what we are leaving out and why we made these choices.

8 The type of models I'm referring to have the core construct in the middle of the horizontal axis, with performance as the single construct to the right, and numerous constructs to the left. In other words, the model contains both an explanation of, and a justification for, our core construct. The only way to totally blunt the criticism that this represents an under-specified explanation of performance is to

eliminate the one-on-one relationship between our core construct and the performance outcome construct in our model (redrawing the model showing all the explanatory variables directly related to performance, including our core construct). However, that defeats the purpose of using the model to tell a story about how the study of X is justified because it is a legitimate path to Y. This conundrum highlights the need to carefully label and describe 'justification relationships'. For example, if our core construct is organizational culture, its relationship to performance might be characterized as, 'the contribution of organizational culture and its antecedents to our understanding of organizational performance', or, if necessary, 'an organizational culture explanation of organizational performance'.

References

Abell, P. (1971) *Model Building in Sociology*. London: Wheiden, Field and Michelson.

Aldrich, H.E. (1999) *Organizations Evolving*. London: Sage.

Arrow, H., McGrath, J.E. and Berdahl, J.L. (2000) *Small Groups as Complex Systems*. Thousand Oaks, CA: Sage.

Asher, H.B. (1976) *Causal Modeling*. Beverly Hills, CA: Sage.

Astley, W.G. and Van de Ven, A.H. (1983) 'Central Perspectives and Debates in Organization Theory', *Administrative Science Quarterly*, 28, pp. 245–73.

Bacharach, S.B. (1989) 'Organizational Theories: Some Criteria for Evaluation', *Academy of Management Review*, 14 (4), pp. 496–515.

Baron, R.M. and Kenny, D.A. (1986) 'The Moderator-Mediator Variable Distinction in Social Psychology: Conceptual, Strategic, and Statisical Considerations', *Journal of Personality and Social Psychology*, 51(6), pp. 1173–82.

Beyer, J.M. (1982) 'Power Dependencies and the Distribution of Influence in Universities', in S.B. Bacharach (ed.), *Research in the Sociology of Organizations*, Vol. 1. Greenwich, CT: JAI Press, pp. 167–208.

Bolman, L.G. and Deal, T.E. (1997) *Reframing Organizations: Artistry, Choice, and Leadership*, 2nd edn. San Francisco: Jossey–Bass.

Cameron, K.S. (1984) 'The Effectiveness of Ineffectiveness', *Research in Organizational Behavior*, 6, pp. 235–85.

Cameron, K.S. and Quinn, R.E. (1999) *Diagnosing and Changing Organizational Culture*. Reading, MA: Addison–Wesley.

Campbell, J.P. (1990) 'The Role of Theory in Industrial and Organizational Psychology', in M.D. Dunnette and L.M. Hough (eds), *Handbook of Industrial and Organizational Psychology*. Palo Alto: Consulting Psychologists Press, pp. 39–73.

Cheng, J.L.C. (1994) 'On the Concept of Universal Knowledge in Organization Science: Implications for Cross-National Research', *Management Science*, 40, pp. 162–8.

Child, J. (2000) 'Theorizing About Organization Cross-Nationality', *Advances in International Comparative Management*, 13, pp. 27–75.

Choi, I., Nisbett, R.E. and Norenzayan, A. (1999) 'Causal Attribution across Cultures: Variation and Universality', *Psychological Bulletin*, 125, pp. 47–63.

Cossette, P. and Audet, M. (1992) 'Mapping of an Idiosyncratic Schema', *Journal of Management Studies*, 19 (3), pp. 325–47.

Cossette, P. and Lapointe, A. (1997) 'A Mapping Approach to Conceptual Models: The Case of Macroeconomic Theory', *Canadian Journal of Administrative Sciences*, 14, pp. 41–51.

Dewey, J. (1929) *The Quest for Certainty*. New York: Minton, Balch.

Dubin, R. (1976) 'Theory Building in Applied Areas', in M.D. Dunnette (ed.),

Handbook of Industrial and Organizational Psychology. Chicago: Rand–McNally, pp. 17–39.

Dubin, R. (1978) *Theory Building*. New York: The Free Press.

Eisenhardt, K.M. (1989) 'Building Theories from Case Study Research', *Academy of Management Review*, 16, pp. 620–7.

Erez, M. and Earley, C.P. (1993) *Culture, Self-identity, and Work*. New York: Oxford University Press.

Fine, M. (1995) *Habits of Mind*. San Francisco: Jossey–Bass.

Follett, M.P. (1924) *Creative Experience*. New York: Longmans, Green and Company.

Goodman, P.S. (2000) *Missing Organizational Linkages: Tools for Cross-level Research*. Thousand Oaks, CA: Sage.

Greenwald, A.G., Pratkanis, A.R., Leippe, M.R. and Baumgardner, M.J. (1986) 'Under What Conditions Does Theory Obstruct Research Progress?', *Psychological Review*, 93, pp. 216–19.

Guetzkow, H. (ed.) (1962) *Simulation in Social Science: Readings*. Englewood Cliffs, NJ: Prentice Hall.

Guttman, L. (1971) 'Measurement and Structural Theory', *Psychometrica*, 36, pp. 329–47.

Hackman, J.R. and Oldham, G.R. (1980) *Work Redesign*. Reading, MA: Addison–Wesley.

Heimer, C.A. (1992) 'Doing Your Job and Helping Your Friends: Universalistic Norms About Obligations to Particular Others in Networks', in N. Nohria and R.G. Eccles (eds), *Networks and Organizations: Structure, Form and Action*. Boston, MA: Harvard Business School Press.

Huff, A.S. and Jenkins, M. (eds) (2000) *Mapping Strategic Knowledge*. London: Sage.

Jacobsen, C., Bronson, R. and Vekstein, D. (1990) 'A Strategy for Testing the Empirical Adequacy of Macro-sociological Theories', *Journal of Mathematical Sociology*, 15, pp. 137–48.

Kant, E. (1998) *The Critique of Pure Reason* (translated and edited by Paul Guyer and Alan W. Wood). New York: Cambridge University Press.

Kaplan, A. (1964) *The Conduct of Inquiry*. New York: Harper and Row.

Kerlinger, F.N. (1973) *Foundations of Behavioral Research*, 2nd edn. London: Holt, Rinehart and Winston.

Klein, K.J. and Kozlowski, S.W.J. (eds) (2000) *Multilevel Theory, Research and Methods in Organizations*. San Francisco: Jossey–Bass.

Kozlowski, S.W.J. and Klein, K.J. (2000) 'A Multilevel Approach to Theory and Research in Organizations', in K.J. Klein and S.W.J. Kozlowski (eds), *Multilevel Theory, Research and Methods in Organizations*. San Francisco: Jossey–Bass, pp. 3–90.

Lewin, K. (1945) 'The Research Center for Group Dynamics at Massachusetts Institute of Technology', *Sociometry*, 8, pp. 126–35.

McKinley, W., Mone, M.A. and Moon, G. (1999) 'Determinants and Development of Schools in Organizational Theory', *Academy of Management Review*, 24, pp. 634–48.

McKinley, W. and Mone, M. (1998) 'The Re-construction of Organizational Studies: Wrestling with Incommensurability', *Organization*, 5, pp. 169–89.

McGuire, W.J. (1983) 'A Contextualist Theory of Knowledge: Its Implications for Innovation and Reform in Psychological Research', in L. Berkowitz (ed.), *Advances in Experimental Social Psychology*. Orlando, FL: Academic Press, pp. 1–47.

Miles, R.E. and Snow, C.C. (1978) *Organizational Strategy, Structure and Process*. New York: McGraw–Hill.

Mohr, L.B. (1982) *Explaining Organizational Behavior*. San Francisco: Jossey–Bass.

Morecraft, J.D.W. and Sterman, J.D. (1994) *Modeling for Learning Organizations*. Portland, OR: Productivity Press.

Morgan, G. (1986) *Images of Organization*. Newbury Park, CA: Sage.

Nagle, E. (1961) *The Structure of Science: Problems in the Logic of Scientific Explanation*. London: Routledge and Kegan.

Osigweh, C.A.B. (1989) 'Concept Fallibility in Organizational Science', *Academy of Management Review*, 16, pp. 579–84.

Paul, R. and Elder, L. (2001) *Critical Thinking: Tools for Taking Charge of Your Learning and Your Life*. Saddle River, NJ: Prentice Hall.

Pfeffer, J. (1993) 'Barriers to the Advance of Organizational Science: Paradigm Development as a Dependent Variable', *Academy of Management Review*, 18, pp. 599–620.

Porac, J.P. and Thomas, H. (1990) 'Taxonomic Mental Models in Competitor Definition', *Academy of Management Review*, 15, pp. 224–40.

Roethlisberger, F.J. (1977) *The Elusive Phenomena*. Cambridge, MA: Harvard University Press.

Rousseau, D.M. (1978) 'Measures of Technology as Predictors of Employee Attitude', *Journal of Applied Psychology*, 63, pp. 212–18.

Rousseau, D.M. and Fried, Y. (2001) 'Location, Location, Location: Contextualizing Organizational Research', *Journal of Organizational Behaviour*, 22, 1–13.

Sastry, M.A. (1997) 'Problems and Paradoxes in a Model of Punctuated Organizational Change', *Administrative Science Quarterly*, 42, pp. 237–75.

Scott, W.R. (2001) *Institutions and Organizations*. Thousand Oaks, CA: Sage.

Simon, H.A. (1955) 'A Behavioral Model of Rational Choice', *Quarterly Journal of Economics*, 69, pp. 99–118.

Sterman, J.D. (2000) *Business Dynamics: Systems Thinking and Modeling for a Complex World*. Boston, MA: Irwin McGraw–Hill.

Sutton, R.I. and Staw, B.M. (1995) 'What Theory Is *Not*', *Administrative Science Quarterly*, 40, pp. 371–84.

Tushman, M.L. and Romanelli, E. (1985) 'Organizational Evolution: A Metamorphosis Model of Convergence and Reorientation', in L.L. Cummings and B.M. Staw (eds), *Research in Organizational Behavior*, Volume 7. Greenwich, CT: JAI Press, pp. 171–222.

Van de Ven, A.H. and Poole, M.S. (1995) 'Explaining Development and Change in Organizations', *Academy of Management Review*, 20 (3), pp. 510–40.

Waldman, D.A. and Yammarino, F.J. (1999) 'CEO Charismatic Leadership: Levels-of-Management and Levels-of-Analysis Effects', *Academy of Management Review*, 24, pp. 266–85.

Weick, K.E. (1995) 'What Theory Is *Not*, Theory *Is*', *Administrative Science Quarterly*, 40, pp. 385–90.

Weick, K.E. (1989) 'Theory Construction as Disciplined Imagination', *Academy of Management Review*, 14, pp. 516–31.

Whetten, D.A. (1989) 'What Constitutes a Theoretical Contribution?', *Academy of Management Review*, 14, pp. 490–5.

Whetten, D.A. (1980) 'Organizational Decline: A Neglected Topic in Organizational Science', *Academy of Management Review*, 5, pp. 577–88.

Whetten, D.A. and Bettenhausen, K. (1987) 'Diversity in University Governance: Attitudes, Structure, and Satisfaction', in John Smart (ed.), *Higher Education: Handbook of Theory and Research*, Volume 3. New York: Agathon Press, pp. 242–70.

Whetten, D.A. and Cameron, K. (2001) *Developing Management Skills*. Saddle River, NJ: Prentice Hall.

Whetten, D.A. and Godfrey, P.C. (1998) *Identity in Organizations: Building Theory Through Conversations*. Thousand Oaks, CA: Sage.

Williamson, O.E. (1985) *The Economic Institutions of Capitalism: Firms, Markets, Relational Contracting*. New York: The Free Press.

4

Learning to be a Successful Writer

Anne Sigismund Huff

Overview

My efforts to be an active, publishing scholar are facilitated by four gradually won insights.

- *Scholarship is based on community and conversation.* In retrospect, the first papers I wrote had an intended audience of one. Not surprisingly, these papers did not get published. They bristled with academic references, but the references reflected an idiosyncratic search to satisfy my idiosyncratic interests. Now, I know that articles and books get published because they grow out of and contribute to shared interests. A cornerstone of every project therefore must be a decision about the scholars I intend to join. There are always many attractive alternatives. Over time I have involved myself in different conversations. That evolutionary process is critical, but each new involvement comes at a high price. I understand more of, and can more fully use, the efforts of fellow travellers when I have been following their linked ongoing exchanges. Similarly, my colleagues are more likely to pay attention to what I want to contribute if I have been in the conversation for a while.
- *Writing is a form of thinking, and thus a tool to use from the very beginning of a research project.* Early in my career, I did not begin to write until my library research was completed, data gathered and conclusions reached. I start much earlier today, because I have discovered that each aspect of scholarship – the way enquiry is framed, the literature that is brought into the argument, the research design, data analysis, etc. – is improved by the discipline writing brings. When I put ideas on paper, it is easier to both simplify my arguments and increase their detail. Even more important, formally articulating an argument gives me needed distance from 'my' ideas. What I am thinking at this moment is a *possible* contribution to scholarly conversation; it is not (at least until very late in the game) a corporal extension of myself that I need to protect.
- *It makes sense to seek advice throughout the writing process.* I sought advice in graduate school, though not as often as I should have. Once an assistant

professor, I assumed my job was to independently identify research ideas, carry them out and write up the results. That typically meant I had little direct input for several years on each project I undertook. By then I was not only heavily committed to a perspective I had established with considerable effort, I was so pressed for time that reviewers became my (very expensive) advisers. Once I started thinking about the community and conversational bases of academic work, I realized that I was foolishly independent. Successful papers, with very few exceptions, are honed by interaction with others before formal submission.

- *Management is required.* I started my scholarly career with a 'sherry-sipping' view of academic life. As a consequence, it did not occur to me to draw on the managerial skills I used outside of the ivory tower. I hoped for inspiration, and tried to develop insight. Experience taught me, with difficulty, that inspiration and insight depend on preparation, organization and persistence. Today, I try hard not to schedule classes or appointments in the morning, for example, because that is the time when I write most easily and quickly. I leave home, so the laundry will not sidetrack me, but I don't go to my office, because other chores wait there. A local coffee house often is the destination, and I make sure that I have enough material to support a long stay. Each scholar similarly must decide how to organize their writing lives, including a decision about financial investments that will improve the quantity and quality of what they write.

When I became a part-time faculty member at Cranfield School of Management, I used these four ideas as the basis for a book called *Writing for Scholarly Publication* (Sage, 1999). It is an overly rational but practical guide that outlines many steps in the writing process, from developing a title to responding to reviewers. I will not summarize it here. Rather, I want to outline four additional insights that have grown out of my subsequent writing workshops and seminars.

I enjoy teaching in this area because it generates conversations on issues I still need to address in my own writing efforts. The intended audience of this chapter is thus a broad one, from current students to established scholars. However, I would like to thank the students in my current University of Colorado seminar, whose writing projects are used to illustrate several points that follow.

This is a semester course, on the cognitive foundations of strategic management, but the students' primary output does not have to be on a cognitive topic. They are enrolled in several different departments, and they each work on a paper that will advance their career goals. Participants turn in a writing assignment almost every week, culminating in formal submission to an appropriate conference or journal.

Formal output may seem to be an overly demanding requirement, especially for first year students, but at the end of every course, even shorter Cranfield Writing Workshops, a number of papers are accepted. A well-thought-out start is the key, followed by persistent development up to the point of submission.

THINK BEFORE YOU WRITE

A number of pitfalls lie at the beginning of almost every writing project. For example, I sometimes begin working on projects that I have to drop as the deadline for another commitment looms. Unfortunately, once I stop working on a paper it takes time to get back into the mindset completion requires; sometimes I never get back. I find myself in another difficulty if I begin writing with a particular audience and contribution in mind, but then lose focus and begin to follow other attractive but tangential topics.

We fall into these and other traps because we begin writing too soon, before thinking adequately about the full portfolio of our obligations and interests, and before thinking adequately about the audience we most want to attract. Thus, in what follows I emphasize what writing should do.

Commit to and draw on an intellectual identity

I wish I had said more about the importance of intellectual grounding in the Sage book. Too many people are unclear about their intellectual 'home'. (I am talking here about identification with a field of enquiry, rather than a more specific, often interdisciplinary, conversation on a particular topic.)

People who are grounded in a broader area of enquiry are more likely to make forceful and credible contributions in their writing. The broader context might be a recognized discipline (like sociology, or organization theory), a strong theoretic base (like systems theory), or an area of enquiry that is just developing disciplinary status and theory (like entrepreneurship). This broader context provides ontological and epistemological grounding. It offers tool kits for enquiry, and exemplary articles that help focus and elaborate contribution.

Sometimes the work already done in an established academic field becomes a strait-jacket that overly restrains subsequent efforts. But an equally confining position, and one that is increasingly likely in an era of interdisciplinary training, is to work with superficial knowledge from many fields, but insufficient grounding to really benefit from any one.

Fields of enquiry, broadly defined, provide an institutional basis for sustaining conversation over time. Meetings are held on a regular calendar, often subdivided into sub-fields that use the occasion to advance their own identity. Journals grow in and around these associations. This context makes a difference in finding an audience. Participants in an intellectual conversation are able to communicate because they have some common background. They are able to interest each other in new ideas because they know what will be considered surprising and interesting.

Because the field influences the sense people can make of a phenomenon (Weick, 1995), I now begin writing courses by asking participants to 'map' their location in *the*, one, larger area of enquiry they identify with most. This can be done in many different ways. One person might put themselves on a historical timeline of developing theoretic paradigms and offshoots. Another might develop a kind of Dewey decimal system that focuses on logical rather than temporal connections. A third possibility is to take a genealogical approach, listing advisers, and their advisers. A variant would map networks more generally, perhaps in an institutional framework. The breadth of the effort varies with the proclivity of the individual, their career stage and the time we are willing to give to the effort. I am happy to have people work on informal or fanciful drawings, but even a casual map is often more difficult to draw than people think it will be.

The exercise can only be considered a success if participants become more aware of and committed to a broader intellectual effort. Jeanne McPherson, for example, started a PhD in communications after a number of years as a consultant and science writer. That background is helping her move fast. In her first year she took an overload of theoretical courses, from several different faculty in her department, and chose an adviser for her dissertation. In her second year, she is already gathering data for a larger project she has under way. It is action research that draws on Jeanne's consulting skills, and she expects to use data collected as a participant observer for her dissertation. Jeanne's current intellectual map is a set of six separate islands. Each is a topic that interested her in coursework, and appears very relevant to her fieldwork. She already has a rather extensive set of names and articles to provide topical detail in each of these areas. This list is sub-divided by whether the writer is within the communications area or not. But at this point she sees either too many or too few links between islands.

I think the current state of this map is a primary reason why she is having difficulty defining a topic for her paper in my course, and a focus for her dissertation. As she begins to analyse her field data, she has too many possible categories in mind, and they do not easily coalesce. Even if she makes a hard decision to restrict herself to one or two perspectives for the paper (which so far has proven to be difficult, because she finds more topics compelling), her next research project is likely to be drawn from another perspective, which will diminish her ability to draw effectively on what she is learning now.

Thus, my strong advice to Jeanne is that she put *one* (and only one) of her islands in the foreground, connect it with one or two other areas of enquiry that most interest her, and then firmly delegate other subject matter to the background. She is reluctant to do that, because she feels affinity with each area and does not want to relinquish possible help early in her fieldwork. (A more established scholar might be similarly reluctant because they are aware of the political pitfalls of aligning oneself with one set of scholars rather than another.) These are both valid concerns, but indecision poses its own difficulties. I urge people to make a commitment. If the fit is not good, it can be changed. Aligning oneself with a specific intellectual territory increases a sense of connection with academic endeavours. As long as she feels like a foreign visitor, she is less likely to feel like a person who can dare write. It is much easier to think of an interesting contribution to conversation if one feels at home.

Make a purposeful choice from a portfolio of writing projects

Though mapping intellectual territory takes time, in my experience it is worth taking yet more time for a second management task. That task is to develop and compare a set of writing alternatives before choosing *one* paper to work on now. I used to begin writing with the assumption that many important details would reveal themselves as I progressed. The problem, as I have already mentioned, is that I too often began things I could not finish, and ended up moving in directions I had not anticipated. In both cases, the initial frame I was using became a trap I could only escape by cutting and abandoning a lot of written material. I still feel that writing is a useful way to work out detail, but now I try to make a more purposeful start, so that I waste less effort.

When I wrote *Writing for Scholarly Publication*, I suggested that people identify three writing alternatives, then compare them in terms of four criteria. I still like the criteria, but feel the number of papers to compare is too artificial. Better to start by listing all the papers one is writing, or thinking about writing. Then, compare the set along the following dimensions:

- *Your passion* for the subject. 'Passion' is a strong word, but writing is a long and often lonely business; it takes a lot of interest to complete a manuscript.
- The project's *relevance to an academic field*. As said above, I strongly urge writers to connect their intellectual effort to a specific, established area of enquiry – an area they see as the 'home base' of their ongoing intellectual efforts. The competition for journal space is going up; it is more and more important to deeply understand the issues that a given field thinks are important. It also is more important to know how to use popular methods of enquiry. Establishing an intellectual identity allows the writer to say something about a specific subject that a larger group will find interesting, something that challenges received wisdom.
- *Relevance to practice.* Writers in a professional field are often asked to justify a proposed project in terms of practitioner interest. I believe it is our obligation to make this connection, but virtue tends to be rewarded by greater access to data, and more involvement with people who can ground the academic's necessarily more removed insights.
- *Importance to career goals.* If I make the decision to commit to a project after explicitly considering all the other things I must, should and would like to do, it is more likely that it will continue to be my priority. I will devote what is always too little writing time to a project I am most suited to do well, one that I am most likely to learn from.

The last point deserves further elaboration. It is not easy to decide on the single paper that most deserves writing attention. For example, Cecil Peterson, who is looking for a job as he finishes his dissertation, brought five possible papers he might develop to my class:

1 Conference paper delivered last month.
2 Conference paper to be delivered in two months.
3 Dissertation results chapter.
4 Job talk for an academic audience that relates fieldwork to the dominant paradigm in the field.
5 Job talk for a practitioner audience.

Each of these paper possibilities is compelling, but when he came to class, Cecil was inclined to work on either paper 1 or paper 2. Both presentations are in a field where Cecil has worked for some time. He already has a published track record in this area. He not only knows some key players, they know him. Although he has decided he is more interested in other subjects, he recognizes that some employers will be attracted to his skills in this area. Furthermore, a lot of organizing work has been done to prepare for the presentations; therefore he is confident he can complete either paper in the time frame of the course, even though he has to give most of his attention to finishing his dissertation and getting a job.

That is the reason I was inclined to support paper 3. Finishing the dissertation would seem to be the single most important thing he should do now; anything else is a distraction. Furthermore, an important way to speed publication from a dissertation is to write results chapters with publication in mind. However, Cecil is not working in my college, and it quickly became apparent that he is committed to a dissertation format in which results are first summarized with minimum researcher interpretation. He has to write at least one more chapter after the one he is working on now before he adds his own analysis, thus, it is hard for him to imagine completing either a conference presentation or a journal article in the next few months.

Presentation or journal submission is the output required for the course. It might seem that I should relax this requirement for a student like Cecil, but I am reluctant to do so, because I think almost all academics today are pressured to publish an article or two a year, and we must accept this target as a permanent fixture in our lives. Midway in the class discussion of this reality, Cecil changed his emphasis to paper 4, which relates his data to the dominant paradigm in his field. He is confident that faculty in different specialty areas will recognize and appreciate it, even though he has decided he is personally more attracted to another, more contemporary theoretic approach. Unfortunately, this preferred framework is much more complicated than the dominant paradigm, and he is not quite sure how easily he will be able to use it to analyse his dissertation data.

There is a last complication: Cecil is also considering possible employment in a consulting firm. As he pursues that option he needs to talk about his dissertation work in a way that is more action-oriented and practical. He has already had informal conversations with one private sector employer, and this is the most exciting opportunity he has yet identified. Paper 5, which does not have to be that long, might be critical in actually landing such a job. Perhaps that paper should be his focus. He could also draw on past work in the subject field of papers 1 and 2 as a reminder of other skills he can offer to an employer.

That is a short, but complicated story. I find it easier to follow because its general outline is so familiar. I am perpetually pulled in multiple directions. When I step back, I see the same problematic dichotomies over and over again. I wonder if I should:

- Further investigate topics that I know something about, or work on more attractive but higher risk new projects?
- Develop practical frameworks, or work on more abstract, theoretic ones?

- Respond to immediate demands, or work on projects that might be more rewarding in the long run?
- Work on something that I really want to do, or respond to external interests and opportunities?

There is no easy answer to these alternatives. Over time, most of us move back and forth to satisfy different career pressures, and develop different competencies. Trying to be multi-faceted is laudable, though it can be distracting. External pressure also causes attention to oscillate, often with less positive developmental results.

The successful scholars I know minimize unnecessary bounce. They decide what they are going to work on now. (I underline 'ci' to emphasize that a decision literally cuts away alternatives. The same root can be found in 'incisors' and 'scissors'.) Interestingly, Cecil ultimately decided on a sixth paper project, one that he had not considered before specifying and analysing the portfolio of papers he had in progress. This paper focuses on the new, more avant-garde theoretic framework that really interests him. Although he does not yet have extensive empirical data to present, he can discuss several compelling examples from his dissertation data that convinced him to go beyond the dominant paradigm.

Paper 6 will be of immediate use as the basis for a job presentation to academic audiences. That makes sense because he does not want to jump into a consulting career without exploring academic possibilities. Time on the paper is doubly valuable, because he wants to conclude his dissertation by applying this framework. Hopefully he will feel confident enough to distribute the paper he is working on now to academic employers.

This choice of paper 6 makes sense to me, and prompts me to offer several other pieces of advice:

1 *Work on what is most important to you.* If you do what is easy, or merely interesting, as Cecil was tempted to do when he thought of turning a conference presentation into a paper, you risk never getting to the work that will make a difference. A similar risk accompanies the decision to work on a project that logically precedes the paper you really want to do, as Cecil was tempted to do when he thought about first using an accepted paradigm to look at his dissertation data. The problem is that academic projects take on a life of their own. They almost always take more time and energy than you hope. They may change your trajectory by inviting consulting work, or generating offers to speak or write on a subject that is not central to your interests. Even when you do get to what you wanted to do, it may not go as well as it would have if you had given it more time.

2 *Draw writing projects together.* One attraction of Cecil's ultimate project is that it 'kills two birds with one stone': it is a document that will be of immediate use in the job market, and an input to the final chapter of his dissertation. I have observed that successful scholars often take advantage of such overlaps, in fact they make them happen. If Cecil had decided to develop papers 1 or 2, for example, I would have asked him whether a stronger paper could be written by combining both presentations into one

(adequately focused) paper. Quantity is sometimes a measure of success among academics, however, and he might be reluctant to follow this advice. I would counter that remembered articles and books tend to be rich in detail. Given how little time there is to write, and how long writing takes, the ultimate project is more likely to be memorable if it draws on all the resources you have available.

3 *Consider dropping projects in less important areas.* 'Triage' is a method of dividing medical patients into three groups – those who will die anyway, those who will get well anyway and those who are most likely to benefit from medical attention. A similar approach can help focus attention when evaluating a writing portfolio. Cecil had already established his credentials in one area. He recently decided that he didn't need to do any more in this area, rather, it was more important to develop other interests. He can choose to develop papers 1 and 2 at another time; they could be very attractive to him as a young faculty member who needs to show productivity quickly, for example.

The overall message is that thought and planning before beginning to write can save a great deal of time. Time is a scarce resource. It does not make sense to begin a writing project until you are convinced that the project you are working on deserves your priority. Different people have different styles, and almost all of us are working on more than one writing project at any given time. Still, it is easy to be lured beyond our multi-tasking limits. Clear decisions not only minimize wasted time, they use career priorities to highlight the most important project to work on right now.

STAND BACK FROM WORK IN PROGRESS

Once writing begins, scholars often find themselves totally immersed. That involvement is the great pleasure of academics, but it also makes sense to vary this by connection with a more distanced, managerial perspective. Two ideas make it easier for me to do that.

Focus attention on a limited, but compelling message

Academic projects typically begin with an internal monologue, often in multiple voices. Part of me wants to begin an interesting new project, for example, while another part of me cautions that I already have too many commitments. Inner conversation gets more interesting as it becomes more substantive. I wonder if an empirical study would be the best way to explore a new subject of interest, but I can also see a compelling argument for first working out a theoretical argument; or, perhaps I should begin by systematically reviewing existing literature? But which methodology? Which theory? Which literatures? How should they be combined? The thing I hope to hear is an internal voice that says, '*That* is interesting!'

Delving into the literature with a specific project in mind shapes my emerging thoughts and continues the dialogue. Does this paper advance theory? Does the empirical design match the research objectives? Does it support or contradict my ideas? Does it lead into directions I have not considered? The most compelling questions grow directly out of what I want to achieve as a scholar.

Other ideas come from conversations with friends and advisers. If they are interested in an idea I am working on, I become more interested, and the ideas they add shape my own. More questions and interesting ideas develop in these conversations.

In short, the topic that becomes a formal research project almost always has survived the winnowing process of conversation – its content has been shaped by many voices. My early career insight, as mentioned at the start of this chapter, is that successful research projects and publications continue this conversation in a more public forum. Typically there are several choices available.

Dawn Detiene, for example, is writing a paper for my current seminar based on a data set that has already been collected. She is interested in explaining performance across three high-tech industries, and has data on a number of variables, including innovation decisions, CEO characteristics, organizational processes and organization culture. Her analysis could be framed in a variety of ways. To keep it simple, consider two alternatives: she could write a paper addressed to those interested in innovation in high-tech environments, or to those interested in the relationship between culture and performance. If she clearly makes a choice, it will help shape many subsequent writing tasks. What is an interesting finding in a high-tech discussion might not attract much attention among those interested in culture, for example, and vice versa.

Choice is not the only issue in continuing a research project. Even when I have made a clear decision about the conversation I want to join, and have identified a specific set of articles and books as an immediate focus (two things that help prune detail), my papers tend to be too complex. The problem, I think, is that they still carry too much weight from previous conversations with myself, and with various friends, advisers and literatures. Many of these are not from the primary conversation I hope to join. Thus it is necessary to establish and re-establish focus. Detail and complexity overburden the paper, especially for less intensely involved readers. The papers I most admire have breadth and detail, but only where it matters.

Persist, but know when to stop

Scholars who bring their writing projects to closure get the time and space they need from those around them. When my writing is going well, the things I want to say often seem fairly clear. That vision fades with amazing speed if I am interrupted. Distraction can bring new ideas, but it is more often the enemy of writing well.

As a reminder of the need for time and space, participants in the writing workshops I run receive a symbolic coffee mug. They are made so that the outside face shows the message on the door of the seminar rooms we use. That message is: 'Please do not disturb'.

Often, writing does not seem like 'real work' when compared to more tangible scholarly tasks, like teaching. Writers sometimes have to remind themselves that writing is indeed work with significant time and space demands. The importance of time and space has to be conveyed to department heads, programme organizers and others. Administrators in many universities *say* they want writing output. In practice, however, they undermine sustained writing with various requests and distractions. It often seems to outsiders (and even to the writer) that writing is something that can be postponed. In fact, interruption is often very costly.

Once we get to work, we must think about how work can be sustained, and when it should stop. Workshop participants see a second message on their side of the mug, which is:

I will DE<u>C</u>IDE:

1. To WRITE
   One paper from a portfolio
   Offering a few 'shiny things'
   To specific conversants
   In a particular forum
2. To KEEP WORKING
3. To STOP WORKING & <u>SUBMIT</u>

It is as simple as that. But that is not simple. Annie Dillard, a novelist, says that:

> Writing a book is like rearing children – willpower has very little to do with it. If you have a little baby crying in the middle of the night, and if you depend only on willpower to get you out of bed to feed the baby, that baby will starve. You do it out of love. Willpower is a weak idea; love is strong. You don't have to scourge yourself with a cat-o'-nine-tails to go to the baby. You go to the baby out of love for that particular baby. That's the same way you go to your desk . . . Caring passionately about something isn't against nature, and it isn't against human nature. It's what we're here to do. (Dillard, 1987: 75–6)

I am delighted with this passage, which I think applies as much to scholars as to novelists. It is not too far-fetched to think of what I am writing now as my baby, part of a larger loving family who share my interest in seeing it develop.

But as I began to quote this passage to others, I realized that my enchantment with Dillard's words revealed how long it has been since I, in fact, have got up to feed a baby. Love was not always my driving emotion when I got up for our young children. Furthermore, I did not leave a warm bed as easily for our second born, and he learned to become a civilized, sleep-through-the-night-child more quickly as a result.

I still agree that successful writers love their work. That is what drives them to find the time and space to work on their current paper. If they do not love it, they end up paying more attention to teaching, to administration, to consulting, to the theatre. Whatever.

But successful writers also keep working on those days when they are less enchanted with their baby. Persistent productivity is based on habit and duty as well as love. If successful writers are not inspired, they work on tasks that require less inspiration. When love is low they work on bibliography, format tables and the like. The baby lives because it gets regular attention, flourishes because it is loved, because it gets priority over other attractive alternatives.

Eventually, however, writers must decide they have done what they can and send their child out into the world. Some scholars have their greatest difficulty at this last transition point. After the planning and research, after the framing and connecting with the literature, after the analysis and footnotes and charts, they still keep polishing their manuscript. They seem to love their progeny too much. If we take Dillard's words to heart, and start thinking of a manuscript as an entity that deserves a life of its own, it may be easier to let go. Submission is critical. We keep scholarly conversation alive only if we send our work to others.

Conclusion

Above my desk I have a brief quote attributed to Charlie 'Bird' Parker, the famous jazz musician. It says:

> I could hear the music before I could play it, and I could play it before I understood it.

A very similar feeling motivates me to write. Initially, I only partially perceive the nature of a subject that interests me. My curiosity begins to be satisfied through sustained enquiry, but it is only as I write about a topic that I begin to understand it.

Of course, I don't ever 'really' understand the complicated things that interest me. That is why I continue to choose a scholarly career, and more specifically, why I choose to keep writing. I want to get as close to understanding as I can, and I feel that I am making progress. I suspect Parker felt the same way about jazz. My objective is to reinforce the same passion in writing-workshop participants and readers of this chapter. The music comes into being as we play together; scholarship is a community activity.

Study questions

1 What is the 'map' of the intellectual territory I most identify with, most want to be a part of now and in the future? Where are my particular interests located in this territory?
2 What writing projects do I hope to achieve over the next few years? Which ones are most important to me? Which ones are most likely to appeal to the field I have just mapped? Which ones are likely to interest practitioners? Which ones should I work on now, given my stage in career, and the other things I have to or want to do?
3 What should I decide to write now?

Recommended further reading

Huff, Anne (1999) *Writing for Scholarly Publication*. Thousand Oaks, CA: Sage.
Hart, Chris (1998) *Doing a Literature Review*. London: Sage.

References

Dillard, A. (1987) 'To Fashion a Text', in William Zinsser (ed.), *Inventing the Truth: The Art and Craft of Memoir*. New York: Book-of-the-Month Club.
Weick, K. (1995) *Organizational Sensemaking*. Thousand Oaks, CA: Sage.

5

Acknowledging the Individual in the Researcher

Kim James and Susan Vinnicombe

> The beliefs and the behaviours of the researcher are part of the empirical evidence for (or against) the claims advanced in the results of the research . . . [which] . . . must be open to critical scrutiny no less than what is traditionally defined as relevant evidence. (Harding, 1987: 9)

OVERVIEW

Why does anyone do management research? One might argue that researchers, who are intelligent and diligent on the whole, could have interesting and better-paid jobs with good prospects in many organizations. In our experience, most management researchers are driven by curiosity to enquire into a phenomenon that has aroused a personal interest. This is particularly true in doctoral work, and even when doctoral research is sponsored, researchers can still shape their project to fit their own interests. Indeed, supervisors encourage students to find their own area of interest within the domain of the supervisor's own research field. This is because the student must be motivated by the research for several years, and the project will probably constitute the founding research frame for the individual's future career.

Does the personal involvement of the researcher in the subject of the research matter? In this chapter we will argue that the individual behind the role of 'researcher' does indeed matter, in a variety of ways, and that it is particularly important in the management research field to account for individual preferences.

Our views reflect the theoretical perspectives from which we come. Kim as a managerial psychologist, and Sue as a feminist, share a number of research values which shape this chapter.

Elsewhere in this book ontology and epistemology are discussed. Those whose ontological assumptions and epistemological approach lead them to positivist research designs may assume that they do not need to bother much with this chapter. However, we would argue that there are various ways in which all researchers need to be reflexive so that their research has rigour and validity – we need to understand that written research is not just an outpouring of one's prejudices onto paper in the guise of objective study.

Some self-awareness is appropriate in all research design, although qualitative research requires high levels of reflexive behaviour that clearly need to be articulated in the writing up of the results (see, for example, Golden-Biddle and Locke, 1997).

This chapter explores the individual in the role of researcher. We identify three ways of highlighting the individual and relate these to examples of recent Cranfield doctoral research projects. Briefly the three aspects are:

PERSONAL INTEREST AND PERSPECTIVES   Personal interest might lead the researcher to research certain topics and phenomena. It will influence the way the question is framed and the context of the study. This view challenges the notion of the 'interchangeable scientist', that anyone could do this research – it just happens to be this researcher, but if any other person had done it, the research would have addressed the same issues in the same way.

PERSONAL RELATIONSHIP TO DATA   How data are collected, what is collected and its quality may depend in complex ways on the individual's understanding, their involvement with the topic and the people contributing to the research. How the individual interrogates the data and interprets their findings also requires self-knowledge. This particularly applies to interpretive approaches. Acknowledgement of the individual's involvement in the research needs to be accounted for in the presentation of the research, in a way that does not pretend detachment.

PERSONAL CHARACTERISTICS   Personal characteristics may lead the researcher to choose particular strategies and designs. This challenges the notion that the research question and phenomenon of interest determine these. We hear students assert, 'I am a positivist', or, 'I am an interpretivist', long before their research topic is developed and as though these are personality traits. We need to understand how these assertions influence the way research is carried out.

We now look at each of these in turn.

Personal interests and perspective

Acknowledging the individual in the choice of topics and research design could be a break with the traditional ways research is reported. Natural science approaches have often been adopted for social and psychological processes. Much psychological research is concerned with avoiding observer bias in a study. When studying human behaviour it is recognized that error can creep in, from problems associated with gathering the data to the subject trying to 'help' the experimenter by guessing what outcome is predicted. Thus, for example, if you want to see whether people can memorize better after some experimental manipulation, giving them a pre-test and a post-test, you need to know if change has merely resulted from getting better from practice in the test. To account for this you may have a classic experimental four control group design. If you are studying group behaviour, having you sitting in the corner of the room as an observer may affect what people do, and you may therefore want a two-way mirror so you can watch unobtrusively. You may worry that your subjects (note the terminology) may be influenced by the nature of the research, so although you may want to study aggression you tell them you are looking at perception or learning. Some famous studies where researchers have gone to great lengths to avoid the subject knowing what is being studied include Asch's (1955) work on conformity, Festinger and Smith's (1959) work on cognitive dissonance and Milgram's (1974) studies of obedience to authority. Another approach to getting objective and controlled data is to survey a large sample suitable for the study so that data can be statistically manipulated. Rigour and reduced bias are attained through carefully choosing a sample and by attention to appropriate questions and scales for measurement.

Yet even in experimental research there may be no such thing as the completely detached observer. Milgram did not just 'happen' upon his research. His own social background led him to be puzzled and horrified by the events committed in the Second World War. He saw horrifying events in Vietnam and could not find an adequate psychological explanation for their occurrence. He had a personal investment, as well as a professional interest, in confronting the world with the knowledge that we can all do morally wrong acts in obedience to authority and that this needs to be brought to our attention. However, from a positivist perspective the knowledge that would be recognized needed to come from an objective, scientific experiment, with bias and confounding factors eliminated as far as possible. Whether we like his method or not – and he does acknowledge the ethical issues his method raises – we probably feel that this work adds to our understanding of human behaviour. But we may also feel it is important to understand the personal background of the researcher and the wider context within which the data were collected. The personal context helps you understand the motivation for the research.

Personal aims are never very far from the shaping of a research topic. Thus we would argue that researchers need to be aware of their own values, aims, biases and experiences whatever kind of research they undertake, and they need to understand how these impact on their studies.

Feminism is a theoretical perspective that helps us understand these issues. Conventional wisdom in feminist research holds that 'the story behind the story' is crucial to understanding research, because all research – feminist or otherwise – is value laden and cannot escape being influenced by the history, life-situation and particular world-view of the researcher. Millman and Kanter (1987) refer to the children's tale of the emperor's new clothes. In this famous fable the townspeople persuaded themselves that the emperor was elegantly costumed. Yet a child, possessing an unspoilt vision, showed the citizenry that the emperor was 'really naked'. The story reminds us that collective delusions can be undone by introducing a fresh perspective. Social movements often parallel this story of the emperor and his fine clothes, in that they allow people to see the world from a fresh perspective. The women's movement is one such example. Millman and Kanter go on to say that, 'In the last decade no social movement has had a more startling or consequential impact on the way people see and act in the world than the women's movement. Like the onlookers in the emperor's parade, we can see and plainly speak about things that have always been there, but that formerly were unacknowledged' (1987: 30).

Harding (1987) suggests that reflection on how social phenomena get defined as problems reveals that there is no such thing as a problem *without* a person who has this problem. One distinctive characteristic of feminist research is that it generates its problems and research questions from the perspective of women's experiences. Further, it is women who should be expected to be able to reveal what women's experiences are. It is 'women's experiences' in the plural, since they vary across class and race. The issues women research, as a historically oppressed group, reflect how they seek to change the conditions in which they live. As a result, feminist research projects often originate in broader political struggles.

We are reminded by Harding that the best feminist research insists that 'the researcher be placed in the same critical plane as the overt subject matter, thereby recovering the entire research process for scrutiny in the results' (1987: 9). Thus, at the start of feminist research projects, researchers usually make explicit their gender, race, class and culture and how this has shaped the research project. In this way 'the researcher appears to us not as an invisible, anonymous voice of authority, but as a real historical individual with concrete, specific desires and interests' (1987: 9).

This is a response to the recognition that the cultural beliefs and behaviours of feminist research shape the results of their analyses no less than do those of sexist and androcentric researchers. The beliefs and behaviours of the researcher are part of the empirical evidence for or against the claims proposed in the results. Harding frames this in a provocative way:

> Introducing this 'subjective' element into the analysis in fact increases the objectivity of the research and decreases the 'objectivism' which hides this kind of evidence from the public. (1987: 9)

The relationship between researcher and the object of research is usually discussed under the heading 'reflexivity in research'. Harding refers to it as a new subject matter on enquiry to emphasize the unusual strength of this form of the reflexivity recommendation.

Fletcher (1999) goes further in arguing the importance of acknowledging the researcher's personal standpoint, since it invites readers to join the interpretative process as partners. Researchers, no matter how comprehensive their studies are, can only hope to tell one part of the story, or one story among many others that could be told. When a researcher's standpoint is made explicit, it helps readers understand what particular story is being told and invites them to connect this story to other perspectives they hold. The feminist tradition is therefore concerned with invitation and joint enquiry.

Examples of gendered research abound in the management field. Wilson (1995) brings together numerous examples, including the famous work by McClelland (see Wilson, 1995). In McClelland's study of achievement motivation he originally collected data from males and females. The female data were so mixed he threw them out and thereby constructed his famous theory based exclusively on male data. Shown ambiguous pictures, such as a figure that could be an executive working, subjects wrote stories which were scored for the level of achievement motivation they demonstrated. He then studied the 'high achievers'. Women were not found to project the same degree of achievement images. They were therefore neglected in the research and McClelland's theories were subsequently based solely on males. Women were treated as a non-standard population of lesser interest. However, an alternative perspective is that women do have high achievement motivation, but that it is demonstrated through different images and stories and under different conditions of elicitation. Further, there are now data which show that the achievement motives of women are often suppressed in groups, especially mixed sex groups, but are enhanced when women perform alone or are convinced that their achievements will not be noticed by, or offend, men.

Following this feminist tradition, Singh (1999: 15–17) recounted the story behind her doctorate, in which she studied personal definitions of commitment in male and female engineering managers:

> This study started after personal experiences led to a question which never seemed to get resolved. Why, despite equal education, similar early career patterns, and increased social support for mothers, were there so few women managers approaching the tops of companies, particularly engineering companies. It could be argued that with the right background, degrees, training, technical skills, competences and ambition, women would be just as well placed in the promotion tournaments as their male counterparts. But they were not there.
>
> The personal experiences occurred over a long period. First, there was a long period as a non-working 'company wife' in several international companies where my husband was employed in the UK, Sweden and Norway. In the 1970s and 1980s, these companies were gender segregated both hierarchically and horizontally; women were not to be found at the top, or even the middle, and they were clustered in support roles such as secretaries and draftswomen.
>
> Later, I took a technology foundation year at university, where I noticed how the women on the course (about 20% of the class) were the ones to take the notes in practical work, to organise what was needed, to tidy up afterwards. The male students naturally took charge, some protective of the females, others aggressive and dismissive when the females did or said something wrong. Why were the women (including myself) behaving like this – organising, tidying, taking the secondary role whilst the men did the action, despite the women achieving high grades in assignments and examinations? Thinking about these questions led to my transferring to sociology, to gain a better understanding of the situation, both of the women in engineering, and of myself. As I grew more interested in research methodology, I decided I wanted to undertake a PhD to explore these issues. As an undergraduate I took a women's studies option to learn about the sociological structures and processes which impact women in management, and particularly women managers in engineering companies. I then became a female manager in a male-dominated technical university, and could apply some of the

learning from the social science degree course to my own experience as a woman manager.

My research started by looking at the barriers to women managers in engineering companies. The project fitted well with a line of women in management doctoral research projects being undertaken at Cranfield School of Management. I started asking men and women engineers about the barriers for women. As by now my husband was an engineering professor, I came into frequent social contact with engineers and engineering students from all over the world, and I took every opportunity to find out what the situation was in the various countries. I found that male engineers talked frequently about women having equal competence but not as much commitment as men. Women said they were extremely committed, and that this was demonstrated by their remaining in the profession, despite difficulties in the male dominated workplace.

Clearly, these personal experiences would impact the undertaking of the research project.

PERSONAL RELATIONSHIP TO DATA

In addition to choice of research topic, we would argue that in social research, recognizing personal involvement in the data need not be construed as bad practice or bias but as a source of data in its own right, particularly when rich, qualitative data collection methods are used. Researchers who want to avoid biased data collection but at the same time to use their experiences need constantly to review their motives and involvement.

How data are collected, what count as data, how the individual interrogates the data and interprets the findings, are all affected by the assumptions made by the researcher.

Some research methodologies explicitly address the individual in the researcher as an integrated part of the research design, data collection and data management. Clinical research (Schein, 1987, 1993, 1995), based on participative action research methods, is one approach that helps us understand this. Schein's ideas initially derived from a seminar in which researchers at Sloan MIT were describing the knowledge they had gained about organizations. They found that they used their consulting experience more than their research to 'know' organizations. This also builds on Schein's process consultation work. Certainly researchers are not 'expert' consultants with solutions to sell. However, Schein argues that client-led process work can and should be considered appropriate management research. The advantage of the clinical approach is that it is relevant to the client and builds in the notion of intervening in a system to understand it, and vice versa: to understand a system one studies the impact of one's interventions.

There are a number of criteria for clinical research, including:

- 'Clinical' implies some form of pathology in the organization; the organization has identified that it needs help, not the researcher. Thus the work is client-demanded not researcher-led and is oriented to pathology and health. (An analogy might be that if you go to a psychologist and say you are depressed, the psychologist treats you for the symptom that concerns *you.* They have not, for example, come to your house and said they have met you at a party, have decided you are an interesting case and asked if they can treat you.)

- Researchers need process consulting skills not just data collecting and data analysing skills.
- Researchers need self-insight to get in touch with their own biases and perspectives that will influence their observations.
- Rigour is developed by re-framing and revising hypotheses about what is going on and by observing the results of interventions (including everything the researcher engages with in the organization, not just formal research interviews or observations but including casual conversations and feelings of being in the organization.)
- Only the client can know what should be done and the consultation/research should build the relationship so that dependency is not the outcome of the work.
- The researcher should raise the consequences of interventions.
- Enquiry comes from the clinician's theory of health.
- Data are deep not broad, involving confidential matters.
- Validation is achieved through predicting responses to interventions.
- Data are analysed through case conferences and sharing with colleagues.
- To avoid malpractice, ethical and legal responsibility are acknowledged.

Such a research approach requires reflexivity, an awareness of one's own experience as data as the research unfolds, and of one's relationship to the data as sense-making takes place.

Long (1999) suggests the aim of 'pure objectivity' is problematic because such research addresses dynamic and changing social systems. The researcher both impinges on the system and is a source of change even when the researcher is no more interventionist than being in the minds of people. The researcher aims to study the organization as encountered and the effects of the interactions between researcher and researched are part of the data that aids understanding. Long goes on to say that in participative action research, close collaboration between researcher and those in the organization is essential and the distinction between researcher and researched becomes less distinct:

> the researcher is able to study and document the changes that occur in his or her relations with the organization as the research proceeds . . . the experience of the researcher will be shaped by the system entered (now a system with a researcher) . . . The experience of the researcher and the relatedness of the researcher/researched, through a process such as transference, mirroring and the activation of social defences, are available for study and feedback as is any other information gathered. (1999: 263)

Participative action research engages a capacity in the individual to find multiple positions within the self to avoid the alternative of splitting and projecting these multiple positions on to either researcher or researched. To avoid this, which would lead unconsciously to an outgroup on to whom fantasies and anxieties would be projected, requires psychological sophistication and maturity.

Such an approach was taken in Jarrett's (1998) PhD. He undertook three case studies in the public sector in order to study the psychodynamics of top teams and their impact on strategic organizational learning. Using a clinical approach to his research, he identified throughout his thesis how his personal motivations and thoughts were engaged in the cases he looked at. This allowed the reader to see how his interpretations were guided and influenced by his personal insights and learning, in addition to using his experience as data. His theory of organizational health, from which the propositions for his research evolved, was systemic psychodynamic theory. This provided a rationale for the exploration of the impact on him of the organizations studied and of his understanding of the groups and individuals studied.

For example, reflecting on one of his case studies he writes:

> The process of engaging with [the organization] has been rich with learning and insights. Thus I am choosing to be selective on the top key themes that emerge from my reflections.

> - My identification with the notion of a strong, clear-thinking and courageous change agent (the CEO) was high. I enjoyed our cosy chats and liked the role of confidant. This relates to my inner preference to be in the circle of influence but not necessarily to front things. I feel that influence is more important to me than power; and recognition and achievement more important than fame or glory. This helps in the research or consultant role but may provide personal challenges in a more proactive leadership role.
> - My relationship with the group was a steady process of gaining trust and meeting commitments – delivering on promises. My natural tendency and the way I had construed the role suggested I should stay on the boundary and be emotionally distant as a researcher. However, both the research process and earlier learning in the NHS Trust case study [presented earlier in the thesis] helped me to realize that active engagement, initiated by me, was required to build the relationship and therefore gain greater insights into the reality of the people I worked with on this exercise. (1998: 515)

He describes how what he observed, what was described to him and his own experience of a crisis with the group were able to give him insight into the issues that they described.

> Thus, my experience of the organization in relation to its environment was one of calm and operational effectiveness. It did not seem to be under threat from its environment, which did not appear as turbulent . . . It did not feel chaotic, more like quiet co-operation at best or plotting in some instances between the Director and Chair. I did not experience the system as chaotic. There was one exception when towards the end of the research I was asked to change role and act as a process consultant. The request came out of a crisis of mismanagement and poor communication so it was to happen 'next week'. I declined, pointing out what seemed to be another defensive routine. [The manager] accepted the point and the session was re-planned and they used their usual consultant. However, in those series of many telephone calls I could see and feel how easy it was to get caught up with a minor crisis that arose out of poor planning, agendas not yet fully negotiated or opportunism. Thus, I concluded that the environment was not chaotic as

a system nor turbulent. However, operational issues could easily spiral into strate-gic or political issues where priorities and differences had not been resolved. It was this element that was more like a minefield – its unpredictable internal nature. (1998: 510)

He gives another example of how awareness of personal experience might affect his understanding of one of the organizations studied:

I also had very positive associations to it. Two years earlier it was where our first child was born and the standard of care in a difficult situation was good. I did men-tion this to some members of the group [the top team being studied] but it was not a conscious thought as I worked with them. But it was no doubt in the background. Thus, I wanted them to succeed. (1998: 406)

In all the places where these contributions are made they are clearly labelled as personal insights. The reader can therefore understand how they add to the other data collected.

Thus, in Jarrett's research he explored his own feelings and reactions to his contact with the organization. These were recorded as data. In psychoanalytic terms the data are the feelings and reactions evoked in the researcher *as a result* of interactions with people in the organization rather than thoughts and feelings brought by the researcher to the organization from outside. The use of this approach requires the researcher to make a distinction between the feelings and thoughts they bring from their own life experience and from thoughts and feelings evoked by others. Training is required to enable researchers to do this. In psychoanalytic terms the researcher is examining projections and transference and defence mechanisms (Obholzer and Roberts, 1994).

Personal characteristics

At the start of another recent Cranfield doctoral thesis the following statement is made:

I recognize there is something about my own ontology which leads me down this path of enquiry and influences the type of research I undertake. (Weight, 2001: 1)

One way researchers can account for the individual in the development of the research and in its methodological choices is to examine personal pref-erences, not in terms of interests or experiences as we have outlined above, but in terms of preference styles which may influence methodological choices.

Most writers on research quite rightly encourage researchers to identify their phenomenon of interest and the knowledge gap to which to contribute, to work out a researchable question, to work out what evidence will answer that question and *then* design a method to collect that evidence. This is a neat and logical flow of work and indeed is an approach to aspire to.

However, we have evidence from many years of teaching and supervising management research students that whatever the final write-up of many theses might say, this is not how research is designed in practice. Within weeks of first encountering the words 'ontology' and 'epistemology' students are describing themselves as positivists or interpretivists and are keen to state, long before their literature review has confirmed a research gap, and before the phenomenon of study is clear, that they will be doing qualitative or quantitative studies. One perspective on this is that their supervisors should get a grip on them and make them do their research 'properly'. However, this may cover up important underlying preferences which shape research and which could more beneficially be explored and used with awareness.

As we observe researchers from close quarters as colleagues and supervisors we can see that there are personal preferences at work. For example:

- Some people are keen to get out and talk to interviewees; others prefer to stay in the library.
- Some want to collect rich, ambiguous data with expressions of emotion and depth of experience; others want clear, orderly, factual data.
- Some are keen to keep the world at an arm's length through survey data; others want to get 'out there' to get a feel for the organization 'on the ground'.
- Some have a preference for statistical analysis, as their confidence in the findings rests on this kind of rigour; others want to see and feel the patterns in what they observe and are told, distrusting numbers as 'garbage in, garbage out'.
- Some want to get a broad overview of what is happening in an industry or in a whole organization; others seek a more intimate, local perspective.
- Some want a clear project plan with Gantt charts from day one; others are comfortable with a more iterative design.
- Some pursue researcher detachment and maintenance of control over the data; others place value on taking the researched into their confidence, involving them in the research and its path.

In the eventual design of research studies researchers may go against their grain, or they may go with their flow, but acknowledging these choices can help them to see the extent to which their research has been shaped by decisions that are intentional and appropriate. The influence of colleagues or supervisors who have different preferences can be detrimental if left undiscussed in managing the relationship.

A helpful model for understanding natural preferences is the Myers Briggs Type Indicator (MBTI) (see, for example, Briggs-Myers and Myers, 1993). The MBTI is a starting point for exploring how one likes to go about data collection and decision-making, how one uses energy and sets priorities. It is not an assessment of capability and so can be used for self-awareness in a non-threatening way. None the less, like all such tools a personal profile should be undertaken with a qualified consultant. This tool is used extensively at Cranfield School of Management for this purpose. It will not predict the eventual choices that are made, because many factors influence such decisions. It will, however, predict how comfortable one may be with choices, how one may like to go about making choices and what might seem either alien or comfortable ways of seeing the world.

The MBTI is an instrument based on Jung's theory of personality type. The essence of the theory is that much apparently random variation in human behaviour is actually quite orderly and consistent as it is linked to certain basic differences in the way individuals prefer to use perception and judgement. 'Perception' is defined as the process of becoming aware – of things or people or occurrences or ideas. 'Judgement' is the process of coming to conclusions about what has been perceived. If individuals differ systematically in what they perceive and the judgements they reach, they may as a result show corresponding differences in their reactions, in their interests, values, needs and motivations in what they like best to do.

Starting from this premise the MBTI aims to gauge, from a self-completed questionnaire, individuals' basic preferences with regard to perception and judgement. The MBTI contains separate dimensions for determining each of four basic preferences that, according to Jung, are one of the structures in the individual's personality. In the account that follows, we have presented these fairly simply. You may be forgiven for thinking you are 'a little bit of everything'. In a profound sense this is true and the dynamics of these types can be explored in a full consultation. However, preferences are not intended as 'boxes', but do indicate how individual differences affect choice and comfort. An analogy with being right- or left-handed illustrates this. You have a hand you habitually write with. It is, for most people, easier and quicker and more readable to others and requires less conscious effort if you use this hand. However, you use both hands for lots of tasks and if you lose the use of one hand, the other can learn to take over. This is not dissimilar to the psychological preferences Jung identified.

The first dimension, extroversion and introversion, identifies a preference for using energy in the external world or the inner world. Extroverts enjoy putting their energy out into the world of people and things, actively taking part. Introverts tend to be more interested in reflecting, shaping and crafting their ideas before they put them out into the world. The introvert therefore frequently finds strange or irritating the extrovert habit of sharing half-thought-through ideas with others as a way of developing them fully. The extrovert finds the introvert's habit of waiting until their ideas are well-formed before speaking about them difficult to understand. Extroverts like to be out and about interviewing, conferencing and networking whereas introverts prefer the writing and crafting of ideas. Of course no one is completely introvert or extrovert. With a basic preference for one over the other, we still need a balance. People with extrovert preferences do shut their doors and get on with writing, or go to the library – but comparatively less frequently, or less comfortably than their introvert preferenced colleagues. People with introverted preferences will brainstorm their ideas with their supervisors, but may prefer to prepare a paper for considered discussion. They will go to conferences and network, but will probably have enjoyed preparing their paper and running through more drafts than their extroverted colleagues who may have found chatting about and presenting their ideas much more fun. Whilst extroverts or introverts may decide to do in-depth interviews for their research, introverts are in our experience much less 'gung ho' about setting off down this line, preferring more reflective preparation. Extroverts tend to see this as just another comfort zone!

The second dimension is sensing and intuition, which relate to our perceptual preferences. As the term suggests, sensing people do have a preference for making sense of the world through their five senses. They ask questions about the size and shape of problems, even when they are abstract. They 'concretize' data collection. That is, they feel comfortable if something can be measured, quantified and operationalized in a practical, systematic and standardized way. They would prefer to get a strong sense of an issue before they begin to theorize or play with ideas. People with an intuitive preference, by contrast, like to take an imaginative perspective beyond the reach of the senses. They like to see possibilities, attribute meanings, make sense of patterns, frequently ignoring facts in search of a bigger picture offering a creative perspective. They use their 'sixth sense'. In research, both preferences are called for. And although we can all access both we do, again, have a preference for one over the other and this will influence the relative amount of time, energy and enthusiasm we have for various aspects of research. As researchers we have handled a large amount of data, poured over statistics and fiddled around to get the detail right. But with an intuitive preference the generation of ideas and the building of models holds a lot more appeal. We have to guard against the desire to skip the factual data in favour of the intuitive patterns and meanings we can see. Researchers with sensing preferences have strength in data collection and detail, but may need to stop every now and then to really question what the data might actually mean beyond the categories and labels they have been sorted into. They need to check that they can answer the all-important question about the research outcomes – so what?

The third dimension is thinking and feeling, which relates to the way we make decisions. Thinking preference focuses on logic, detached analysis and objectivity. In decision-making and dealing with data, thinking preference focuses on standing back and applying general principles to making sense of the data collected. The feeling preference is concerned with values and beliefs and how these impact on people as a key part of taking a decision. In making sense of the data the feeling-preferenced person may want to immerse themselves in the data and understand what people are saying from their unique and subjective standpoint. This does not mean that thinking people cannot work with feelings, nor that feeling people cannot be analytical. However, it is the standpoint from which the analysis is done that distinguishes the preferences. Thus thinking researchers may be comfortable detaching themselves from their data and trying to establish objective criteria for assessing the meaning of their data, using statistical techniques. Even when thinking-preferenced researchers do rich qualitative research, they frequently feel the need to go back and quantify what they have found. Feeling researchers are more likely to want to immerse themselves personally and use their own experiences to help them interpret the data from their respondents. They are more likely to enjoy a more interpretivist approach, such as phenomenology. They may recognize the difficulty of separating the respondents' and their own views and so may resolve this by adopting a co-enquiry approach. This approach explicitly recognizes that there is an interaction between researcher and respondents. They are often frustrated with having to use analytical tools to demonstrate what they 'know' from the data.

The last dimension is judging or perceiving. These are choices about how to make time priorities. The priorities referred to here are either those about gathering information or making decisions. Those who have a preference for making decisions like to structure their world and have a plan for the future. Those who have a preference for gathering data are much more happy to keep things open-ended and less planned and are likely to leave things to a more spontaneous unfolding. These preferences may be reflected in how the whole research project is carried out; those with a judging preference are more likely to manage their research as a project, with an end point clearly in view. Those with a perceiving preference like to have lots of different avenues to pursue, and are less focused on the finished outcomes. Perceiving researchers are more comfortable handling lots of complex data and ambiguity. There may be many interpretations that can be drawn from the data and they often enjoy studying these rich possibilities. Judging researchers like clarity and order, and are more concerned with completing tasks. They are more comfortable with data that lend themselves to discrete analyses leading to clear answers.

These descriptions give only a flavour of the MBTI typology and further consideration can be given to the possible combinations of preferences and the way the less-preferred aspects are used. However, knowing one's personal preferences is often invaluable in researchers' understanding of how they are likely to engage with the research process. The model also provides a helpful basis to negotiate the supervisory relationship.

CONCLUSION

We have looked at some of the issues that provide a starting point for acknowledging the individual in the researcher. We have observed and believe that undertaking research, particularly for a doctorate, can be a profound personal development journey. As Weight (2001: 1) observed: 'This journey is coming to its end, and many people have helped me along the way. Without them, I would not have discovered so much about the world and myself, as well as about the subject of this thesis. For this enrichment of my life, I am grateful.'

Self-awareness and insight are essential for the choice of research topic and methods, for the shaping of ideas and the capacity to make sense of rich data in a meaningful way. The journey can be long and with many highs and lows. Acknowledging that this is a very personal and emotional experience rather than just a straightforward cognitive task is often a very important step in making the journey an enriching one.

Study questions

1 How is the research shaped by your own personal interest and, if applicable, the interests of your sponsoring organization? Has this influenced the framing of the research question and the context in which the research was carried out?
2 How did you collect your data? What did you collect? How have you managed 'objectivity' in the data analysis? How did you check your findings?
3 How did you engage with the whole research process? What aspects came easily and were there challenges in completing the research? What have you learned about yourself in the process?

Recommended further reading

Briggs-Myers, I.B. and Myers, P. (1993) *Gifts Differing*. Palo Alto, CA: Consulting Psychologists Press. (A good follow-up book on the MBTI)
Golden-Biddle, K. and Locke, D.K. (1997) *Composing Qualitative Research*. London: Sage. (An interesting book for all qualitative researchers, which includes a valuable chapter on 'characteristics of the story teller')
Johnson, P. and Duberley, J. (2000) *Understanding Management Research*. London: Sage. (Includes an excellent last chapter on reflexivity in management research)

References

Asch, S.E. (1955) 'Opinions and Social Pressure', *Scientific American*, 193, pp. 31–5.
Briggs-Myers, I.B. and Myers, P. (1993) *Gifts Differing*. Palo Alto, CA: Consulting Psychologists Press.
Festinger, L. and Smith, J.C. (1959) 'Cognitive Consequences of Forced Compliance', *Journal of Abnormal and Social Psychology*, 58, pp. 203–10.
Fletcher, J.K. (1999) *Disappearing Acts: Gender, Power and Relational Practice at Work*. Cambridge, MA: MIT Press.
Golden-Biddle, K. and Locke, D.K. (1997) *Composing Qualitative Research*. London: Sage.
Harding, S. (1987) 'Is There a Feminist Method?', in S. Harding, *Feminism and Methodology*. Milton Keynes: Open University Press, p. 9.
Jarrett, M. (1998) 'The Psychodynamics of Top Teams and the Impact on Strategic Learning: Three Case Studies in the Public Sector', unpublished PhD thesis, Cranfield School of Management, UK.
Long, S. (1999) 'Organizations in Depth', in G. Yannis (ed.), *Action Research: Participative Action Research and Action Learning in Organizations*. London: Sage.
Milgram, S. (1974) *Obedience to Authority: An Experimental View*. New York: Harper and Row.
Millman, M. and Kanter, R.M. (1987) 'Introduction to Another Voice: Feminist Perspectives on Social Life and Social Science', in S. Harding (ed.), *Feminism and Methodology*. Milton Keynes: Open University Press, pp. 29–36.
Obholzer, A. and Roberts, V.Z. (1994) *The Unconscious at Work*. London: Routledge.
Schein, E.H. (1987) *The Clinical Perspective in Fieldwork*. Newbury Park, CA: Sage.
Schein, E.H. (1993) 'Legitimating Clinical Research in the Study of Organization Culture', *Journal of Counselling and Development*, 71 (July/August), pp. 703–8.

Schein, E.H. (1995) 'Process Consultation, Action Research and the Clinical Inquiry: Are They the Same?', *Journal of Managerial Psychology*, 10 (6), pp. 14–20.

Singh, V. (1999) 'Exploring Male and Female Managers' Perspectives on the Meaning and Assessment of Commitment: Cases from Leading British and Swedish Engineering Companies', unpublished PhD thesis, Cranfield School of Management, UK.

Weight, P. (2001) 'Strategic and Professional Leadership: The Study of Role Duality', unpublished PhD thesis, Cranfield School of Management, UK.

Wilson, F. (1995) *Organizational Behavior and Gender*. New York: McGraw–Hill.

PART 3

Approaches and Techniques

6

Qualitative and Quantitative Issues in Research Design

Phyl Johnson and Don Harris

OVERVIEW

This chapter offers a discussion of both qualitative and quantitative issues in research design within the broad field of management studies. The chapter will take the reader through various stages and levels of consideration in their choice of appropriate research designs.

The chapter begins with a general discussion of the different types of phenomena of interest and research questions a management researcher may be focused upon. We make the observation that there may be more or less known about a researcher's particular phenomenon of interest and that this state of extant knowledge will be the initial guide to the appropriateness of either a qualitative or a quantitative design. This is directly opposed to the strategy that many have fallen prey to in the past: being wedded to a particular design or method irrespective of the nature of the research question.

The chapter then moves on to the second and third sections that individually discuss first quantitative then qualitative research designs. Each section begins with general descriptions of what is usually defined as qualitative or quantitative research. Basic families of methods of data collection and analysis are then discussed. Finally, each section will conclude with an insight into the pros and cons of qualitative and quantitative research designs in practice.

A START POINT: THE RESEARCH QUESTION

The start point of research in any field is the *research question* or problem. For example, in physics one might ask, 'How is the speed of sound affected by the density of the medium through which it is transmitted?' In psychology a research question might be, 'At what stage of development do children uniformly first appear to have identities of self?' In management studies, a research question might be, 'What are the key elements of organizational culture that CEOs choose to address during organizational change?' Whatever the field, research questions tend to be loose at the outset of a piece of research and become tighter as the work progresses. Initially, there may only be a phenomenon of interest, for example the speed of light, child development or organizational culture. The research question then emerges from the particular phenomenon of interest and is gradually tightened by a process of iteration with extant literature to identify research gaps and interesting questions. In this way one moves from being simply interested in organizational culture to asking a specific question about the elements of culture CEOs seem to see as important during organizational change.

It is the nature of a research question that will guide many of the significant choices throughout the duration of a research project. Of these choices, the one most directly influenced is the choice of research design – how the research will be done. That is, whether the research is theory-testing or theory-generative, predominantly qualitative or quantitative in terms of data collection and analysis, and focused on single or multiple units of analysis.

Although all research questions do to some extent begin loosely – we don't know exactly what we are asking until we begin to ask it – there are variations in terms of their initial looseness and the extent to which they do eventually become tight. It is this initial distinction that can give the first clues as to whether a qualitative or quantitative research design is likely to be appropriate in terms of operationalizing the question(s) being asked.

For instance, if a particular phenomenon of interest is one where there is little extant knowledge, then the research question itself is more likely to be loose. That is, there is unlikely to be enough knowledge to pin down specific constructs, variables and relationships to be *tested*. Instead, the job of a piece of research in an unknown area is to begin to uncover what the important constructs, variables and relationships might be and, in effect, *generate* theory. Here, the research is likely to be qualitative and data will be collected in an open-ended loose fashion.

The opposite is true for quantitative research. That is, in an area where there is a reasonable amount of existing knowledge, specific constructs and relationships between them can be isolated. Hypotheses can be generated and operationalized usually as items on a survey instrument of some kind. This form of research is tighter and more structured than its counterpart.

The choice of predominantly qualitative or quantitative research design is then a matter of which is *appropriate* in the light of the research question being asked. The reality of research in the social sciences is that it takes time to build up expertise in a particular research method. It then becomes difficult to abandon that method in favour of a more appropriate method which may be unfamiliar. However, developing eclectic methodological ability that can be appropriately applied to a range of questions is an essential part of research training.

It is important to recognize that quantitative and qualitative research methods need not live in total isolation from each other. The two approaches should not be seen as discrete either/or options. They can be viewed as labels that describe two ends of a continuum. The two methodologies can complement each other.

QUANTITATIVE RESEARCH DESIGN

WHAT IS QUANTITATIVE RESEARCH? Most quantitative management research will involve a questionnaire or survey of some kind, although this is not the only approach to quantitative research in a managerial setting, and neither are the results of questionnaires the only source of quantitative data. Company measures such as annual financial returns or absenteeism rates can also be used in conjunction with survey data. For instance, frequent use has been made of economy- and industry-wide financial performance data as well as individual company reports and historical 'archive' data (for example in board research as summarized by Dalton et al., 1997). In addition, in terms of structured data, it has been common – especially in the United States where databases are well developed – to use detailed demographics as dependent variables in top team exploration (see, for example, Hambrick and Mason, 1984). For the most part in what follows, it will be assumed that the quantitative technique to be employed is questionnaire-based.

Quantitative research is best characterized by the analytical approach to the data that are generated. Quantitative research *always* involves the numerical analysis of data. This may be as simple as the production of frequency histograms or as complex as the multivariate statistics of structural equation modelling. The requirement to be able to perform statistical procedures on data means it is necessary that they are collected in a highly structured manner.

There are three broad types of quantitative research: descriptive, comparative or prescriptive. *Descriptive research* involves no comparison between groups. It is essentially a simplified description of some phenomenon, facilitated by using numbers. At one extreme descriptive data analysis may be as straightforward as frequency histograms or reports of means and standard deviations. Alternatively, descriptive techniques also encompass the multivariate techniques of principal components analysis and confirmatory factor analysis. All of these approaches describe underlying structures in the world; they do not compare between groups or predict what the likely outcome of an action will be.

Comparative research involves the statistical comparison of data between two (or more) groups. As an example, the objective of such an approach may be to establish if one management technique or another leads to higher employee job satisfaction or increased productivity. There is a dependent variable (or variables) and an independent variable (or variables). The independent variable refers to the different groups (categories) you wish to compare; the dependent variable is what is measured – in the previous examples, job satisfaction or productivity. Differences in the dependent variable are taken to be a result of hypothesized differences between the groups specified in the independent variable.

It is often argued that the ultimate objective of science of any kind should be prediction. *Prescriptive data analysis* has this objective embedded within it. Prescriptive statistical approaches range from simple regression to complex structural equation modelling-based approaches, such as path analysis. Some researchers are now even beginning to use neural networks and genetic algorithms for research of this kind (see Garson, 1998). Implicit within any prescriptive approach to quantitative research is an underlying predictive model of *cause and effect*. This model may be simple or complex, but for it to be verifiable through quantitative methods, it must be explicit and it must be capable of being described in the form of mathematical equations.

Issues in quantitative research

Questionnaires embody a basic principle of quantitative research that is both its principal strength and its fundamental weakness. *You only get the answers to the questions that you ask.* This may sound obvious but it is often forgotten. If a vital question is omitted from a survey instrument you will never know what (potential) effect it would have had. Unlike the interview situation, where the interviewee may spontaneously proffer additional, often vital information, this is not possible with a self-completion survey instrument. While this may initially seem like a drawback, it does encourage theoretical rigour and data discipline in the researcher.

Quantitative research requires that the researcher asks the right questions of the participants in the study. To ask the right questions the researcher must know what the right questions are. This is usually achieved in two, non-mutually exclusive ways: by undertaking qualitative interviews with members of the target sample, and/or extensive reviews of relevant published literature. However, not only must the researcher be aware of the potential relationship between the predictor and the criterion variables, he or she must also be aware of any potential interactions with other variables or the confounding effects of other variables.

As relationships between variables must be expressed formally, the means of measurement must also be expressed formally. This means that the study should be replicable by a third party or at another point in time by the same researcher. The results of such research can be compared directly to the previous research. *Replicability* is an essential feature of the scientific method. If results cannot be replicated then either the original research is of questionable quality or it is of limited generalizability. Replicability is much easier to achieve in quantitative research where the process is more structured and the raw data are less dependent on the analyst's interpretive skill.

When dealing with hypothetical constructs and their measurement, *reliability* is a key issue. Reliability refers to the ability of a measurement instrument to produce the same answer in the same circumstances, time after time. Imagine the problems you would have if, when you were trying to measure the size of this book, the length of one centimetre on your ruler varied. Your problems become compounded when you are trying to measure something that is changing. Instead of a book, imagine trying to measure the growth of two sets of seedlings, one grown in fertilizer and one that isn't. Are any differences due to the fertilizer or down to the ruler? You cannot do quantitative research without a reliable measuring instrument. Your problems are compounded further when you are trying to measure a hypothetical construct, such as job satisfaction or stress. In this case you don't even know what units your ruler is calibrated in! There are techniques to enhance the reliability of your measures and assess their reliability (see Moser and Kalton, 1971 for a good review).

When measuring any hypothetical construct it is advisable not to use a single item. Single-item measures are less reliable than multi-item measures (scales) and are also less valid. If you consider a concept such as 'employee satisfaction' it is likely to have many sub-dimensions, for example satisfaction with the nature of the work, satisfaction with management, or satisfaction with the office environment. A summated scale comprised of several items each tapping a slightly different aspect of satisfaction will provide a more reliable and more valid measure. The test–retest reliability of such a scale can be established by correlating the responses from respondents on two occasions. High correlations are indicative of a reliable scale. Split-half reliability may be more practical in management studies when there may only be one opportunity to access the sample of informants. This method involves splitting the items in a scale purporting to measure a single construct into two halves and correlating the results from each half with each other. If the correlation is high, then both parts of the scale are measuring the same construct.

Split-half reliability is a variation on a theme of the internal consistency of a scale. The internal consistency of the scale (that is, the extent to which all the items are measuring the same construct) can be established by calculating coefficients such as Cronbach's alpha. A high Cronbach's alpha (above 0.7, where this coefficient runs from zero to unity) indicates that the scale is internally consistent. An analysis of the individual items can help to identify 'rogue' items. If the Cronbach's alpha value increases when an item is deleted from the scale this item is decreasing the internal consistency of the scale and should be dropped.

Establishing the *external validity* of the measurement of a hypothetical construct is far more difficult than assessing its reliability. External validity is concerned with establishing whether a measure actually measures what it is purported to measure. There are various types of external validity, the most common being content validity, construct validity, concurrent validity and predictive validity. However, it is important to note that validity of any kind can only be inferred – it can never be truly established.

For a scale to have content validity, its components must encompass all the pertinent aspects of the domain to be assessed. This requires a systematic assessment of the domain at the outset of the scale's development. A thorough review of the literature and extensive qualitative interviewing of a sample of participants drawn from the target population are essential precursors to the development of a scale for use in quantitative research and are vital to ensure its content validity.

Construct validity refers to the degree of association shown by the scale to other theoretically associated variables. For example, a scale purporting to measure extroversion should also predict that high scorers are more likely to engage in social behaviours than low scorers.

Concurrent and predictive validity are very similar concepts. To establish if a scale has either of these forms of validity, it must be related to an observable phenomenon. As an example of concurrent validity, it may be proposed that a scale measuring the motivation of staff will be associated with higher productivity. There would be evidence of concurrent validity if motivation scores were highly correlated with output in existing staff. The same scale might be used in a selection application where it would be predicted that highly motivated candidates, if employed, should show higher productivity than less motivated job-seekers. If this is true, then there is evidence that the scale exhibits predictive validity.

Internal validity is really an issue in the fundamental design of the study. Internal validity addresses the question, can it reasonably be assumed that A causes B? Many purists would argue that in management studies, which typically uses an *ex post facto* or retrospective approach (in other words it involves the study of concomitant variance rather than causality), there is a fundamental threat to internal validity as it cannot be positively established whether A causes B. Campbell and Stanley (1966) and Kerlinger (1973) offer detailed discussions.

SAMPLING CONSIDERATIONS

There are many sampling techniques, the simplest and most theoretically rigorous being simple *random* sampling. In this approach, a random sample of people is extracted from the pre-defined population of interest. The sample should proportionately reflect the characteristics of the population from which it was drawn. Ideally, this technique requires an exhaustive list of all the potential respondents, although this may not always be possible.

Instead of obtaining a random sample, a slightly easier approach is *systematic* sampling, where every *n*th person is sampled, where *n* is the proportion of the population to be included in the sample. While this is easy it can be subject to periodicity effects. Consider a satisfaction survey sampling every *n*th seat on an aeroplane, which has its seats arranged three-abreast each side of the central aisle. If every fifth seat is sampled there would be no periodicity effect. However, if every sixth seat is sampled only people sitting in window seats may be included in the final sample. Sitting next to a window may, for example, significantly increase their satisfaction with the flight.

Cluster sampling is useful when the groups of interest are geographically dispersed, although it needs to be assumed that they are all similar in composition. An example might be the staff of franchises. Clusters of franchises may be defined – perhaps those in the north, south, east and west of the country – and staff working in randomly selected franchises in each of the clusters included in the sample.

In the above cases, if the sample required is relatively small there is still a chance that certain respondents from relatively small sub-groups in the population will be under-represented (for example, people from small departments within a large company). *Probability proportionate to size* techniques avoid this problem. If the size of the sub-groups in the population is known, then a random sample of the required proportion can be obtained from each of these sub-groups.

All of the above techniques should produce a representative, probabilistic sample of respondents, the responses from whom should be generalizable to the whole population. However, in certain circumstances a non-probabilistic sample may be required, for example when it is necessary to obtain a sample of sufficient size to undertake a meaningful analysis from a sub-group of specific interest. Quota sampling is an example of such a technique, where the aim may be to obtain a sample of at least 20 respondents from each division of a company, irrespective of the relative size of each of these divisions. Although this ensures that each sub-group is adequately represented, care should be taken when drawing conclusions from the results that relate to the wider population. For example, if such an approach is used to assess employees' attitudes towards performance-related pay, it would be wrong to conclude that $x\%$ of the total workforce are in favour. It may, however, be possible to draw such a conclusion from a probabilistic sample of the workforce. *Purposive sampling* is another non-probabilistic technique where a certain sample is taken to be representative of the whole population, for example one university may be taken to be typical of all universities of a particular type. Some conclusions may be drawn about the generalizability of results from such a case, but what represents a 'typical' sample is very much a product of expert judgement and may be difficult to defend. Indeed, in all these sampling approaches, unless your sample is chosen carefully, there will always be considerable threats to the validity of any results and the generalizability of any conclusions.

ANALYSIS OF QUANTITATIVE DATA

The target in quantitative research is to collect data using *reliable* and *valid* measures from a *representative sample* of respondents. The way these data are analysed reflects the aims of the research, whether descriptive, comparative or prescriptive. This section describes the range of statistical approaches that are available. It *does not* tell you how to undertake each test. For details of test application, you will need to resort to a statistics textbook.

In quantitative analysis, the first thing to recognize is that not all quantitative data are the same. The type of quantitative data gathered dictates the analyses that can be performed and in turn the types of research question that can be answered. A hierarchy containing four general categories of data can be described. Note that a greater variety of more powerful statistical procedures can be applied to higher orders of data.

The lowest level of quantitative data that can be collected are *nominal* data. Nominal (also known as categorical) data signify the presence or absence of a pre-defined category in a case, for example being either male or female, or being a junior, middle or senior manager.

Ordinal data are a slightly higher level, consisting of the *ranking* of observations. For example, people coming through a door first, second and third. Ordinal data make no comment about parameters such as the amount of time between people coming through the door – there may only be five seconds between the first and second person entering the room but half a minute or half a day may elapse before the third person arrives.

With *interval* data the 'distance' between intervals is the same. But note that doubling the distance will not necessarily mean twice as much. The most commonly cited example of this type of data is temperature, measured in degrees Centigrade or Fahrenheit. In both cases, the interval between 1° and 2° is the same as the interval between 2° and 3°; however, as absolute zero is not at zero degrees on either scale, 20° is not twice as hot as 10°.

The highest level of data that you can collect are *ratio* data. There are many examples of this category of data, for example, length in centimetres, time in seconds or number of units produced per hour. This category of data has exactly the same properties as interval data; however, as the zero point is actually at zero, doubling the value *does* mean twice the amount.

Collecting the highest order of data that you can for all variables will widen the range of possible statistical procedures that can be employed and will allow for a greater range of questions to be asked of the data. It is important, however, to recognize that questionnaire surveys are the most common source of quantitative data in management research, and that data do not often fall comfortably into any of these categories. Data from survey items are certainly likely to be of a higher level than ordinal data, but could not be considered interval level (see Figure 6.1). For example, there is no guarantee that the size of the interval between 'strongly agree' and 'agree' is the same as that between 'agree' and 'no strong feelings'. Data of this kind are sometimes referred to as *scalar* data.

Tables 6.1–6.3 present a guide to the more common statistical procedures used and their objectives. In these tables, the column headed 'order of data' refers to the order of data of the measures taken as the predictor (or dependent) variable. The column headed 'numbers of groups' refers to the number of samples. Where there are more than one group, this usually implies comparison of some sort (for example between line workers and managers). Single group designs can be either descriptive or prescriptive.

My manager always listens to my suggestions about how I could do my job better
(Tick *one* box that best reflects your opinion)

Strongly agree	Agree	No strong feelings	Disagree	Strongly disagree
☐	☐	☐	☐	☐

FIGURE 6.1   *Example questionnaire item*

TABLE 6.1 *Descriptive statistical analytical approaches for the analysis of quantitative data*

Order of data	Number of groups	Quantitative method	Purpose
Nominal	One	Frequency count	Simple description
		Π^2 'Goodness of fit'	To assess if the frequency distribution of elements in a sample conforms to that in a known population
	Several	Cross-tabulation	Simple description, broken down by category
Ordinal	One	Spearman's correlation	To assess the degree of concomitant association between two variables
Scalar, interval or ratio	One	Pearson's correlation	To assess the degree of concomitant association between two variables
	One	Principal components analysis or factor analysis	To uncover any latent, underlying structures in a set of many variables
		Confirmatory factor analysis	To confirm if a hypothesized underlying structure in a set of many variables actually exists in a data set
		Cluster analysis	To identify homogeneous sub-sets of respondents on the basis of many variables
	One (or several)	Median or mean (with standard deviation)	Measure of central tendency, and dispersion of sample scores around the mean

TABLE 6.2 *Comparative statistical analytical approaches for the analysis of quantitative data*

Order of data	Number of groups	Quantitative method	Purpose
Nominal	Two	Π^2 test of association	To establish if observations in a certain category for a certain group are under- or over-represented
Ordinal	Two	Mann–Whitney 'U' test	To establish if there is a difference between two groups in the rank ordering of cases on a variable
	More than two	Kruskal–Wallis test	To establish if there is a difference between n groups in the rank ordering of cases on a variable
Scalar, interval or ratio	Two – with a single predictor variable (dependent variable – DV)	t-test	To establish if there is a difference between the means of two groups on a variable
	More than two – with a single predictor variable (DV)	One-way analysis of variance (ANOVA)	To establish if there is a difference between the means of n groups on a variable. (May also be used as a crossed, or factorial, design)
	Two (or more) but with several predictor variables (DVs) used in combination	Multivariate ANOVA	To establish if there is a difference between n groups using a weighted linear combination of variables

TABLE 6.3 *Prescriptive statistical analytical approaches for the analysis of quantitative data*[a]

Order of data	Number of groups	Quantitative method	Purpose
Scalar, interval or ratio	One – with a single predictor variable	Regression	To predict the score on a criterion variable from a given score on a predictor variable
	One – with several predictor variables	Multiple regression	To predict the score on a criterion variable from scores on a number of predictor variables
	One – with several predictor variables	Path analysis	To predict the score on a criterion variable from scores on a number of predictor variables, taking into account the effects of mediating variables that have a complex relationship with the criterion
	Two (or more)	Discriminant function analysis	To predict the group of a categorical criterion variable from scores on a number of predictor variables

[a] NB: There are no prescriptive techniques available for lower orders on data.

MISCONCEPTIONS ABOUT QUANTITATIVE RESEARCH

Many people tend to think of quantitative research approaches as being an 'objective' rather than a 'subjective' approach to research. Wrong! Quantitative research is a different kind of subjective approach. The subjectivity lies in the scales included in the questionnaire (or perhaps more importantly those not included), the samples obtained and the data reported and analysed.

There is also an assumption that quantitative measures are meaningful in absolute as well as relative terms. Again, this is not necessarily true. Production rates and absenteeism may be meaningful in absolute and relative terms; however, it would be a brave researcher who would suggest that they can produce an absolute measure of hypothetical constructs such as workload, stress or job satisfaction. This is not to say that these measures are worthless but they may only be meaningful in comparative terms.

On a similar note, there is also an *illusion of precision* about quantitative data. Quantitative management research usually requires respondents to record their attitudes, opinions or beliefs, often using a five- or seven-point scale. Researchers frequently report means for these data to two decimal places (or even more). But what does a mean score of 3.27 represent when the division between scale point 3 and scale point 4 is the difference between 'no strong feelings' and 'disagree'?

There is a danger when interpreting quantitative data that the numbers produced begin to have a life of their own. It is absolutely vital to remember what the numbers actually mean and where they have come from. There can be a tendency for the quantitative researcher to lose perspective, focusing on the numbers and not their meaning. Numbers are simply a way to summarize and describe facets of the world. They are not, by themselves, reality.

QUALITATIVE RESEARCH DESIGN

WHAT IS QUALITATIVE RESEARCH?   A qualitative research design is one where the data are collected in the form of words and observations, as opposed to numbers. Analysis is based on the interpretation of these data as opposed to statistical manipulation. Qualitative research is associated with research questions and phenomena of interest that require exploration of detailed in-depth data, aimed at description, comparison or prescription. For example, research might be concerned with a detailed description of innovation processes in an organization that is recognized as outstandingly cutting-edge. Alternatively, research might compare two innovative organizations in different industries to uncover either uniform or similar processes.

The case for prescriptive work is cloudier. In order to be prescriptive, the findings of a study usually have to be 'data-generalizable' in that the relationships uncovered in data taken from a sample of the target population have to be generalizable to the whole population. Issues such as sampling and sample size are key. In qualitative research, the aim is usually to provide detail, and large sample sizes are not normally feasible. Consequently, prescription is not normally seen as directly compatible with qualitative research as it is with quantitative. However, this does not rule it out. For instance, a researcher may just have one single question to ask, for example, 'in your organization how do you negotiate with financial institutions when writing annual reports?' This is a specific question but one that cannot be reduced to questionnaire items as we simply know very little about how senior executives do negotiate with financial institutions during annual report writing. The question could be asked of all the top teams of firms in a particular industry which appear in a stockmarket index, for example telecommunications. This might produce more than 100 short interviews. The results of the study could then be used in a prescriptive fashion.

In the main, qualitative research tends to be either descriptive or comparative. However, even though qualitative research is not usually prescriptive, this does not mean it is not generalizable. Generalizability can be associated with either data generalizability or theory generalizability. In the former, researchers should be able to demonstrate that their findings will be replicable in all similar cases. With theory generalizability, the ideas and theoretical contributions reached at the end of the work are generalizable to future work that can advance progress already made. Quantitative research can have both data and theory generalizability, whereas qualitative research usually has just the latter.

Whether it is descriptive or comparative, qualitative research is usually exploratory, in-depth and can contain some or all of the criteria listed below (Miles and Huberman, 1994).

- Intense and prolonged contact in the field.
- Designed to achieve a holistic or systemic picture.
- Perception is gained from the inside based on actors' understanding.
- Little standardized instrumentation is used.
- Most analysis is done with words.
- There are multiple interpretations available in the data.

With its aims to see the world from the point of view of the informant, become immersed in their detail and get close to the phenomena of interest, qualitative management research has a foundation in ethnography. Ethnography in organizations can be undertaken by simply 'hanging around' the organization, talking in corridors or over lunch, being a 'fly on the wall' at meetings, or in a more structured way as a direct participant in the activities being studied. Ethnographic data usually take the form of fieldnotes written up by the researcher, and, where available, transcripts of transactions. Chapter 7 contains a fuller discussion of ethnographic approaches.

In management studies the most common means of qualitative data collection are structured interviewing, semi-structured interviewing, unstructured interviewing, non-participant observation, company documents already written and documents written specifically for the research, for example diaries and journals. Note that in each of these cases, whether the data are a document, a transcript or a set of notes, they exist in their rawest form in words. However, this does not mean that they can't be categorized and subjected to statistical analysis.

Qualitative research is not necessarily small scale, looking at a single event, individual, group or organization; it can make comparisons across numerous units. In general, the more units that are included, the less depth is achievable, and this is the trade-off. Usually though, sample sizes are much smaller than in quantitative research. For instance, whereas a questionnaire might be mailed to 700 people a qualitative research design might be targeting only 30 informants. There are no rules about how many is enough. The number of interviews, observations diaries or surveys needed depends on the research question and the limitations of time, money and researchers available to collect and analyse the data.

ISSUES IN QUALITATIVE RESEARCH

STAYING OPEN TO SURPRISE   Qualitative research has at its core a strength that counterbalances one of the weaknesses of structured, quantitative research. That is, qualitative research is capable of answering not only the questions asked, but if executed in a relatively unstructured fashion, also answering those not originally asked. For instance, at the outset of exploratory work, a researcher is unlikely to be entirely sure what they are asking and what may or may not be important to that enquiry. Further important questions, constructs and relationships are likely to emerge as a project progresses. Many qualitative researchers will experience the element of surprise as important factors and questions begin to emerge during fieldwork or analysis. The key is for the researcher to ensure that they stay open to being surprised and not devoted to their initial set of expectations.

There has been a lot of debate over the extent to which researchers can or should remain entirely free of preconceptions, allowing key constructs and relationships to 'emerge' from the data via systematic grounded analysis. The argument that people are capable of being a 'blank slate' is difficult to sustain. Perhaps the best a researcher can do is try to remain as theory/expectation-free as possible. Trying to stay 'free' is in fact one of the arts (Wolcott, 1995) of qualitative research, and, as with any other skill, this requires practice. Concrete things can be done to help guard against being overly assumptive early on in research. These include: (1) engage in supervision, that is, get another individual to challenge your ideas as they are developing; (2) when a pattern is first emerging, look for negative instances and deliberately explore those in more detail; (3) listen to your own intuition, especially when it is telling you that you might be following the wrong scent.

LARGE AMOUNTS OF DATA   Undertaking qualitative research carries a health warning that should be taken seriously before commencing a project of any kind: data overload. The amount of words a researcher can end up having to interpret can accumulate at a worrying rate. For instance, for every hour of taped interview, one can expect to spend approximately another 10 hours working on it. The first four of these can be spent transcribing the tape (depending on typing speed and/or number of people talking). There are some useful tips. First, get the best recording equipment you can, this makes transcription considerably easier. Be sure you need to transcribe all the data. There may be peripheral interviews that may never be needed; wait until you are sure you need them before transcribing. Finally, if it won't compromise your data for someone else to transcribe and there are funds available, delegate this task. Once transcription is complete, the remaining six hours of effort are expended in the analysis of the data. This will usually involve multiple iterations of: reading, coding, re-coding, re-reading and comparison of the transcript.

RELIABILITY AND VALIDITY   Reliability and validity in quantitative research have been discussed in the first half of the chapter. However, these concepts change their meaning somewhat when associated with qualitative work. For instance, in quantitative research, it is commonly viewed that validity is scarified for reliability. That is, the control and simplification necessary to achieve reliability can lead the researcher to ignore the fundamental complexity of social phenomena (Walker, 1985). Blumer describes this more harshly: 'inside of the "scientific" protocol, one can operate unwittingly with false premises, erroneous problems, distorted data, spurious relationships and inaccurate concepts' (1969: 29). In short, the fact that quantitative designs are not embedded in the world of the informant can challenge their basic validity.

Even though reliability is not usually addressed directly, that does not mean that the qualitative researcher is not rigorous. After all, bad research is bad research. In qualitative research it is more often the case that there is less of an expectation that another individual (or perhaps even after a period of time has elapsed, the same individual) could find the same interpretation in the data. None the less, trustworthiness and quality of findings are important. In qualitative research there are fewer established norms to generate trust automatically than in quantitative research (for example, Cronbach's alpha greater than 0.7). However, although still not established as standard practice – and there are many who argue that standard practice has no place in qualitative research – measures can be taken to maximize trustworthiness.

The first of these is *confirmability*. This is effectively concerned with *transparency* in data interpretation: can someone else follow your audit trail of evidence? Confirmability does not necessarily mean that another individual would reach the same conclusions as you (in other words, adopt the same interpretation of the data). Rather, that they can clearly see where your interpretation comes from, and, supported by the fact that you were in the field, trust that it is the most compelling interpretation. Demonstrating *parallel meanings* across the data set can also generate confirmability. That is, showing that your interpretations are applicable across all the data (from all units and all forms of data) rather than choosing to support your conclusions from one aspect of the data. One give-away that findings are not applicable across the data would be multiple quotations from one interview when several were available. Another would be multiple citations from one time period in a longitudinal design at the expense of the other time periods when data were collected. One final aspect of confirmability concerns quality checking for *systematic confirmatory bias*. Here, evidence would be given that either multiple methods converged on the same interpretation in spite of any bias the researcher may have, or that multiple individuals (coders) converged on the same interpretation. However, for some qualitative researchers, attempting to produce multi-coder convergence is allowing the rules and language of quantitative research to bound qualitative research unnecessarily. To reduce rich, highly complex data to a set of a few basic relationships that a group of individuals can reliably agree upon undermines the point of qualitative research. Consequently, it is less common to find trustworthiness generated via multiple coding.

The second means of generating trustworthiness in qualitative research is to directly examine (either by asking questions of oneself or asking a colleague to do so) the *authenticity* of the interpretations gained from the data. Miles and Huberman (1994), suggest several questions to ask.

- 'Are the descriptions gained "thick" enough'? In other words, are they contextually rich, is there a lot of information and insight drawn specifically from the research site?
- 'Do the descriptions ring true', or do they seem in any sense improbable or highly unlikely?
- 'Have the rules for interpretation been made specific'? Were they stated ahead of time and if they were changed was that change justifiable?
- 'Have rival explanations been considered', or has only one explanation been considered from the start?
- 'If there is an element of prediction, were the predictions accurate', or did the events that unfolded fail to confirm the interpretations offered?
- 'Do the original informants agree with the interpretations?' Have they been asked and is there a record of their views about the conclusions drawn?

If the answers to some or all of the questions above indicate authenticity and there have been some efforts to establish confirmability, then generally, qualitative research can be argued to be both valid and, in the language of quantitative research, reliable. A major sticking point in qualitative research is that a standard practice has yet to emerge and if a new researcher looks for a format or exemplar to follow, either in journals or a thesis, they will be disappointed. To a large extent this is a result of the variable nature of qualitative research, but more importantly it is the result of the relative novelty of published qualitative management studies in comparison with quantitative.

QUALITATIVE ANALYSIS

In the analysis of qualitative data, there are two important factors to bear in mind. First, there is little standardization in terms of data collected across studies – each analysis will to some extent be a uniquely designed event. Second, there are multiple interpretations (and ways of arriving at them) available in the data – there are no absolutes that can be encompassed in table form as is the case in quantitative research (see Tables 6.1 to 6.3) where a type of data relates to a type of analysis. The way in which data are analysed in qualitative research depends on the research question, the way the data were collected and, ultimately, what is appropriate to achieve the objectives of the research.

None the less, there are two very basic families of data analysis in qualitative research that offer a general choice before project-specific aims and objectives are taken into account. The first of these is *content analysis*. In this form of analysis, the contents of the data collected are explored to uncover either emergent patterns, evidence of expected patterns or pattern matching between multiple cases. There are various software tools available that help *manage* this process but will not (unless the analysis is as simple as a word count) do the analysis for you. These include NVivo and Atlas, as well as other data-specific tools such as Decision Explorer which handles cognitive maps (see Chapter 10). When using packages such as NVivo, each instance of a particular pattern can be collected under one node in a model and kept entirely cross-referenced. Once the entire data set is coded having searched for expected, emergent and matched patterns, what is created is a model of nodes behind which sit all the data. The nodes can then be manipulated to begin to create a conceptual account of the data. This process, although benefiting hugely from computer support, is after all cognitive and can be done manually with cards, coloured pens and a lot of handwriting. The former is often preferable and moreover helps improve the trustworthiness of the analysis by showing the kind of transparent audit trail of interpretation described earlier.

The other basic family member of qualitative analysis is *grounded analysis* (the subject of Chapter 8). This form of qualitative analysis comes from a particular approach to management research – grounded theory (Glaser and Strauss, 1967). In this approach, the researcher's objective is usually highly exploratory, targeted at answering a particular research question by allowing findings and interpretations to emerge from the data, whilst searching for unexpected/emergent patterns. Grounded analysis offers a series of guided stages to be followed in order to reach the point where the model of explanation generated can be said to truly account for the data collected. In this way grounded analysis has many advantages. However, it is rare for a piece of written up grounded research to display all of the stages undergone. Consequently, books and papers such as Johnson (1981, 1987) and good quality doctoral theses, are useful guides.

Whichever family of qualitative analysis is adopted, and whatever project-specific tasks are completed as part of it, the centrally important aspect of qualitative analysis is that it is an insightful and in many ways intuitive process. Wolcott (1995) describes it as art and calls for researchers to listen to and not be afraid of their instincts. He offers a quote from Michaelangelo talking about his sculpting of David which is suggested to capture the experience of qualitative analysis: 'I just chipped away at anything that wasn't David'. This may sound hollow until qualitative analysis has been experienced. The particular explanation or interpretations that finally make sense of all the elements of the data can simply dawn upon the researcher. Everything clicks but it may never become exactly clear how and why such an idea began to take shape. These intuitive leaps are simultaneously the core strength and weakest point of qualitative research.

CONCLUSION

This chapter has presented an overview of the quantitative and qualitative methods available for use in the social sciences. The particular focus has been on the practicalities and realities of conducting research in a management environment. In the first part of the chapter the several key messages about the nature of quantitative research in managerial settings were addressed. These were mostly concerned with identifying the type of quantitative research to be undertaken (descriptive, comparative or prescriptive) and assessing the reliability and validity of any psychometric measures obtained. The type of measures obtained (the level of data) has important implications for the analytical strategy to be employed. It was also made explicit that quantitative research often builds on the foundations laid by prior qualitative research. Quantitative research is highly dependent upon theoretical structures for its rigour; however, these theoretical structures have to come from somewhere, and that somewhere is often qualitative research.

In the second half of the chapter five important aspects of conducting qualitative research in a managerial environment were considered. First, qualitative research is designed to operate well in areas that are complex, messy, causally ambiguous and where there is little extant knowledge. In the field of management there are many areas which fall into this categorization and which therefore lend themselves to qualitative research designs. Second, qualitative research is usually descriptive or comparative but may also be prescriptive. Third, qualitative research is conducted from the point of view of the informant and a high degree of engagement with the informant's world is central to its success. Consequently most forms of qualitative data collection provide very rich data sets. Fourth, as a result of the richness of the data, there are many interpretations available at the point of analysis. The challenge of qualitative analysis is to provide the most compelling interpretation of the data. To be compelling, qualitative researchers need to pay attention to transparency and trustworthiness whilst holding on to intuition and insight. Fifth, both qualitative data collection and analysis rely on the development of skill. That is, skill to attend to, extract and gather rich information and skill in uncovering the insights that lie within the data. In short, qualitative research is perhaps the 'art' form that Wolcott (1995) describes rather than the reliance on technical expertise that characterizes quantitative research.

The aim of this chapter has not been to play one major form of research design off against another. Rather it has been to demonstrate that the most important factor in choosing a research design is what is appropriate to answer a particular research question. Often the two types of research work complement each other to produce such an answer.

Study questions

1 Do you have a current preference for qualitative or quantitative research? No matter how mild that preference, sit back and ask yourself why you are drawn to one approach more than the other. Consider what is at the root of what you like and dislike about each.

2 Take a research question or research theme that you are currently working with. Challenge yourself to think of how that project might emerge if you took (a) a qualitative approach, and (b) a quantitative approach. What have you learned about the pros and cons of each for your work?

3 If you intend to adopt either a qualitative or quantitative approach, think about how you can make sure that you stay open to surprises in your data collection and analysis. Come up with five danger signals that would alert you to your becoming blinkered or biased.

4 Numbers or indeed snippets of text in themselves have no meaning. Think of strategies that you could employ ahead of data collection to make sure you capture and protect the meaning in your data.

Recommended further reading

Kerlinger, F.N. (1973) *Foundations of Behavioral Research*. New York: Holt, Rinehart and Winston.
McCall, R. (2000) *Fundamental Statistics for Behavioural Sciences*. London: Wadsworth.
Miles, M. and Huberman, A.M. (1994) *Qualitative Data Analysis: An Expanded Sourcebook*. London: Sage.
Wolcott, H. (1995) *The Art of Fieldwork*. London: Sage.

References

Anastasi, A. (1990) *Psychological Testing*, 6th edn. New York: Macmillan.
Blumer, H. (1969) *Symbolic Interactionism: Perspective and Method*. Englewood Cliffs, NJ: Prentice Hall.

Campbell, D.T. and Stanley, J.C. (1966) *Experimental and Quasi-Experimental Designs for Research*. Chicago: Rand–McNally.

Dalton, D.R., Daily, C.M., Johnson, J.L. and Ellstrand, A.E. (1997) 'Number of Directors on the Board and Financial Performance: A Conceptual Synthesis and Meta Analysis', paper presented to Academy of Management Conference, Boston.

Eden, C. and Ackermann, F. (1998) *Making Strategy. The Journey of Strategic Management*. London: Sage.

Frost, P. and Stablein, R. (1992) *Doing Exemplary Research*. London: Sage.

Furnham, A. (1984) 'Personality and Values', *Personality and Individual Differences*, 5 (4), pp. 483–5.

Garson, D.G. (1998) *Neural Networks: An Introductory Guide for Social Scientists*. London: Sage.

Glaser, B.G. and Strauss, A.L. (1967) *The Discovery of Grounded Theory*. Chicago: Aldine.

Hair, J.F., Anderson, R.E., Tatham, R.L. and Black, W.C. (1998) *Multivariate Data Analysis*, 5th edn. Saddle River, NJ: Prentice Hall.

Hambrick, D.C. and Mason, P.A. (1984) 'Upper Echelons: The Organization as a Reflection of its Top Managers', *Academy of Management Review*, 9 (2), pp. 193–206.

Hays, W.L. (1994) *Statistics*, 5th edn. Fort Worth, TX: Harcourt Brace.

Johnson, G.N. (1987) *Strategic Change and the Management Process*. Oxford: Blackwell.

Johnson, G.N. (1981) 'The Application of Grounded Theory to a Study of Corporate Growth', The University of Aston Management Centre Working Paper Series, No. 212.

Kerlinger, F.N. (1973) *Foundations of Behavioral Research*. New York: Holt, Rinehart and Winston.

McCall, R. (1994) *Fundamental Statistics for Behavioural Science*. London: Harcourt.

Moser, C.A. and Kalton, G. (1971) *Survey Methods in Social Investigation*. Aldershot: Gower.

Miles, M. and Huberman, A.M. (1994) *Qualitative Data Analysis: An Expanded Sourcebook*. London: Sage.

Popper, K.R. (1963) *Conjectures and Refutations*. London: Routledge and Kegan Paul.

Robson, C. (1983) *Experiment, Design and Statistics in Psychology*, 2nd edn. Harmondsworth: Penguin.

Schwandt, T.A. and Halpern, E.S. (1988) *Linking Auditing and Meta-Evaluation. Enhancing Quality in Applied Research*. Applied Social Research Methods Series, Vol. 11. Newbury Park, CA: Sage.

Walker, R. (1985) *Applied Qualitative Research*. Aldershot: Gower.

Wolcott, H. (1995) *The Art of Fieldwork*. London: Sage.

7

Ethnographic Approaches to the Study of Organizations

Val Singh and John Dickson

OVERVIEW

This chapter introduces ethnography, literally the scientific description of a culture. Ethnography is used in a variety of fields including social and cultural anthropology, education, sociology and human geography. In studies of organization and management, ethnography is the direct *observation* of a particular phenomenon of interest within an organization or business context, the *interpretation* of those observations and the *description* written in the context of the whole environment.

An ethnographic approach looks at the world through a particular lens, allowing the researcher to uncover the socially significant in a holistic way. It uncovers meaning which is inaccessible through other forms of enquiry, using interpretation, interaction, context, emotion and aesthetic experience. Unstructured data, including observations of behaviour and recorded speech, are analysed and interpreted by the researcher, resulting in an explanation of meaning in its situated context. The written ethnographic account is then interpreted again by the reader, who is challenged to examine critically the evidence for its arguments.

In contrast to researchers who are concerned with representative samples that will reflect the 'objective world', ethnographers look for unusual or inexplicable study settings, working with small populations. They seek to develop explanations and theories rather than test pre-existing theories. Ethnography shares with grounded theory (see Chapter 8) the purpose of generating understanding through iterative comparisons of data and theory, and both approaches aim to develop theoretical ideas which are grounded in data before the ideas are considered in the light of existing theory. Ethnography differs from broader grounded theory in that ethnographic findings are always kept within their specific context, without seeking to formalize and generalize theory through theoretical sampling in multiple contexts. The components of an ethnographic study are usually participant observation, a holistic construct of the 'culture' or 'society' under examination, context sensitivity, a sociocultural description, and some element of theory (Stewart,

1998). Earlier ethnographies were often based on non-participant observation, and some modern studies still follow that approach.

In the first part of the chapter, we describe the historical origins of ethnography, its underlying theoretical principles, and its development into a range of approaches from objective to subjective styles of research. We discuss the concept of culture, an essential ingredient of ethnographic studies in organizations, and discuss the role of the researcher, as situated in the research setting. The second part of the chapter deals with the practical steps involved in the conduct of ethnography. We consider issues relating to identifying and gaining access to the research setting, and describe the different kinds of data which are available. We offer advice on the undertaking of fieldwork and analysis, as well as hints on writing up ethnographic studies for journals, books and dissertations. In the final part of the chapter we present two ethnographic case studies.

Origins and development of ethnography

Ethnography has its roots in applied, cultural and social anthropology and sociology. It is a relatively recent research tradition, influenced strongly by hermeneutics – the study of the principles of understanding historical texts. A key tenet of hermeneutics is the recognition that people inhabit different cultural worlds and have different cultural experiences. In hermeneutics, researchers draw on their own experiences to understand those other world meanings.

In the nineteenth century, the field of cultural studies experienced tensions in its positioning between the sciences and the humanities. Scientific results were accorded higher status, whereas the anthropological account was seen as part of a literary genre where richness of writing was sometimes more important than accuracy of interpretation. To counter this criticism, many anthropologists tried to remain partially detached, resulting in limitations in their understanding of what they observed.

Early ethnography was more anthropological in nature, seeking to explore and describe whole cultures in their own settings. The nineteenth- and early twentieth-century ethnographers' relationship as scholars to the people under their scrutiny shows a particular sociopolitical discourse embedded in those relationships. Scholars lived close by but not integrated within their subject community, seeking to maintain their scientifically valued objectivity. 'Going native' was regarded as unscientific and to be avoided at all costs. Early ethnographers assumed authority over their subjects, and in remote communities, even carried out scientific tests on them as well as observation. The Western scientists presented their written interpretations of the 'culture', whilst refusing and silencing the native voice. Yet sometimes they missed valuable evidence, by their own prior assumptions about who or what was important as a source of information. Often women's voices were not heard, reflecting the male scientists' work environment where women did not have legitimacy as researchers at that time. The ethnographers often removed as evidence valuable and even sacred artefacts (and on some occasions, even live natives) for Western universities, museums and collections.

The modern ethnographic tradition was underpinned in part by studies undertaken from the 1920s onwards within the 'Chicago tradition' of sociology (Atkinson and Hammersley, 1994), although the researchers there still struggled with the dichotomy of scientific and hermeneutic influences. From those roots, George Mead led the post-1940s movement of symbolic interactionism, with its emphasis on interpretation and shared meanings, closely related to ethnography. A classic ethnographic study of that period is Whyte's (1955) study of street corner society in Boston. This study paints a portrait of the world as seen and understood by a particular group of marginalized people. The rich description creates the background upon which Whyte explains how this 'society' works. Its values and assumptions as well as external forces make the consequent actions and customs understandable to the reader. Through this approach, the inexplicable can be explained. In this case, middle-class social workers could gain insight into the problems and constraints of a group they wished to assist but with whom they shared little in terms of world-view, life experience and life expectation.

The interpretivist, and especially symbolic interactionist, approaches have led to greater appreciation of the need to work closely with the research participants in their daily lives. Ideally, they do this for as long as it takes to gain the data and interpret the meanings which the subjects have accorded the events and phenomena of interest. However, Bate (1997) comments that few researchers these days are willing to invest the essential time away from base needed for immersion, participation and reflection in organizational life, given the politics and pressures in academia for quick turnaround of publications.

The nature of the ethnographic approach and the lack of impact of its results on social and organizational policy has led to a call for more collaborative research using this method (Atkinson and Hammersley, 1994). Whyte (1991) recommends participatory action research (PAR) as a form of ethnography, because it is likely to be more fruitful, since the members of the organization studied are actively engaged in the quest for information and ideas to guide their future actions. Whyte says that a key benefit of PAR, when carried out with high standards, is that the researcher together with the participants can simultaneously pursue truth and solutions to concrete problems. He undertook a PAR study with Mondragon (a set of inter-related cooperative organizations in Spain), providing the foundation for major organizational change. Cooperative members were the change drivers, facilitated by the ethnographers. Members used their own experiences and judgement to evaluate the PAR progress, and they also started to set their own research agenda, eventually producing a book and organizing a conference. Their findings were acknowledged, especially by other practitioners, as highly accurate representations of cultural change at Mondragon, with relevance far beyond the boundaries of the organization. However, Atkinson and Hammersley remind us that the goal of ethnography is to produce knowledge, and that not all social, political and organizational goals for change are desirable.

Even the modern ethnographic approach is challenged by some feminists, who consider that most social research reflects masculine experiences of the world. They claim that male researchers' understandings are limited by a male world-view of the topic. Clearly all researchers will bring bias into their studies, whether through gender, culture, class or experience. Consequently, it is essential for researchers to understand the limitations which prior assumptions and experience may impose on them, and that every effort is made to maximize sensitivity within the field, allowing sufficient time for in-depth reflection during the fieldwork and when writing up the study.

ORGANIZATIONAL CULTURE AND ETHNOGRAPHY

THE IMPORTANCE OF CULTURE   The aim of an ethnographic study is to observe, interpret and report cultural phenomena of some particular kind within their context. There are numerous definitions of culture, which broadly fall into two groups. One group sees culture as referring to the total way of life of a people, including their interpersonal relations as well as their attitudes (for example, Geertz, 1973). The second group views culture as composed of values, beliefs, norms, rationalizations, symbols and ideologies (for example, Louis, 1983), in other words, as a set of mental products.

From a behavioural perspective, part of the latter group, organizational culture exists in the minds of the people in the organization, socially constructed as a result of antecedents, behaviours and perceived consequences in those minds, and evolving over time (Thompson and Luthans, 1990). The organization is seen as a culture-producing phenomenon or milieu, with internal systems (rules, structure, norms, rites, myths, heroes and stories) which actively shape it (Louis, 1983). There may be many subcultures, including a dominant culture, within the organization, all of which are dynamic and changing, as people interact with it (Bate, 1997).

The ethnographer seeks to understand and interpret the culture of a social system, through the reading of observed behaviours and interpretation of the meanings held by its participants. The subject makes the first interpretation, which is 'read' and systematized at the second order level by the researcher, who writes an ethnographical account for the third order interpretation by the reader. The outcome should be a 'thick' or rich description of the signals and structures of the culture, focused on the phenomenon of interest. Hatch (1993) describes this process as 'making the familiar strange', indicating the paradox for the researcher in terms of challenging prior assumptions.

ORGANIZATIONAL ETHNOGRAPHY   Ethnographers see organizations as settings within which social relations take place between actors focused towards a set of goal-oriented activities, where rules are constructed and their meaning interpreted by the actors for that particular context. Within an organization, particularly a larger one, there is a plurality of settings, and multiple frameworks of meaning, but the settings are partial and specialized. The organizational culture is not only researched and described as a whole, as in 'classic' ethnography, but usually studied in a particular context to understand a phenomenon of interest.

Van Maanen (1979: 540) described the aim of organizational ethnography as to 'uncover and explicate the ways in which people in particular work settings come to understand, account for, take action, and otherwise manage their day-to-day situation'. By definition, such studies are longitudinal, seeking to observe and translate as much as possible of the flow of action, meanings and interrelationships of the relevant respondents in the time available. Key stages are observation, interpretation and then iterative reflection as the study is analysed and written up. The recording of observations transforms the behaviours of day-to-day events into an account which can be re-consulted, rewritten as understanding deepens, and reinterpreted by first the writer and then the reader.

Bate (1997) asserts that more researchers claim to be doing organizational ethnography than is the case in practice. He does not consider as ethnographies the kinds of studies where the researcher makes a few short visits to an organization, rather than being located on site over several months. However, for many reasons it is difficult to undertake ethnographies of the 'total immersion' kind. There is a trend in management research to observe particular events such as board meetings or the rolling out of change projects, where the researcher is not on site all the time to understand its actors and pick up the nuances of the context.

The big advantage of using ethnography in organizational studies is that it does not rely on artificial settings. It takes account of the living history of the phenomenon under exploration. It accesses what people do in their everyday business, not just what they say they do in surveys or what the organization states in mission statements and corporate literature, though these may be complementary to an ethnographic study. Ethnography does not reduce meaning to what is observable scientifically, nor does it treat subjects and situations as static. It allows exploration, linking the individual and the social, at the micro and macro level. It rejects speculation through hypotheses in favour of first-hand empirical investigation – 'learning by going' as Geertz called it. Bate (1997) further argues that going into the field is the best way forward, rather than prior consultation of numerous textbooks of qualitative methods. However, we recommend some prior understanding of ethnographic method before entering the field.

THE ROLE OF THE RESEARCHER

PARTICIPANT AND NON-PARTICIPANT OBSERVATION   The researcher can be seen as an instrument through which the data are observed, interpreted and transformed into an ethnographic account. The researcher needs to keep close enough to see the detail, whilst distant enough to retain an objective insight, although the level of distance may vary depending upon the philosophical world-view of the researcher as well as the context of the study. Figure 7.1 shows four broad research approaches within the ethnographic tradition: realist observation, observation as participant, participant observation

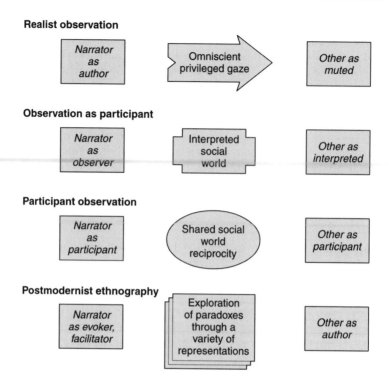

FIGURE 7.1   *A range of ethnographic approaches*

and postmodern ethnography. These are better seen as points on a continuum of subjectivity to relative objectivity rather than as discrete approaches.

Realist or non-participant observation is undertaken by an expert narrator, who observes and describes from a position of authority. Observation as participant is undertaken by a researcher included in but on the fringe of the activity, who seeks understanding through similarity of experience without being a real participant. Participant observation is a more subjective design based on mutual respect and shared social understandings. In the postmodern approach (as well as in participatory action research), the researcher helps to bring forth understanding by giving voice to the informant.

RESEARCHER IDENTITY AND REFLEXIVITY   Observation is not simply seeing what goes on, but requires a heightened sense of awareness to notice the actors (including you, the researcher) and their performances in their various roles and settings. Over several observations of the phenomenon, patterns in the context (such as the extent to which meanings are understood and/or shared in line with the power dynamics of the situation) may start to emerge. The observations from that sense of awareness have then to be translated into intense reflection on reasons for the behaviours and events observed. This allows the researcher to speculate about and then seek confirmatory and disconfirmatory evidence about the necessary conditions for the phenomenon. The purpose is to discover the hidden processes within the culture, the tacit knowledge, to gain contextual understanding that can be explained within a social theoretical framework.

There are several roles which the individual researcher may play: straight researcher, co-worker, helper, management spy, management tool, or driver of change. Serious consideration should be given to how you will behave in the field, and what identity you will assume. The impact of your participation or observation on group behaviour should also be considered, especially at the early stages before trust has been built. Respondents may react differently in one-to-one conversations compared to group responses.

In your chosen role, you will find critical use of reflexivity to be one of the best tools in your ethnographer's toolkit. Easterby-Smith and Malina (1999: 84) state that the two processes of *mirroring* and *contrasting* are helpful. Through mirroring, 'observation of another leads to the realization that the features observed can also be attributed to the observer'. Contrasting means focusing on another in order to understand how the observer is different. Easterby-Smith and Malina found these two processes useful in understanding cultural differences between UK and Chinese research teams as well as interpreting the results of their studies within respective organizations. Such reflexivity exposes hidden assumptions and tacit knowledge both within yourself as researcher, and in the way you gain understanding of your respondents' ideas, values and motivations, as well as assumptions which they may be making in expressing to you their culture.

You should examine carefully any assumptions which you hold about the issue and its setting, which might influence the research process and its outcome, as these will have to be acknowledged later. Consider your personal identity (for example, gender, age, class, relationship with power structures and individuals in the organization under observation) and define your role in the research to yourself. Clarifying identity will allow you to reflect on the biases which you introduce to the data collection, the analysis and the reporting.

INTERACTION WITH RESEARCH PARTICIPANTS   Researchers usually make clear to the subjects of their research who they are and why they are there. However, there may be times when it is better not to inform them, for example, where the presence of an academic outsider would disrupt the normal behaviour of the group so that the phenomenon would be inaccessible, or if trying to uncover corrupt practices. Unless you are taking an under-cover role as full participant, you will be asked in what capacity you are at the research site. If you do not make your chosen role explicit, subjects' assumptions may make the research task more difficult by limiting their openness as they try to second-guess why you are there.

Issues of anonymity and confidentiality have to be dealt with at an early stage of the ethnographic project, so that subjects and their organizations can trust you to ensure that individuals are not damaged by the research intervention and reporting. You should work within a code of ethics, guided by your supervisor in the case of research students, and/or drawn up by the relevant professional bodies such as the British Psychological Association.

ETHNOGRAPHY IN PRACTICE

IDENTIFYING THE PHENOMENON AND GAINING ACCESS   An ethnographic study usually starts with concern about a particular phenomenon in organizational life, which is not accessible by hypothesis-testing. The issue may be raised in a number of ways, for example by the organization's management, policy-makers, the researcher, or suggested in previous research as being worthy of deeper exploration. To capture the phenomenon in its setting, access has to be gained into an appropriate organization and its particular sub-components if necessary. This may be straightforward where the organization has sought help with an issue or the implementation of a major change project, as the organization will be keen to provide access to the appropriate people. However, if you have identified a phenomenon of interest from the literature, and then need to find an appropriate research site, it may take time to find access to a suitable location, especially where particular infrequent events within specific organizational structures are key to the design.

LOCATING THE SETTING   Whilst the broad setting may be determined at the start by the interest in the phenomenon, you have to identify the actual location for participation and/or observation in the organization. This might be the organization as a whole, particularly where the organization is relatively small, but is more likely to be a unit within a larger organization. Examples would include studies of culture or subcultures within a business unit, a site, project, team, tier of management, department, or division. Alternatively, the subject of interest might be a phenomenon which cuts across many subcultures, for example, information and communication flows. You have to judge which would be the most revealing places to observe the events, and then gain access.

Whilst formal interviews may be part of the study and take place in informants' offices or workshops, you should encourage informal conversations. There are two reasons for this. First, you will very often hear personal views in a conversation after work that would not be shared in an interview or in the workplace. Second, you may not be asking the right questions. In Dickson's research (see case study at the end of the chapter), he stumbled a number of times on critical pieces of information through chance comments in casual conversations. So consider where and when such informal conversations might take place: for example, over coffee prior to meetings, in a workplace cafeteria, in a local bar or gym after work. Then it is up to you to build relationships with the potential informants. Ethnography is exploratory research, so initially a wide-angle lens on the phenomenon of interest is best. After all, 'you don't know what you don't know'. As you become familiar with the issues and the environment, a focus should gradually be obtained.

SELECTING INFORMANTS   One of the key decisions you have to make concerns who are appropriate informants. The ideal informant is an insider who is comfortable with you, well enough placed to have the knowledge and understanding to clarify anomalies, and open to talk about the delicate issues that no one else will mention. Clearly not all informants will fit these criteria, but correct selection is critically important. If you are researching a particular culture, the selected respondents must have the information which is sought, even if it has to be drawn out over time. They must be in a position to know about the phenomenon and if they have only access to hearsay, then you must recognize it as such. You should also be aware that respondents may have particular reason to present their views in a misleading way or deliberately to lie. A sample of key informants may give sufficient depth of information and understanding from their perspective, but there may be other angles that require tangential sampling. For example, the study may depend on interviews with senior managers, but would be enriched with corresponding accounts from middle managers or from the board.

GENERATING DATA   The specific methods used in ethnographic research are not tightly specified but are developed as the project itself develops. Interviews with key respondents, and observation of everyday behaviour and/or meetings and events over a prolonged period, are the most common methods, together with informal conversations with a wider range of informants. The setting details should be noted, including physical location, persons present, their personal details such as age, gender and job position, their inter-relationships, the time of day and duration, with the exact order of any events and interruptions during the observation or interview.

Interviews reveal not only the substantive content of comments made by the respondents, but also how they use language, the stories and myths told, the humour, the naming and labelling of things, and the metaphors in common use. You should bear in mind that in an actor-centred study, it is the way in which the respondents make sense of these actions, words and events – their meanings – which are to be interpreted.

A considerable amount of other data is usually collected, providing multiple evidence or triangulation. The more agreement you find in the different sources, the more confident you can be of the veracity of your account. Also, the more important the assertion, the more critical it is to have good data triangulation. Evidence includes written data such as corporate material, including externally available items (annual reports, brochures, press coverage, advertising, website pages) and internal documents (such as minutes of meetings, memos, reports, organization charts and procedural manuals).

Other sources include artefacts of organizational symbolism, such as leadership styles, technology and human resource management policy. Corporate events, rituals and ceremonies give access to the history of the organization and its current aspirations, and how those impact its present-day culture. The logo of the company says something about its culture, as do the site locations, the built spaces, the external façade, the design and décor, the internal rooms, public and private offices, even the art (if any) on the walls. Previously, ethnographers often used pen and ink drawings of research settings, but you now have a variety of tools, including audio and video tape recordings, and photographs, all of which may form part of the final report. The seeking out of evidence beyond that given in interviews and in observed behaviours is important, as you should look for disconfirming material enabling you to make judgements about the quality of your data and analysis.

FIELDWORK NOTES   You should try to gain approval for tape recording of all interviews, although permission is not always given, despite promises of confidentiality. Avoid recording without permission. It is unethical, and when you are inevitably discovered, it will destroy any trust established. Do tape record if possible, because the quality of transcribed data directly from the taped words of the respondent will inevitably be richer than that of handwritten notes. Nuances such as emotions, pauses and repetitions can be identified and incorporated into the analysis. Fieldnotes can easily miss small signs that point the enquiry in new directions and raise new questions. In one interview of a senior manager on a sensitive topic, the respondent tapped keys against the table at several points, indicating stress. Others laughed nervously or hilariously at various points. Such behaviours should be noted in the transcript to heighten your sensitivity when later reviewing the text. Taped and transcribed interviews also have the benefit of inclusivity rather than subjective selectivity, very important if the focus of the study has not yet been tightly defined, as there may be hidden linkages to underlying phenomena.

A powerful research technique is to listen to the taped interview immediately afterwards, definitely within 24 hours of the interview, to make notes of your own impressions and insights as well as emotions, thoughts and puzzlements during the interview. This one technique will be a source of insight – gold dust, not to be lost. You should also transcribe the tapes personally, as that slow process also provides a uniquely rich opportunity for preliminary interpretation and theorizing. Where tape recording is not allowed, you should take notes during the interviews, and write up the interviews as soon as possible, before other events or data cloud your recollection of the event. As far as possible, the respondents' words should be noted verbatim.

Keep detailed records of what was observed as well as spoken, and of your own state of mind during the event. Sometimes it may be easier for you to tape record your own comments rather than writing them down at that particular time, transcribing them later. As well as interview records and descriptive notes, another set of fieldwork notes, sometimes called the 'field journal', should be kept for developing ideas, reflections and theorizing about underlying processes and events as they unfold. This should be kept readily available, as a notebook to carry around, and transferred to computer on a frequent basis. It should be open whenever transcribing or coding data, as fleeting insights need to be recorded. It is essential to keep the descriptive notes separate from the theoretical field journal, so that the origin of the data is easily established. A separate fieldwork diary should be maintained for the day-to-day arrangements and minutiae of the practical aspects of the research.

Be sure to make duplicate copies of your notes and computer files, and label tape cassettes clearly. The nature of ethnography is that the researcher is in the field often and possibly away from office facilities for some time. Back-up computer disks should be kept separate from the computer, but just as important are written notes. Dickson used a notebook with carbon paper and tear-out duplicate pages when photocopiers were not available. Each week he would send the carbon copies for word processing while retaining the originals. There are documented cases of ethnographers losing all their data through computer theft, fire or other mishap. It is easy and wise to protect your efforts with carbon copies or photocopies and back-up disks.

ANALYSING THE DATA   Soon after entering the field, the neophyte researcher will be amazed at the daunting volume of information that quickly accumulates. This is the point when it is wise to temporarily withdraw from data collection to begin sorting information, reflecting on possible new directions of investigation and making initial attempts at theory development. Ethnographic analysis is a reflective and iterative process of identifying categories developed from extracts of the various data sources. Having inductively identified a category or theme, the researcher then takes a deductive stance and attempts to prove or disprove it. For a detailed description of this process, see the section on analysis in Huberman and Miles (1998).

Software packages such as NVivo, QSR NUD.IST and The Ethnograph can be helpful for those who wish to use them,[1] whilst others prefer to organize their analysis within their usual word processing package. We strongly recommend the use of NVivo as it is now very user-friendly, facilitating not just the analysis (it now has a modelling function), but, importantly, the data management and writing up of the research, often major hurdles for new researchers. The analysis is both continual, impacting future fieldwork, following up hunches and unexpected leads, and sequential, refining the problem issue, tightening the concepts and incorporating findings into the draft model of the phenomenon in its setting.

At the start, the coding is inclusive, particularly of incidents, and as it continues, higher-level groupings of similar codes begin to form an analysis structure from which initial theorizing can begin. It is essential to keep an open mind at this stage, so that the hidden processes and structures may be identified. The theoretical codes may be integrated into the structure at an early stage or later on, after the literature has been consulted. You should note your working definitions of the concepts you are coding so that future coding can be accurately targeted. This also allows you to review the evolution of your thoughts and analysis months later when your recollections may not be as precise as you would wish.

In analysing the data, you should look at the frequency and distribution of the phenomena, any patterns in and between cases, and their typicality. Data that do not fit the identified patterns may be highly significant (though not always), so consideration should be given to outlying data and any surprising responses or negative instances. Specific locations and temporal situations may provide further insight, as may the level of shared understanding of phenomena. There may be multiple types of evidence surrounding a phenomenon. For example, different types of data may confirm or disconfirm tentative hypotheses, further refining potential explanations. You should be aware of the weighting of particular situations, respondents and types of data when selecting evidence for propositions to explain the phenomenon. An excellent source of guidance for analysing qualitative data of various kinds is Lofland and Lofland (1995).

One of the advantages of being on-site during the initial analysis period which overlaps with the data-gathering is that you can easily feed back possible explanations and puzzles to the respondents, asking them to comment on the analysis, to gain their views. This strengthens your resulting report.

REFINING THE ANALYSIS   As you gain increasing confidence in the analysis, through much iteration and reflection, it may be helpful to lay out the evidence in a more structured way. The data may be reassembled under their coded headings, where patterns are often very obvious. Where appropriate, tables may be constructed of the patterns found within different contexts. Sometimes even counts of respondents, occurrences and co-occurrences (for example) may be made for plausibility, and although there is a risk of confusing counts with quality, such action does counteract possible bias from over-influence due to one or two particularly strong or memorable interviewees. Miles and Huberman (1994) provide guidance on tabulating the evidence, but are criticized by some ethnographers for an emphasis on fragmentation and pattern-seeking rather than understanding the whole phenomenon. Miles and Huberman defend their position, stating that without pattern-seeking, there is a high risk of accumulating a large volume of unstructured data from which it will be easy to build description but difficult to build theory.

EXITING THE FIELD   Eventually you will reach 'saturation point', when little new information is emerging from the fieldwork. At this stage, you should withdraw, and start a period of intense reflection and reorganization of the data. Good relations should be maintained with the respondents where possible, to continue the checking and feedback process. If reports have been promised to the organizational or financial sponsor of the project, then the timing for those should be agreed. Where the work is for an academic degree such as PhD, you will minimize the stress if you ensure that the academic and sponsor reports do not have conflicting deadlines. The writing up of such studies is a long and complicated process.

DEALING WITH VALIDITY   Ethnographers seek to provide as 'true' an account as possible of the phenomenon studied. They have to answer whether they have really observed what they describe. Stewart (1998) calls this the 'veracity' of the account. Yet the data cannot be verified, are not stable because they are situational, cannot be replicated, and are gathered through participant involvement. The objectivity of the account (in conventional terms, its reliability) can be enhanced by alertness and sensitivity to others, and should transcend the perspectives of both the researcher and the informants. Stewart also uses the term 'perspicacity', instead of generalizability and external validity, for the transfer of findings from the observed site to a higher level of abstraction, which should reveal insights into other similar circumstances.

In some fields, there may be calls for coding checks to be made, with other researchers taking a section of the data and coding against the definitions given by the originator, resulting in a percentage similarity of codes. However, ethnographers may well argue against this process, as it is their own individual interpretation which matters. Nobody else is likely to have exactly the same background, experiences and insight in the field. Nevertheless, you need to give a clear account of how you reached your conclusions so that others can judge the quality of your findings and the resulting explanations – the so-called 'audit trail'.

BUILDING THEORY   The main output of ethnographic research is not prediction but the mobilization of evidence that explains the phenomenon of interest within its setting. Geertz (1973) says that 'the aim is to render obscure matters intelligible by providing them with an informing context', to uncover the conceptual structures that inform the behaviour of the respondents, and to build an explanatory framework, based on theory, within which the phenomenon takes place.

As the patterns (whether foreground or contextual) or possible explanations start to emerge, you should try to map out the social system of interest, transforming it into a theoretical model of interconnections and contexts, both formal and informal. You should seek evidence for the model, proposing possible explanations underpinned in theory. A key part of this is for you, the researcher, to challenge the emerging model, by asking yourself how you know what you claim to have found. What are the links between data and theory? How valid is the evidence produced? What is the quality of the data and the findings, and what biases have been acknowledged and minimized? Do the data come from more than one source, confirming or disconfirming other evidence? NVivo's modelling capability is extremely useful for checking the analysis, as it allows you to jump immediately to the coded text fragments (from all of the interviews) underlying any node in the model, to check for validity and consistency in the data and analysis.

The actual theory-building is inevitably small-scale, because of its unique but limited location. It should be located in a body of previous work, in which it has in some way extended knowledge. Reference therefore needs to be made to current and previous literature, and findings set into that theoretical context. Often, ethnographic studies have been left at the descriptive stage, but completion is reached only when the contribution to knowledge has been clarified and reported. Sometimes, more than one organizational case study may be undertaken, with the selection of a second based on a theoretically derived difference from the first case. However, few studies comprise more than three cases, and most are single organization case studies.

Becker and Geer (1982) suggest a number of theoretical statements to be made in the explanation: (1) complex statements of the necessary and sufficient conditions for the existence of the phenomenon; (2) statements that the phenomenon exercises an important influence on the organization; and (3) statements identifying the phenomenon as an instance of a more abstract concept described in sociological theory.

WRITING UP THE ETHNOGRAPHIC ACCOUNT   This stage can be overwhelming, given the volume of material collected, examined, analysed and used or discarded. For this reason, the best advice is to start writing early in the fieldwork phase. With good fieldnotes and progress diaries, a logical first step might be to tell the story of the study and its actors, identifying the major turning points and key insights. This will give you a framework on which to hang the theory and analysis.

Books have been the traditional output from ethnographic studies, because the length allows space for sufficient detail of the methods, findings and explication of the contribution to knowledge and practice. An excellent example of a well-structured book is Kunda's (1992) study of an engineering company culture (see case study at end of this chapter). The book starts with an introduction to the whole study, followed by a general overview of the company setting. He describes the substance and form of the managerial ideology of the culture, and then analyses the practices through which the culture and ideology are implemented. He next documents how people make sense of their experience and their roles. The final chapter provides an overview of findings, reviewing what has been learnt from a theoretical point of view, and considers the study in a wider context. An appendix details the history of the project, the methodology and Kunda's personal experience, as well as dealing with bias.

Where the work is to be written up as a dissertation, you are advised to follow your university guidelines and conventions. A good way to start is to look at some theses in your field using similar methods. The traditional chapter order is introduction, literature review, philosophical approach and methodology, findings, analysis, discussion and conclusions.

For many, it is difficult to report such rich work within the constraints of journal article format and length. Golden-Biddle and Locke (1997) provide insightful guidance on crafting the written report from qualitative research, particularly on turning the collection of evidence into articles that stand up to scrutiny and approval by reviewers. They point out the importance of knowing for whom you are writing, and emphasize that 'the major task of writing our journals' texts involves working out how to make *contextually grounded theoretical points that are viewed as a contribution by the relevant professional community of readers*' (1997: 20; emphasis in original).

For journal articles, we suggest that you first look at articles in your field in quality journals that report ethnographic approaches, or if they are difficult to find, then look at good articles using other qualitative methods. Look at the structure, the balance between issue, setting, findings and theoretical discussion. A possible structure is to give first the natural history of the research, its original purpose and how it developed over time, followed by a summary of the fieldwork roles, settings and relations. An account of the data selection, collection and recording should then be given, followed by the findings and a clear account of the analysis process. You should present an appropriate level of evidence of participant-derived and literature-derived concepts, backing up explanatory statements with relevant quotations. In the conclusions section, the implications of the findings for theory (existing and new) should be reviewed, as well as for practice, and you should make suggestions for further research.

Where there is a contribution to practice, you should consider how best to inform the relevant community of the results. Shorter or more descriptive pieces can be written up for practitioner journals and magazines for quick dissemination, without the need for the theoretical aspects to be highlighted.

Two case studies

We conclude with a summary of two ethnographic case studies as illustrations of this methodological approach, one undertaken in a remote business community, and the other in a high technology company in the United States.

'A Different Model of Doing Business in a Subsistence Community: Experience from Madang, Papua New Guinea', PhD thesis by John Dickson (1995)

Western models of enterprise promotion have been used all over the world, but often inappropriately in different cultural settings, resulting in unsuccessful ventures and wasted funds. After three years working as a rural business adviser in Papua New Guinea (PNG), John Dickson spent nearly a year living in a rural PNG community researching the motivations and expectations of rural businessmen and the communities they lived in. The reason for the research was the contradictory experience of intense community interest in business combined with high business failure rates. Traditional business research had identified the many business failures but raised more questions than answers. Familiarity with rural business problems suggested to Dickson that his research method must somehow incorporate not only the businessmen and their businesses but the surrounding community as well. He used cultural theory to guide his analysis, in which his key finding was the overwhelming influence that community values had on the local business process and on the success of individual businesses. One consequence of the strong community influence was that an outsider who had moved to the community had a greater chance of business survival because he had fewer community responsibilities and pressures. Another consequence of the strong community ethos was for the businessmen to use unusual coping mechanisms to deal with the impact of these values. The multiple business allowed the businessman to achieve profit while continuing to show the expected generosity to his community. The disappearing business encompassed a number of conflict avoidance mechanisms. These differences from traditional Western models provided an explanation as to why so many assisted projects failed in the past, and provided suggestions for more relevant models in the future. Dickson made a case that enterprise planning, development and evaluation should not take place in deliberate ignorance of the social and cultural processes within which they are immersed, but should be designed to support and intensify existing business activities. His thesis thereby made a contribution both to knowledge and practice, as well as providing a rich description of local community business life.

Engineering Culture: Control and Commitment in a High-Tech Corporation, *by Gideon Kunda (1992)*

This book has received praise as a fine account of an organizational ethnography, and is recommended reading for any new ethnographer. Kunda studied corporate culture in two sites of a major high technology company, where most employees were male graduates in their late twenties to mid-thirties. The atmosphere was informal, with well-paid workers showing self-confidence and commitment, regularly working long hours. Kunda found that there was a managerial rhetoric of corporate culture working as an informal organizing principle alongside the formal structures and processes. The managers viewed the culture as something to be engineered ('researched, designed, developed and maintained') to achieve corporate goals. Individuals used 'the strong culture' to explain or make sense of their lives. As people accepted the culture, there was less need for visible control as they worked with self-direction and emotional attachment to the company goals. The control was subtle, and the employees were left with a feeling of free choice. He comments:

> Although it is not immediately apparent, the price of power is submission: not necessarily to demands concerning one's behavior, as is typical of low-status work, but to prescriptions regarding one's thoughts and feelings, supposedly the most cherished belongings of autonomous beings. (1992: 214)

Kunda calls his study 'an ethnography of lay ethnographers', those managers who were consciously trying to manipulate control through culture. Kunda examined the way the culture was imposed, the presentation rituals, as he called them, noting how power and dominance were manifested in talking down, talking across and talking around rituals in social interactions. His findings are set in context with previous literature on culture and control. Kunda describes his methodology chapter as a 'confessional' in contrast to the realist description of the research findings which blur the subjective nature of the study, however well designed and carried out. He reflects on his evolving role in the project, from doctoral student associated with an MIT academic consultancy task to participant observer with office facilities and a free run of the headquarters, although still viewed with suspicion by many of the engineers. Through taking part in both formal and informal activities within the organization, Kunda managed to share many of the experiences and thoughts of his temporary colleagues, at the same time finding space and time for personal reflection. Two major issues arose during the fieldwork. Kunda noted that he was less able to gain access at the most senior levels, until he was invited to observe a vice president, after which senior access became easier. Secondly, his access to the informal aspects of life was somewhat limited because much of it took place outside the immediate site, and so he had to rely on hearsay rather than observation. None the less, after a year, he had accumulated vast amounts of data of various kinds. He then entered a process of reading and cataloguing his field notes, categorizing and organizing the data, searching for meaning. Analytical categories emerged from this process around ideology, rituals and the self. As he started to write up his work, Kunda had to move from the purely descriptive writing towards an explicit analytic framework in the final thesis. Kunda then developed his book, after three years of intensive rewriting, and clearly achieved his aim for an ethnographic report which brought forth hidden meanings and offered interpretations for debate.

Study questions

1 Consider a particular issue of interest, such as the impact of a new customer interface scheme in a large organization. How best would that be researched? Suggest three or four ways, then critically examine them – do any of them find 'the truth'? Consider the people, the timing and the location – who, when, for how long, what would be studied where? Would observation or participation be more fruitful – what advantages and disadvantages would there be?

2 Practise non-participant observation in your own organization, or when you are visiting elsewhere. Stand at the reception desk and think about what information you can glean there about the organizational culture. Observe what is going on, how visitors are greeted, how the surroundings form the first image of the organization. Consider the various data types discussed in this chapter, both physical and symbolic. Does there appear to be a hierarchy, is the atmosphere formal or friendly, is it quiet or 'buzzy', professional or muddling along, what about the furniture and the walls? What are the theoretical properties and dimensions of the features observed? Such an exercise can start to sharpen up perceptual skills, making additional evidence available which normally your eye does not see, because it is so normal.

3 A favourite exercise often given by Professor Mary Jo Hatch – write 1,500 words about your desk. This really taxes the creativity of some students, and is an excellent exercise in raising symbolic awareness.

Recommended further reading

Atkinson, P. and Hammersley, M. (1994) 'Ethnography and Participant Observation', in N.K. Denzin and Y.S. Lincoln (eds), *Handbook of Qualitative Research*. London: Sage, pp. 248–61. (A theoretical but accessible overview of the subject)

Bate, S.P. (1997) 'Whatever Happened to Organizational Anthropology? A Review of the Field of Organizational Ethnography and Anthropological Studies', *Human Relations*, 50 (9), pp. 1147–75. (An excellent article relating to management studies)

Becker, H.S. and Geer, B. (1982) 'Participant Observation: The Analysis of Qualitative Field Data', in R.G. Burgess (ed.), *Field Research: A Sourcebook and Field Manual*. London: George Allen and Unwin, pp. 239–50. (Good advice on the kinds of data to be collected, and what to do with them)

Easterby-Smith, M. and Malina, D. (1999) 'Cross-cultural Collaborative Research: Towards Reflexivity', *Academy of Management Journal*, 42 (1), pp. 76–86. (Insight into the importance of reflexivity, particularly in very different cultural settings)

Geertz, C. (1973) *The Interpretation of Cultures: Selected Essays*. New York: Basic Books. (Essential for a deeper understanding of culture in its holistic sense)

Kunda, G. (1992) *Engineering Culture: Control and Commitment in a High-Tech Corporation*. Philadelphia: Temple University Press. (You are strongly advised to read this book, especially the methodology chapter, before setting out on an ethnographic route)

Prasad, P. and Prasad, A. (2000) 'Casting the Native Subject: Ethnographic Practice and the (Re)production of Difference', EGOS Colloquium, Helsinki, Finland, July. (A very thought-provoking discussion of ethnography, history and discourse)

Rosen, M. (1991) 'Coming to Terms with the Field: Understanding and Doing Organizational Ethnography', *Journal of Management Studies*, 28 (1), pp. 1–24. (An excellent overview of ethnography in organizational settings)

Stewart, A. (1998) *The Ethnographer's Method*. London: Sage. (A slim volume giving more general methodological advice for budding ethnographers. Includes very useful comments on how such studies are evaluated by reviewers for journals and funding bodies, and suggests that agreement on the criteria for evaluation will be modest)

Van Maanen, J. (1987) *Tales of the Field: On Writing Ethnography*. Chicago: University of Chicago Press. (Lots of fieldwork experiences, useful for new ethnographers)

Whyte, W.F. (1991) *Participatory Action Research*. Newbury Park, CA: Sage. (Essential reading if you plan to undertake participatory action research)

Note

1 QSR NUD.IST, QSR NVivo and The Ethnograph are all distributed by Scolari, Sage Publications Ltd, 6 Bonhill Street, London EC2A 4PU. Free demonstration versions can be downloaded from the Scolari website (www.scolari.co.uk).

References

Atkinson, P. and Hammersley, M. (1994) 'Ethnography and Participant Observation', in N.K. Denzin and Y.S. Lincoln (eds), *Handbook of Qualitative Research*. London: Sage, pp. 248–61.

Bate, S.P. (1997) 'Whatever Happened to Organizational Anthropology? A Review of the Field of Organizational Ethnography and Anthropological Studies', *Human Relations*, 50 (9), pp. 1147–75.

Becker, H.S. and Geer, B. (1982) 'Participant Observation: The Analysis of Qualitative Field Data', in R.G. Burgess (ed.), *Field Research: A Sourcebook and Field Manual*. London: George Allen and Unwin, pp. 239–50.

Dickson, J. (1995) 'A Different Model of Doing Business in a Subsistence Community: Experience from Madang, Papua New Guinea', unpublished PhD thesis, Cranfield School of Management, Bedfordshire, UK.

Easterby-Smith, M. and Malina, D. (1999) 'Cross-cultural Collaborative Research: Towards Reflexivity', *Academy of Management Journal*, 42 (1), pp. 76–86.

Geertz, C. (1973) *The Interpretation of Cultures: Selected Essays*. New York: Basic Books.

Golden-Biddle, K. and Locke, K.D. (1997) *Composing Qualitative Research*. London: Sage.

Hatch, M.J. (1993) 'The Dynamics of Organizational Culture', *Academy of Management Review*, 18 (4), pp. 657–93.

Huberman, A.M. and Miles, M.B. (1998) 'Data Analysis and Management and Analysis Methods', in N.K. Denzin and Y.S. Lincoln (eds), *Collecting and Interpreting Qualitative Materials*. London: Sage.

Kunda, G. (1992) *Engineering Culture: Control and Commitment in a High-Tech Corporation*. Philadelphia: Temple University Press

Lofland, J. and Lofland, L.H. (1995) *Analysing Social Settings: A Guide to Qualitative Observation and Analysis*. Belmont, CA: Wadsworth.

Louis, M.R. (1983) 'Organizations as Culture-bearing Milieux', in L.R. Pondy, G. Morgan and T. Dandridge (eds), *Organizational Symbolism*. London: JAI Press, pp. 39–54.

Miles, M.B. and Huberman, A.M. (1994) *Qualitative Data Analysis: An Expanded Sourcebook*. London: Sage.

Stewart, A. (1998) *The Ethnographer's Method*. London: Sage.

Thompson, K.F and Luthans, F. (1990) 'Organizational Culture: A Behavioral Perspective', in B. Schneider (ed.), *Organizational Climate and Culture*. San Francisco: Jossey–Bass, pp. 319–44.

Van Maanen, J. (1979) 'The Fact of Fiction in Organizational Ethnography', *Administrative Science Quarterly*, 24 (4), pp. 539–50.

Whyte, W.F. (1955) *Street Corner Society: The Social Structure of an Italian Slum*. Chicago: University of Chicago Press.

Whyte, W.F. (1991) *Participatory Action Research*. Newbury Park, CA: Sage.

8

Grounded Theory

David Partington

OVERVIEW

In qualitative management studies few research monographs are as famous
and enduring as Glaser and Strauss's *The Discovery of Grounded Theory:
Strategies for Qualitative Research*. Since its appearance in 1967 the book has
inspired and informed a stream of grounded theory publications, both empirical and methodological, from a growing list of scholars. The output includes
notable further offerings from Glaser and Strauss themselves, as well as from
their disciples and others who have sought to apply and develop the
approach. Despite this proliferation, the original exposition remains the most
widely cited reference to grounded theory methodology and method.

The Discovery of Grounded Theory was written at a time when speculative,
doctrinaire 'grand theories' of culture and social structure dominated the
output of the sociological elite. Sociologists who advocated theorizing from
data, as opposed to 'armchair' theorists who worked from a priori assumptions and logical argument, felt the need to fight hard against certain
members of the academic establishment to justify their approach. Perhaps as
a result of this prevailing climate of adversity – which has since faded somewhat – the passion and clarity of Glaser and Strauss's famous polemic have
never been surpassed in grounded theory writing.

Fundamentally, *The Discovery of Grounded Theory* is about being systematic
with qualitative data. Employing a wealth of terminology, the book is concerned with the application of procedures and guidelines for a rigorous
approach to using qualitative data for building theory, rather than just description. However, despite the frequency with which it is cited, by no means all of
those who refer to the work are true to its purpose, which was to achieve the
fine balance between procedural rigour and creativity. Now, in qualitative
management research, the term 'grounded theory' has taken on a more generic
meaning, tending to embrace all theory-building approaches which are based
on the coding of qualitative data. An inevitable consequence of this broaden-
ing of meaning has been a certain loss of attention to the key principles of the
Glaser and Strauss approach, and to their underlying purpose.

One of the reasons why the legacy of Glaser and Strauss has become
dimmed and diluted is that their approach is difficult to grasp, particularly

for novice qualitative researchers. Glaser and Strauss were clearly aware of the dilemma inherent in describing in the linear format of a practically applicable research monograph what they knew to be a highly personal, iterative procedure. This awareness is evident in their repeated statements of the need for intangible qualities such as insight and 'theoretical sensitivity' (1967: 46). For Glaser and Strauss that essential element in a sociologist's armoury comes not from the following of procedures but from a combination of the sociologist's innate ability to conceptualize and formulate theories, from their personality and temperament, and from knowledge of their area of research.

Despite such difficulties, several factors combine to make the original approach eminently suitable to the purposes of contemporary management research. The twin pillars of grounded theory methodology are *constant comparison* and *theoretical sampling*. By exploring and exemplifying these two basic tenets in the context of management research I offer a set of guidelines which is based on assumptions about contemporary forces of supply and demand in management theory. I aim to make certain important characteristics of Glaser and Strauss's original grounded theory approach accessible to management researchers.

In the following sections I briefly trace the origins and development of grounded theory and explain why it is becoming a popular strategy for management researchers. The main focus of the chapter is a series of guidelines for employing the approach in practice, and throughout I offer advice on building grounded theories that are both rigorous and, because they are built from data, capable of practical application. I conclude with some observations about the kinds of personal and temperamental characteristics which are necessary for scholars embarking on grounded theory studies and bringing them to a successful conclusion.

ORIGINS AND DEVELOPMENT

The application of qualitative methodologies to management research has a long track record. For several decades interpretive, qualitative approaches to management research and theory have grown in popularity, and have developed as an important part of what Denzin and Lincoln (1998: vii) refer to as the 'quiet methodological revolution' in the social sciences. Despite its lengthening history, however, the field of qualitative management research is still characterized by inconsistencies and contradictions, and the precepts for conducting and evaluating such work are less clear than those of quantitative studies which are underpinned by the established norms of positivism and inferential statistics.

One of the consequences of this lack of uniformity is that every qualitative researcher tends to develop their own individual approach. However, consistency of approach holds certain attractions, particularly to those who seek the promise of legitimacy and rigour. Further, some management scholars have expressed concern that if we are to build on the work of others we need explicit, practical methodological ground. Pfeffer (1995), for example, refers to Weick's influential work on sensemaking (see Weick, 1993). He suggests that, admirable though it may be, Weick's strongly creative style makes it difficult for others to pick up and develop his work.

There is no doubt that building grounded theory requires a strong element of creativity. The extent to which it is possible to combine creativity with following a step-by-step process has been the subject of some debate. In general grounded theory literature there is some evidence of attempts to address the need for methodological consistency which is offered by a proceduralized approach. Strauss and Corbin (1990), for example, argue that spelling out procedures and techniques in step-by-step fashion is useful, particularly for novice researchers. But because their approach is aimed at fulfilling the needs of social scientists and professionals from all disciplines, it can be bewilderingly complex for many who attempt to use it for the specific purposes of certain styles of management research.

Many theory-building management studies have certain characteristics which make it possible to simplify attempts to formalize and spell out grounded theory procedures. In this section I present a set of detailed, step-by-step guidelines for building grounded management theories which are firmly based on Glaser and Strauss's original work, but which are adapted to suit those characteristics. The guidelines are based on a set of assumptions which, in my experience, characterize most theory-building management studies. In particular, I am concerned with the application of procedural rigour to case studies in which mainly interview data are used for building theoretical models of management action which are guided by an ontology and epistemology which are both explicit and appropriate.

My aim is to set out a framework for doing grounded theory management studies which is simple and accessible, but which has sufficient inherent flexibility to allow individual researchers to build in the essential ingredient of creativity, and to develop the methodology for their own purpose. The guidelines are presented in five sequential parts: getting ready, getting started, moving forward, reaching theoretical saturation and conveying credibility. They are illustrated with examples from theory-building studies.

GETTING READY TO DO GROUNDED THEORY

Before you begin to collect, code and analyse data, four fundamental elements of your research project should be in place. You should start with a clear *purpose*, one or more research *questions*, a *theoretical perspective*, and an outline *research design* (see Figure 8.1). Because these four fundamental elements all relate to one another, they should constantly be reviewed, and should be allowed to evolve and develop over the course of the research project. However, unless they are kept in alignment with one another it will be difficult to bring the study to a successful conclusion.

Purpose

A clear purpose is an essential element in any research project. There are several possible levels of purpose, and you should aim to be clear on as high and

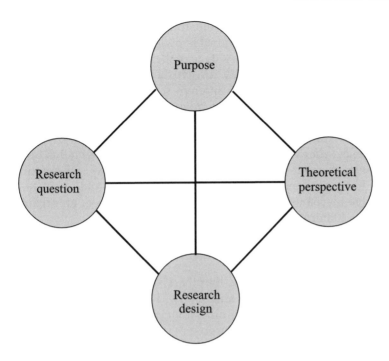

FIGURE 8.1   *The research process: four elements in alignment*

as many levels as possible. It could be argued that the ultimate purpose of all formal management research is to benefit society. Taking this view implies the notion that improved understanding of organizations will lead to some form of progress other than the purely academic. In turn, this presupposes the possibility of 'progress', or at least of limiting decline by updating knowledge to meet changed circumstances. Yet even this view is not without problems. Silverman (1993), for example, argues that uncritical belief in progress in society is dangerous, because even obvious examples of the phenomenon may, on closer examination, reveal themselves to be paradoxical.

Whatever your view, you should try to articulate your theory of management in relation to your proposed study. You may find this challenging, since it should entail a critical examination of your own values and basic assumptions. But whether you define your purpose as emancipation, increased corporate profitability, advancing knowledge for its own sake, or some other ultimate goal, you should be explicit about it, since it will underlie the entire design and conduct of your research.

The purpose of a particular piece of research may be considered at another level, which is concerned with the content of the desired output. Blaikie (1993) places research purposes on a continuum which relates broadly to the existing level of knowledge of the topic and the pre-existence of theory. From the most basic level of *exploration* of a phenomenon about which knowledge is scarce, purposes range through *description, understanding, explanation* and *change* to *evaluation of change*.

The guidelines that follow are illustrated with examples from a current cross-sector study into organizational knowledge management (Partington et al., 2001). In the first, exploratory stage of the study we are using a grounded theory methodology. The study revolves around 20 willing participating organizations from a variety of different sectors, including manufacturing, aerospace, electronics, food and beverages, construction and health care. The purpose of the study is to enable these disparate organizations to become more effective at what they strive to do, be that growth, survival, profitability, efficiency, effectiveness or whatever. They will achieve this by learning across sectors about how specific types of individual and organizational knowledge are gained, retained, transferred or lost, and about how these knowledge mechanisms are linked to specific features of an organization's external and internal environment.

Research question

The second essential element is that there should be one or more research questions to guide the enquiry and to provide focus. It is worthwhile spending time articulating and refining concise, carefully worded research questions which closely fit the purpose of the research.

In the knowledge management project, we are working with a set of organizations whose managers hold a common belief that studying, discussing and disseminating knowledge management processes in contrasting environments will provide opportunities for cross-sector learning. Our first task as researchers is to understand the key features of the strategic and operational environment of each of our participating organizations. We want to observe and listen to managers and other organizational actors to discover what is important to them. Later in the study we will develop a generic set of contextual dimensions which can be used to map the position of an organization in relation to its context and the knowledge management practices to which it should aspire.

The initial research questions are: *What are the key characteristics of each participating organization, and what do these characteristics reveal about the organization's knowledge needs and knowledge sources?* Later, as the study moves into a more action-oriented mode, further questions will be advanced which relate to the application of theories developed in the initial, grounded phase.

Theoretical perspective

A misconception which sometimes hampers grounded theorists is that they are somehow expected to put aside all their experiences, preconceptions and knowledge of existing theory. Apart from the obvious impossibility of such a theory-neutral state, management researchers attempting to operate from a 'clean slate' would be facing the impossible task of operationalizing an infinitely large number of potential variables. If you are building a theory it is important to start out with an explicit framework on which that theory can be developed. The framework should suit both your purpose and your research questions.

Theoretical frameworks in management research come in many different forms. They can range from elaborate multivariate conceptualizations and models to simple relationships between a few basic concepts. They can have the benefit (or encumbrance) of a strong research tradition with its origins in more established disciplines like economics, sociology, psychology and anthropology, or they can be relatively naive. They can be partial and fragmented, or they can be philosophically harmonized and complete.

Theoretical frameworks which make explicit the researcher's ontological and epistemological assumptions provide the best foundation on which to construct and defend a theoretical argument. Much management research is conducted in the positivist tradition, which holds that through observing regularities researchers can make generalizations, within defined limits, of relationships between variables. The purpose of the generalizations then becomes prediction. For many grounded theorists the purpose is also prediction, but from the different viewpoint that the social world cannot be experimentally closed and does not operate according to a set of scientific laws, and therefore predictive *certainty* is not possible. In the social world, observed regularities can do no more than express *tendencies* caused *by underlying generative mechanisms* which may or may not be brought into play in a given situation.

This theory of reality is exemplified by Bhaskar's (1975) 'critical realist' ontology. Taking this view of the social world and applying it to the study of management the researcher's job is to speculate about plausible underlying generative mechanisms. Such a *mechanism* is the existence of external and internal forces or stimuli which, provided they or their effects are attended to, may lead to a purposeful response. Without such attention the mechanism remains dormant. With it, the response is enacted in the form of a series of observed or reported events, whether or not these are experienced at first hand by the researcher. The events, and their links to the stimuli which gave rise to them, are discovered through fine-grained analysis of data, particularly from observation and unstructured interviews. Through this analysis the researcher's job is repeated speculation and enquiry. The *speculation* will involve asking what plausible, understandable cognitive processes are intervening between stimulus and action or intent. The *enquiry* will be the unfolding study and the search for consensually valid explanations.

In the first, grounded theory part of the knowledge management project we are adopting this critical realist position. We are starting with the following fundamental assumptions, which both inform and form our theoretical framework:

1 A basic underlying mechanism of knowledge needs and sources in organizations exists which is common to all our participating organizations.
2 In an organization, the enactment of different parts of the mechanism may be prevalent or dormant depending on the nature of the organization.
3 An important part of the mechanism in an organization is a set of key characteristics of the organization and its environment, which provide the stimulus for action or intent.

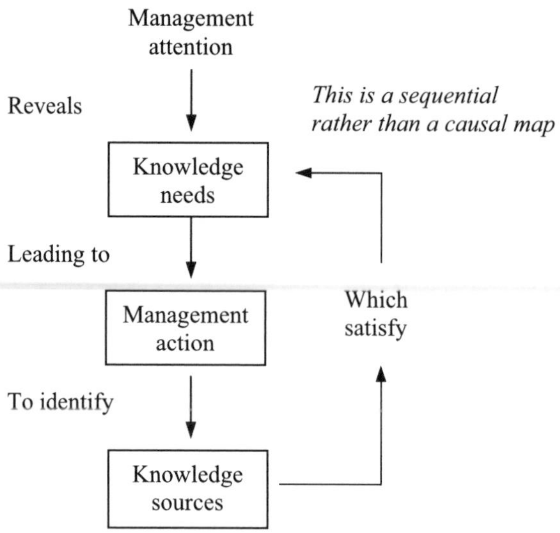

FIGURE 8.2   *Knowledge needs and sources revealed by the focus of management attention*

4 The key characteristics in an organization will be revealed by the allocation of organizational actors' scarce attention in open-ended interviews and other data sources.
5 Each key characteristic in an organization will create and reveal needs for certain specific kinds of knowledge. These needs are satisfied wholly, partially or not at all from knowledge sources created and revealed by other characteristics.
6 By aggregating the key characteristics of all 20 organizations a set of generic characteristics may be developed, each of which is possessed to a greater, lesser or opposite extent by each organization.
7 The key characteristics and the knowledge needs and sources in the aggregate model will enable managers to understand the knowledge mechanism that exists in their organization. It will also enable them to learn from the mechanism in operation with similar or opposite characteristics in other organizations.

The framework is summarized in Figure 8.2.

Research design

The fourth essential element in the preparatory phase of a study is the research design. A fully developed research design will embody the researcher's purpose, questions and theoretical framework. In case study research, it will define the primary unit of analysis, the selection of at least the first case to be studied, and the data collection strategy and analytical approach for at least the first case.

Initial designs for grounded theory studies are likely to be sketchy and incomplete. This is because of the distinctive feature of grounded theory known as *theoretical sampling*, whereby the data collection strategy is not defined up front but is allowed to be driven by emerging ideas. The process of theoretical sampling, which can operate at several levels, is explored in more detail later in the chapter.

Continuing the example, we view knowledge management not as a simple, technology-based activity but as a cluster of cognitive and behavioural routines which might, for example, identify, articulate, codify and share information. The managers in our participating organizations explicitly share our view, that knowledge management is a social phenomenon, not a technological one. In the first stage of the study, where we were mapping organizational contexts, our unit of analysis was the *characteristic* of the organization's external or internal context. The initial set of cases consisted of the organizations that had been invited to participate in the study, and had accepted. The first informants were the most senior managers in each case. Since its outset the design of the knowledge management project has developed considerably, as I will describe in the following sections.

GETTING STARTED WITH DATA CODING AND ANALYSIS

Having defined your purpose, research questions, theoretical perspective and outline research design, the next step is to begin the joint processes of data collection, coding and analysis. It is important to remember that theorizing is not something that is done only during the final stages of a study, after all the data have been collected and the analysis is complete. The theory-building process starts right at the beginning, when the study is in its early, conceptual stages, and continues throughout.

Because the knowledge management research is a multi-researcher project it has been important for the members of the team who are involved in the detail of the grounded theory part of the study to maintain close communication with one another, especially in the early stages of theorizing. We have developed an approach that allows us to be as individually creative as we want to be, coming together regularly to discuss our various emerging contributions and bringing them into alignment before moving on.

It is a good idea to keep a methodological diary recording developments in the theory-building process. If you do this from the start you will have a record of how important early ideas about theory and data iterated and moved forward towards your final conclusions. This will enable you to be explicit, and therefore more convincing, about the methodological processes you employed. Here is an example of such a diary entry from the knowledge management project:

> Following meeting with MY decided that the initial coding schema for [organization X] was inappropriate. Predefining TEAM and KNOWLEDGE as level 1 categories works less well than the schema which emerged from the initial coding of the first page of BM's interview, because most statements about work in the

organization are about ROLES, not easily mapped to TEAM or KNOWLEDGE. Four kinds of roles emerged, labelled R1 to R4 (see Version 2 of coding schema). Agreed with team that any developments to the level 1 codes beyond those in Version 2 will be discussed and agreed so that we proceed in parallel.

Conducting and analysing an open-ended interview early in the study will help you to become sensitized to what is important to your informants. In grounded theory work this is usually more useful than what is important to you, since your purpose is to understand the world from your informants' point of view. In management research, you will often find that the more senior the manager the more useful the interview data, but be careful not to 'use up' your best informants in pilot interviews unless you are sure that they will consent to further interviews.

Interviews should be recorded on audio-tape if possible. Unless the subject matter is particularly sensitive, either personally, politically or commercially, most managers will readily agree to the use of the tape recorder. It helps if it is introduced in a non-threatening way. A casual remark such as, 'you don't mind if I use this tape recorder do you?', can be less intimidating than a lengthy speech promising absolute security and integrity. Many managers have never been the subject of a formal research interview. It can be an enjoyable, even therapeutic, experience to be interviewed by someone who is prepared to listen sensitively and without interruption to one's recollections and views for what can be quite long periods.

Recording interviews has four significant advantages over the main alternative, taking notes during and immediately after the interview. First, when you listen to the tape you will realize that the sense and the theoretical implications of a surprisingly large part of what was said were missed by you at the time. Second, it allows you to think about and note ideas for further questions during the interview without the need to worry about missing important data. Third, you have the tape available for repeated listening for voice tone and emphasis. Fourth, it allows you to reflect critically on your interviewing style, and thus to improve your technique.

Transcribing audio-taped interviews is time-consuming. Depending on your purpose, and on the talkativeness of the respondent, most interviews take somewhere between 30 and 90 minutes to conduct, although some run to several hours. They can take many times that duration to transcribe and analyse, particularly if your typing skills are rudimentary. The transcription process can be tedious at times, especially if the detailed content of the interview is not inherently fascinating. However, there is a serious advantage to transcribing interviews yourself, which you will only experience if you have the patience to do it. The joint process of transcription, coding and analysis offers an extraordinary opportunity to become sensitized to the full richness of your data. The very slowness of the process somehow contributes to the theoretical depth which it is possible to achieve. If you get someone else to transcribe your interviews you will lose this opportunity. Transcribing as many of your interviews as possible can ultimately speed up the almost miraculous process of turning what starts out as an unwieldy mass of data into an understood whole.

In some qualitative research it is important to transcribe every utterance, pause and even gesture. Silverman (2000) describes work with clinician/patient encounters where this minute level of detail was important to the research. In much management research this level of attention to detail is unnecessary. Indeed, if you are concerned with developing a deep understanding of a complex organizational environment, transcribing and reporting every 'um' and 'ah' can be distracting to the reader and irrelevant to the theory.

The guiding maxim is to make your transcription style fit your purpose. As you become more sensitized to your data and to your emerging theories, you may become more selective about which words or passages in an interview are worth transcribing in full, which can be paraphrased, and which can be left out altogether. However, in the early stages of a study, when you do not know for certain what is important to you or to your informant, it is better to transcribe everything, thereby maximizing opportunities to become familiar with your data and with your informant's world.

Many researchers use word processing software for transcribing interview data and coding it into theoretical categories. Word processors have the advantage that coding can be entered directly into the transcript, perhaps using a distinctive typeface or symbol. Specialist software packages for managing qualitative data offer similar advantages (see Chapter 7). Some researchers, particularly those who are new to qualitative research, are lured by the promise of such packages providing a combination of guidance and legitimation of their approach. But qualitative research software packages do not do qualitative research; they merely provide a fairly free-form structure within which to manage data. The main problem for new researchers using such tools is the need to learn qualitative data collection and analysis at the same time as mastering powerful new software. There is a danger that technical issues can obscure the researcher's purpose, making it difficult to stay sufficiently focused on the data and alert to theoretical ideas.

Most experienced qualitative analysts started out with simple manual analytical techniques using cards, sticky notes, cut-and-paste text and scribbled margins. Many still prefer simple approaches over sophisticated specialist software. If you are planning to use a qualitative approach, you should consider developing your research skills first, at least to the point where you know what you want to do with your data, before you attempt to master a qualitative research software package.

Now consider the following extract from an interview with a contract manager in a privatized highway maintenance firm, transcribed and coded in a word processor file:

These tend to be younger people, and also people from the general construction industry [MEMO DOUBLE BLOW AS EX-PUBLIC SECTOR PEOPLE REACH RETIREMENT AGE] who don't have a clear picture of what our job is [K1-WHAT HIGHWAY MAINTENANCE IS]. Our parent company, in the early days a lot of people there took the rise out of us really – they thought our job was picking up dead hedgehogs [GOOD QUOTABLE QUOTE] and was really not very exciting at all [C2-WORK ATTRACTIVENESS-NOT EXCITING]. To a degree they're not far out, and the opportunity's not always there to do exciting work, or to work long hours and have high earnings [C2-WORK ATTRACTIVENESS-LONG HOURS] [C2-WORK ATTRACTIVENESS-HIGH EARNINGS], which is another problem. If we could guarantee people 50 or 60 hours work a week I think we would have less trouble retaining them. [K6-RETAIN STAFF THROUGH WORK ATTRACTIVENESS] [MEMO IN THIS FIRM WORK ATTRACTIVENESS MAY BE RELATED TO K7].

The passage contains examples of many aspects of coding and analysis, in this case entered in distinctive upper case text within square brackets. The first entry, [MEMO DOUBLE BLOW AS EX-PUBLIC SECTOR PEOPLE REACH RETIREMENT AGE], is a theoretical *memo* which acts as a reminder and consolidator of analytical thought. Memos are used to keep a record of the researcher's internal dialogue. They should be used freely to record thoughts and ideas as they occur. They should be self-contained statements. They will contribute in important ways to the eventual written theory. Starting each memo with a consistent 'flag' (in this case [MEMO . . .) makes it easy to search and retrieve them.

At the time this passage was coded, the constantly evolving *coding schema* consisted of a list of 13 high-level *categories*. Each high-level category has a shorthand code. The categories are labelled and defined in Table 8.1.

The second entry, [K1-WHAT HIGHWAY MAINTENANCE IS], is an example of the categorization of an *instance* of *data* as an individual recruit's knowledge need. The manager states that recruits from the general construction industry do not have a clear picture of what the highway maintenance job entails. This specific instance of data, which may indicate a knowledge need at the individual level, is given the initial shorthand category K1. This is an example of a *self-generated* category, where the researchers have used their own terminology to describe the category.

The third entry, [GOOD QUOTABLE QUOTE], will be used to locate a memorable quote at the writing up stage, as it could provide a vivid illustration of a phenomenon that characterizes the organization's environment. The informant feels that work in the firm has an unattractive, low-status image by comparison with its parent company's mainstream operation, which operates at the more glamorous, big project end of the construction industry.

The fourth entry, [C2-WORK ATTRACTIVENESS-NOT EXCITING], is an example of the high-level category INTERNAL CONTEXT, which has the shorthand code C2 (see Table 8.1). The *property* of internal context to which the informant refers is work attractiveness, and the *dimension* of work attractiveness in this firm is that it is not attractive. This property of the category C2 (internal context), and its associated dimension, are recorded in a running list, either by expanding the high-level coding schema or as a separate table (see Table 8.2).

The dimensional scale 'not attractive . . . attractive' is an example of *in vivo* coding, where the words of the informant have been used to label the dimension. *In vivo* categories, properties and dimensions are useful for 'staying close to the data', an essential feature of creating and conveying convincing grounded theory.

TABLE 8.1   Shorthand codes, categories and definitions in an early example of a coding schema

	Category	Definition
R1	Role–individual–own	Statements about the informant's own roles, responsibilities, actions and intentions
R2	Role–individual–other	Statements about another individual's roles, responsibilities, actions and intentions
R3	Role–collective–team	Statements about the collective roles, responsibilities, actions and intentions of a team
R4	Role–collective–organization	Statements about the collective roles, responsibilities, actions and intentions of the organization
C1	External context	Statements about environmental factors outside the organization to which attention is paid
C2	Internal context	Statements about environmental factors inside the organization to which attention is paid
K1	Knowledge–need–individual	Statements about an individual's need for knowledge
K2	Knowledge–need–team	Statements about a team's need for knowledge
K3	Knowledge–need–organization	Statements about the organization's need for knowledge
K4	Knowledge–source	Statements about sources of knowledge
K5	Knowledge–transfer process	Statements about processes for knowledge transfer
K6	Knowledge–retention process	Statements about processes of knowledge retention
K7	Knowledge–loss process	Statements about processes of knowledge loss

TABLE 8.2   Category, property and dimension

Cat	Property	Dimension	
C2	WORK ATTRACTIVENESS	NOT ATTRACTIVE	ATTRACTIVE

The process of allocating properties and dimensions to categories is a highly effective way of becoming sensitized to extreme characteristics in the data. *Constant comparison* of categories, properties and dimensions is at the core of grounded theory methodology. The constant comparison process works in the following way. Each time a new instance of an existing category, or property, is found in the data, it is compared with previous instances of the same category and property and with their definitions. If the new instance does not fit the definition, then either the definition must be changed so that it fits the new instance and all previous instances, or a new category, property or dimension (with definition) must be created.

Another example of analysis leading to the identification of several properties associated with a single category arose in a study of the implementation of planned organizational change in contrasting organizational contexts. One of the important choices that managers had in the implementation process was found to be the level of formality they employed in the definition and communication of plans and controls in the change project. Four properties of this category were generated by the constant comparative process (Table 8.3). The dimensions of each property reflected the spectrum of formality.

TABLE 8.3   *Four dimensioned properties of planning formality*

Property	Dimensions
Level of detail	Broad . . . Detailed
Flexibility	Flexible . . . Rigid
Pre-definition	Emergent . . . Predetermined
Desirability	Desirable . . . Undesirable

By considering the range of properties and dimensions, the conditions under which they are maximized or minimized, their major consequences and their relation to other categories, theoretical ideas are developed. It emerged, for example, that one of the reasons for high levels of predetermination of project plans was the desire to objectify the project, thereby distancing its undesirable consequences from management intent.

The fifth and sixth entries in the data passage, [C2-WORK ATTRACTIVENESS-LONG HOURS] and [C2-WORK ATTRACTIVENESS-HIGH EARNINGS], are further examples of coding, the first self-generated and the second *in vivo*. Both are examples of coding at three levels, plus a dimension, for example as follows:

Level 1:	C2 (internal context)
Level 2:	WORK ATTRACTIVENESS
Level 3:	EARNINGS
Dimension:	HIGH

The manager is saying that both these properties, which are related but subtly distinct features of work attractiveness, are absent in the organization. The two new properties are added to the table of properties and dimensions (see Table 8.4).

There is no need to be consistent throughout your coding schema about the number of levels and sub-levels you use. You may find that some aspects of your analysis lead you to code at more levels than others.

The final two entries are [K6-RETAIN STAFF THROUGH WORK ATTRACTIVENESS] and [MEMO IN THIS FIRM WORK ATTRACTIVENESS MAY BE RELATED TO K7]. The manager appears to be concerned that people (and, therefore, knowledge) are being lost because the work is unattractive. The memo expresses a tentative theoretical proposition that might be developed through comparison with work attractiveness in other organizations.

As well as acknowledging the inevitability of the process of theorizing being an ever-present feature at all stages of a grounded theory study, you should not delay starting analysis of your data any longer than necessary. If you are conducting a series of interviews do not wait until you have done them all before you start the process of transcription and analysis. You may well discover threads in your earlier interviews that will determine how you conduct later ones, even in the same case study.

The use of diagrams and data maps is helpful in starting the process of

TABLE 8.4   New properties, sub-properties and dimensions

Property	Sub-property	Dimension	
WORK ATTRACTIVENESS	OPPORTUNITY TO WORK OVERTIME	HIGH	LOW
WORK ATTRACTIVENESS	EARNINGS	HIGH	LOW

understanding your data. Three types of diagram are commonly used by grounded theorists. The first type is a *time-scaled representation of events*, which is particularly useful in understanding change over time. Instances of data that pinpoint the respondent's recollection of the chronology of events can be coded with a simple indicator, for example [CHRON]. All such indicators can be searched and events placed on a time-scaled diagram covering the period of interest. Particularly 'busy' parts of the diagram can be expanded in more detail in further diagrams. When two or more respondents' accounts show disagreement over the timing of events this can be a phenomenon of interest in its own right, and can lead the researcher to seek explanations and further, confirmatory data from other sources.

The second type of diagram is referred to by Strauss and Corbin (1990: 163) as a 'paradigm model'. It consists of a systematized cause-and-effect schema which the researcher uses to map instances of data and explicate relationships between categories. Strauss and Corbin's paradigm model contains six elements arranged as a sequential model:

causal conditions → phenomenon → context → intervening conditions →
action/interaction strategies → consequences

The third type of diagram is called a *conditional matrix*. To aid the identification of relationships between data instances, Strauss and Corbin recommend the graphical tracing of *conditional paths* on a *conditional matrix*. The conditional matrix represents a set of *levels* drawn as eight concentric circles, each level corresponding to different aspects of the social world. Moving from the outer circle to the inner, the levels are labelled as follows (Strauss and Corbin, 1990: 163):

(1) International (2) National (3) Community (4) Organizational and Institutional (5) Sub-Organizational and Sub-Institutional (6) Group, Individual, Collective (7) Interaction (8) Action.

A simpler form of paradigm model, with only three components, can be useful for management researchers who are concerned with stimulus–organism–response patterns (see Figure 8.3). The model places the informant's cognitive process (organism) at centre stage, between environmental stimulus and their action or intent (response). Similarly, the conditional matrix may be simplified for the specific purposes of a particular study.

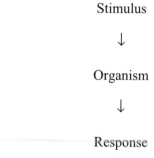

FIGURE 8.3   *The simplified paradigm model*

MOVING FORWARD

The previous section was about getting started with data collection, coding and analysis. When generating grounded theory it is essential that these three operations are done simultaneously, from the beginning of a study to its end. At the start, somewhat more emphasis will naturally be placed on data collection, but as the study progresses the balance will shift towards analysis. The analytical process gradually pervades all research activity. Analysis become easier and more purposeful, even during the act of data collection. As a narrowed set of data categories and their relationships draws into focus it becomes clearer how *theoretical sampling* can help to enrich the theory, make it more generalizable and draw the study to a conclusion.

Theoretical sampling is one of the key features of grounded theory methodology. It is a fundamentally different concept from statistical random sampling, where researchers are both guided and restricted by the well-established rules of statistical inference. Statistical samples are required to be representative of some population, and large enough to draw conclusions that are statistically significant at a stated level. Grounded theorists are unrestricted by such rules. They can and should take full advantage of opportunities for theoretical sampling, allowing the data collection strategy to be driven by emerging theoretical ideas. The role of theoretical sampling is to enable the researcher to maintain control over the theory development process. This is achieved by deliberately seeking to *maximize* or *minimize* selected *differences* and *similarities* between cases, and thus between instances of data that underlie categories and their properties.

Maximizing selected similarities (and minimizing selected differences) from one case to the next enables the researcher to collect more similar instances of data which could support the existence of a category and its theoretical properties. At the same time it provides the opportunity to seek out important new differences which were not revealed in previous cases. For example, different organizational units or sub-units of a similar size may be studied. This can highlight and confirm theoretical properties relating to size, and determine the conditions under which those categories exist. At the same time it can emphasize differences which are independent of size. Another example of the strategy of maximizing similarities is to study more than one case in the same firm. Data from two similarly sized workgroups in the same organization could confirm properties relating to workgroups of that size in the organization as a whole, whilst drawing attention to further categories and properties relating to differences in, for example, workgroup task or leadership style.

Maximizing selected differences (and minimizing selected similarities) between cases increases the likelihood that new and unexpected data will be found relating to a category. At the same time it can reveal unforeseen similarities in apparently contrasting case settings. For example, in a study of change management (reported in Partington, 2000) data collected in a public sector hospital case setting pointed to important categories and properties arising from its public nature. The next case, which was selected because the company was similarly sized but privately owned, happened to be a heavy engineering company. This example of maximizing difference enriched understanding of categories and properties relating to the public/private ownership dimension. At the same time it allowed the development of further important categories and properties concerning the fact that both organizations employed a large number of highly qualified technical specialists.

Theoretical sampling can operate within cases as well as between them. For example, early interviews in an organization might lead to the identification of some important additional informants who had not been considered at the start. Even within an interview, theoretical thoughts and ideas can suggest new avenues of enquiry.

SOLIDIFYING THE THEORY

As the study progresses, the joint processes of constant comparison and theoretical sampling lead to consolidation and simplification of the grounded theory. This happens in three ways.

First, the analytical approach changes from comparing new instances with previous instances, to comparing new instances with previously identified properties. Picking up the *formality* example from a previous section, later incidents were compared with the property that formality of communication of organizational change project plans was avoided under certain circumstances, especially when formal plans were seen to be a way of judging the failure of a project. Wilful avoidance of formality became a property which then became integrated into the analysis. By the end of the study the properties themselves had become integrated. The properties for *formality* were combined into a single property relating simply to its extent of enaction, with avoidance being linked to dimensions of personal control, the core, integrating construct of the study.

Second, *theoretical saturation* is reached. Theoretical saturation is achieved when no new categories or properties are found, and all further instances of data merely add to the bulk of specific instances of already-discovered categories and properties. When this point in the analytical process is reached, it becomes instinctively clear to the analyst that the time has come to allow the emerging theory to solidify.

Third, there is a *reduction in the list of categories and properties* in the coding schema. The typical pattern is that, in the early stages, the coding schema grows rapidly to accommodate a mass of instances which do not fit existing categories and/or their properties. As the theory solidifies, the analysis becomes focused on a core, over-riding set of categories which form the new theory. Some categories are seen to be unimportant and are discarded. Others are found to overlap and are combined. The process of integrating categories with their properties is a key element in this later analytical stage.

To complete the change management example, the study's conclusions may be summarized in three statements. First, managers implementing initiatives of planned organizational change apply a general repertoire of six common management processes, each of which is employed to a greater or lesser extent at any time (response). Second, the extent of enaction of each process element may be considered as an expression of the change drivers' possession or pursuit of personal control over the change (organism). Third, feelings of personal control are partly determined by managers' attention to selected issues which arise from key characteristics of the organization and its sector (stimulus). The final list of categories were combined into an integrated model of change management. Further theoretical output of the study was a series of propositions linking S–O–R combinations in 'trios'.

The key point about the solidification stage of grounded theorizing is to suspend conclusion as long as possible, and in particular, until the three stages described above have fully happened. There can be a temptation to close the analysis too soon, before the full theoretical richness of the data has been allowed to inform the theory. Premature closure is often accompanied by a tendency simply to search for confirming examples of theoretical ideas in the data, and to offer these as evidence in the written theory. Grounded theorists should search relentlessly for instances which do *not* fit emerging categories, properties, definitions and theories, and therefore necessitate changes in order to accommodate them. The aim is to produce a theory which fits *all* the data, rather than one which *usually* works.

A common issue for grounded theorists who are learning their research skills concerns the extent to which they should go back to recode and re-analyse all their earlier data in the light of emerging coding schemas and theoretical developments. Usually there is no need, provided the new categories become saturated. If they do not, there may be a need to recode earlier data, especially if the unsaturated category is core to the theory. The decision whether or not to recode also relates to the way in which the final written theory will be presented. If the aim is to present a series of case studies which have been carefully constructed to a common format to allow for ease and transparency of *comparison*, then recoding earlier data (and rewriting earlier case study drafts) to the final form will result in an output that is more consistent and therefore easier to understand. If the intent is to focus on the solidified theory, drawing on selected instances from a variety of cases, recoding will not be so important.

TABLE 8.5   *Ten examples of grounded theory studies in the field of management and organization*

Authors	Subject matter
Brown and Eisenhardt (1997)	Product development
Hargadon and Sutton (1997)	Innovation
Burgelman (1994)	Strategic business exit
Gersick (1994)	Pacing strategic change
Yan and Gray (1994)	Joint ventures
Prasad (1993)	Work computerization
Gioia and Chittipeddi (1991)	CEO's role in change
Kram and Isabella (1985)	Peer relationships
Dunn and Swierczec (1977)	Planned organization change
Turner (1976)	Information complexity and disasters

CONVEYING CREDIBILITY

Conveying the credibility of a grounded theory study presents its writer with two major challenges. The first is getting the reader to understand what the theory is. The second is communicating a convincing trail of evidence from data to theory. This section examines these challenges and concludes with a summary of practical guidelines and criteria which are commonly used for judging the quality of written grounded theory.

What is the theory?

Different scholars have held different views of what theory is, and the essence of the debate is conveyed in Chapter 3 of this book. Published grounded theories appear in a variety of forms, often using combinations of fine grained description, abstract models or frameworks, concepts and theoretical propositions. In order to appreciate this variety it is useful to look at some exemplars of published work. Locke (2001) traces the adoption and adaption of grounded theory approaches in published studies of management and organization through three decades, from its first appearances in the domain in the early 1970s. In her thorough, scholarly text she identifies a variety of more or less formal ways in which grounded theory processes have been applied to the study of a range of topics, from a range of perspectives, including modern, interpretive and postmodern. The selection of ten empirical exemplars listed in Table 8.5 gives an idea of the range of this work. It is beyond the scope of this chapter to analyse the different forms of theoretical output in these and other publications. However, in one of the chapter's study questions you will be invited to examine one or more of these papers and test them out against the set of quality criteria which concludes this section.

What is the trail of evidence from data to theory?

The second challenge in writing grounded theory is presenting a vivid, credible trail of evidence showing exactly how the theory was developed from the data. Large volumes of qualitative data do not easily lend themselves to neat summarization, and it is common for grounded theory writers to lead their readers through several stages of data reduction, each representing a progressively higher level of theoretical abstraction. For example, in multiple comparative case study work the stages of reduction might consist of some or all of the following:

1 written individual case studies, each in the same format for easy comparison, using quotes from data to illustrate points;
2 a summary tabulation at the end of the case, again in a common format;
3 a descriptive cross-case comparison which draws together all cases;
4 a summary tabulation of the cross-case comparison;
5 summary models and theoretical propositions.

It is important at all stages to stay close to the data, and not to make leaps of faith. A useful device is to ask, for each new assertion, 'exactly where in the data does it say that?'.

The growth in application of qualitative research methods has been accompanied by a concern that reports based on such methods should be of good quality. Miles and Huberman (1994: 277) state that the concern is not just that of convincing positivists that 'naturalistic enquiry is no more biased or inaccurate or imprecise than their methods', but that issues of quality in qualitative studies deserve attention on qualitative researchers' own terms. Miles and Huberman (1994: 278–80) offer a number of helpful pointers for judging the quality of qualitative research. These are grouped into four sets, listed below.

1 Issues of *objectivity/confirmability*, including the explicit description of methods and procedures, and of assumptions, as well as a clear linking of conclusions to condensed data displays.
2 Issues of *reliability/dependability/auditability*, including the clarity of research questions, of the researcher's role, and the specification of basic paradigms and analytic constructs.
3 Issues of *internal validity/credibility/authenticity*, including the comprehensiveness and plausibility of the account, the use of triangulation or the existence of a coherent explanation for not using it, the seeking of negative evidence and rival explanations, and the agreement by informants of essential facts and evidence.
4 Issues of *external validity/transferability/fittingness*, including the explicit identification of informants, the diversity of cases, the consistency with readers' experiences, the 'thickness' of description, the generic nature of processes and outcomes described in conclusions.

CONCLUSION

A common way of classifying approaches to generating theory is to distinguish between inductive and deductive theorizing, and the term 'grounded theory' is often used generically to denote inductive theorizing. In practice, the neat distinction between induction and deduction is of limited use since theorizing will always involve the iterative use of both processes, with the added ingredient of inspiration (Langley, 1999).

Doing grounded theory is not an easy option. Because of its emphasis on fine-grained analytical detail it does not naturally suit all temperaments. It demands a high degree of persistence, patience, sustained concentration and mental flexibility. The analytical process can be worryingly messy. It can generate feelings of weariness and lack of control, particularly in the early stages of a study. Suspending conclusion in such a process is particularly difficult, and can result in a tendency to draw weak theoretical conclusions too early.

However, for those who are forearmed with courage, a clear purpose and a realistic view of the time and intellectual effort required, grounded theory research can be both exciting and rewarding. The payoff comes as the moment of theoretical solidification is approached, characterized by the flowing release of theory that is powerful, realistic and, because it is grounded in data, difficult to refute. The ever-changing contextual backdrop of organization and management presents a limitless succession of opportunities for building new grounded theory.

Study questions

1 The section in this chapter entitled 'Writing grounded theory' lists several published studies of organization and management which claim to have used a grounded theory approach. Take one or more of these and assess them against Miles and Huberman's checklist of criteria.
2 Conduct an audio-taped unstructured interview with a manager, with the purpose of discovering what is currently important to them in the workplace. Transcribe and code the interview. Develop a coding schema with categories and, where possible, properties and dimensions. Be self-critical of your interviewing style.
3 Conduct a similar study as in study question 2, but collect data by shadowing a manager for a day and recording your observations.

Recommended further reading

Glaser, B.G. and Strauss, A.L. (1967) *The Discovery of Grounded Theory: Strategies for Qualitative Research*. Chicago: Aldine. (An influential text still in print and a must for anyone who wants to understand the origins of grounded sociological theory)

Locke, Karen (2001) *Grounded Theory in Management Research*. London: Sage. (A thorough, scholarly exposition which places grounded theory in context, discusses its processes and procedures, and explores its application in organization and management studies)

Strauss, A.L. and Corbin, J.M. (1990) *Basics of Qualitative Research: Grounded Theory Procedures and Techniques*. Beverley Hills, CA: Sage. (Aimed at social scientists from all disciplines, and especially novice researchers, and offering a step-by-step approach)

References

Argyris, C. (1979) 'Richard Neustadt and Harvey V. Fineberg: The Swine Flu Affair: Decision Making on a Slippery Disease', *Administrative Science Quarterly*, 24 (4), pp. 672–9.

Bhaskar, R. (1975) *A Realist Theory of Science*. Leeds: Leeds Books.

Blaikie, N. (1993) *Approaches to Social Enquiry*. Cambridge: Polity Press.

Brown, S.L. and Eisenhardt, K.M. (1997) 'The Art of Continuous Change: Linking Complexity Theory and Time-paced Evolution in Relentlessly Shifting Organizations', *Administrative Science Quarterly*, 42, pp. 1–34.

Burgelman, R.A. (1994) 'Fading Memories: A Process Theory of Strategic Business Exit in Dynamic Environments', *Administrative Science Quarterly*, 39, pp. 24–56.

Dunn, W.N. and Swierczec, F.W. (1977) 'Planned Organization Change: Toward Grounded Theory', *Journal of Applied Behavioral Science*, 13, pp. 136–57.

Eisenhardt, K.M. and Bourgeois, L.J. (1988) 'Politics of Strategic Decision Making in High Velocity Environments: Towards a Midrange Theory', *Academy of Management Journal*, 31, pp. 737–70.

Gersick, C.J.G. (1994) 'Pacing Strategic Change: The Case of a New Venture', *Academy of Management Journal*, 37 (1), pp. 9–45.

Gioia, D.A. and Chittipeddi, K. (1991) 'Sensemaking and Sensegiving in Strategic Change Initiation', *Strategic Management Journal*, 12, pp. 433–48.

Glaser, B.G. and Strauss, A.L. (1967) *The Discovery of Grounded Theory: Strategies for Qualitative Research*. Chicago: Aldine.

Hargadon, A. and Sutton, R.I. (1997) 'Technology Brokering and Innovation in a Product Development Firm', *Administrative Science Quarterly*, 42, pp. 716–49.

Huber, G.P. and Power, D.J. (1985) 'Retrospective Reports of Strategic-level Managers: Guidelines for Increasing their Accuracy', *Strategic Management Journal*, 6, pp. 171–80.

Kram, K.E. and Isabella, L.A. (1985) 'Mentoring Alternatives: The Role of Peer Relationships in Career Development', *Academy of Management Journal*, 28 (1), pp. 110–32.

Langley, A. (1999) 'Strategies for Theorizing from Process Data', *Academy of Management Review*, 24 (4), pp. 691–710.

Locke, Karen (2001) *Grounded Theory in Management Research*. London: Sage.

Miles, M.B. and Huberman, A.M. (1994) *Qualitative Data Analysis*. Thousand Oaks, CA: Sage.

Partington, D. (2000) 'Building Grounded Theories of Management Action', *British Journal of Management*, 11, pp. 91–102.

Partington, D., Tranfield, D., Young, M., Bessant, J. and Sapsed, J. (2001) 'Mapping Contexts of Application: A Grounded Approach to Understanding the Key Dimensions of Organizational Environments.' Paper presented at *Academy of Management*, Washington DC, August.

Pfeffer, J. (1995) 'Mortality, Reproducibility, and the Persistence of Styles of Theory', *Organization Science*, 6, pp. 681–6.

Prasad, P. (1993) 'Symbolic Processes in the Implementation of Technological Change: A Symbolic Interactionist Study of Work Computerization', *Academy of Management Journal*, 36, pp. 1400–29.

Silverman, D. (1993) *Interpreting Qualitative Data: Methods for Analyzing Talk, Text and Interaction*. London: Sage.

Silverman, D. (2000) *Doing Qualitative Research: A Practical Handbook*. London: Sage.

Strauss, A.L. and Corbin, J.M. (1990) *Basics of Qualitative Research: Grounded Theory Procedures and Techniques*. Beverley Hills, CA: Sage.

Turner, B.A. (1976) 'The Organizational and Interorganizational Development of Disasters', *Administrative Science Quarterly*, 21, pp. 378–97.

Van Maanen, J. (1979) 'Reclaiming Qualitative Methods for Organizational Research: A Preface', *Administrative Science Quarterly*, 24 (4), pp. 520–6.

Weick, K.E. (1993) 'The Collapse of Sensemaking in Organizations: The Mann Gulch Disaster', *Administrative Science Quarterly*, 38, 628–52.

Yan, A. and Gray, B. (1994) 'Bargaining Power, Management Control, and Performance in United States–China Joint Ventures: A Comparative Case Study', *Academy of Management Journal*, 37 (6), pp. 1478–517.

9

Case Study Research

Alan Harrison

OVERVIEW

Many management students associate 'case studies' with hours spent arguing over such epics as *The Cola Wars* and *How Chrysler Corp Came Back From the Dead*. Apart from their well-known teaching uses, case studies are also widely used for management research. Here, however, the track record is less consistently favourable, and case study research is sometimes criticized as being comparatively weak. Much of this criticism is related to variability in the nature of scholars' claims that their research is 'case study-based'. There are perhaps too many examples where case studies have been used to parade 'best practice' which has been derived from relatively superficial evidence and analysis. Yet some of the major contributions to theory in the social sciences have been based on evidence from case studies. Examples of such contributions include Whyte's (1955) *Street Corner Society* and Allison's (1971) *Essence of Decision: Explaining the Cuban Missile Crisis*. Studies such as these are often lengthy and resource-intensive in nature, and yet, depending on the scope of the phenomenon being studied, case study research does not have to emulate such a level of detail. Nevertheless, the researcher who seeks to conduct case-based social enquiry of a quality that is competitive with other approaches should start by understanding that there are no short cuts.

In spite of such health warnings, to those of us who are proponents of case study methods, there is no more satisfying or enjoyable way to carry out management research, and there are several clear advantages. First, there is a continual 'reality check' with what is being researched. What you see and hear poses a constant challenge to your emerging theoretical ideas. Second, there is an almost endless choice of research methods – both qualitative and quantitative – that can be deployed under the case study banner. Third, because it is essential to draw a boundary around your study, the circumstances under which the conclusions apply are normally apparent.

Case study research is of particular value where the theory base is comparatively weak and the environment under study is messy. Both these criteria apply to research into operations management (OM), and as an active researcher in that field of management studies I will be using a number of OM examples to illustrate the issues at stake.

This chapter explores the strengths and weaknesses of case study research from the point of view of research design, and examines the practicalities of conducting case study research. Readers will develop their understanding of:

- What case study research is and what it is not.
- How case study research interfaces with other methods of social enquiry.
- Applications of case study research in theory development.
- Designing case study research.
- What makes for good case study research.

While the initial sections investigate case study theory issues, the last section on carrying out case study research is essentially practically-oriented.

THE CASE STUDY 'POINT OF VIEW'

A key issue for the researcher is how to get to grips with the chosen research questions. Two time-honoured 'solutions' are *induction* and *deduction*. Inductive enquiry moves from observation to the development of general hypotheses, while deductive research uses general statements derived from a priori logic to explain particular instances. Arguments have raged about which of the two approaches represents true scientific method, but Wallace's combination of inductive and deductive strategies, shown in Figure 9.1, suggests that both inductive and deductive methods are intimately related in the activities of doing empirical research and theorizing.

In this conception of the cyclical relationship between theory and evidence, the distinction between induction and deduction becomes blurred. Blaikie (1993: 156) asks, 'is it possible to combine these two strategies and thereby [to] capitalize on their strengths and minimize their weaknesses?' Wallace argues that both theory-generation and theory-testing processes are inevitably part of science. Further, he asserts that one can start research at any point on the cycle. While Wallace's scheme may not explicitly have been applied to social constructs, it helps to promote thinking on the possible cyclical nature of theory-building and theory-testing. The importance of such thinking to case study researchers is that they are placed in an environment where such interplay between building and testing theory is not only feasible, but is characteristic. This is what I referred to as a 'reality check': researchers are being constantly challenged to confirm or disconfirm theory from the wealth of evidence that surrounds them. The strategy that is used to describe the interplay of induction and deduction is called *retroduction* (see for example Blaikie, 1993: 162ff; Ragin, 1994: 47). Observed relationships between phenomena lead to postulation of the existence of structures or mechanisms which, if they existed, would explain the relationships. These are then tested by further research activity designed to isolate or observe them, or to eliminate alternative explanations.

Another research strategy that helps to underpin the case study researcher's point of view is *analytic induction*, which directs researchers to be attentive to evidence that challenges or disconfirms their emerging theoretical ideas. The

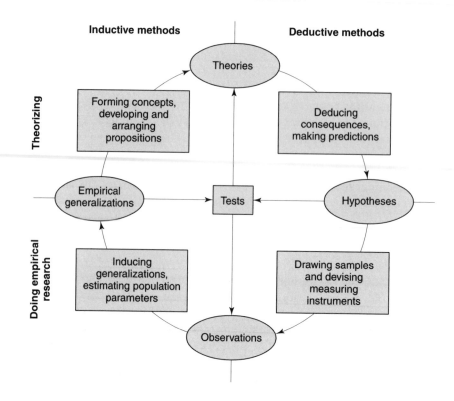

FIGURE 9.1 *Combining inductive and deductive strategies (after Wallace, 1971)*

constant comparative, grounded theory method described by Glaser and Strauss (1967) uses the establishment of similarities and differences among incidents to define and refine concepts and categories, but normally stops short of testing theory. Analytic induction uses a comparative approach, but goes a step further by both generating and testing theories. Ragin (1994: 93 and 183) defines analytic induction as 'any systematic examination of commonalities that seeks to develop concepts or ideas across a limited number of cases'. Katz (1982) comments that analytic induction is poorly labelled because it is not a technique of pure induction. Researchers work back and forth between theory and evidence, trying to achieve what Katz calls a 'double fitting' of explanations and observations.

The cyclical or spiral process of analytic induction has been depicted by Meredith (1993: 4; see Figure 9.2). Adding to his basic model, a continuous, repetitive cycle from exploration to description to explanation to testing is conceived. 'Throughout this iterative process, descriptive models are expanded into explanatory frameworks which are tested against reality until they are eventually developed into theories ... the result is to validate and add confidence to previous findings, or else invalidate them ...' (Meredith, 1993: 3). If explanation is ignored, he argues, we have 'black boxes' where there is no understanding of the phenomena. If testing is ignored, we have

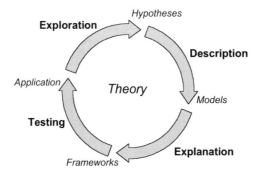

FIGURE 9.2   *Exploration – description – Explanation – testing cycle (after Meredith, 1993)*

'war stories', where each new explanation takes the field into a new direction. Ignoring the description phase leads to 'ivory tower prescriptions', where research findings are disconnected from reality. Meredith's conceptualization of an iterative process underlines the special opportunity with case study research for a rich dialogue between ideas and evidence. It also highlights the need for frequent overlap between data analysis and data collection.

Theory development

Meredith et al. (1989: 300) comment that 'OM research has failed to be integrative, is less sophisticated in its research methodologies than the other functional fields of business, and is, by and large, not very useful to operations managers and practitioners.' This lack of practical usefulness has been blamed by several authors on the prescriptive solutions derived from application of operations research/management science (OR/MS) methods in OM research. Such methods are characterized as heavily quantitative in nature and based on applications of multivariate statistical techniques.

These concerns are not limited to OM, and Ragin (1987) has articulated similar views in relation to sociological research. A summary of his views is presented in Table 9.1, which draws distinctions between *variable-oriented* and *case-oriented* research. Variable-oriented research is based on the application of multivariate statistical techniques, delivers broad generalizations and seeks average influence across a variety. Case-oriented research is based on the application of multiple methods that seek to account for all deviating cases. While creating a rich dialogue between theory and evidence, conclusions are specific to the (relatively few) cases examined. As always, you can't have it all ways!

But Starbuck (1995) raises some complementary issues which are relevant here.

- A true statement about a population may not apply to any individual case.
- Generalizing impedes true understanding: properties shared by all organizations are superficial, obvious or unimportant.

TABLE 9.1   *The dichotomy between variable-oriented and case-oriented research in the social sciences*

Issue	Variable-oriented	Case-oriented
Basis of research	Quantitative Multivariate statistical techniques Many data sets	Multiple methods to establish different views Qualitative and quantitative Few data sets
Scope	Wide categories Broad empirical generalizations based on heterogeneous samples Comparability ignored/skirted	Narrow classes of phenomena Several combinations of conditions may yield a certain outcome
Causality	Disaggregated into variables and distributions Based on analysis of entire population or sample	Probabilistic relationships not accepted Must account for all deviating cases
Conclusions	Vague and abstract 'Unreal quality' of conclusions More concrete questions do not receive the attention they deserve	Few general conclusions Separate contexts
Theory/ data link	Radically analytic Strictly a priori Link between research and actual empirical processes strained	Rich and elaborate dialogue Strong link between research and actual processes
Aggregation	Breaks into parts – variables which are difficult to reassemble into wholes. Not combinatorial	Holistic: parts related to context of whole
Complexity	Average influence across a variety	Sensitive to complexity and historical specificity, but difficult to sustain attention to complexity across a large number of cases
Relevance	Broad: general statements linked to abstract theoretical ideas about generic properties	Narrow: findings specific to few cases examined

Source: After Ragin, 1987

- Following averages can lead us to being misled into thinking how organizations are the same, when what matters is *how they are different* (emphasis added).
- Large samples and statistical significance generate 'significant' findings that have no meaning.
- Large sample statistics deflect attention from individuality, complexity and variety.

Survey-based research of large populations necessarily adopts many of the deficiencies of variable-oriented research. All too often, the output – while accurate – is dull, bland and uninteresting. Lawler (1985) states that 'organizations are studied by researchers that never see them! The result is rather antiseptic descriptions of organizations and the development of theories from these. To a degree, broad brush is the enemy of research that influences practice' (1985: 11).

A further problem with such research is that of assuming comparability of elements in what are, in reality, very disparate samples, whatever Cronbach's alpha coefficient may indicate! For example, Bratton (1992) comments on survey-based organizational behaviour (OB) research into Japanization in mechanical engineering establishments listed under Standard Industry Classification 32:

> the classification includes a wide range of firms from low technology 'metal bashing' workshops, to high-technology precision engineering establishments. Equally, it became clear that the respondents' understanding of terms like 'new technology', even when closely defined in the questionnaire, proved to be different . . . (1992: 13)

Overcoming the problems of bias in sample selection, in completion of questionnaires, in how issues for the questionnaires themselves are selected and worded, and in reliability and validity analysis are familiar problems of survey research. But most problematic of all is the artificial disaggregation of variables into questions, accompanied by some assessment scale that requires the respondent to distinguish between such criteria as 'high, medium and low'. It is the task of the researcher to abstract from the particular (12% labour turnover last year) to the general ('high'). Mintzberg (1979: 587) states: 'I believe the researcher shirks his [sic] responsibility when he expects the manager to do the abstracting.' Apart from creating problems of interpretation and data collection for the individual who has the onerous task of filling in the questionnaire, such disaggregation denies the dynamic and holistic nature of operations systems and fails to address the complexity of the interconnections involved. Such problems are compounded by the relative remoteness of the researcher, who may pay only token visits to the firms involved.

As Swamidass (1991: 798) argues, 'field based research can narrow the gap between practice and research because it takes the researcher to the field for dialogue and observation'. He continues by contesting that 'some OM topics that are too fuzzy and messy, for example . . . JIT implementation, are under-researched because they are unsuitable for deductive methods of research'. In an area where the theoretical base is weak, 'field based approaches are the best ways to find out about the issues, describe the problems, discover solutions and generally ground our theory in the complex, messy world of real organizations' (McCutcheon and Meredith, 1993: 248).

THE POSITION OF CASE-BASED RESEARCH

It is appropriate at this point to review the position of case-based research with respect to other approaches in OM. A helpful framework has been adapted for OM by Meredith et al. (1989: 309) after Mitroff and Mason (1982), shown here as Figure 9.3.

Sources and kind of information used in the research

Natural _____ Artificial

	Approach to knowledge generation	Direct observation of object reality	People's perceptions of object reality	Artificial reconstruction of object reality
Axiomatic				• Reason/logic theorems • Normative/descriptive modelling
Logical positivist/ empiricist	• Field studies • Field experiments	• Structured interviewing • Survey research	• Prototyping • Physical modelling • Laboratory experimentation • Simulation
Interpretive	• Action research • Case studies	• Historical analysis • Delphi/expert panel • Intensive interviewing • Introspective reflection	• Conceptual modelling

(left axis top: Rational; bottom: Existential)

FIGURE 9.3   *Framework for research methods (Meredith et al., 1989)*

Two dimensions shape the framework and define the philosophical basis for research activity. First, the *rational/existential* dimension (the *y* axis) defines truth from 'out there' (independent of human experience) to 'in here' (based on individual interpretation). At the 'rational' pole, research tends to be deductive, formally structured and concerned with coherence with 'laws'. At the 'existential' pole, the research process is more inductive, more subjective and concerned with correspondence with the real world rather than with existing laws. Second, the *natural/artificial* dimension (the *x* axis) defines the source and nature of data used in the research. At the 'natural' pole, the research process is more concerned with the 'real' phenomenon and with validity, less concerned with reliability, closer to reality and more current. At the 'artificial' pole, the research process uses highly abstracted and simplified models, is highly controlled and efficient, but is less current.

Meredith et al. (1989: 308) go on to assert that the critical issue is between reliability and external validity, stating that, 'survey instruments provide very reliable data but their validity in actually measuring constructs is sus-pect . . . the most valid information is obtained by direct involvement with the phenomenon'. While I find Meredith's framework a useful rationalization of a complex web of possible research processes, case study research is actually an envelope for several possible research methods – more accurately referred to as a *research strategy*. Thus, structured interviews, field studies and surveys are all possible methods which can be deployed under the case study banner. As Yin (1994: 92) points out, 'the case study enquiry . . . relies on multiple sources of evidence, with data needing to converge in a triangulating fash-ion . . .'

There is, however, a cautionary note to the application of under-utilized research methods in a new area. Of the three types of case study research identified by Yin (descriptive, exploratory and explanatory), Swamidass (1991: 797) argues that 'an inspection of published field-based empirical articles by OM researchers shows that they are predominantly exploratory and use the most rudimentary form of analysis . . . for the most part, the collection of empirical research in this area is not driven by the desire to test and establish one or more well-known OM theories'. Flynn et al. (1990: 251) observe that, 'although the proportion of empirical OM research is increasing relative to OM modelling research, empirical research with a strong conceptual and methodological base is less common'.

Rigour in case study research

Such concerns argue for rigour in case study research. Yin (1994: 33ff) lists four tests 'commonly used to establish the quality of any empirical social research'. These are discussed below.

- *Construct validity*: establishing correct operational measures for the concepts being studied. While you may select a set of measures in your research design, case study research is relatively forgiving. Hartley (1994) refers to the 'open ended nature of much data gathering' – if things don't add up, try something else. It is difficult to get it right the first time, so I favour studies based on multiple sources of evidence.
- *Internal validity* (for explanatory case studies): establishing a causal relationship whereby certain conditions are shown to lead to other conditions as distinguished from spurious relationships. As indicated above in Figure 9.2, one is circulating between theory and evidence, so case study research provides an ongoing opportunity to test causal relationships. Throughout the data gathering process keep asking yourself 'does this make sense?' – against your hypotheses, against other data and against existing theory.
- *External validity*: establishing a domain to which a study's findings may be generalized. Table 9.1 suggests that the relevance of case study findings is narrow, because findings based on a single case are hard to generalize. Instead, case study research can be generalized to theory: one 'non-conforming' case is sufficient to challenge a theory that should encompass it!
- *Reliability*: demonstrating that the operation of a study – such as the data collection procedures – can be repeated with the same results. It is usually impossible to repeat data collection exactly, because the conditions have changed. But demonstrating that you have the detailed evidence available (for example, taped interviews, transcripts and coding) and that you have analysed that data in a systematic way that others could repeat is a key reliability test. Other reliability tests such as having interviewees to check over transcripts, and repeating the coding with independent researchers, are further examples of good practice.

Eisenhardt (1989) proposes a roadmap for theory-building from case study research, shown as Table 9.2. This process contains much sound advice for assuring rigorous research design. Eisenhardt argues that the theoretical

TABLE 9.2 *Process of building theory from case study research*

Step	Activity	Reason
Getting started	Definition of research question Possibly a priori constructs Neither theory nor hypotheses	Focuses efforts Provides better grounding of construct measures Retains theoretical flexibility
Selecting cases	Specified population Theoretical, not random sampling	Constrains extraneous variation and sharpens external validity Focuses efforts on theoretically useful cases – i.e. those that replicate or extend theory
Crafting instruments and protocols	Multiple data collection methods Qualitative and quantitative data combined Multiple investigators	Strengthens grounding of theory by triangulation of evidence Synergistic view of evidence Fosters divergent perspectives and strengthens grounding
Entering the field	Overlap data collection and analysis, including fieldnotes Flexible and opportunistic data collection methods	Speeds analyses and reveals helpful adjustments to data collection Allows investigators to take advantage of emergent themes and unique case features
Analysing data	Within-case displays Cross-case pattern search using divergent techniques	Gains familiarity with data and preliminary theory generation Forces investigators to look beyond initial impressions and see evidence through multiple lenses
Shaping hypotheses	Iterative tabulation of evidence for each construct Replication, not sampling, logic across cases Search evidence for 'why' behind relationships	Sharpens construct definition, validity and measurability Confirms, extends and sharpens theory Builds internal validity
Enfolding literature	Comparison with conflicting literature Comparison with similar literature	Builds internal validity, raises theoretical level, and sharpens construct definitions Sharpens generalizability, improves construct definition, and raises theoretical level
Reaching closure	Theoretical saturation when possible	Ends process when marginal improvement becomes small

Source: Eisenhardt, 1989

insights of case study research arise from methodological rigour and multiple-case logic. While I support the point about methodological rigour, it is possible to substitute subsets within a single corporation, as she herself argues in a subsequent paper (Eisenhardt, 1991). The key point is to provide the variety that is needed to test emergent case study theory from several different perspectives. As Ragin observes (1987: 52), 'notions of sampling and sampling distributions are less relevant to [the case study] approach because it is not concerned with the relative distribution of cases with different patterns of causes and effects. More important than relative frequency is the *variety* of meaningful patterns of causes and effects that exist.' Case study

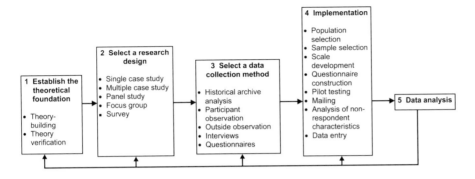

FIGURE 9.4   *A systematic approach for empirical research (after Flynn et al., 1990)*

research does not accept probabilistic relationships: *all* deviating cases must be accounted for. The guiding principle, as Yin (1994: 45) points out, is one of replication, not of sampling logic. Case selection should be on the basis of *literal replication* (which predicts similar results), or *theoretical replication* (which predicts contrasting results but for predictable reasons). Replication with other cases highlights similarities and differences that demand further investigation or explanation. Such thinking adds to the strength of case study approaches in terms of 'building new theories and synthesizing existing theories' (Ragin, 1987). This goes to the heart of the *comparative method* of social science: explaining variation.

Figure 9.4 presents a seven-stage process for conducting empirical research (Flynn et al., 1990: 254). At stage 1, a theory-building or theory-testing foundation is selected. At stage 2, the empirical research design is selected, and at stage 3 appropriate data collection method(s) to go with the research design are determined. At stage 4, the research is operationalized, and at stage 5 the data are analysed. Finally, the research is published. I have added feedback loops to interconnect stages 1 to 5.

Unit of analysis

A problem in conducting case study research is where to draw the line. You enter a treasure trove of fascinating data and can be dragged off in any one of numerous directions. Sooner or later you have to determine the *boundary* of your research. Defining the case as the unit of analysis, Miles and Huberman (1994: 25) describe the boundary as 'somewhat indeterminate'. In practice, the boundary will often define itself reasonably well if you have clarified your research objectives. In my study at Rover Cars, a massive car assembly process employing thousands of people was linked to many off-line processes such as design and production planning. By determining that the focus of the research was to be the flow of materials and information within the factory, the boundary eventually defined itself. Figure 9.5 shows how it turned out.

The definition of the project boundary was key to operationalizing the research. It had to be painstakingly discovered by a familiarizing process of

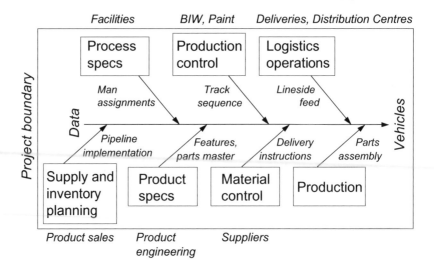

FIGURE 9.5   *The unit of analysis at Rover Large Cars*

interviewing a lot of people and sense-checking against the research objectives. The boundary defined what had to be investigated in further detail, and what processes (such as suppliers, body in white (BIW) and product engineering) would be excluded.

Triangulation

Many management research textbooks refer to the advantages of mixing qualitative and quantitative approaches. For example Firestone (1987) proposes that quantitative studies de-emphasize individual judgement and stress the use of established procedures, leading to more precise and generalizable results. Qualitative research, on the other hand, produces rich depiction and strategic comparison across cases, thereby overcoming the 'abstraction inherent in quantitative studies'. These considerations address the increasing concerns of researchers in the OM area about the imbalance between qualitative and quantitative methods and the poor link between theory-building and theory-testing research. Jick (1979: 608) lists four advantages of multi-method research:

1 Researchers can be more confident of their results.
2 Deviant or off-quadrant dimensions of a problem may be uncovered, leading to enriched explanation of the research problem.
3 Synthesis or integration of theories is facilitated.
4 Triangulation may serve as the critical test, by reason of its comprehensiveness, for competing theories.

The significant thread linking these benefits is the closeness and sensitivity that qualitative methods bring to the triangulation process: 'Qualitative data and analysis function as the glue that cements the interpretation of multi-method results' (Jick, 1979: 609). The researcher seeks *convergence* between qualitative and quantitative perspectives of the same phenomenon.

Analytical framework

Pettigrew (1990, 1992) stresses the need for a 'meta level' analytical framework to enable change to be studied in different environments without theory limitations in comparative case study research. There are three primary considerations: context, content and outcome variables. First is the *context* in which the long-term change process takes place. There are two aspects to consider: the *outer context*, which includes the economic, social, political and sectoral environment in which the firm is located, and the *inner context*, which refers to features of the structural, cultural and political environment through which ideas for change proceed. Second is the *content* of the parcel of interventions that comprise the 'change' (the 'what'). Content also describes the *process* by which the change is delivered (the 'how'). Process is here defined as 'a sequence of events that describes how things change over time' (Van de Ven, 1992). Pettigrew (1992: 10) argues that, while they have traditionally been researched separately in the field of organizational change management, content and process are best regarded as inseparable. The 'historical, developmental perspective . . . which thereby focuses on the sequences of incidents, activities and actions unfolding over time' provides a mechanism for tracking the emerging differences between two or more units of analysis. These differences emerge as *outcome variables*, the third consideration of the meta-level model. Outcome variables describe what it is that is being explained. There are 'great advantages to having a clear outcome to explain in strategy research'. An example of an outcome variable was the differential rate of change between health authorities who confronted similar, centrally imposed reorganizations. While the change content (the reorganization) was the same for each, the outcome variables (for example, service levels) differed – suggesting that different change strategies had been followed. The challenge for the researcher is to describe the process of change, and to link it to the different outcomes. Again, this demonstrates the power of the comparative method combined with case study research: explaining the causes of variation between different outcomes.

Pettigrew's research design seeks to control complexity by building constancy into the study by controlling the content, and by defining a constant unit of analysis to facilitate cross-case comparison. The outcome variables must be clearly identified and measured. Finally, as implied above, Pettigrew stresses the basic importance of time ('truth is the daughter of time', 'catching reality in flight', and so forth). It is necessary to make decisions on the time frame of the research (retrospective, historical, real time, longitudinal).

CARRYING OUT CASE STUDY RESEARCH

As Hartley (1994) states, there has been a dearth of advice about the practical steps of carrying out case study research. A useful starting point is to consider the fit between the researcher's style and the context of the phenomenon under study. Taking the researcher's style first, this could be broadly categorized as a range between two extremes.

- *Structured*: the researcher develops a detailed 'game plan' in the research design, identifying all of the variables against which data will be collected, together with an interview framework and possible coding scheme. An example is Teagarden et al.'s study (1995) of an international human resources management project.
- *Unstructured*: the researcher chooses not to make any detailed game plan, but to view the research as a 'voyage of discovery' which should have no preconceived format that may otherwise act as a restriction to what is observed. An example is Delbridge's (1998) ethnographic study of 'life on the [assembly] line'.

Equally, the context of the phenomenon under study can be categorized as a range between:

- *Fixed*: the phenomenon under study is comparatively stable. Some researchers prefer to study the effects of change processes after they have settled down, perhaps 2–3 years after the package of changes was introduced. An example is my study of the changes resulting from introduction of the Honda-designed Rover 600 automobile onto manufacturing processes designed for the traditional Rover 800 (Harrison, 1998).
- *Dynamic*: the phenomenon under study is evolving rapidly. Examples are the formation of supplier associations (Aitken, 1998) and the virtual organization as an instrument of change (Franke, 1999).

These categories can be combined in a matrix of different research strategies, as suggested in Figure 9.6. The researcher with a preference for unstructured methods such as grounded theory (see Chapter 8) would, for example, address an unchanging ('fixed') phenomenon in a heuristic way. The phenomenon exists, but the researcher adapts the method to the context. In a changing environment with a dynamic phenomenon under study, the researcher with a preference for unstructured methods is faced with a 'Two-way' voyage of discovery in that both the research method and the phenomenon are evolving. To the researcher who prefers unstructured work, the risk is to become 'overwhelmed by data and/or to be drawn into narrative rather than theory building' (Hartley, 1994: 219). A focus for the research is needed, as indicated above under the *unit of analysis* subsection. To the researcher who prefers a highly structured research framework, the risk is to close one's mind to new or emerging possibilities because they are not 'in the game plan'.

Here are some tips from my own research and from that of some of our doctoral students, arranged in five stages suggested by Yin (1994). These are: selecting the case; conducting the study; analysing the case study evidence; developing the conclusions; reviewing the data collection protocol.

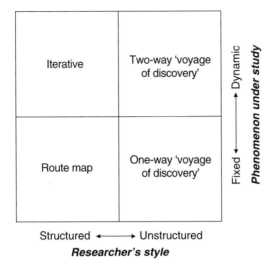

FIGURE 9.6   *Four possible research strategies*

Selecting the case

Once it has been decided that a case study approach will be used, the research objective should be the starting point for selecting which case to use. For Bolumole (1999), this narrowed the field to just three. She researched the role of third party logistics providers in facilitating the integration of convenience retail supply chains, and there just aren't that many. For most other researchers, there are many possibilities and the problem is how to select the 'best'. 'Best' in practice actually means not only the best environment for exhibiting the phenomenon under study, but also the best from a point of view of ease of access and of management support. The latter is often the scarcer resource! Personal knowledge and contacts are often valuable to start with. Carrying out your first case study in an organization you already know well saves a lot of time in understanding the context, and in developing contacts. Thus, Koulikoff-Souviron used her former employer as the proving ground for research design (Koulikoff-Souviron and Harrison, 2001). While this was planned as a prototype case that would yield limited results, she found that the high level of support, help in selecting relevant parts of the organization to carry out the research and familiarity with the context have combined to provide a bonanza of rich data. This significantly raises expectations for the selection of the next case!

Another effective way to select case studies is to carry out a preliminary survey. In a study of innovation in German organizations, Lohmüller (in Goffin et al., 2000) discovered that survey results could be categorized according to percentage turnover of new products (number of new products divided by total number of main products in the portfolio) and the innovation rate (the proportion of last year's sales revenues arising from significantly new products launched during the past three years). This is shown in Figure 9.7.

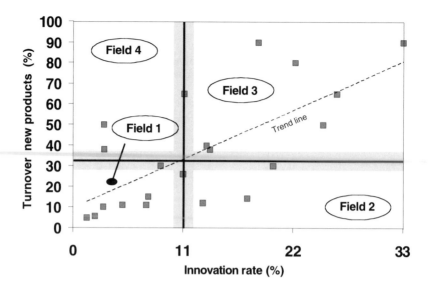

FIGURE 9.7   *Initial survey data suggest a trend and 'outliers' that merit
further investigation*

Extreme positions in either or both of these categories suggested firms that should be selected for deeper, case-based research. Organizations tend to respond positively to unsolicited approaches if you have a clear purpose and they can see the potential relevance and value of your research output to them. There will be disappointments from time to time, for example due to preoccupation with a major reorganization. However, in many organizations the prospect of a bright, theoretically informed student investigating in depth a phenomenon of current interest is normally irresistible!

Conducting the case study

Even if you are a researcher with a preference for a structured approach, a period of orientation in a new case environment will be essential. Here, an internal project champion will be of great benefit, and someone who has worked with the organization a long time, who knows everyone and who is familiar with the area you want to research is often preferable to a member of the top team. Apart from you getting to know the organization, the orientation period is also the opportunity for the organization to get to know you. This is a period of 'heavy duty communications' – becoming familiar with the research context and explaining your interests and plans to those who need to know.

The orientation period closes when you feel confident that you have gained enough knowledge to begin your research. You know in which groups interviewees could be selected, how to extract data from the IT systems, which meetings to attend and so on. A key output from this period is the identification of the unit of analysis – what will form the 'case' in your project. This identification may well benefit from further iterative work to refine your initial ideas, but it is a key consideration, helping to answer the important question 'what is/what is not included?'

Qualitative aspects of case study research have much in common with comments on grounded theory and action research in Chapters 8 and 13 of this book. An excellent framework is also included in Miles and Huberman (1994: 50ff). For case study work in particular, it is important to ensure variety, and that you have sampled sufficient points of view to develop a balanced picture. Pettigrew (1990: 277) states 'crucially, data collection is concerned with observation and verification'. A helpful guideline for selecting interviewees is Pettigrew's concept of 'supporters, opponents and doubters'. When selecting informants, try to obtain a range of views from a wide body of opinion. In my experience, it is the opponents who present much richness of data – it is they who will tell you what is wrong with a process, or challenge or disconfirm the prevalent view. Identification of these polar types will come from the orientation period, by preliminary informal interviews with each member of a group, or by asking who they are. A further consideration in selection is how many to choose? Clearly, case study research does not claim to yield results that are statistically significant. But the sampling must reflect the need for observation and verification. Thus, one would expect to interview informants from all seven of the sub-processes in the unit of analysis in Figure 9.5.

Facts and figures, or supporting 'quantitative' evidence, come from a variety of sources. For the purposes of comparative research, it is essential to have a robust research design that allows evidence to be collected for comparable variables. However, data that are easy to collect in one case are often very difficult and laborious to find in another. I determined that one of my measures of material flow was to be overall equipment effectiveness (OEE, Nakajima, 1989), which measures the percentage of total available hours a production line is creating value (that is, it isn't broken down, producing scrap or running slower than targeted!). In my pilot study, OEE was a nightmare to measure: there were no systematic data – for example the maintenance fitters only recorded the hours they had worked on the equipment, not the total time the equipment had been idle. Collecting satisfactory data was difficult and time-consuming. In a second case, OEE was the key measure used for measuring the performance of the factory. It was systematically calculated each month, so data collection was easy. Two conclusions can be made:

- Data are often unavailable in the form needed by your research. Stick to your research plan, and find a way round the difficulties.
- Comparative research creates particular challenges in this area. What is readily available in one case may be difficult to collect in another.

A further corollary would be: don't be excessively ambitious about your research design – keep it practicable within the limits of your resources.

Finally, don't be tempted to become a complete 'expert' in the case. There is a trade-off between knowledge and time, as suggested in Figure 9.8. There is an optimum point at which to conclude your work before the data analysis

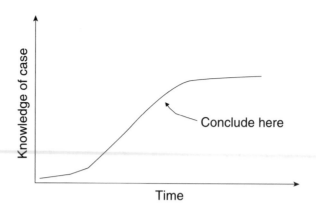

FIGURE 9.8 *Knowing when to conclude*

becomes excessive and the same points keep repeating themselves. You understand this from experience – you have reached the point of diminishing returns, but have not explored every nook and cranny.

Analysing case study evidence

Statistical methods cannot be applied to broad case study conclusions because there are more variables than cases. Instead, analysis begins in the field as the researcher records notes of what has been perceived, makes initial interpretations and tests hypotheses during subsequent phases of data collection. The initial focus is therefore on the pattern of variables within a case, that is, on the parts in relation to the whole. For a piece of qualitative research, the variables may have been derived from predetermined codes, developed during data analysis of transcribed interviews using aids such as NVivo (Richards, 1999) or by analysing fieldnotes. If additional data have been obtained from 'hard' variables (in other words continuous variables such as line speeds and inventory levels), then these may provide further evidence. This can be very valuable in the analysis of case study data when different outcomes demand explanation. For example, part of the evidence in one of the cases I studied was provided by the different performance records of two production lines in the same factory that had shared the same changes in organization structure. The comparative outputs in tonnes/day of the two lines over the same 18-month period after these changes had been introduced is shown in Figure 9.9.

It was apparent that Line 7 was pursuing some kind of 'mis-strategy' – the output had actually been deteriorating ever since the changes had been made. Line 4, on the other hand, had been relatively stable, but had returned some of its best-ever results in recent months. Armed with this information, I returned to the qualitative data collection and analysis to find out what were the different management policies on the two lines and what those who worked in the process thought of them.

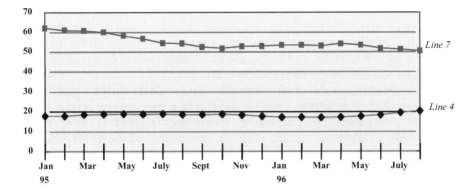

FIGURE 9.9   *Trend in outputs (tonnes/day) for two production lines in the same factory*

Whether data are hard or soft, qualitative or quantitative, the case study researcher is faced with the challenge of dealing with complexity. You have to get to grips with the complexities of the real world, and then make sense of them. Data analysis is made practicable by a robust game plan. Pettigrew (1990: 282) calls this 'routes to structured understanding', some of which are listed here:

1 Be clear about research objectives
   –   build on strengths
   –   be aware of limitations.
2 Be clear about the unit of analysis and study questions.
3 Come to terms with time.
4 Make your research method explicit.
5 Make your meta-level analytical framework explicit.
6 Make explicit the character of the generic propositions you are seeking.
7 Identify analytical themes that cut across the data.
8 Use techniques of data reduction and display.

In other words, excellence in analysis is dependent on excellence in the build-up to the analysis. The challenge of data reduction and display is thereby greatly facilitated. Miles and Huberman (1994) propose various analytic techniques such as data arrays, creating displays and tabulating the frequency of events. In comparative case-based research, consistency in data collection and analysis is essential. Yin (1994) states that every investigation should have a general analytic strategy to guide the decision as to what will be analysed and for what reason.

Developing conclusions

Developing conclusions involves linking all the variables into a 'more holistic theory' (Easterby-Smith et al., 1991: 111). This requires moving back and forth between existing theory and the patterns, themes and possible explanations that have emerged from your study. Such an iterative process helps your conclusions to take on a more grounded and explicit form. It helps to present your initial conclusions to your colleagues, to your industrial 'project champion' and at an academic conference. External critique helps you to re-evaluate your conclusions.

While conclusions will emerge from the data analysis within a given case, a greater challenge is provided by developing conclusions across cases. Extending the general analytic strategy across cases is referred to as *replication* (Yin, 1994). This means focusing on the overall pattern of results and the extent to which the observed pattern of variables matches a predicted one. If identical results are predictably obtained over multiple cases, literal replication has been obtained. If different results are obtained over multiple cases, theoretical replication has been obtained. Using a general analytic strategy greatly facilitates the task of replication.

When faced with this prospect in writing the cross-case comparison section of my doctoral dissertation, I was concerned that nothing new would emerge. The three units of analysis were completely different, and the prospect of making connections between them appeared daunting:

- *Case study 1*: unit of analysis = manufacturing cell in a tractor plant, repeated over five cells.
- *Case study 2*: unit of analysis = planning, control and assembly of cars (see Figure 9.5), repeated over two models.
- *Case study 3*: unit of analysis = production line for polypropylene film making, repeated over two lines.

While these cases had been deliberately selected for variety, one can become bogged down between such widely different products and processes. But the research task is to rationalize such differences, and to advance theories that place them in perspective to each other. Thus differences and distinctions are as important as similarities; both have a role to play in advancing knowledge. In my study, cross-case comparison was facilitated by considering:

- *Elements in common*, which provided evidence about what might indeed be 'universal best practice'.
- *Uniqueness*, which provided evidence about opportunities for application of specific practices in given situations. Uniqueness also suggested that there were potential pitfalls, which acted to reduce competitiveness.

My conclusions went on to suggest that it is the elements in common that are becoming widely shared commodities, and that it is the uniqueness area that requires special attention.

Review of data collection protocol

Review and critique are always a cleansing and reinvigorating process. No matter how good your study in terms of what was achieved, you can always do better next time. And reviews should be conducted before – as well as after – the study has been completed. During the review, several issues can be addressed, for example:

- The data cannot be collected as originally planned. This may call for an adjustment to a particular variable, or it may mean a major re-think. One of my students found that the expected data were simply not available – unknown to the project sponsor the method of production had been changed two years previously! However, it was possible to extract the needed data from archival sources, and as a bonus, to compare it with the current method. Such tactics are often important in conducting case study research.
- The data analysis process proves to be inefficient, and a new method may be called for. When analysing my first case, I used an unstructured data analysis software package. While this may have been appropriate for my colleagues in unstructured qualitative research, it was unhelpful to my more structured approach. It added little value to my method, and took a long time to learn and to operate. A more efficient way for me was to enter the codes into interview transcripts in a word processing package, and to use search, and cut and paste features. While progress in the design of qualitative data analysis software is constantly being achieved, in-depth analysis by the researcher should not be short-circuited.
- Opportunities are being missed. While distractions must be avoided, there may be occasions when important opportunities present themselves. The test is the extent to which such opportunities help to advance the achievement of research objectives.
- Conclusions conflict with the literature. While this may be perfectly valid (you are right and your forbears are wrong – although such black and white distinctions are unusual in the social sciences), this is a challenge to 'build internal validity, raise theoretical level and sharpen construct definitions' (see Table 9.2).

The review process is a challenge for continuous improvement of the research design, and is thus an integral part of carrying out case study research.

CONCLUSION

Case study research is more aptly described as a strategy than a method. It sets out to address the understanding of a phenomenon (unit of analysis) within its operating context. Of necessity, case study research is about engaging with the complexities of the real world, and about making sense of them. The researcher is faced with the challenge of coping with large amounts of data, defining the scope of the study, collecting data in a coherent way, analysing data in a replicable way and condensing the complexity into something that is logical and understandable to others. These are no mean challenges, but the rewards are deeper insights into reality than are possible with other approaches to social enquiry. Case study research is flexible and can be adapted to many areas of knowledge creation. And the researcher is continuously confronted with the question 'does this make sense?'

Study questions

1 Why is it important to have a structured research design in comparative case-based research? Does this conflict with a desire to use theory-building approaches to data collection?
2 Review Eisenhardt's roadmap in Table 9.2. What helps to create high-quality case study research?
3 Review and critique two papers from the literature in which case study methods have been used. Use Eisenhardt's roadmap to help in your analysis. What are the strengths and weaknesses of the methodology used?

Recommended further reading

Miles, M.B. and Huberman, A.M. (1994) *Qualitative Data Analysis*, 2nd edn. Thousand Oaks, CA: Sage. (Produced by two educationalists, an essential *vade mecum* for conducting qualitative research in the social sciences. An excellent all-round text that takes the reader from the contribution of qualitative methods through to data display)

Ragin, C.C. (1987) *The Comparative Method: Moving beyond Qualitative and Quantitative Strategies*. Berkeley: University of California Press. (Another excellent text that lays down the rationale for qualitative research and how it compares with research based on multivariate statistical methods, written from the perspective of a 'poacher turned gamekeeper')

Yin, R.K. (1994) *Case Study Research: Design and Methods*, 2nd edn. Thousand Oaks, CA: Sage. (A systematic text that takes the reader through many of the aspects of case study research. Robert Yin has consistently promoted case study methods from an era when they were little used. An 'essential read')

References

Aitken, J. (1998) 'Integration of the Supply Chain: The Effect of Inter-Organisational Interactions between Purchasing-Sales-Logistics'. PhD thesis, Cranfield University.

Allison, G.T. (1971) *Essence of Decision: Explaining the Cuban Missile Crisis*. Boston, MA: Little Brown.

Blaikie, N. (1993) *Approaches to Social Enquiry*. Cambridge: Polity Press.

Bolumole, Y. (1999) 'Outsourcing Logistics: The Supply Chain Role of Third Party Service Providers'. Proceedings of the 3rd Annual Conference of the Logistics Research Network, The Institute of Logistics and Transport, Corby.

Bratton, J. (1992) *Introduction to Japanization at Work*. London: Macmillan, pp. 1–16.

Delbridge, R. (1998) *Life on the Line in Contemporary Manufacturing: The Workplace Experience of Lean Production and the Japanese 'Test' Model*. Oxford: Oxford University Press.

Easterby-Smith, M., Thorpe, R. and Lowe, A. (1991) *Management Research: An Introduction*. London: Sage.

Eisenhardt, K.M. (1989) 'Building Theories from Case Study Research', *Academy of Management Review*, 14 (4), pp. 532–50.

Eisenhardt, K.M. (1991) 'Better Stories and Better Constructs: The Case for Rigour and Comparative Logics', *Academy of Management Review*, 16 (3), pp. 620–7.

Firestone, W.A. (1987) 'Meaning in Method: The Rhetoric of Quantitative and Qualitative Research', *Educational Researcher*, 17, pp. 16–21.

Flynn, B.B., Sakakibura, S., Schroeder, R.G., Bates, K.A. and Flynn, E.J. (1990) 'Empirical Research Methods in Operations Management', *Journal of Operations Management*, 9 (2), pp. 250–84.

Franke, U.J. (1999) 'The Virtual Web as a New Entrepreneurial Approach to Network Organizations', *Entrepreneurship and Regional Development*, 11, pp. 203–29.

Glaser, B. and Strauss, A. (1967) *The Discovery of Grounded Theory: Strategies of Qualitative Research*. New York: Aldine.

Goffin, K., Lohmüller, B., Pfeiffer, R., Szwejczewski, M. and New, C. (2000) 'Exploring the Relationship between Innovation Rate and Revenue in German Manufacturing Companies', 7th International Product Development Conference, Leuven, Belgium, 29–30 May.

Hartley, J.F. (1994) 'Case Studies in Organizational Research', in C. Cassell and G. Simon (eds), *Qualitative Methods in Organizational Research: A Practical Guide*. London: Sage.

Harrison, A.S. (1998) 'A Comparative Study of Lean Production Metrics in an Automotive Assembler', *International Journal of Logistics – Research and Applications*, 1 (1), pp. 27–38.

Jick, T.D. (1979) 'Mixing Qualitative and Quantitative Methods: Triangulation in Action', *Administrative Science Quarterly*, 24, pp. 602–11.

Katz, J. (1982) *Poor People's Lawyers in Transition*. New Brunswick, NJ: Rutgers University Press.

Koulikoff-Souviron, M. and Harrison, A. (2001) 'Human Resource Practices in Supply Chain Relationships: An Empirical Study'. Proceedings of the Sixth International Symposium on Logistics, Salzburg.

Lawler, E.E. (1985) 'Doing Research that is Useful in Theory and Practice', in *Challenging Traditional Research Assumptions*. San Francisco: Jossey–Bass, pp. 1–17.

McCutcheon, D.M. and Meredith, J.R. (1993) 'Conducting Case Study Research in Operations Management', *Journal of Operations Management*, 11, pp. 239–56.

Meredith, J. (1993) 'Theory Building through Conceptual Methods', *International Journal of Operations and Production Management*, 13 (5), pp. 3–11.

Meredith, J.R., Raturi, A., Amoaka-Gyampah, K. and Kaplan, B. (1989) 'Alternative Research Paradigms in Operations', *Journal of Operations Management*, 8 (4), pp. 297–326.

Miles, M.B. and Huberman, A.M. (1994) *Qualitative Data Analysis*, 2nd edn. Thousand Oaks, CA: Sage.

Mintzberg, H. (1979) 'An Emerging Strategy of "Direct" Research', *Administrative Science Quarterly*, 24 (4), pp. 582–9.

Mitroff, I.T. and Mason, R.O. (1982) 'Business Policy and Metaphysics: Some Philosophical Considerations', *Academy of Management Review*, 7 (3), pp. 361–71.

Nakajima, S. (ed.) (1989) *TPM Development Programme*. Portland, OR: Productivity Press.

Pettigrew, A.M. (1990) 'Longitudinal Field Research on Change: Theory and Practice', *Organization Science*, 1 (3), pp. 267–92.

Pettigrew, A.M. (1992) 'The Character and Significance of Strategy Process Research', *Strategic Management Journal*, 13, pp. 5–16.

Ragin, C.C. (1987) *The Comparative Method: Moving beyond Qualitative and Quantitative Strategies*. Berkeley: University of California Press.

Ragin, C.C. (1994) *Constructing Social Research*. Thousand Oaks, CA: Pine Forge Press.

Ragin, C.C. and Becker, H.S. (eds) (1992) *What is a Case? Exploring the Foundations of Social Enquiry*. New York, NY: Cambridge University Press.

Richards, L. (1999) *Using NVivo in Qualitative Research*. London: Sage.

Starbuck, W. (1995) 'Learning from Accidents and Extreme Cases', keynote address to BAM Conference, Sheffield.

Swamidass, P.M. (1991) 'Empirical Science: New Frontier in Operations Management Research', *Academy of Management Review*, 16 (4), pp. 793–814.

Teagarden, M.B., Glinow, M.A., Bowen, D.E., Frayne, C.A., Nason, S., Huo, Y.P., Milliman, J., Arias, M.E., Butler, M.C., Geringer, J.M., Kim, N.-H., Scullion, H., Lowe, K.B. and Drost, E.A. (1995) 'Toward a Theory of Comparative Management Research, an Idiographic Case Study of the Best International Human Resources Management Project', *Academy of Management Journal*, 38 (5), pp. 1262–87.

Van de Ven, A.H. (1992) 'Suggestions for Studying Strategy Process: a Research Note', *Strategic Management Journal*, 13 (Summer Special Issue), pp. 169–88.

Whyte, W.F. (1955) *Street Corner Society: The Social Structure of an Italian Slum*. Chicago: University of Chicago Press.

Yin, R.K. (1993) *Applications of Case Study Research*. Thousand Oaks, CA: Sage.

Yin, R.K. (1994) *Case Study Research: Design and Methods*, 2nd edn. Thousand Oaks, CA: Sage.

10

Cognitive Mapping

Mark Jenkins

OVERVIEW

The purpose of this chapter is to introduce the reader to the technique of cognitive mapping as a basis for conducting management research. Whilst I have attempted to be as even handed as possible in terms of giving a balanced overview of some of the alternative approaches, I have inevitably focused on those aspects which I have found worked for me as a researcher. Management research is a highly personal process and one in which the researcher has to decide what will work for them in a given project. With this in mind, the objective of the chapter is to provide an insight into the approach of cognitive mapping and to consider its strengths and weaknesses as a research tool. It is not intended to be an authoritative review or a definitive account, it is simply a perspective which will, I hope, inform the reader as to whether or not this is an approach that warrants further exploration.

It is also fair to say that a secondary objective is to encourage 'good' mapping research. Whatever epistemological biases you may have it is always possible to distinguish good research from superficial or inherently biased approaches. I therefore hope that this chapter encourages the reader to consider cognitive mapping as a research approach, but at the same time enhances their understanding of some of the issues in developing high-quality management research.

COGNITION AND MANAGEMENT RESEARCH

In order to understand the principles that underpin cognitive mapping we first need to reflect on the role of cognition in offering insights into managers, their behaviours and the organizations within which they operate. The concept of cognition originates from the field of psychology and more specifically cognitive psychology. It developed as an alternative theory of human behaviour to that of the behaviourists (Skinner, 1938), so called because their explanation of human behaviour used the stimulus–response (S–R) model, the position being that the behaviour of an individual could be wholly explained by the stimulus which was applied. The field of cognitive

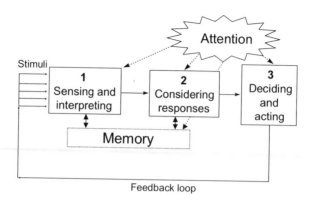

FIGURE 10.1 *A simple schematic of the cognitive process (developed from an original model by Wickens, 1984)*

psychology developed as an alternative perspective placing greater emphasis on concepts such as perception, attention and memory and therefore considered the S–R explanation of behaviour too simplistic. The cognitive perspective is based on the intervening effect of the 'organism', and specifically cognitive processes such as perception, attention and memory, between stimulus and response. This is therefore referred to as the S–O–R model (Broadbent, 1958). A simple representation of the cognitive process is shown in Figure 10.1.

In Figure 10.1 we see a series of stimuli which are 'sensed' by the individual, this sensing being combined with a process of perception by which we first become aware and then 'make sense' of the stimuli based on our previous experience. For example, a pricing move by a competitor would be first identified, then interpreted as a tactical move to improve their year-end figures, or as a shift in strategy to build long-term market share. This process draws on prior experience held in memory and allows us to determine whether or not we need to act and if so in what way. These actions are then reviewed to see if the desired outcomes are achieved. The concept of attention is an important one in that it assumes cognitive processing ability as a limited resource and therefore one which we direct to the areas that we see as more beneficial to us. In a novel situation attention would be focused on receiving stimuli in order to gain a better understanding, but in more routine situations attention may be given more to accessing prior experience in memory than to new information being received.

The study of cognition is therefore based on the premise that there are intervening processes between stimulus and response that we have to understand in order to explain human behaviour. In a management context these assumptions translate into the notion that a manager's cognitive processes will determine the external stimuli to which they are more sensitive, the way in which they 'make sense' of such stimuli, and the actions they choose to pursue in response to the stimuli. Whilst the causal relationship between thought and action is still largely conceptual rather than empirical, it is important to recognize that, as a methodology, cognitive mapping is founded on the position that a cognitive processing function or, if you prefer, 'conscious mind', both exists and directly influences behaviour or actions of individuals operating within organizations. If we accept the role of a cognitive process – which may not always be appropriate, such as in the behavioural or 'impulsive' aspects of consumer behaviour (Foxall, 1997) – the epistemological question which follows is how do we begin to represent these processes in a valid and reliable way? This is one of the questions cognitive mapping seeks to address. In this context the term cognitive is used relatively loosely to encompass a range of domains and approaches which represent aspects of these processes. For example, a causal map is a cognitive map that is concerned with representing cognition as a series of causal connections between concepts; a repertory grid is also a cognitive map in that it identifies how a stimulus is mapped on a construct. Some cognitive maps may also represent shared cognitions (Langfield-Smith, 1992) and are therefore underpinned by socio-cognitive rather than purely cognitive concepts (Ginsberg, 1990). In this sense the term cognition is used in a way that would probably appal many cognitive psychologists. However, management research is more often concerned with richly complex settings and the cognitive approach provides a very important perspective for how individuals and groups deal with this complexity. The emphasis of cognitive mapping is to attempt to capture a situation through the eyes (or minds) of those organizational actors who are engaged in interpreting and responding to the situation. The application of cognitive mapping approaches is essentially based on an interpretivist philosophy which is concerned with how individuals interpret their environment.

As the concept of cognition assumes some form of cognitive structure various authors have attempted to develop their own terms, either to generically capture the concept of structure, or to imply some particular aspect or application of cognitive process. Terms you may well come across which are synonymous with a cognitive structure are: schema (Brewer and Nakamura, 1984; Cossette and Audet, 1992); mental model – a term often used to refer to categoric approaches to understanding individual views on competitive environments (Hodgkinson and Johnson, 1994); belief system (Sproull, 1981; Walsh, 1988); frame (Minsky, 1975) or frame of reference (Shrivastava and Mitroff, 1983); cognitive map (Tolman, 1948; Eden, 1992); heuristic, a term normally associated with judgements in decision-making (Sherman and Corty, 1984), or script, which represents behaviours or sequences of action that are appropriate in particular situations (Gioia and Poole, 1984). Whilst the frameworks outlined so far have tended to be concerned with individual or managerial cognitive structures, researchers have also applied these ideas to the organizational level of analysis. There is clearly an issue around applying theoretical concepts developed to represent individual cognitive structures to the organizational level, however this has not dissuaded researchers from reifying the organization to have human cognitive qualities such as memory (Walsh and Ungson, 1991) and frames of reference (Shrivastava and Schneider, 1984) and allowing them to be represented as cognitive maps (Weick and Bougon, 1986).

The application of cognitive mapping approaches to the management field is a relatively recent phenomenon. Early work on cognitive mapping in organizational contexts can be traced back to work in the public policy area in the 1970s (Axelrod, 1976), but most of its application to the management and business contexts has taken place over the past 20 years. The momentum for this has been a desire to balance the objectivist perspective of disciplines such as economics with a greater development of interpretivist research. The following call for researchers to adopt cognitive mapping approaches is illustrative of this motivation:

> Even though managerial cognition must figure prominently in strategy-making, top managers' thinking is seldom explicitly mentioned in the academic or business literature on strategic management ... ... Since Strategic Management studies the activities of managers, and since managers must think about strategy, why don't researchers allocate more research to studying how strategic managers think? (Stubbart, 1989: 326)

COGNITIVE MAPPING APPROACHES

I provide here an illustration, rather than an exhaustive account of some of the more widely applied – or perhaps more accurately, more widely published – applications of cognitive maps.

In Anne Huff's seminal book on cognitive mapping, *Mapping Strategic Thought* (Huff, 1990), she reviewed the field by defining five categories of maps. These are outlined in Figure 10.2. The first category refers to maps that assess attention, association and importance of concepts. These would be approaches that might quantitatively compare the occurrence of concepts in interviews or other material, in other words a basic form of content analysis – for example, a PhD student at my institution compared organizations by the frequency of use of the term 'empowerment' in meetings and corporate documentation to try to evaluate their focus on giving employees more autonomy. The second group involves maps that show dimensions of categories and cognitive taxonomies. In this group the maps are concerned with representing the way in which concepts are grouped both in terms of how abstract or specific these groups are (taxonomies) but also in terms of the criteria being used to assign membership to a particular group. For example, if a manager defines an event as a threat rather than an opportunity what criteria is he or she using to make this allocation? The third group involve maps that show influence, causality and systems dynamics. An example of this might be a CEO's view of business which is represented by a virtuous circle where higher levels of service provide greater levels of customer satisfaction which generate greater levels of business, which in turn allow more investment in staff development which increases the level of service. Here what is being mapped is how an individual believes the business operates in terms of a system of concepts that affect each other in a positive or negative direction. The fourth category involves maps that show the structure of argument and conclusion – here we have a greater focus on decision-making which draws on areas such as philosophy, rhetoric and linguistics. Finally, the fifth category

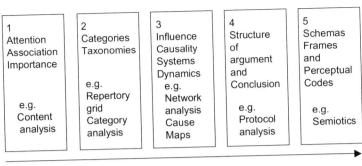

1	2	3	4	5
Attention Association Importance	Categories Taxonomies	Influence Causality Systems Dynamics	Structure of argument and Conclusion	Schemas Frames and Perceptual Codes
e.g. Content analysis	e.g. Repertory grid Category analysis	e.g. Network analysis Cause Maps	e.g. Protocol analysis	e.g. Semiotics

Increasing interpretive input from researcher

FIGURE 10.2   *Anne Huff's five categories of maps (Jenkins, 1998: 234)*

is concerned with maps that specify schemas, frames and perceptual codes. This is the most complex form of map and one which draws on linguistic structure and cognitive psychology more directly, involving more complex inter-relationships between concepts and assumes the existence of a deep underlying structure. A more detailed discussion of these groupings is available in Chapter 1 of Huff's (1990) book.

Studies that use and apply cognitive maps

In order to discuss some of the issues in applying cognitive mapping approaches I have selected two of these categories: maps that are concerned with categorical and taxonomic structures and maps that are concerned with causal structures. The reason I have focused on these two areas is that this is where most of the existing research has focused and therefore new researchers have a reasonable body of literature to draw on. I have also selected these types of map as they particularly lend themselves to applications in practical contexts where we are interested in the more detailed perspective of individuals in a managerial situation. I personally find category 1 lacking in the richness that I am interested in exploring, but I also find that categories 4 and 5 require a great deal of interpretation by the researcher in order to create a coherent map. This can be very useful in some situations, but as I am generally more interested in understanding individual interpretations of situations, then these approaches tend to move too far away from the views as expressed by the individual for my own preference.

I have used three studies as examples of cognitive mapping research and review this section by drawing on some of the contrasts between the studies.

Cognitive maps as taxonomies

The construction of categories, taxonomies or typologies is widely accepted as being a fundamental cognitive activity. In order to make sense of a concept I need to categorize it in order to understand how I need to respond. To undertake this process I look for attributes which are similar to other concepts I have experienced in the past or which I have learned about from other sources. For example, if I come across an ostrich for the first time I will probably try to work out what kind of animal (overall category) it is – is it a bird (it has wings) or is it a mammal (it doesn't fly)? Work by Eleanor Rosch and colleagues considers the processes by which we categorize concepts and the consequences of so doing (Rosch (et al., 1976), 1978). In the context of management research this work allows us to explore how managers categorize concepts and surmises on the implications of such processing. Porac and his colleagues have undertaken a range of studies which are concerned with the way in which managers create cognitive taxonomies of their competitive environment. One of their most widely cited studies is that on the Scottish knitwear industry (Porac et al., 1989). By mapping the way in which the CEOs of Scottish knitwear businesses viewed their competitive landscape the study showed how they focused on those who were geographically and demographically similar to themselves: 'From their point of view, no other producers can manufacture the kinds of sweaters that they manufacture. Thus when asked to discuss their competition, they focus mainly upon each other' (Porac et al., 1989: 407).

The approach used by Porac et al. in this paper involved a series of discrete stages. First they targeted 17 firms manufacturing high-quality knitwear. They used primary (interview) and secondary data to identify 'core beliefs' about how to deal with other firms in the sector. These beliefs about other firms were then used to construct a 'top-down' taxonomy working from the generic grouping of 'textiles' to identify subgroups and then subgroups within these subgroups and so on. An elicited 'cognitive taxonomy' of one of the respondents from the study is shown in Figure 10.3.[1]

The conclusion of the study revolves around the existence of 'cognitive oligopolies'. Here the authors adopt a term drawn from economics relating to industry structure to represent a phenomenon where managers cognitively limit their competitive set to those whom they are familiar with and can predict their competitive tactics. In this way taxonomies provide us with a mechanism for representing how managers organize and populate their domains. The real value of this process is that it enables us to see how managers actually see things, rather than how some of our well-honed management theories imply they should be. Another example of this is Reger's study of the Chicago banking sector, in which she looks at the dimensions managers use to evaluate competitors (Reger, 1990). One of the key findings of this study is that managers use a number of dimensions to chart competitive position which had hitherto not been emphasized in academic theory. This is really the essence of how cognitive mapping can add to management research – simply by allowing us greater insights into how managers really see things, rather than how we (as academics or researchers) think they should.

Cognitive maps as causal networks

In considering cognitive maps as causal networks I can draw on a study which is more familiar to me, as it is the basis of my earlier doctoral work and

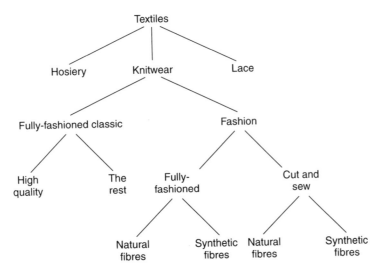

FIGURE 10.3   *Elicited 'cognitive taxonomy' of one managing director of a Scottish knitwear firm (Porac et al., 1989)*

applies a particular form of cognitive map – one that focuses on the causal connection between concepts, referred to as a causal map. The terms causal map and cognitive map are often used interchangeably. For example, one of the first collections of mapping managerial research is Axelrod's (1976) book, which focuses on public policy issues and uses entirely causal maps, which are throughout referred to as cognitive maps. Axelrod in turn draws on the work of Maruyama (1963) and Harary et al. (1965), who use mathematical approaches to understanding networks, systems and directed graphs. However, whilst most of these theoretical ideas are essentially concerned with structure rather than sense-making, in that they provide a basis for examining the cognitive maps as systems rather than as a collection of thoughts, attribution theory provides a psychological explanation for considering cognition as a series of causal relationships. Developed in social psychology, it provides a basis for understanding an individual's interpretation of actions and events through the cause and effect relationships which they believe to exist (see Augoustinos and Walker, 1995: 60–96).

One of the real strengths of causal maps is that they allow the researcher to develop a more dynamic representation of managerial cognition, in that they allow ideas to be linked together and their relationships defined in a causal sense. The idea of a virtuous or vicious circle can easily be represented on a causal map and they therefore allow us to show in more detail the way managers or groups of managers are understanding their situation. Another useful aspect of the causal map is that it lends itself to being a facilitation device, rather than solely a way of empirically representing data. Whilst there have been some very detailed analyses carried out on causal maps – for perhaps one of the more extreme examples of this see Bougon et al.'s (Bougon et al., 1977) paper on the Utrecht Jazz Orchestra – causal maps can also be used in a more interactive research approach, where they are used to facilitate debate and discussion rather than just represent data. Colin Eden's work has been particularly influential in applying causal mapping approaches to this kind of context, and his excellent book with Fran Ackermann, *Making Strategy* (1998), provides a detailed account of this process.

In a study of small business owner-managers (Jenkins and Johnson, 1997) we were interested in whether we could discern differences in the cognitive maps of businesses that were growing compared to those that were stable or declining. The sample involved 30 small retail businesses and included butchers, greengrocers, jewellers and sports shops. We used semi-structured interviews employing the laddering technique (Eden, 1988: 5; see also Chapter 12 in this volume) to develop a series of cause–effect relationships concerning the respondent's view of the business. This was achieved by undertaking a series of exploratory interviews to establish the ways in which owner-managers felt they could develop their businesses, for example these included such issues as refitting the premises, increasing the product lines covered and manufacturing their own products. These were then put on cards and at the start of each interview the respondent would be asked to identify those ideas which fitted most closely with their views on developing their business. The laddering technique simply involves the interviewer asking why a particular approach is important, the response to this question providing a causal 'ladder' to the next concept in the map. For example, if a respondent picked 'open more outlets' the interview would ask 'why is this important to you?' and the response may be 'to reduce my overheads', creating a causal linkage between these two concepts, as shown in Figure 10.4.

The interview was completed when all the issues the respondent felt were relevant had been covered and they felt they had fully explained why these were important. This semi-structured format allowed for a fair amount of discussion and digression, but it enabled the respondent to describe the business, as they saw it, which was essentially the purpose of the process.

The interview was then transcribed and a series of coders were used to review the interview transcripts and to identify the key concepts used by the respondents and the causal relationships between them. In effect, this was a form of data reduction with the coders providing a distillation of the interview data in the form of a causal map. An example map is shown in Figure 10.5.

The coders had also grouped the concepts within the maps into a series of preset categories, such as concepts that related to customers, to business measures or to personal aspirations. We were then able to group the maps based on the growth performance of the business and test out a number of a

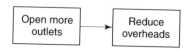

FIGURE 10.4 *Example of a causal ladder*

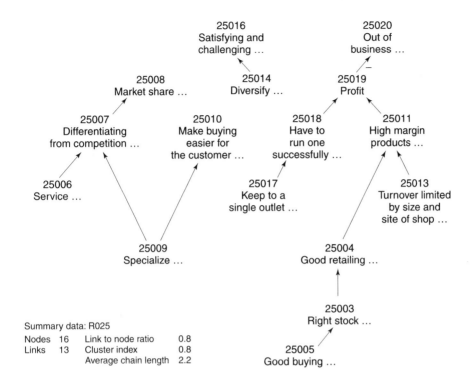

FIGURE 10.5   *Example of emergent entrepreneur (R025) (Jenkins and Johnson, 1997)*

priori propositions about what differences we might expect between the maps. For example, the literature on market orientation implies that owner-managers who are more customer-oriented are likely to be more successful and grow their business more effectively; we therefore operationalized this proposition by comparing the proportion of customer-oriented concepts in the maps of businesses that were growing compared to those that were not. We also conducted a deeper inductive analysis of the maps to generate some new questions which we framed as propositions. We were able to do this due to the rich nature of the transcripts; if we had simply asked respondents to causally connect one concept with another then we would not have been able to access this richer stream of data provided by their reflections on how the business operated. This particular study used a total of 30 causal maps, one for the owner-manager of each business. In other studies there have been fewer maps but these have involved a far more detailed assessment and complex map.

A contrasting causal mapping study to Jenkins and Johnson (1997) is that undertaken by Barr, Stimpert and Huff (1992). This study illustrates a series of causal maps which are derived solely from documentary evidence. The advantages of this approach are that it does not require access to the managers within the organization and that it also enables maps to be compared over longer periods of time, as is the case with this study, which focuses on the changing environment faced by US railroad companies in the 1950s. Researchers also argue that using secondary data concerning an organization makes the map a closer representation of the cognitions of the organization, rather than simply aggregating individual maps. However, the concerns of such an approach relate to the notion of whether an organization can have a 'cognitive map' or whether such data provide the insights into the organization which the mapping approach is concerned with eliciting. Whilst there are arguments on either side, this particular study is an excellent example of what can be achieved from such an approach. It also provides some clear conclusions on the linkages between such maps and how organizations change. The methodology used by Pam Barr and her colleagues was to use mapping as a form of content analysis using letters to shareholders from two comparative companies over a 25-year period. Data from annual reports was also used to develop a logic to each of the firm's strategies. These data sources were then assumed to provide a representation of the mental models of the top managers running each of the railroads. Once the data were collected a highly structured coding approach was applied (Huff et al., 1990; Wrightson, 1976) to create a map for each of the railroads, an example of which is shown in Figure 10.6.

Each of the three studies outlined above illustrates some of the mapping decisions researchers need to make depending on the question they seek to explore. Decisions on the nature of the source data are concerned with validity and reliability, but also the practicalities of gaining access to the right people for an appropriate length of time. These trade-offs have to be made in the context of individual research questions, the preference of individual researchers, decisions on the type of map which is to be created and the way in which the map will be developed. Porac et al. (1989) used a relatively loose and opaque process which moved from interviews and secondary data to some example maps and conclusions. In contrast, the cause mapping studies used far more explicit approaches, moving from the raw data to the creation and analysis of the maps. Again there is no one answer, but these are decisions which have to be considered depending on the aims of the study.

RESEARCH DECISIONS IN APPLYING COGNITIVE MAPS

In order to explore some of the practical steps and trade-offs that need to be made in a research study using cognitive mapping, I now focus on a framework that I introduced in a previous piece on mapping approaches (Jenkins, 1998). I refer to this framework as the mapping shield. The mapping shield is shown in Figure 10.7 and provides a useful basis for structuring the issues that the researcher needs to consider.

Step 1: Define the research context

If we consider the mapping process as a series of steps then the first has to be concerned with the research context on the right-hand side of the shield. A clear question or phenomenon should also address the issue of scope (the boundaries of the research) and the level and unit of analysis. Unless these questions are clearly addressed then no amount of complex argument or analysis will get you through a doctoral process. For example, is the study concerned with what managers do or what they think? If you are interested in what they do then find another methodology; if you are interested in what they think then you have to be clear about the domain – think about what? In the earlier study I was interested in how they thought about growth; not survival, not selling their business, but growth. This meant I needed to frame the method within the scope of the research. Level of analysis is also critical here. In my study I was concerned with an influential individual (influential in terms of their impact on the business) but you may be interested in a group process – or even, as with Barr et al. (1992), an organizational level of analysis and related data sources.

Step 2: Resolve the methodological issues

What are the ontology and epistemology which support your approach? What is cognition? How can we measure it? Is it really cognition? What theories inform the way in which the maps should be created? George Kelly's (1955) personal construct theory provides the basis for a number of approaches, including Eden's (1988), but there are others, such as Heider's (1946) theory on causality or Festinger's (Festinger, 1954) theory of social comparison. I stress the importance of being clear about a theory of cognition rather than just a theory of cognitive structure. For example, cybernetics is a theory of structure, and therefore helps us to do a great deal of analysis, but the question needs to be resolved as to what is the theory of cognition which underlies your mapping approach. From this we then move to the more challenging questions of validity and reliability. For me, validity is concerned with how close we are really getting to representing an individual's cognition. Reliability is concerned with the distribution of error and the replicability of the research. In my view much of the published work sacrifices validity for the sake of reliability. Whilst it is important to do 'good' research it is also important to do 'true' research that gets as close as possible to the phenomenon of interest. All too often we see complex approaches to analysis which produce a map that is far removed from the respondent or respondents it is claimed to represent.

One of the decisions you will have to consider concerns the use of a coding process and external coders. Mary Tucker Wrightson outlines an excellent coding scheme in Axelrod's book (Wrightson, 1976) and this is also developed in Anne Huff's book (1990: ch. 13). The adoption of coders is quite popular when documentary data sources are used. By using external coders the researcher is distancing him or herself from the detailed analysis to ensure that they are not 'directing' the analysis in any way. This is consistent with ontologies where the role of the researcher is detached from the data, but alternative approaches have been where the researcher engages in the analysis and interpretation in an open and transparent way.

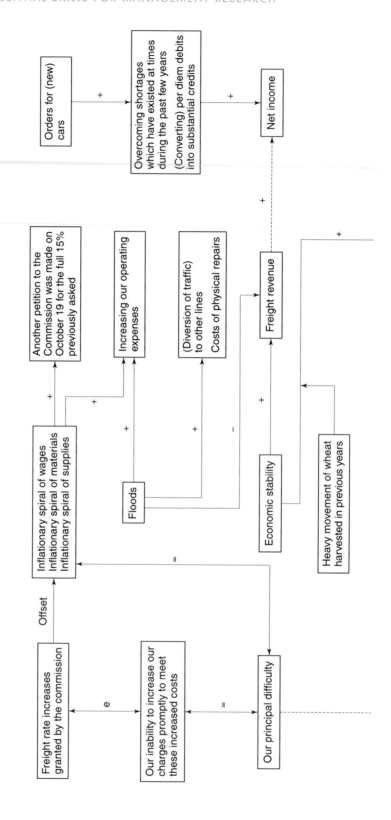

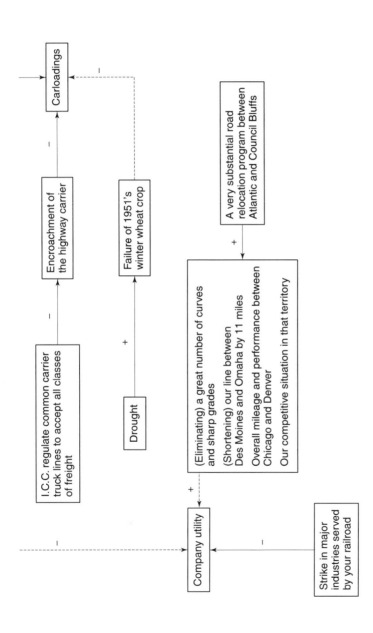

FIGURE 10.6 Example of a cause map for the Rock Island railroad company, 1951 (Barr et al., 1992)

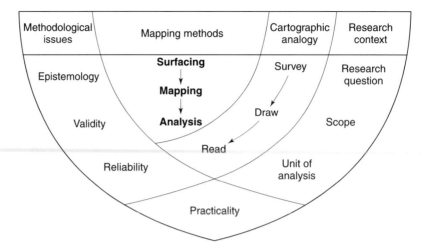

FIGURE 10.7   *The mapping shield for research decisions (Jenkins, 1998)*

Step 3: Try it out – can it be done?

This is the acid test. All too often we develop our research design away from the challenges of the research field and find that in reality our design is too unwieldy or simply that we cannot get the access to informants needed to achieve our aims. At this point we might need to review the position and perhaps reflect on the constructions of Steps 1 and 2 in order to create a research design that can actually be carried out. This question can only be addressed by some form of pilot or exploratory interview. How long does the process require? What makes it easier for the respondent? I once attended a seminar in which a researcher announced that the interviews were very thorough and some lasted as long as eight hours! Clearly other than your own family (and this may also be a problem) you are unlikely to get anywhere near this level of access and so approaches need to be effective in quickly getting into the issue. For example, in my own research on growth I had a whole list of constructs which I had derived from the literature to create a very complex process. In the first five minutes I realized that my process was destroying any level of insight I might have obtained because the respondents were trying to fit their view of the world into my complex framework – and it wouldn't go! I therefore moved to a more open process which enabled them to express their views more freely.

Of course, the problem then becomes one of how you begin to evaluate all of this data. I dealt with the more open nature of the data by using coders to identify concepts and the causal linkages between these concepts. On reflection this became a very time-consuming and arduous process, but because it was one which allowed the data to be as close to the respondent's view as I could make it, it was a price worth paying.

CONCLUSION

This chapter has reviewed some of the background, properties and approaches of cognitive mapping to enable researchers to make more informed choices about some of the issues they face. I stated at the outset that I present a particular view based on my own experience rather than an exhaustive account. There are many other excellent approaches which have not been discussed here. However it is hoped that the list of recommendations for further reading at least gives the reader some ideas as to where to go next if they are interested in pursuing the mapping approach.

The challenge of cognitive mapping is its relatively open architecture as a research method. Unlike approaches such as the repertory grid, where there are well-established norms, in cognitive mapping there is an array of approaches, all of which bring particular strengths and weaknesses to the research process. I hope, if nothing else, you have at least formed the view about whether or not you want to discover more.

Study questions

1 Try to construct a causal map of a research project. Start with the outcome of the research and map the factors which are needed to create this outcome.
2 Create a set of hierarchical categories for an area of literature you are interested in. For example, if you start with 'strategy' how many different categories can you create to organize your thinking on the domain?
3 Using the Mapping Shield work through three alternative mapping approaches for a piece of research and identify which is the strongest approach.

Recommended further reading

Huff, A.S. (ed.) (1990) *Mapping Strategic Thought*. Chichester: Wiley. (A seminal text for anyone looking to undertake management research using this perspective. It is a valuable collection of mapping studies, concentrating on the field of strategic management, written in a clear and accessible way. Its strength lies in the fact that it contains outlines of the mapping approaches used by the contributors in step-by-step detail)

Huff, A.S. and Jenkins, M. (2002) *Mapping Strategic Knowledge*. London: Sage. (An update of Anne Huff's original that also emphasizes the linking between cognitive mapping and the growing domain of knowledge management)

Walsh, James P. (1995) 'Managerial and Organizational Cognition: Notes from a Trip Down Memory Lane', *Organization Science*, 6 (3), pp. 280–321. (A comprehensive review of the field. Now relatively dated but it does provide an excellent starting point for those looking to undertake a literature review of this area)

Hodgkinson, Gerard P. (2001) 'The Psychology of Strategic Management: Diversity and Cognition Revisited', in C.L. Cooper and I.T. Robertson (eds), *The International*

Review of Industrial and Organizational Psychology, Vol. 16. Chichester: Wiley. (A more up-to-date review that is also connected more explicitly to the field of psychology. It provides a useful critique of existing theories and some of the more widely used methods)

Note

1 This taxonomy was generated with a 'top-down' method often used to elicit taxonomic mental structures. The respondent was asked to begin with the category 'textiles' and classify the subtypes of successively more specific categories of textile firms. This and other techniques for generating taxonomic cognitive structures are discussed in Porac and Thomas (1987).

References

Augoustinos, M. and Walker, I. (1995) *Social Cognition: An Integrated Introduction.* London: Sage.

Axelrod, R.M. (1976) *The Structure of Decision: Cognitive Maps of Political Elites.* Princeton, NJ: Princeton University Press.

Barr, P.S., Stimpert, J.L. and Huff, A.S. (1992) 'Cognitive Change, Strategic Action, and Organizational Renewal', *Strategic Management Journal*, 13, pp. 15–36.

Bougon, M.G., Weick, K.E. and Binkhorst, D. (1977) 'Cognition in Organizations: An Analysis of the Utrecht Jazz Orchestra', *Administrative Science Quarterly*, 22, pp. 606–39.

Brewer, W.F. and Nakamura, G.V. (1984) 'The Nature and Functions of Schemas', in R.S. Wyer and T.K. Srull (eds), *Handbook of Social Cognition*. Hillsdale, NJ: Erlbaum, pp. 119–60.

Broadbent, D.E. (1958) *Perception and Communication.* London: Pergamon Press.

Cossette, P. and Audet, M. (1992) 'Mapping of an Idiosyncratic Schema', *Journal of Management Studies*, 29, pp. 325–47.

Eden, C. (1988) 'Cognitive Mapping', *European Journal of Operational Research*, 36, pp. 1–13.

Eden, C. (1992) 'On the Nature of Cognitive Maps', *Journal of Management Studies*, 29, pp. 261–5.

Eden, C. and Ackermann, F. (1998) *Making Strategy: The Journey of Strategic Management.* London: Sage.

Festinger, L. (1954) 'A Theory of Social Comparison Processes', *Human Relations*, 7, pp. 117–40.

Foxall, G.R. (1997) 'The Explanation of Consumer Behaviour: From Social Cognition to Environmental Control', in C.L. Cooper and I.T. Robertson (eds), *International Review of Industrial and Organizational Psychology*, 12, pp. 229–87.

Ginsberg, A. (1990) 'Connecting Diversification to Performance: A Sociocognitive Approach', *Academy of Management Review*, 15, pp. 514–35.

Gioia, D.A. and Poole, P.P. (1984) 'Scripts in Organizational Behavior', *Academy of Management Review*, 9, pp. 449–59.

Harary, F., Norman, R.Z. and Cartwright, D. (1965) *Structural Models: An Introduction to the Theory of Directed Graphs.* New York: Wiley.

Heider, F. (1946) 'Attitudes and Cognitive Organization', *Journal of Psychology*, 21, pp. 107–12.

Hodgkinson, G.P. and Johnson, G. (1994) 'Exploring the Mental Models of Competitive Strategists: The Case for a Processual Approach', *Journal of Management Studies*, 31, pp. 525–51.

Huff, A.S. (ed.) (1990) *Mapping Strategic Thought*. Chichester: Wiley.

Huff, A.S., Narapareddy, V. and Fletcher, K.E. (1990) 'Coding the Causal Association of Concepts', in A.S. Huff (ed.), *Mapping Strategic Thought*. Chichester: Wiley, pp. 311–25.

Jenkins, M. (1998) 'The Theory and Practice of Comparing Causal Maps', in C. Eden and J.-C. Spender (eds), *Managerial and Organizational Cognition: Theory, Methods and Research*. London: Sage, pp. 231–49.

Jenkins, M. and Johnson, G. (1997) 'Entrepreneurial Intentions and Outcomes: A Comparative Causal Mapping Study', *Journal of Management Studies*, 34(6), pp. 895–920.

Kelly, G.A. (1955) *The Psychology of Personal Constructs*. New York: W.W. Norton.

Langfield-Smith, K. (1992) 'Exploring the Need for a Shared Cognitive Map', *Journal of Management Studies*, 29, pp. 349–68.

Maruyama, M. (1963) 'The Second Cybernetics: Deviation Amplifying Mutual Causal Processes', *American Scientist*, 51, pp. 164–79.

Minsky, M. (1975) 'A Framework for Representing Knowledge', in P.H. Winston (ed.), *The Psychology of Computer Vision*. New York: McGraw–Hill.

Porac, J.F. and Thomas, H. (1987) 'Cognitive Taxonomies and Cognitive Systematics'. Paper presented at the annual meeting of the Academy of Management. New Orleans, USA, August.

Porac, J.F., Thomas, H. and Baden-Fuller, C. (1989) 'Competitive Groups as Cognitive Communities: The Case of Scottish Knitwear Manufacturers', *Journal of Management Studies*, 26, pp. 397–416.

Reger, R.K. (1990) 'Managerial Thought Structures and Competitive Positioning', in A.S. Huff (ed.), *Mapping Strategic Thought*. Chichester: Wiley, pp. 71–88.

Rosch, E. (1978) 'Principles of Categorization', in E. Rosch and B. Lloyd (eds), *Cognition and Categorization*. Hillsdale, NJ: Wiley.

Rosch, E., Mervis, C.B., Gray, W.D., Johnson, D.M. and Boyes-Braem, P. (1976) 'Basic Objects in Natural Categories', *Cognitive Psychology*, 8, 382–439.

Sherman, S.J. and Corty, E. (1984) 'Cognitive Heuristics', in R.S. Wyer and T.K. Srull (eds), *Handbook of Social Cognition*. Hillsdale, NJ: Erlbaum, pp. 189–286.

Shrivastava, P. and Mitroff, I. (1983) 'Frames of Reference Managers Use: A Study in Applied Sociology of Knowledge', in *Advances in Strategic Management*. Greenwich, CT: JAI Press, pp. 161–82.

Shrivastava, P. and Schneider, S. (1984) 'Organizational Frames of Reference', *Human Relations*, 37, pp. 795–809.

Skinner, B.F. (1938) *The Behavior of Organisms*. New York: Appleton–Century–Crofts.

Sproull, L.S. (1981) 'Beliefs in Organizations', in P.C. Nystrom and W.H. Starbuck (eds), *Handbook of Organizational Design*. Oxford: Oxford University Press, pp. 203–24.

Stubbart, C.I. (1989) 'Managerial Cognition: A Missing Link in Strategic Management Research', *Journal of Management Studies*, 26, pp. 324–47.

Tolman, E.C. (1948) 'Cognitive Maps in Rats and Men', *The Psychological Review*, 55, pp. 189–208.

Walsh, J.P. (1988) 'Selectivity and Selective Perception: An Investigation of Managers' Belief Structures and Information Processing', *Academy of Management Journal*, 31, pp. 873–96.

Walsh, J.P. and Ungson, G.R. (1991) 'Organizational Memory', *Academy of Management Review*, 16, pp. 57–91.

Weick, K.E. and Bougon, M.G. (1986) 'Organizations as Cognitive Maps', in H.P. Sims and D.A. Gioia (eds), *The Thinking Organization*. San Francisco: Jossey–Bass, pp. 102–35.

Wickens, C.D. (1984) 'Introduction to Engineering Psychology and Human Performance', in C.D. Wickens (ed.), *Engineering Psychology and Human Performance*. Columbus: Charles E. Merrill Publishing, pp. 1–18.

Wrightson, M.T. (1976) 'The Documentary Coding Method', in R.M. Axelrod (ed.), *The Structure of Decision: Cognitive Maps of Political Elites*. Princeton, NJ: Princeton University Press, pp. 291–332.

11

Repertory Grid Technique

Keith Goffin

OVERVIEW

Repertory grid technique is a powerful tool that can be used in many research situations to help respondents articulate their views on complex topics without interviewer bias. George Kelly developed the technique for use in psychology, however, because it is so adaptable, it has been used in many different contexts. The technique is a highly structured form of interviewing which leads to a matrix of quantitative data – the repertory grid.

This chapter covers the design and administration of a repertory grid interview. It begins with a description of the technique in action, discusses Kelly's *theory of personal constructs* and gives a detailed description of grid design, analysis and limitations. The chapter concludes with detailed examples from management research.

The technique in action

Consider a repertory grid interview investigating relationships in the workplace. The interviewee would be asked to name several colleagues with whom they work on a regular basis – we will call them colleagues A, B, C, D, E and F. The colleagues are what are termed the *elements* of the test and each name is written on a separate postcard-sized card, as shown in Figure 11.1A. Note that the cards have been pre-numbered in a random sequence (5, 1, 4, 3, 2 and 6), to enable the selection of random groups of cards. From the diagram it can be seen that the name of the first colleague ('A') has been written on the card numbered '5', whereas Colleague B's name is written on the card numbered '1'.

After the cards have been annotated with names, the interviewee is presented with a set of three cards – termed a *triad*. Figure 11.1B shows the triad consists of cards 1, 2 and 3, corresponding to Elements B, E and D. As the triad is presented, the interviewee is asked, 'Why is working with two of these colleagues similar and different from working with the third?' A typical response – termed a *construct* – could be that two of the people were 'easy to work with', whereas working with the third is 'difficult'. The way in which the interviewee differentiates between the elements in the triad reveals one aspect of how working relationships are viewed. Each of the interviewee's elements (colleagues) is

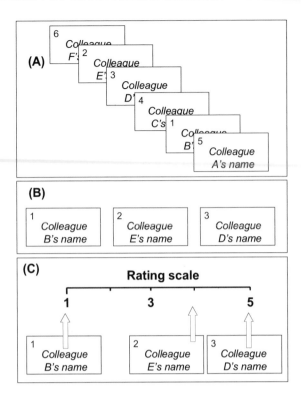

FIGURE 11.1   *Example of a simple repertory grid test: (A) the elements of the test – colleagues – written on cards; (B) the first triad presented to the interviewee; (C) the rating of the elements in the first triad (note all elements will be subsequently rated)*

then rated against this first construct. As shown in Figure 11.1C, this can be a 5-point scale on which Colleague B has been highly rated on this first construct ('1'), whereas Colleague D was given a minimum rating ('5').

Further triads are used to *elicit* further constructs. The interviewee is not allowed to repeat constructs and so each new triad elicits at least one new construct. (Sometimes, a triad may elicit several constructs.) Following the identification of each construct, the interviewee is required to rate all the elements against it using the 1–5 rating scale. These ratings form the repertory grid, as shown in Figure 11.2.

In Figure 11.2 the six elements of the test – Colleagues B to F – are shown across the top of the grid. In an actual interview, the names of the colleagues would be used and the interviewer would treat this information confidentially. Down the side of the grid are the constructs elicited during the interview. It can be seen that the Colleague B is rated as '1' on the construct (Easy to Work With). Similarly, it can be seen that the interviewee's boss (Colleague B) is rated mid-scale ('3') on the construct 'Political' but highly rated on the construct 'Directive' ('1'). The ratings tell us about how an interviewee views their colleagues and indicate the most important constructs. For example, the ratings on the construct 'Experienced' are not as widely spread (they only range from 1 to 2) as those for

| Constructs | Elements | | | | | | Pole |
	CARD 1 Colleague B (Boss)	CARD 2 Colleague E	CARD 3 Colleague D	CARD 4 Colleague C	CARD 5 Colleague A	CARD 6 Colleague F	
Easy to Work With	*1*	*4*	*5*	5	1	1	Difficult
Directive	1	4	5	*3*	*4*	*4*	Relaxed
Clever, Quick	*2*	5	*3*	4	*1*	1	Slow
Friendly	4	*2*	1	*3*	1	*1*	Cold
Political	*3*	*3*	5	1	*5*	5	Fair
Experienced	2	2	*1*	*2*	2	*2*	Inexperienced

FIGURE 11.2   *A repertory grid on working relationships*

'Clever', 'Quick' (where the ratings range from 1 to 5). This shows that this latter construct differentiates more strongly between the elements.

The stars around the ratings in Figure 11.2 indicate which cards were in the triad that elicited particular constructs and, for example, the first construct was elicited by the triad consisting of Cards 1, 2 and 3. All of the triads consist of random groups of cards – this was achieved by assigning the cards random numbers in advance (from random number tables). The first triad was predefined to consist of Cards 1, 2 and 3 and the second was Cards 4, 5 and 6. At least two cards are changed between each successive triad. This gives the interviewee a varied set of elements to compare and elicits more significant constructs.

In addition to the ratings, repertory grid interviewing produces rich qualitative data. The interviewees' comments on their constructs give insights and so it is normal to record and transcribe interviews. For example, the interviewees' explanation of the construct 'Political' would indicate whether a high rating of 1 was perceived positively or not. The meanings of constructs need to be probed and one useful way is to ask interviewees to explain the opposite end of the scale of a construct, which is termed the *pole*. For example, the interviewee might explain the pole of the construct 'Political' as 'Fair'. The grid includes space for the poles, as shown on Figure 11.2.

It is useful to compare repertory grid technique with direct questioning. Although direct questioning is a common way to investigate views and opinions, it has drawbacks. For example, it may be difficult for interviewees to articulate their views on complex topics. In contrast, grid interviewing produces detailed explanations and this is one reason the technique has been so widely used. The Equant case offers an example from consumer research:

Case study: Equant

One company that has used the repertory grid technique to its advantage is Equant, the world's largest data network provider – offering network design, integration, maintenance and support services in over 120 countries. The company always placed a high emphasis on being 'customer-focused' and regularly reviewed the results of customer satisfaction surveys, comparing their performance to competitors'. Although such surveys provided useful 'benchmarks', Equant recognized that it did not measure performance against the criteria that were most important to customers.

In 1996, the company offered excellent network performance and global service availability. Consequently, it received better ratings than its competitors in surveys and this could have led to complacency. However, a project was launched to investigate whether there were aspects of service quality that were important to customers but were not covered by the surveys. Liam Mifsud, Business Support Manager at Equant, designed and conducted repertory grid interviews, in which the elements of the grid were a range of customers' current service providers. Interviewees (IT Directors and Managers) were asked to name nine suppliers that their companies did business with, and these elements were presented in triads. The constructs elicited typically included a wide range of service quality criteria (far wider than those covered by the customer satisfaction surveys).

The results showed that customers' perceptions of service quality were not solely based on technical measures (such as coverage or network performance). Equant were able to identify ten new criteria on which their performance was being judged. For example, customers emphasized intangible elements of service quality, such as the responsiveness and flexibility of account management teams, and the quality and competence of the support staff they came into contact with.

Although repertory grid technique was very useful, Equant found that it was not suitable for use in regular customer satisfaction surveys with a global customer base. The need for face-to-face interviews was too time-consuming. Another drawback identified by Mifsud was that 'some senior managers who were interviewed objected to what they considered the simplicity of the technique'. Nevertheless, Equant views the principle of eliciting satisfaction criteria from customers as excellent, and now has an ongoing programme based on this concept. 'This provides us with a valuable means of understanding the changing needs of customers,' says Mifsud. Through this programme, Equant has been able to achieve real market differentiation and gain market share.

THEORY OF PERSONAL CONSTRUCTS

Repertory grid technique is based on Kelly's Personal Construct Theory (PCT). George Kelly believed that to make sense of our world all humans develop 'rules' by which we view or categorize situations, people, relationships and objects, in fact almost any phenomenon with which we are confronted (Kelly, 1970). The rules by which we make sense of these situations are our constructs. Kelly (1955) defined a construct as, 'a way in which two or more things are alike and at the same time different from one or more things'. Although people constantly generate and modify constructs, they may not be explicitly aware of this. When the grid is completed, interviewees often comment that they understand their own views better – because the process of eliciting constructs has probed to a depth of which they were previously unaware.

The key components of PCT can be summarized as:

1 All individuals develop and test constructs as a way of explaining and anticipating events.
2 Many constructs will be constantly updated, as they prove useful or less useful in interpreting events.
3 Interviewees typically differ in how they construe events (although there will be some constructs that will be shared across interviewees).

4 Social contexts influence individuals' constructs.
5 If one individual construes events in a way similar to another, then both of their psychological processes are similar.

The above key components of PCT can be used during repertory grid design to help avoid reliability and validity issues. For example, points 1 and 3 should remind researchers that the phenomenon they are investigating might involve constructs that are specific to the individual interviewee and so it may not be possible to derive results that are representative of a population. Similarly, point 2 raises the issue that constructs change and are dependent on the time at which they were elicited. Such considerations should be an integral part of the interview design process.

DESIGN OF A REPERTORY GRID INTERVIEW

Fransella and Bannister (1977) said that 'to use a grid is to involve a researcher in a whole series of problems'. However, it is more accurate to say that they involve the researcher in a series of *decisions*. This section will present the five main decisions in the design of a repertory grid interview: selection of the elements; presentation of the elements; construct elicitation; the rating of the elements against the constructs; and the interview administration.

Selection of the elements

Elements must be selected to fit with the aims of the investigation. For the investigation of working relationships discussed earlier, the elements were the interviewee's colleagues, which may seem obvious. However, in other situations the choice may not be so easy. In the Equant example, a range of both 'good' and 'poor' suppliers led to striking triads and elicited more subtle constructs.

Pilot interviews will be necessary to check the elements selected, and the following guidelines are useful:

1 Elements should be specific and discrete (for example, people, objects or events) in order to avoid confusing the interviewee.
2 Simple, clear elements support effective interviewing.
3 The set of elements should be relatively homogeneous – for example, mixing people and objects may cause confusion.
4 Elements should avoid any value judgements, as these increase the potential for misunderstanding.
5 The interviewee must be familiar with the elements.
6 Most importantly, the elements must be appropriate to the topic being studied.

Up until now, all discussions have been based on what are called *personal elements*. These are produced in response to a request from the interviewer to name, for example, colleagues. Personal elements are identified by interviewees and are therefore familiar to them. In one form of repertory grid technique, the interviewee is asked to name people who fit a number of specified roles, such as 'a teacher you liked', 'the most intelligent person you know', etc. Specifying roles is a common approach, used for example by Harris (1997). In the example on working relationships, the set of elements named is likely to be specific to each interviewee. However, if the interviewees all work within one organization, there will be some commonality of elements (colleagues) across the interviews. The degree to which the elements are the same becomes an important issue when comparing grids.

In contrast to personal elements, some repertory grid interviews supply the elements to the interviewee – these are termed *provided elements*. For example, a study of pupils' linguistic skills supplied the names of countries as elements (Lemon, 1975). Similarly, in market research, brand names could be used as elements. As provided elements are identical across interviews, the resulting grids can be more easily compared. However, all interviewees must be familiar with the elements chosen. If this is difficult to achieve, interviewees can choose the elements with which they are familiar from *a pool* of provided elements – this means that different interviewees will have some commonality of elements.

Presentation of the elements

In order to elicit meaningful constructs, the researcher must decide on the most appropriate way to present the elements. A computer can be used to conduct interviews and this will be discussed under the administration of the test. Usually, however, each element is written manually on a card and different triads are presented to the interviewee until all combinations have been covered, or the interview is terminated.

Table 11.1 indicates the number of different triads that are available compared to the total number of elements used. Obviously, if the interviewee can only name three elements, then only one triad can be defined and repeated construct elicitation is impossible. To produce a sufficient number of triads, five or more elements are needed.

The combination of elements in each triad is important because, if successive triads are too similar, it is hard to elicit meaningful constructs. In Figure 11.2, each triad has at least two different cards and the first two triads are completely different. Researchers have found that if only one element is changed between successive triads, then the resulting constructs will be less important (Bender, 1974). Therefore, it is better to change at least two elements between triads. As Table 11.1 shows, there may be a large number of possible triads if the number of elements is high, however in a 50–60 minute interview, the interviewee will typically only be presented with about 10 triads.

Normally triads are used, however, the *dyadic method* (with two elements) has been found to be useful for interviewing children and in psychological testing. In the latter application, 'elements, instead of being individuals, that is, John or Jill, are the relationships between pairs, that is, John in relation to

TABLE 11.1   *The number of possible triads from a fixed number of elements*

Number of elements	Number of possible triads[a]
3	1
4	4
5	10
6	20
7	35
8	56
9	84
10	120
11	165
12	220

[a] This is calculated from the mathematical formula for the number of combinations C of *y* elements (*y* = 3 for triads), that can be selected from a total of *x* elements

$$C = x! \ / \ [y!(x - y)!];$$

where *x*! (called '*x* factorial') = $5 \times 4 \times 3 \times 2 \times 1$, if *x* = 5 and *x*! = $6 \times 5 \times 4 \times 3 \times 2 \times 1$, if *x* = 6.

Jill, John in relation to Elizabeth and so on' (Ryle and Lunghi, 1970). Although this version is reputably highly sensitive, it needs careful application, as the elements are complex. It has remained a specialized approach but one that may be useful in certain management applications.

Elements are normally written on cards, but in the case of provided elements (which are known in advance) pictures or photographs can also be used. Visual stimuli can be useful and, when comparing simple products, it may even be possible to present the actual products themselves in triads, as opposed to cards.

Eliciting constructs

A key part of construct elicitation is the question posed with each triad. The general form of this question is, 'In what way are two of these alike and at the same time different from the third?' However, this will need to be adapted to the research context without introducing observer bias. For example, value judgements such as 'How are two of these "better" than the third?' should be avoided. The question will need to be piloted and is somewhat of a balancing act between guiding interviewees to produce constructs that are relevant (not trivial) and avoiding bias. For example, in consumer research on car performance, the interviewee might be presented with triads of provided elements (different car models with names and photographs). The question posed with each triad could be 'In what way are two of these car models similar and different from the third in terms of performance?' This type of question focuses the interviewee on performance and avoids trivial answers such as 'two of them are blue and the other is red'. However, the use of qualifying phrases such as 'in terms of . . .' requires careful consideration.

The issue of unexpected or trivial answers is a difficult one. Should certain constructs be rejected for being 'irrelevant'? Care is needed as constructs may initially appear unimportant and further questioning may be required. In general, constructs should not be rejected unless there is supporting evidence that they are outside the scope of the research. Researchers need to ask questions to probe the meaning of constructs. *Laddering techniques* (see Chapter 12) can also be used to identify the most important constructs from grid interviews.

There are two types of constructs: *personal* and *provided*. The most common approach in exploratory research is to elicit personal constructs – the interviewee produces their own constructs in response to each of the (triads with no suggestions from the interviewer). Across a group of people interviewed on a particular topic, there will be some *common constructs* – constructs identified by the majority of people. A particular point to note is that care must be taken when grouping interviewees' personal constructs into categories and identifying common constructs. Interviewees may use similar words to describe quite different concepts; the work of Nash (1979) and its subsequent criticism (Open University 1979: 29) illustrate this problem.

Provided constructs are given by the researcher to the interviewee and no further constructs are elicited. The interviewee is simply asked to rate elements against the set of provided constructs. An investigation of the relative merits of the two types of constructs found that interviewees are more able to express their thoughts using personal constructs. Researchers may also choose to elicit some personal constructs and then obtain interviewees' ratings using provided constructs. For an example of this 'mixing' of constructs, see Landfield (1965).

Provided constructs are especially useful in surveys (see, for example, Metcalf, 1974). In market research it is normal to conduct 20–30 interviews to identify how people perceive products. These interviews identify the common constructs, which are then used as provided constructs in a survey of a representative sample (Frost and Braine, 1967). This gives ratings of different products against each of the provided constructs.

Researchers new to repertory grid design should practise construct elicitation. Conducting interviews with friends on simple topics can provide good experience before moving to pilot interviews on the specific research topic.

Rating the elements

In the example on working relationships, each element was rated on a 5-point scale. Other possibilities include a bipolar scale, and ranking elements as opposed to rating them. Ranking appears a simple way to gauge how interviewees perceive elements. However, it is an ordinal measurement that does not allow simple statistical analysis because the difference between each of the ranked elements may not be the same. Consequently, rankings have significant limitations that normally make them unsuitable for management applications. It has also been noted that conducting rankings can be tedious for interviewees (Pope and Keen, 1981: 46).

Ratings are more commonly used, as they can be easily analysed. A bipolar

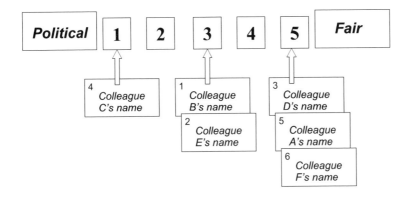

FIGURE 11.3   *Use of additional cards for the ratings*

scale can be used, although for most situations a 5-point scale is appropriate. Wider scales increase the sensitivity of the measurement, provided interviewees can cope with them – Hudson (1974) used an 11-point scale in consumer research. With more points on the scale, extra time is required to rate the elements and this can become boring for the interviewee.

Extra cards labelled with the constructs and poles can be used to help an interviewee conduct their ratings, as shown in Figure 11.3. These additional cards can also be in a different colour (Pope and Keen, 1981: 49). However, researchers should be cautious in applying this approach with managers, who may perceive it as condescending.

The *range of convenience* of a construct is an important concept. Every construct has a limited range of applicability and, at the highest level, a particular construct may only apply to one topic. For example, the construct 'Political' and its pole 'Fair' may only be applied by an interviewee to their working relationships and not, for instance, personal relationships. At a lower level, a construct's range may be limited to certain elements only, that is an interviewee may not be able to rate some elements against a particular construct. Researchers should note on the repertory grid where elements fall outside the range of convenience of a particular construct, normally by entering 'N/A' for 'not applicable'.

Normally it is preferable to have interviewees give their ratings directly after each construct has been elicited. The alternative is to wait until all constructs have been elicited and then have the interviewee complete all of the ratings against each construct. However, if the ratings are left until the end of the interview, there is a danger that the interviewee will pay only superficial attention to the ratings. If this occurs, the quantitative data will be of questionable reliability. Therefore, in most cases, it is better to conduct the ratings after each construct is identified. If the ratings are left until the end of an interview, then yet another decision is needed; should the ratings be made *across* or *down*? In the former, each element is rated against each construct (corresponding to moving across the grid). In the latter, each element is rated against each construct (corresponding to moving down the columns of the grid).

Administering the interview

Despite the many variations of repertory grid interviewing, the underlying administration is the same. It consists of determining the elements, eliciting and understanding each construct, rating the elements against each construct and terminating the interview.

A fundamental decision is whether to conduct the interview manually or to use a computer package, which conducts interviews automatically (as a 'dialogue' with the interviewee). Here the advantages of one-to-one interviews, such as the possibility for the researcher to ask supplementary questions, should not be underestimated. The repertory grid, as indicated earlier, is only part of the data that should be collected in an interview. Responses to further questions are a rich source of data. Therefore, manual interviewing is the best approach for management researchers, unless a large survey makes computer-based interviews the only practical option.

In administering the interview, the researcher has three main tasks that must be conducted in parallel: to produce a comprehensive grid; to understand the meaning of constructs; and to keep the interviewee's attention. Practice is needed to deal professionally with these tasks in parallel. If you are interviewing senior managers, they will have limited patience with a researcher who is muddled in selecting triads or does not pose meaningful questions to clarify constructs. There are two essential tools for interviewing: an interview script and a pre-prepared blank grid. The script includes the introductory explanation for the interviewee and the question to be asked as each triad is presented (for an example see Goffin, 1993: 356). The blank grid can be annotated with the constructs, their poles and the respective ratings, etc.

Earlier, Table 11.1 gave the potential numbers of triads and, with eight elements, there are 56 possible triads. However, many of these will be similar and so only the most varied triads should be selected. Interviewees are likely to become tired after 50–60 minutes and this corresponds to a need for about 10–14 triads. In management research, where the interviewee is often giving up their time voluntarily, a good rule of thumb is to ask for an hour of their time. The grid should be completed within 50 minutes and the remaining time can be used to give the interviewee feedback on the research aims and their grid. At this point managers, although they may have been initially sceptical about repertory grid technique, often want to learn more. This gives the researcher an additional opportunity to collect qualitative data on the interviewee's perceptions of the elements and constructs.

ANALYSING A REPERTORY GRID

At this point a more complex example will be used to discuss analysis issues. It is taken from management research investigating the use of complex equipment in hospitals. Analysis covers both qualitative data (from the transcript) and quantitative data (from the ratings).

The example

Hospitals have devices such as anaesthetic machines that are maintained by engineers. The research aimed to understand how hospital engineers view the different types of equipment, in order to identify how it could be better designed. Fifteen engineers were interviewed and the personal elements were ten pieces of equipment used in the interviewees' hospitals. The elements were written on pre-numbered cards and the random sequence is given as a reminder to the interviewer at the top of the grid, as shown in Figure 11.4. Also recorded is background information such as the interviewee's name (identified as 'B11' for confidentiality reasons) and the number of the transcript tape. Pre-determined triads were used to elicit constructs.

The elements were ten medical devices named by B11, including patient monitors (used in intensive care) and electro-surgery machines (used in the operating theatre). The manufacturers of each of these devices have been disguised in Table 11.4.

Qualitative analysis

From Figure 11.4 it can be seen that eleven constructs were elicited. All ten elements were rated against these constructs on a 9-point scale. Interviewee B11's explanations of his constructs were detailed, largely spontaneous and unequivocal (Goffin, 1994). Based on the transcript, several examples will be given:

- The second triad elicited 'Ease of Repair' (the name of this construct and all others are from the transcript). Comparing the products, B11 said, 'patient monitoring is the easiest for us – we have the least trouble with it . . . The parts, which need to be changed regularly . . . are more "service-friendly". Note, however, that the elements in the triad were rated identically (with '5').
- In explaining Construct 4, 'Ease of Training Users', B11 said, 'Card number 10, that requires really intensive training for the users – that leads to user errors'. His use of the card number rather than using the manufacturer/ product name is interesting. Most of the other interviewees also used the card numbers and the researcher had the impression that this allowed them to be more critical when referring to the company that they knew was sponsoring the research.
- Construct 9 was 'Repair Costs', when a hospital pays for a manufacturer's engineer to repair equipment. On this construct, many elements were perceived as 'too expensive'.
- Construct 11, 'Material for User Training', is an interesting construct because all the ratings were '9'. 'We . . . give regular training for the anaesthesia department. We need better material and graphics to be able to explain the equipment.'

The above explanations are based on quotes selected from the transcript, although content analysis can also be used. Such combinations are particularly powerful in exploratory research.

Date: 1/9/91 **Interviewer:** K. Goffin **Interviewee:** 'B11' **Tape:** #7
Start: 10:30 **Finish:** 12:00 **Duration:** 90 minutes (including several interruptions)
Order of personal elements: 5; 1; 8; 6; 9; 10; 4; 7; 3; 2

The Elements by Card Number

Constructs	1	2	3	4	5	6	7	8	9	10	Pole
1 Periodic Maintenance	*1	*2	*4	3	1	4	4	1	1	3	More maintenance required
2 Ease of Repair	5	1	5	*5	*5	*5	1	1	1	5	Hard to repair
3 Ease of Cleaning	4	4	3	5	3	6	*3	*3	*4	6	Difficult to clean
4 Ease of Training Users	*2	*5	2	7	5	4	2	2	2	*6	Very difficult to train users
5 Availability of Spare Parts	2	3	*1	3	3	*6	1	2	*3	6	Hard to obtain
6 Manufacturer's User Training	?	*3	1	2	*8	3	1	?	5	*3	Low quality
7 Service Documentation	5	2	*1	5	2	*7	1	2	3	*7	Inadequate documentation
8 Contact to Manufacturer	3	4	*1	2	*5	3	*1	5	2	3	Little contact
9 Repair Costs	6	3	3	*7	*9	8	3	*8	3	9	Excessive repair costs
10 Tech. Training for Hospital Engineers	*?	1	1	2	5	8	*1	?	*2	2	Poor training courses
11 Material for End User Training	9	*9	*9	9	*9	9	9	9	9	9	Absolutely no material

FIGURE 11.4 *Repertory grid from a hospital engineer*

Visual quantitative analysis

After the constructs are fully understood, the grid data should be visually inspected. This brings the researcher 'closer' to the data by asking questions about the ratings of both the constructs and the elements, including:

- Which are the constructs that show the greatest spread of ratings? It can be seen that 'Service Documentation' (between '1' and '7'), 'Repair Costs' ('3' to '9') and 'Technical Training' ('1' to '8') all have significant spreads.
- Are there constructs for which the ratings do not cover the whole scale? 'Periodic Maintenance' generally has good ratings and 'Material for End User Training' has only very poor ratings ('9').
- Which elements have particularly high ratings? Elements 3 and 7 have many high ratings.
- Are there elements that did not receive ratings? For instance, Element 8 was not rated against Construct 6 ('Manufacturer's User Training'), since the respondent had no knowledge of the training offered by this manufacturer. This is indicated on the grid by a question mark.

Computer-based analysis

After the visual inspection, the grid data are entered into a software package. These offer numerous possibilities and researchers should make themselves familiar with these *before* collecting data. Collecting data before defining how they will be analysed risks applying statistical methods that are not applicable to the way in which the data were collected. Computer analysis normally provides statistics for the constructs, statistics on the elements and a cognitive map.

It is beyond the scope of this chapter to review the different packages available on the market. However, Flexigrid (details available from Finn.Tschudi@psykologie.uio.no) is one of the most established packages, although it is not Windows-based. Several packages are web-based, such as Webgrid and EnquireWithin (refer for details to http://www.enquirewithin.co.nz), developed by Valerie Stewart, a pioneer of the use of repertory grid technique for management research.

STATISTICS FOR THE CONSTRUCTS   Table 11.2 shows the descriptive statistics for B11's constructs. It can be seen that against Construct 1, 'Periodic Maintenance', the elements were rated from a minimum of '1' to a maximum of '4', had a mean of 2.40 and a standard deviation of 1.28. Construct 1 accounted for 4.54% of the variability of B11's ratings, across all constructs. The variability is an indication of a respondent's most important constructs, as it indicates the ones that differentiate most strongly between the elements (Smith, 1986). It can be seen that B11's most important constructs appear to be 'Repair Costs' (17%) and 'Technical Training for Hospital Engineers' (15%).

A low variability with a high average rating indicates a construct on which all products are highly rated. Such a construct is not the most significant – even if it is one of the first elicited. An example is Construct 1, 'Periodic Maintenance' (with 4.5% variability and a mean rating of 2.40). From the ratings, it appears

TABLE 11.2 Descriptive statistics[a] for hospital engineer B11's constructs

Construct	Best rating on this construct (Min.)	Mean rating on this construct (Mean)	Worst rating on this construct (Max.)	Spread of ratings on this construct (Std Dev.)	Percentage of spread (Variability[b])
1 Periodic Maintenance	1	2.40	4	1.28	4.54
2 Ease of Repair	1	3.40	5	1.96	10.63
3 Ease of Cleaning	3	4.10	6	1.14	3.57
4 Ease of Training Users	2	3.70	7	1.85	9.44
5 Availability of Spare Parts	1	3.00	6	1.67	7.75
6 Manufacturer's User Training	1	3.25	8	2.17	12.97
7 Service Documentation	1	3.50	7	2.20	13.42
8 Contact to Manufacturer	1	2.90	5	1.37	5.32
9 Repair Costs	3	5.90	9	2.51	17.41
10 Tech. Training for Hospital Engineers	1	2.75	8	2.33	15.05
11 Material for End User Training[b]	9	9.00	9	—	—
Average		3.49			

[a] The statistics in this table are reproduced exactly as they are output from *Flexigrid*; the figures are not necessarily significant to this degree.
[b] Construct 11 has identical ratings for all elements.

that the maintenance of all ten pieces of equipment is comparatively easy. Therefore, most companies' products are perceived as easy to maintain.

Constructs with low variability and a low average rating can, however, identify emerging issues. For instance, Construct 11 has zero variability because all manufacturers scored '9' on this. Clearly companies could gain a competitive advantage by offering training material. Obviously this perception is from one engineer and the importance would have to be confirmed with a representative sample.

Table 11.3 shows the correlations between B11's constructs. The correlations above 0.8 are:

- A negative correlation between Periodic Maintenance and User Training from the Manufacturer.
- Correlations between Ease of Cleaning and the two constructs Availability of Spare Parts and Service Documentation.
- A correlation between Availability of Spare Parts and Service Documentation.

Obviously a correlation does not prove causation. The above correlations are probably spurious. For example, more complex devices normally require more maintenance and also more training (as they are complex).

STATISTICS FOR THE ELEMENTS   Table 11.4 shows the statistics for the elements. It can be seen that Element 7 (Company C's micro infusion pump) had a high average rating of 1.80 and low variability (3.79%). This shows that everything about this product and manufacturer is perceived positively from B11's perspective. The product with the poorest average rating is Element 6 (Company F's incubator) with 5.40. The elements that have very good ratings on some constructs but poor ones on others can of course be recognized by their high variability (for example, Company E's patient monitor had 18% variability).

THE COGNITIVE MAP   This is a two-dimensional representation of an interviewee's perceptions of their elements against their constructs. As long as researchers are aware of its limitations, it is a useful way of summarizing data, based on Principle Components Analysis (PCA). Two tables (Tables 11.5 and 11.6) give the data on which the map is based. Table 11.5 shows how the different PCA components cover the variation in the results (called the analysis of *component space*). The first two components account for 67% (46 + 21 = 67) of the variation in the results. If the variation explained by the first two components is not around 70%, then the map is a serious compromise, because the data cannot be well represented in two dimensions – researchers should always check this.

Table 11.6 gives the element and construct *loadings*. These are used to draw the cognitive map, which is shown in Figure 11.5. The position of Element 5 (Company E's patient monitor) can be determined from the loadings (–0.37 on Component 1 and –0.94 on Component 2), as indicated by the dotted lines on the diagram. Similarly, the construct loadings at the bottom of Table 11.6 determine where constructs lie. Construct 3 (Ease of Cleaning) has loadings of

TABLE 11.3 The relationships between constructs[a]

Constructs	1	2	3	4	Construct numbers 5	6	7	8	9	10
1 Periodic Maintenance	1.0									
2 Ease of Repair	0.26	1.0								
3 Ease of Cleaning	0.32	0.43	1.0							
4 Ease of Training Users	0.14	0.42	0.59	1.0						
5 Availability of Spare Parts	0.14	0.37	**0.89**	0.58	1.0					
6 Manufacturer's User Training	**-.84**	0.09	-.12	0.18	0.24	1.0				
7 Service Documentation	0.14	0.56	**0.94**	0.48	**0.84**	0.00	1.00			
8 Contact to Manufacturer	-.66	-.06	-.06	0.22	0.26	0.78	0.05	1.00		
9 Repair Costs	-.17	0.54	0.42	0.49	0.60	0.45	0.59	0.61	1.00	
10 Tech. Training for Hospital Engineers	0.02	0.47	0.42	0.15	0.62	0.43	0.53	0.46	0.64	1.00
11 Material for End User Training	—	—	—	—	—	—	—	—	—	—

[a] Construct 11 has identical ratings for all elements and so it was omitted from the analysis.

TABLE 11.4 *Descriptive statistics for B11's elements*

Element	Element's best rating (Min.)	Element's mean rating (Mean)	Element's worst rating (Max.)	Spread in element's ratings (Std Dev.)	Percentage attributable to product (Variability)
1 Company A: patient monitor	1	3.50	6	1.66	8.98
2 Company B: electro-surgery device	1	2.80	5	1.25	5.09
3 Company C: infusion pump	1	2.20	5	1.40	6.40
4 Company D: anaesthesia machine	2	4.10	7	1.87	11.39
5 Company E: patient monitor	1	4.60	9	2.37	18.41
6 Company F: incubator	3	5.40	8	1.80	10.57
7 Company C: micro infusion pump	1	1.80	4	1.08	3.79
8 Company G: patient monitor	1	3.00	8	2.24	16.32
9 Company H: heated bed	1	2.60	5	1.20	4.70
10 Company J: ventilator	2	5.00	9	2.10	14.36
		3.50[a]			

[a] Overall average.

TABLE 11.5   *The analysis of component space for hospital engineer B11*

PCA component number	Root	As a percentage
1	4.56	46
2	2.15	21
3	1.15	12
4	0.82	8

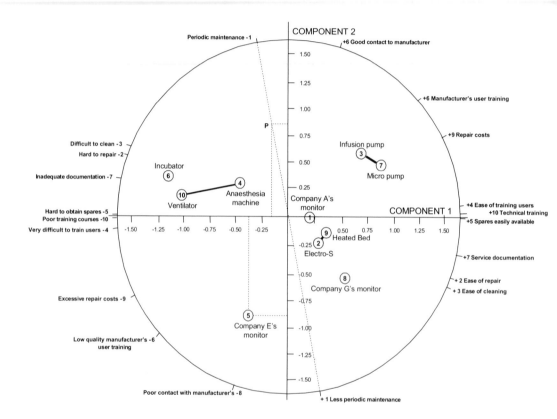

FIGURE 11.5   *The cognitive map for hospital engineer B11*

–0.86 and 0.35, which allows point P to be drawn on the map, through which a line is drawn to identify the position of the construct on the circle. Normally, software packages draw maps automatically.

The circle drawn around the origin is annotated with ten of B11's constructs and their poles (the eleventh construct had identical ratings for all products and was therefore omitted from this analysis). Three constructs (numbers 4, 10 and 5) have very strong correlations with Component 1, whereas two (numbers 1 and 6) are strongly correlated to Component 2. This shows that the interviewee's perception of support is largely explained by the

TABLE 11.6 Element and construct loadings for B11's grid

Elements (Products)	Component 1			Component 2		
	Vector	Loading	Residual	Vector	Loading	Residual
1 Company A: patient monitor	0.10	0.21	0.52	-0.00	-0.00	0.52
2 Company B: electro-surgery device	0.13	0.29	0.40	-0.16	-0.24	0.34
3 Company C: infusion pump	0.33	0.70	0.58	0.40	0.58	0.24
4 Company D: anaesthesia machine	-0.22	-0.46	0.37	0.21	0.31	0.27
5 Company E: patient monitor	-0.17	-0.37	1.30	-0.64	-0.94	0.41
6 Company F: incubator	-0.54	-1.15	0.43	0.24	0.36	0.31
7 Company C: micro infusion pump	0.42	0.89	0.36	0.33	0.48	0.12
8 Company G: patient monitor	0.25	0.54	0.75	-0.39	-0.58	0.42
9 Company H: heated bed	0.18	0.38	0.50	-0.11	-0.16	0.47
10 Company J: ventilator	-0.48	-1.02	0.21	0.13	0.18	0.18

Constructs	Component 1			Component 2		
	Vector	Loading	Residual	Vector	Loading	Residual
1 Periodic Maintenance	-0.07	-0.16	0.98	0.58	0.85	0.25
2 Ease of Repair	-0.30	-0.63	0.60	0.15	0.22	0.55
3 Ease of Cleaning	-0.40	-0.86	0.27	0.24	0.35	0.14
4 Ease of Training Users	-0.34	-0.72	0.48	-0.04	-0.06	0.48
5 Availability of Spare Parts	-0.43	-0.92	0.15	0.01	0.01	0.15
6 Manufacturer's User Training	-0.18	-0.38	0.85	-0.36	-0.53	0.57
7 Service Documentation	-0.40	-0.86	0.26	0.16	0.24	0.20
8 Contact to Manufacturer	-0.12	-0.27	0.93	-0.60	-0.87	0.16
9 Repair Costs	-0.35	-0.75	0.44	-0.26	-0.37	0.30
10 Tech. Training for Hospital Engineers	-0.33	-0.71	0.49	-0.02	-0.03	0.49
11 Material for End User Training						

five constructs related to these two components. Three pairs of products are perceived as similar from the support viewpoint and form what are termed clusters on the cognitive map. These are:

- Company H's heated bed (Element 9) and Company B's electro-surgery device (2) are perceived as similar and easy to support.
- Company C's infusion pump (3) and micro infusion pump (7) are clearly perceived as very similar and easy to support.
- Company J's ventilator (10) and Company D's anaesthesia machine (4) – this similarity is not surprising as both pieces of equipment are of comparable complexity and have a similar medical application.

The position of Element 5 (Company E's monitor) on the map is distinctive. This product is perceived by B11 as having high repair costs and being supported by an organization who provide too little training for the users and have too little contact with the respondent's engineering department.

COMPARING DIFFERENT GRIDS   The previous section demonstrates the breadth of analysis available from a single grid. Cognitive maps were also derived from the 14 other interviews but they cannot be directly compared as the elements and the constructs were often different. However, several maps showed that Company E's repair costs were perceived as high and Company F's documentation was poor – this has implications for the companies concerned. Some software packages allow multiple grid comparisons and the comparison of two grids collected at different times from a single patient is common in psychotherapy (see Fransella and Bannister, 1977).

Forty different constructs were elicited from the 15 interviews with engineers and Table 11.7 shows the 15 most frequently mentioned. Several constructs in this list were identified by B11, such as 'Ease of Cleaning'. From the table it can be seen that 'Service Documentation' was elicited from 11 interviewees (corresponding to 73%). However, the most frequently mentioned constructs are not necessarily the most important. Therefore, the variability averaged across the grids is also given in the table. To compare variability figures from different grids, the figures must be normalized as though all grids had the same number of constructs. These normalized figures can then be compared and averaged. A comparison of the frequency of mention, the weighted variability and the qualitative data (transcripts) was used to identify the most important constructs for hospital engineers: 'Technical Training for Engineers', 'Ease of Repair', 'Price of Spare Parts', 'Repair Costs' and 'Service Documentation'.

In comparing multiple grid data to identify, for example, common constructs, several approaches can be taken. One useful approach is to have a group of interviewees attend a workshop to discuss and analyse the complete list of constructs elicited.

TABLE 11.7   *The 15 most frequently mentioned constructs*

Construct	Mentions	Frequency (%)	Average normalized variability (%)	Order
1 Service Documentation	11	73	11.8	4 =
2 Reliability	10	67	5.9	
3 Ease of Use	10	67	7.3	
4 Tech. Training for Engineers	9	60	18.4	1
5 Ease of Troubleshooting	9	60	8.4	
6 Local Service Organization	9	60	6.2	
7 Periodic Maintenance	8	53	10.1	
8 Availability of Spare Parts	8	53	11.3	
9 Ease of Repair	7	47	15.3	2
10 Ease of Cleaning	7	47	7.0	
11 Repair Costs	6	40	11.8	4 =
12 Mechanical Design	5	33	7.9	
13 Price of Spare Parts	4	27	14.6	3
14 Company Technical Support	4	27	6.6	
15 Equipment Complexity	3	20	11.4	

LIMITATIONS OF REPERTORY GRID TESTING

Although the many advantages of repertory technique have been discussed, it is also important to recognize the following potential limitations:

1 If the number of personal elements that can be identified is low, there are not enough possible triads and the technique cannot be used.
2 Due to the many variations in design and analysis, researchers need to carefully select the most valid approach. (The next section on management applications gives examples of the limitations of certain designs.)
3 The somewhat artificial nature of a repertory grid interview may influence an interviewee's constructs (Open University, 1979: 30).
4 The technique is time-consuming (typically 60 minutes).
5 Managers may be initially sceptical of the technique, as identified in the Equant case and by Harris (1997).
6 The interviewees' ratings of the elements are susceptible to the 'halo' effect (halo effect is the term used for the influence respondents themselves have on ratings. For example, a rating is not objective and its value tells us something about the interviewee as well).
7 The computer analysis can become almost an end in itself, which may disguise weak research design. Fransella and Bannister warn against becoming too fascinated with the figures (1977: 109). The statistical analysis chosen must be valid.
8 The apparent simplicity of diagrams such as cognitive maps may seduce researchers into making invalid interpretations of the data.
9 The interpretation is sometimes problematic, as there are not always clearly accepted ways of analysing data. For example, determining the most important constructs can be based on frequency, variability and cognitive

mapping but there is no 'accepted' method. Researchers will therefore need to consider the alternatives and whether they can be used in combination (to give 'triangulation'). There is still a need for substantial research on the repertory grid technique itself.

EXAMPLES FROM MANAGEMENT RESEARCH

This last section describes eight applications of repertory grid technique in management research, with their advantages and limitations.

Success in Singaporean businesses (Barton, 1995)

Are the attributes of success different for Asian businesses than those for Western companies? Barton developed a list of 17 dimensions of business strategy (such as Clear Direction and Vision) and used these as the provided constructs for interviews with nine university academics. They were asked to rate six companies (the provided elements) against them. The author claimed that the results 'challenge some of the Western concepts regarding the origins of . . . superior performance' (p. 80) and used short case studies of the companies used as elements to prove this. However, from a repertory grid standpoint, the research had several limitations. First, no explanation of how the 17 dimensions of business strategy were developed was given. The dimensions would have been more valid if they had been derived from managers. Secondly, the six elements were all successful businesses. It would have been more revealing to elicit personal constructs from business people, using a selection of successful and less successful companies as elements.

Tourists' images of travel destinations (Coshall, 2000)

What are the main factors that influence tourists in their choice of destinations? Coshall identified the potential for repertory grids to be used in tourism research. One grid was presented – an investigation of perceptions of London's tourist attractions, using galleries, museums etc. as elements. The interesting aspect of this paper is that the provided elements are not necessarily familiar to the interviewee, as the aim of the research was to identify perceptions. 'Destination images are important since they permit tourists to generate a set of expectations about a place before that place is actually experienced' (p. 85).

Rapid product development (Debackere et al. 1996)

In today's competitive environment, rapid new product development (NPD) is crucial for manufacturing companies. Debackere et al. interviewed managers and engineers at various companies, using six recent NPD projects as elements. A total of 53 interviews elicited 59 different constructs. There are two counts on which the use of repertory grid technique can be criticized. First, the way in which the 'importance' of the different constructs was established – interviewees were simply asked to rate constructs on a scale of 10 ('very important') to 1 ('not at all important') at the end of the interviews. Surprisingly, the data from the individual grids were not analysed – although variability indicates the importance of constructs. Secondly, the researchers made no use of qualitative data in their analysis and did not say whether the interviews were transcribed. Despite these limitations, the paper shows the potential of repertory grid technique for investigating NPD.

Career development (Fournier, 1997)

How do graduates' perceptions of career development change during the first four years of their employment? In an ambitious longitudinal study, Fournier interviewed 33 graduates on entering employment (designated time: T1), six months later (T2) and 4 years later (T3). The personal elements of the interviews fitted a number of pre-defined roles, related to the interviewee (e.g. 'myself when I joined the company'), colleagues (e.g. 'a disliked colleague') and acquaintances (e.g. 'a best friend'). Triads were selected to always include the element 'actual self' and these elicited between 10 and 14 personal constructs. With three grids per interviewee, the analysis of the data was complex (readers interested in time series of grids will find it useful to review this paper in detail). At each interview new constructs were elicited and the comparison of these was based on a content analysis of constructs, using a grounded approach.

The research found that graduates' perceptions change significantly when they enter the workplace. Although this paper demonstrates significant rigour in the application of content analysis (for example, two researchers undertook the analysis independently to allow a check on the reliability), an opportunity was missed. The frequency with which constructs are mentioned does not relate necessarily to their importance. It would have been possible to perform some triangulation on this point, through making use of ratings – which were apparently not used. However, this paper demonstrates the use of content analysis and illustrates how Personal Construct Theory can be applied during research design.

Women in international management (Harris, 1997)

Why are women not promoted into international management roles? To examine this sensitive issue, Harris used in-depth case studies of three major organizations. Formal selection procedures for international managers were contrasted with repertory grid perceptions of managers' performance. The personal elements used were male and female managers fitting into the categories of 'highly effective international manager', 'moderately effective . . .' and 'not effective . . .' (up to nine elements in total, three per category). At each company four to six senior managers responsible for selecting employees for international assignments were interviewed. The resulting constructs were analysed to see which were correlated with high performance and to see whether there were gender differences. An interesting aspect of this research was the comparison between the constructs with the formal appraisal criteria for international managers; there were major differences. A limitation with the study is that some interviewees were unable to choose more than one woman as one of their elements. This was a direct result of the phenomenon being studied (that is, few women in management) and meant that gender factors could not be analysed to the level that would have been possible if equal numbers of men and women could have been used as elements.

In reflecting on her research, Harris said that 'a large degree of skill and confidence is needed on the part of the researcher to persuade busy senior managers to sit down and shuffle cards around for over an hour'. However, she ends more optimistically saying, 'in general, once the managers had engaged in the process, they became quite engrossed!' (1997: 114).

Airfreight service quality (Khan, 1993)

What are the important factors when shipping airfreight? Khan used different airlines' airfreight services as elements for interviews with 19 managers. A total of 44 different constructs was elicited. In contrast to Debackere et al. above, Khan determined the most important constructs from both the frequency of mention and from the main components of the cognitive maps (pp. 138–54). Furthermore, Khan's combination of repertory grid technique with trade-off analysis is interesting. After the most important constructs had been identified, a subset was used to identify how shipping managers make trade-offs between price and service quality when choosing between different airlines.

Measuring progress in organizational change (Langan-Fox and Tan, 1997)

How can you measure progress towards a new organizational culture? This is an issue facing many organizations today and a real challenge to researchers. Langan-Fox and Tan investigated an organization, which had introduced a service quality culture. Interviews with 13 middle managers used 'a cross-section of elements' (p. 279), including both parts of the organization and individuals as elements. Such inhomogeneous elements would be expected to lead to confusion but the authors do not explain how they coped with interviewees' reactions. Furthermore, they did not have the elements rated against the constructs because 'the main objective . . . was to elicit personal constructs' (p. 279). However, this omission means that substantial data on the meaning of the constructs were lost – because ratings often stimulate additional comments. Common constructs were identified but the authors were cautious, and 'grouping too many constructs where nuances and differences were perceived was avoided' (p. 280). Overall, a longitudinal design would be needed to achieve the central research aims.

Individuals and team performance (Senior, 1997)

Many aspects of business require successful teamwork. 'Crucial to the performance of teams are the abilities and behaviours of their members' (p. 242) and there are a number of methods for measuring team roles of individuals. However, the measurement of team performance is difficult. To overcome this

Senior studied 11 actual business teams and used repertory grid interviews with individuals to determine team performance. The seven personal elements were a number of teams fitting roles such as 'a good team' and the 'team of interest' (in the research). Interviewees were asked 'to compare and contrast . . . elements in terms of their performance' (p. 249). Following the interviews, composite cognitive maps were produced for each team. However, the validity of this process is unfortunately not discussed. For each of the 11 composite maps (one per team), the position of the 'team of interest' on the map was used as a proxy for team performance. Overall, the results show some evidence that a balanced mixture of different types of individual in a team correlates with higher team performance. However, Senior is cautious in drawing her conclusions and clearly identifies the limitations in the study and the need for further research.

CONCLUSION

Repertory grid technique has many advantages when used in management research, including its ability to uncover interviewees' understanding of complex issues. The technique is highly flexible and therefore researchers must identify the most appropriate and valid method for data collection. Just as there are numerous ways in which repertory grid data can be collected, there are many ways to analyse data. Consequently, researchers will need to understand a range of statistical approaches, with their advantages and limitations, in order to make the most effective use of their data. However, for those who take the time to understand the subtleties of repertory grid technique, and combine qualitative and quantitative analysis, the rewards can be substantial.

Study questions

1 A major construction company wants to improve the efficiency of the projects it manages throughout the world. Twenty project managers will be available for interview. Design a repertory grid interview to establish what are the typical points that managers learn from construction projects. What would be the elements and how would you analyse the data?

2 In a repertory grid study investigating relationships in the workplace, how could laddering be used to enhance the data generated during the interview?

3 You are interested in how cultural awareness training influences employees' views. A multinational corporation and the police force of a European country have agreed to cooperate with your research. Both are introducing cultural awareness training (the former due to friction between US and German engineers working on joint projects and the latter in response to criticism in the press of racist attitudes in the police). How could repertory grid interviews investigate the effectiveness of cultural awareness programmes?

Recommended further reading

Fransella, F. and Bannister, D. (1977) *A Manual for Repertory Grid Technique*. London: Academic Press. (Key handbook which covers the main issues in grid design, reliability and validity)

Stewart, V. and Stewart, A. (1981) *Business Applications of Repertory Grid*. London: McGraw-Hill. (This useful book is out of print, but an updated version of some of the chapters is available on the website http://www.enquirewithin.co.nz)

Pope, M.L. and Keen, T.R. (1981) *Personal Construct Psychology and Education*. London: Academic Press.

Note

Thanks to Liam Mifsud for his assistance with the Equant example and to Cheryl Freeman, Ursula Koners, Fred Lemke and Nick Reed for commenting on the first draft of this chapter.

References

Barton, C.E. (1995) 'Success in Corporate and Entrepreneurial Organizations in Singapore', *Journal of Small Business Management*, 33 (4), pp. 80–9.

Bender, M.P. (1974) 'Provided versus Elicited Constructs: An Explanation of Warr and Coffman's Anomalous Finding', *British Journal of Social and Clinical Psychology*, 13, pp. 329–30.

Coshall, J. (2000) 'Measurement of Tourists' Images: The Repertory Grid Approach', *Journal of Travel Research*, 39 (1), pp. 85–9.

Debackere, K., Vandevelde, A. and Van Dierdonck, R. (1996) 'Understanding Critical Success Factors in the Design–Manufacturing Interface: Lessons from Field Research using a Repertory Grid Approach', Proceedings of the 3rd International Product Development Conference, INSEAD, 15–16 April 1996, pp. 229–44.

Fournier, V. (1997) 'Graduates' Construction Systems and Career Development', *Human Relations*, 50 (4), pp. 363–91.

Fransella, F. and Bannister, D. (1977) *A Manual for Repertory Grid Technique*. London: Academic Press.

Frost, W.A.K. and Braine, R.L. (1967) 'The Application of the Repertory Grid Technique to Problems in Market Research', *Commentary*, 9 (3), pp. 161–75.

Goffin, K. (1993) 'Planning Product Support for Medical Products', PhD thesis, Cranfield School of Management, Bedfordshire, UK.

Goffin, K. (1994) 'Understanding Customers' Views: A Practical Example of the Use of Repertory Grid Technique', *Management Research News*, 17 (7/8), pp. 17–28.

Harris, H. (1997) 'Women in International Management: An Examination of the Role of Home Country Selection Processes in Influencing the Number of Women in International Management Positions', PhD thesis, Cranfield School of Management, Bedfordshire, UK.

Hudson, R. (1974) 'Images of the Retailing Environment: An Example of the Use of the Repertory Grid Methodology', *Environmental Behaviour*, 6 (4), pp. 470–94.

Kelly, G.A. (1955) *The Psychology of Personal Constructs*, Vols 1 and 2. New York: W.W. Norton.

Kelly, G.A. (1970) 'A Brief Introduction to Personal Construct Theory', in D. Bannister (ed.), *Perspectives in Personal Construct Theory*. London: Academic Press.

Khan, A. (1993) 'Perceived Service Quality in the Air Freight Industry', PhD thesis, Cranfield School of Management, Bedfordshire, UK.

Landfield, A.W. (1965) 'Meaningfulness of Self, Ideal and Other as related to Own versus Therapist's Personal Construct Dimensions', *Psychological Reports*, 16, pp. 605–8.

Langan-Fox, J. and Tan, P. (1997) 'Images of a Culture in Transition: Personal Constructs of Organizational Stability and Change', *Journal of Occupational and Organizational Psychology*, 70 (3), pp. 273–94.

Lemon, N. (1975) 'Linguistic Developments and Conceptualisation', *Journal of Cross-Cultural Psychology*, 6 (2), pp. 173–88.

Metcalf, R.J.A. (1974) 'Own versus Provided Constructs in a Reptest Measure of Cognitive Complexity', *Psychological Reports*, 35, pp. 1305–6.

Nash, R. (1979) 'Pupils' Expectations for their Teachers', in M.J. Wilson (ed.), *Social and Educational Research in Action: A Book of Readings*. London: Longman, pp. 291–307.

Open University (1979) *Block 4 Data Collection Procedures*, DE304 Research Methods in Education and the Social Sciences Series. Milton Keynes: Open University Press.

Pope, M.L. and Keen, T.R. (1981) *Personal Construct Psychology and Education*. London: Academic Press.

Ryle, A. and Lunghi, M.W. (1970) 'The Dyad Grid: A Modification of Repertory Grid Technique', *British Journal of Psychiatry*, 117, pp. 323–7.

Senior, B. (1997) 'Team Roles and Team Performance: Is There "Really" a Link', *Journal of Occupational and Organizational Psychology*, 70 (3), pp. 241–58.

Smith, M. (1986) 'An Introduction to Repertory Grids – Part Two: Interpretation of Results', *Graduate Management Research*, 3 (2), pp. 4–24.

12

Laddering: Making Sense of Meaning

Susan Baker

OVERVIEW

Laddering is an in-depth, probing interview technique, so called because it forces the respondent up a ladder of abstraction, linking relatively concrete meanings at an attribute level with abstract meanings of more pervasive existential importance. It is based on the concept of ordination, that is, the hierarchical organization of personal constructions ranging from the peripheral to more central dimensions of meaning.

Researchers adopting a social constructivist approach to science will find laddering an appropriate, and moreover, appealing, technique. It is in keeping with the belief that each person creates his or her own reality based on individual preconceptions, giving rise to the existence of multiple realities. Researchers seek neither to impose values nor to find one true, generalizable law. They are more concerned with pattern recognition and meaning in context, hence the use of the term 'subjective paradigm'. Laddering provides a means of accessing these personal systems of meaning, or patterns of thought; the technique helps make sense of meaning.

This chapter uncovers the stepping stones in the stream of literature, highlighting the pathway from Kelly's Personal Construct Theory (PCT) through the early development of laddering technique to a point of confluence with the domain of values research. Here a PCT/laddering-based approach to values elicitation, known as the micro approach and dominated by Gutman's means–end model, has spawned a rich body of literature in marketing. Typically, means–end analysis is used to understand how consumers differentiate between products. The results of laddering studies are often used for purposes of market segmentation and positioning, important stages in the building of successful brands.

The second half of this chapter graphically illustrates the practice of this approach by presenting in some detail a research study carried out among purchasers of perfume in the UK and Germany. This offers insights into the processes of data collection and analysis and, furthermore, demonstrates the powerful benefits of laddering technique.

ON THE SUBJECT OF MEANING

> Meaning is an experience of persons; it refers to the (experience of) relationships between things. (Wright, 1970)

If we accept this statement, then it is only when we see a thing in context that it has meaning. This meaning may be privately held and idiosyncratic; it is an individual creation and subjective. It cannot, therefore, be objective, and something 'out there' to be researched in the positivist manner.

Positivism is an approach derived from the natural sciences where the aim of studying natural phenomena is to seek causal relationships and to explain and predict events. Wilhelm Dilthey, the German philosopher (1833–1911), used the verb *erklären* to describe this quest to explain. This leads to an emphasis on empiricism, quantifiable observations and statistical analyses in the pursuit of social enquiry. Positivists maintain that there is only one view of reality, and they are concerned with the objective representation of that view, giving rise to use of the term the 'objective paradigm'. In contrast to this, the 'subjective paradigm' focuses on 'understanding'. Dilthey coined the term *Geisteswissenschaften* (which translates as 'the humanities' or 'the arts') to describe the study of expressions of human life. He argued that, in contrast to an emphasis on *erklären* in the study of nature, the study of human conduct should be based on *Verstehen* (or understanding) to enable researchers to grasp the subjective.

An interpretive approach to social enquiry is built upon the tenet that there is a fundamental, qualitative difference between the subject matters of the natural and social sciences and that a different scientific method is, therefore, required. Acceptance of this difference is based on the argument that society is more complicated than nature, and that understanding society is conceptually and logically different from understanding nature.

This particular theoretical framework is exemplified by the writings of sociologist Max Weber (1864–1920), who was concerned to establish an objective science of the subjective, that is, to blend the interpretive and positivist approaches. Drawing on Dilthey's work, Weber discerned four modes of understanding: the rational, which he divided into direct and motivational types, and the empathetic or appreciative. He was most concerned with rational understanding. 'Direct understanding of a human activity is like grasping the meaning of a sentence or thought. . . . Motivational understanding of social action is concerned with means and ends; it is the choice of a means to achieving some goal' (Blaikie, 1993: 38). This latter definition provides a direct epistemological link to PCT, laddering technique and means–end theory, thus enabling the researcher to position them within a defined philosophical framework.

Further impetus in defining an interpretive view of the social sciences is given by the philosopher Ludwig Wittgenstein (1889–1951), whose work explores the entwined relationship of language and action. In *Tractatus Logico-Philosophicus* (1921), he asserts that everything that can be thought can also be said. The limits of language are, therefore, the limits of thought.

In his view, we live our language and it, in turn, is a reflection of the way we live our lives. Language therefore lies at the heart of the debate about thought processes – extending Karl Weick's well-known aphorism 'How can I know what I think until I hear what I say' (quoted in Huff, 1990: 27). This suggests that an examination of the language used by subjects would provide an understanding of their thought processes. According to Morgan (1993), if we accept that knowledge results from some kind of implicit or explicit 'conversation', 'dialogue', 'engagement' or 'interaction' between the interests of people and the world in which they live, then the challenge facing researchers is to become skilled in the art of seeing, understanding, interpreting and reading the situations we face. In attempting to understand how individuals, or groups of individuals, make sense of things, the researcher needs to find a way of gaining entry to their system(s) of meaning. Laddering presents itself as a powerful tool for accessing these.

Personal Construct Theory and laddering technique

As a means of understanding behaviour, the school of psychology known as behaviourism focused on studies where the behaviour of individuals was unambiguously observable and preferably measurable. In Russia behaviourism was closely identified with physiology and the reflexes of the brain so famously studied by Ivan Pavlov. In America it was launched in 1913 by J.B. Watson and is probably best represented by the work of J.B. Skinner. The term *behaviouristic* came to refer to the environmental control of behaviour under laboratory conditions which forced the subject into a passive role with limited freedom of choice.

In direct contrast to the behaviourist theories dominant at the time, Kelly's *The Psychology of Personal Constructs* (1955) proved a seminal work: 'When Kelly was writing, behaviourism constituted the orthodox psychology, the mind was a psychological no-go area, and it was revolutionary to suggest that people may be able to reflect on and direct their conduct' (Butt, 1995). Writing as a researcher in the field of psychotherapy, Kelly constructed a general theory, based on 25 years of clinical experience, of how people go about interpreting and anticipating their personal experiences. His theory of personality comprised a fundamental postulate that 'a person's processes are psychologically channelized by the ways in which he [sic] anticipates events' and a further 11 corollaries elaborating on these processes. The first of these is the Construction Corollary: 'Construing. By construing we mean "placing an interpretation": a person places an interpretation upon what is construed. He erects a structure, within the framework of which the substance takes shape or assumes meaning. The substance that he construes does not produce the structure; the person does' (Kelly, 1955: 50).

Staying with this analogy, it was Hinkle's thesis (discussed extensively by Bannister and Mair, 1968) which defined laddering technique. This tool enables the researcher to ascend a person's 'structure' and to understand the edifice of personal meaning. This in-depth, probing technique elicits data that illustrate how subordinate constructions link with the superordinate; the ladder thus becomes a sample view of the subject's life.

Kelly is credited with having adopted a 'credulous approach', based on his maxim that 'if you do not know what is wrong with a person, ask him; he may tell you'. This demonstrates a belief in the view that the elicitation of verbal data from a subject would best aid the clinician in formulating initial and subsequent diagnoses. This links with the modern model of qualitative market research which holds that 'consumers are able to tell you what they do, feel and think, particularly with the aid of indirect questioning techniques which allow the interviewer to probe more "heartfelt" responses' (Gordon, 1999.)

Kelly's Personal Construct Theory has been used extensively in the psychotherapeutic process, together with laddering, to uncover the meaning of certain behaviours, linking the superficial to deeper levels of core role structure. Outside this field of application, his work opened up the domain of cognitive interpretation and the belief that some sort of internal processes – thoughts, images, constructs – are responsible for people's conduct.

COGNITIVE PSYCHOLOGY AND CONSUMER BEHAVIOUR

Cognitive psychology has had an epochal influence on understanding consumer behaviour in the domain of marketing, where it became the dominant paradigm for social psychology over the latter part of the twentieth century. In adopting this cognitive approach to understanding consumer buyer behaviour, researchers deem mental factors to be the predominantly controlling variables as opposed to a behaviourist approach, which would hold these to be mere mediators. As a cognitivist, the researcher seeks logical relationships and statistical significance through studying mental structures and processes in the mind, based on verbal data, rather than looking for a socially significant amount of behavioural change, based on observations of overt behaviour. The matrix depicted in Figure 12.1 can be used to explore the two approaches.

	Behaviourist approach	Cognitivist approach
Role of environmental factors	Primary	Secondary
Role of cognitive factors	Secondary	Primary

FIGURE 12.1   *Research approaches to consumer behaviour: matrix*

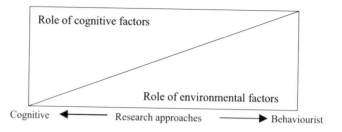

FIGURE 12.2   *Research approaches to consumer behaviour: continuum*

Debate with academic researchers and practitioners in particular over a period of years leads me to suggest that as some find this positioning too polarized, as the variables are ranked and not rated in any way, it may be more useful to conceptualize the two approaches as opposite ends of a continuum, as depicted in Figure 12.2. This shows two distinct extremes with many variations of emphasis in between and provides a means of accommodating most, if not all, consumer behaviour researchers and practitioners in their paradigmatic leanings.

Researchers commonly label all stimuli in the environment as 'information' and use an information processing model to describe how consumers' cognitive systems take in and handle these stimuli. 'From an information processing perspective, cognition concerns (1) how people interpret information and transform it into knowledge or meaning (patterns of thought), and (2) how they use this transformed information to form judgements of objects and events to make decisions about appropriate behaviors' (Peter and Olson, 1990: 49).

Theories about information processing are frequently expressed in the form of a flowchart that sets out the flow of information through the cognitive system. Some of these systems are expressed quite simply while others are more sophisticated. An example of a more complex model is illustrated in Figure 12.3. This model emphasizes the interaction between two key processes – interpretation and integration – and stored knowledge in memory.

Cognitive processes are stimulated when a consumer is exposed to an external stimulus in the environment or feels an internal stimulus such as an affective response.[1] To the consumer both types of stimulus constitute 'information'. Consumers then interpret this information in terms of their own interests, values and knowledge, which may be organized and stored in long-term memory as knowledge structures. Parts of this knowledge may then be activated for use in the interpretive process. This is then followed by the integration process which is concerned with how consumers combine and use information. The output of this is the formation of attitudes and intentions to act. These include intentions to purchase, to recommend a brand to a friend, and so on. As the model illustrates, information processing is an iterative process and the flow of information is not believed to take place linearly.

This process is, for the most part, carried out at a subconscious level and the task of the researcher becomes one of uncovering all or, more usually, part of it.

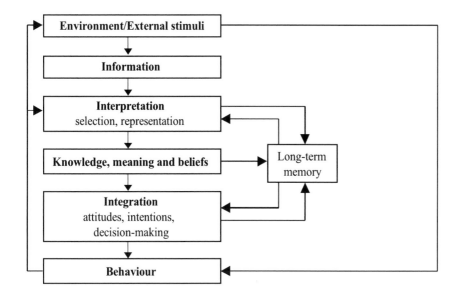

FIGURE 12.3   *How consumers choose brands: the information processing model (adapted from Peter and Olson, 1990)*

THE IMPACT OF **PCT** AND LADDERING ON VALUES RESEARCH

Where PCT and laddering meet the domain of values research, particularly as this is applied to understanding consumer behaviour, we see the development of an alternative research approach to values elicitation, known as the micro approach and dominated by the means–end model. A historical perspective on values research is summarized briefly in three parts to illustrate the ways in which the use of the PCT/laddering-based approach significantly impacted this body of literature.

1   *The role of values in management research*

The values concept is often used to identify unknown or underlying variables in individual actions and it is this ostensible uncovering of the cognitive path between personal values and behaviour that gives values research its significance to management researchers. 'Values are an integral and daily part of our lives. They determine, regulate, and modify relations between individuals, organizations, institutions, and societies' (Agle and Caldwell, 1999). The intangible nature of the concept makes definition difficult and it is cognitive psychology that provides a ready framework for exploration.

The role of values in understanding behaviour was given impetus by Milton Rokeach (1973), who defines them as 'an enduring belief that a specific mode of conduct or end-state of existence is personally or socially preferable to an opposite or converse mode of conduct'. A value system, he argues, is 'an enduring organization of beliefs concerning preferable modes of conduct or end-states of existence along a continuum of relative importance'. Rokeach differentiates between means and ends, and classifies 36 values into two sets of 18: terminal values and instrumental values. Terminal values are concerned with preferred end-states of existence, for example, happiness, security and accomplishment, while instrumental values are related to modes of behaviour, such as honesty, courageousness and broadmindedness, which are effective in achieving those end-states. The inter-relation between 'means' (instrumental) values and 'ends' (terminal) values is referred to as a values system.

This a priori classification of values into two groups constitutes a key assumption in using the Rokeach Value Survey (RVS), which is a view of the values concept that is not always upheld. For example, Gutman (1982), among others, does not draw a distinction in this way. In his model, values, as preferred end-states of being, are a type of consequence for which a person has no further (or higher) reason for preference. He classes Rokeach's instrumental values rather as consequences, therefore giving rise to the assertion that consequences gain a meaningful role in the model through their ability to move the consumer towards an end-state.

2   Values research – the macro perspective: the RVS and other inventories

In the literature, the classification of values indicators has followed two tracks – the macro and the micro, the latter having its roots in PCT and laddering.

The macro perspective uses values to profile respondents using some pre-existing inventory or list of general human values. The methodological advantage of this is that it enables researchers to describe in a quantitative fashion the values of virtually any group and to compare and contrast these with the values of any other group. The main underlying assumption is, however, that respondents can deal with a priori value orientations and are satisfied with using the statements they are given to reflect their own personal orientations. This implicitly assumes that respondents are in touch with their personal feelings and that they choose to respond accurately. Examples of this approach include the Rokeach Value Survey (Rokeach, 1973), Values and Lifestyles (Holman, 1984) and List of Values (Kahle et al., 1986).

In the realms of consumer research, two of the inventories have received much attention: Values and Lifestyles (VALS) and List of Values (LOV). VALS was first presented as part of a proprietary programme offered by SRI International in 1978 and applications of this survey have seldom been reported in the academic literature. Its roots lie largely in Maslow's hierarchy of needs and in the concept of social character. A comprehensive overview of the typology is presented by Holman (1984). LOV was culled from Rokeach's list of 18 terminal values, Maslow's hierarchy of needs 'and various other contemporaries in value research' (Kahle and Kennedy, 1988), resulting in a listing of nine values. Table 12.1 provides a comparative listing of both the RVS and LOV. It remains unclear from the literature which of the three value surveys – the RVS, VALS or LOV – provides the most effective means of measuring consumer values; VALS would appear to have been operationalized least frequently.

Despite the seminal nature of Rokeach's writings on the subject, few researchers have used the RVS in the way originally intended. Many have

TABLE 12.1 *The Rokeach Value Survey and List of Values compared*

Terminal values	Instrumental values
A comfortable life	Ambitious
An exciting life	Broad-minded
A sense of accomplishment	Capable
A world at peace	Cheerful
A world of beauty	Clean
Equality	Courageous
Family security	Forgiving
Freedom	Helpful
Happiness	Honest
Inner harmony	Imaginative
Mature love	Independent
National security	Intellectual
Pleasure	Logical
Salvation	Loving
Self-respect	Obedient
Social recognition	Polite
True friendship	Responsible
Wisdom	Self-controlled

List of Values (LOV)
(no distinction is made between terminal and instrumental values)

Self-respect	Sense of belonging
Sense of accomplishment	Fun and enjoyment in life
Being well respected	Self-fulfilment
Security	Excitement
Warm relationships with others	

adopted a scaling (or rating) approach, as opposed to Rokeach's prescribed ranking method (1973), which provides a topic of considerable academic debate. Scaling supports the view that macro methods of values elicitation are largely driven by the notion of preference.

3 Values research – the micro perspective: the means–end model

Widely promoted as the alternative approach to values elicitation, the micro perspective obviates the need for using pre-established lists of values by utilizing in-depth qualitative methods, based on PCT and laddering technique, to understand respondent motivations. The focus is on identifying those values that can be linked to attributes. These values will be described in the respondent's own language and may be less general, less abstract and perhaps more behaviour-oriented.

This approach has been developed largely in the field of consumer research where an attempt has been made to understand buyer behaviour through the satisfaction of personal values. It is means–end theory which enables the researcher to describe how the three levels of knowledge – products as bundles of attributes, as bundles of benefits and as value satisfiers – can be organized to form a simple, associative network. This is depicted in Figure 12.4.

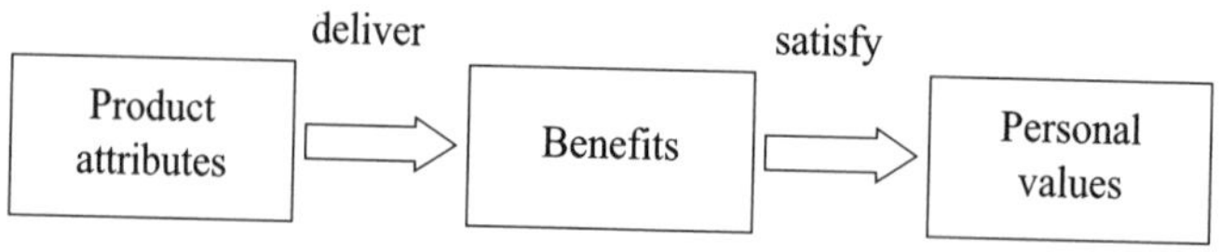

FIGURE 12.4   *The means–end model*

A means–end chain is a simple knowledge structure containing inter-con-nected meanings through which product attributes are seen as the means to an end, or personal values. It is important to note that embodied in this model is the concept of levels of abstraction: lower-level attributes link with higher-level benefits or consequences which, in turn, link with still higher-level values, reflecting Kelly's notion of the links between subordinate and super-ordinate constructs. The attributes, consequences and values become nodes in the network and the linkages between the three levels are the associations or arcs of the network, descriptive labels which are 'borrowed' from causal – or attribution – theory and management cognition where the cognitive process is considered to behave as a semantic network. Means–end theory is closely associated with Gutman, although the roots of his work can be traced back to Young and Feigin (1975) and Vinson et al. (1977). In his seminal paper, Gutman (1982) presents a version of the means–end model based on two assumptions about consumer behaviour.

First, values play a dominant role in guiding choice; consumers choose actions that produce desired consequences and minimize undesired conse-quences. Second, consumers reduce the complexity of choice by grouping products into sets or classes. It is this categorization process that explains how consumers organize their thinking about specific product alternatives, enabling them to treat non-identical stimuli as equivalent. To attain values, consumers group products into different categories depending on which fea-tures they emphasize and which they ignore, an assumption that has its roots in categorization theory (Rosch and Mervis, 1975; Rosch et al., 1976).

In order to elicit higher-level responses, as well as to understand the linkages between the lower-level descriptors and higher-level consequences and values, Reynolds and Gutman (1984, 1988) utilize laddering technique, the results of which can be graphically represented in a tree diagram, or hierarchical value map, by means of a dominance, or implications, matrix (Jolly et al., 1988).

Throughout the 1990s the means–end model has been extended through a body of research that focuses first on application (and is largely descriptive in nature) and secondly on methodology.

OPERATIONALIZING MEANS–END ANALYSIS: UNDERSTANDING PERFUME PURCHASE

In order to illustrate the practice of this PCT/laddering approach to values research, a study using the means–end model is now presented in some detail to enable the reader to gain an overview of the data collection and analysis

PROCESS   **OUTCOME**

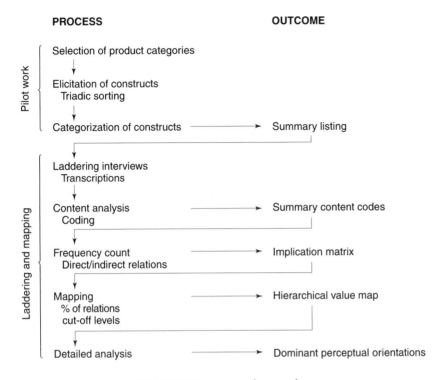

FIGURE 12.5   *Research procedure*

process. In addition, it is intended that this study should demonstrate the powerful benefits of adopting the approach. An overview of the research procedure is illustrated in Figure 12.5. This shows its separate stages in terms of processes and outcomes and can be used as a guide to the fieldwork reported in this and the following sections of the chapter. The analysis of the data was undertaken using a manual approach; a software package known as Laddermap (Gengler and Reynolds, 1989) has been created, although it is felt that in setting out each stage of the analysis procedure a fuller appreciation of the technique is conveyed.

The study was conducted among UK and German subjects who had recently purchased women's perfume, with the aim of exploring the meaning or patterns of thought behind their choices.

FIELDWORK STAGE **1:** ELICITING CONSTRUCTS

Data collection procedure

Using an amalgamated list of both UK and German brand leaders in the women's perfume category enabled respondents across the two markets to start from exactly the same set of stimuli. This amalgamated list is shown in Table 12.2.

TABLE 12.2   *Brands used to represent the product category*

Perfume brands
Anais Anais
Beautiful
Coco
Joop!
Loulou
No. 5
Roma
Vanderbilt
Youth Dew
Bath & Beauty
Berlin
Eternity
Le Bain
Opium
Paris
Tresor
White Linen

Eliciting constructs

The first stage in the process starts with a differentiation task where subjects are asked to explain their personal basis for making distinctions between objects. In this study, the initial interviews produced a set of distinctions made by individual respondents concerning perceived meaningful differences between the brands. Responses were elicited using the triadic sorting technique (Kelly, 1955). By this means, respondents were presented with sets of three brands on cards. They were then asked to name 'the odd one out' by stating one way in which two of them were alike yet different from the third. The bases for similarity (the emergent pole) and difference (the implicit pole) were recorded. Respondents were then repeatedly presented with different triads, or sets of three brands, until they could no longer think of any reason why two of them were different from the third.

A total of 29 interviews was carried out, 16 in the UK and 13 in Germany, each of which typically lasted 25–45 minutes.

Categorization of constructs

Following scrutiny, one interview was rejected because of insufficient demographic data. The number in each cell was then reduced through random selection to ten, to establish a common base across the two markets. The constructs elicited from respondents were then listed, resulting in a total of 127 (56 for the UK and 71 for Germany).

The next step was to reduce the data by identifying commonality of meaning. It was decided to complete this task using external judges to avoid too much bias being exercised by the researcher. Three native speakers per country were employed to code the constructs by category heading.

TABLE 12.3   *Summary listing of constructs elicited*

Perfumes
for older/younger women *
light/heavy or fragrance *
modern/classic *
country of origin
flowery/other
packaging *
advertising and promotion *
from Chanel/not from Chanel *
long-lasting
feminine/masculine
designer fragrance/not a designer fragrance
sweet/other

* = repeated in both countries

After this categorization process, a simple frequency count resulted in a list of the top nine constructs for the product category/country. These lists were then amalgamated across the countries and commonalties identified. Following this, a definitive summary listing of the constructs elicited was produced in English for the product category. These are shown in Table 12.3. The summary listings were then translated into German by the researcher for use in the second stage of the fieldwork.

The outcome of this categorization process was a listing of 12 attributes for perfume that could be used to form the starting point of the laddering interviews carried out in stage 2 of the fieldwork.

FIELDWORK STAGE **2:** LADDERING AND MAPPING

Laddering interviews

In order to carry out the laddering interviews, respondents were recruited by cascading contacts in both countries. Interviews were completed mainly at place of work, with the remainder being split between at home and at leisure. Effectively, a quota sample was created as respondent samples for the product category were matched on three criteria: gender, employment and whether the purchase was for themselves or intended as a gift (it is estimated that 40% of sales of perfume in the UK are gift purchases).

To elicit the laddering data, the personal approach was chosen rather than a more recently developed pencil and paper technique. With the latter, respondents are issued with a questionnaire consisting of laddering-type questions and left to fill in the responses themselves. Using this impersonal technique assumes respondents can cope with the instructions. In addition, the pencil and paper method may restrict the amount of data gathered (as researchers typically provide space for a ladder consisting of three steps only – and respondents may wish to record more). However, the advantages of the paper and pencil method are that the data are easier to work with, in terms of categorization, as transcripts do not have to be made and the salient elements of the data are labelled by respondents.

A further decision was required prior to starting the laddering interviews regarding the use of elicited versus provided constructs, or bi-polar dimensions. In the original use of the repertory grid technique, the method was to elicit both constructs and elements from the same respondent (Kelly, 1955). 'There is . . . considerable evidence that the constructs which are elicited from subjects individually are more personally meaningful to those subjects than are constructs supplied to them from other sources' (Adams-Webber, 1979: 23). However, the main advantage of supplying constructs elicited previously to respondents is that it permits a higher degree of standardization in comparing different sample populations but it does represent a major departure from Kelly's own emphasis on the personal nature of each individual's construction process. Researchers must make an informed decision here of their own when planning their studies.

Despite this breach with Kelly's protocol, it was decided to use the previously elicited constructs to start the laddering interviews in order to gain the benefits of standardization across the different national samples.

After gathering background information, the session was started by giving respondents a sheet listing the salient constructs for the product category. Respondents were asked to name those constructs of most importance to themselves when making a purchase. They were then asked to name their preferred pole and this was then followed with the question 'Why is that important to you?'. Thus, the laddering interview began. Most interviews were taped (the only exceptions being due to malfunctioning of the tape recorder on two occasions). In the style of a young child, this question was repeated obsessively until the respondent could provide no further material.

As highlighted by Reynolds and Gutman (1988), the main problems encountered with the laddering interviews related to respondents not 'knowing' the answer when asked why a particular attribute or consequence was important to them, or when they were struggling to articulate an answer. Under these circumstances, it is difficult for the interviewer to assist without putting words into the mouths of respondents and thereby biasing the interview. As Reynolds and Gutman (1988) suggest, it was useful to ask what would happen if the attribute or consequence *were not* delivered. Kelly himself suggests alternative ways of asking the question by adopting an 'invitational mood'. Secondly, some respondents found that because of their responses the interview took a more personal approach than they had perhaps anticipated. This created a certain uncomfortableness on their part that was alleviated largely through confidentiality reassurances given by the interviewer, or the particular topic was returned to later in the interview.

A total of 24 interviews was carried out, 12 per country. Each typically lasted 60–90 minutes and a maximum of three per day was carried out. An extract of an actual interview is shown in Figure 12.6.

Which of these aspects are important for you? A

I last bought perfume to take on holiday so I was looking for a small package.
And I didn't want to spend a lot. A

What did you choose? A A

A flowery one. Modern feminine. No special advertising.

How would you describe flowery? A A

Sweet, like flowers. Not musky or spicy.

Why was it important to you to buy a flowery perfume?

Because I knew I would like it.

Why do you like flowery perfumes?

I only like scented ones – not the heavy fragrances.

Why is this? A C

Because heavy ones may give you a headache. Light ones are nice and refreshing.

Why is that important to you?

It's other people who can smell it – to be honest, I can't smell it.

Why is it important to you to feel refreshed? C

Well, when you're with other people, you don't like to be thought smelly! Not like some people who've got BO.

That's not how you like to feel? C

No! In the morning after a shower, talced and refreshed – with some perfume – you feel more confident. It makes you walk tall. Look forward to the day. C

Why is this important to you?

So that you can go through the day full of confidence and get on with your work and bring it up to standard. It makes you feel good. V

You mentioned that you prefer the modern perfumes – how would you describe modern? A

It was in a modern plastic bottle – plastic is modern as opposed to glass and it had a spray nozzle rather than a stopper. A

What is the advantage of this? C C

You only need to put a touch of light perfume on, it's less wasteful. Plastic doesn't break in the bag so you don't lose the contents. It's much lighter than glass. You can see how much you've got left. C

You said you prefer feminine fragrances – how would you describe these? A

I don't know what the dictionary says – nice and refreshing and light – nothing heavy.

Was there any other aspect which was important to you?

I didn't know what the country of origin was.

Would this matter to you? A

It wouldn't matter. I'm not quite sure how long the smell would last – I haven't tested it.

What would you expect?

Certainly several hours. A

Why is that? C

You don't always have time to go and refresh yourself in … popping to the loo every 5 minutes to spray yourself. You can't do it.

Is there any other aspect which is important to you?

No, I don't think so.

FIGURE 12.6 *Example of a laddering interview*

Content analysis

The purpose of content analysis and data reduction is to make the data more manageable. With the means–end model (illustrated in Figure 12.4), this is achieved by following Gutman (1982) and subdividing it into the constituent elements of attribute (A), consequence (C) or value (V) and labelling it accordingly. This coding process is followed by a categorization procedure that takes place within the three main groupings (that is, attribute, consequence, value). Here, the purpose of the task is to reduce down the amount of data through an iterative process of identifying commonality of meaning.

To begin with, the English language interviews were transcribed by the researcher while the German language tapes were transcribed by a German secretarial service. This was to ensure that coders had 'perfect' scripts to work on and would not be distracted, or indeed misled, by any errors in transcription. The interviews were then sent out to coders for coding. An instruction pack was prepared and briefings given on an individual basis over the telephone. Two coders per country were employed to code the interviews. Inter-coder reliability was checked using a simple exercise and no problems were reported with the set task.

Data reduction

Table 12.4 illustrates the total number of elements identified in the transcripts by the coders and also shows how these were subdivided within each cell.

Following coding, each individual element highlighted in the interview was listed under one of the three headings that had been assigned by the coders (attributes, consequences, values). These lists were then passed back to the coders for categorization. To assist in this task, an initial list of category headings was prepared and translated by the researcher with coders offered the opportunity to create additional categories to those provided (this appeared to be more necessary for the German responses). Thus, it was at this stage that the translation process was effectively begun (further details on managing language issues can be obtained directly from the author). Again, majority decisions predominated and where differences arose, the researcher made the final decision.

TABLE 12.4   *Summary of elements recorded*

	Attributes	Consequences	Values	Total
UK	120	113	22	255
Germany	114	133	43	290

Summary content codes

The main task to be achieved with categorization is to create categories distinctive enough into which all elements fall easily. However, one does not want to end up with too many categories otherwise meaning through

TABLE 12.5 *Summary content codes – English version*

Perfume		
Attributes	Consequences	Values
1 Nature of the fragrance	11 Personal hygiene	26 Sense of belonging
2 Brand name	12 Self-expression	27 Confidence
3 Packaging	13 Evokes memories	28 Self-satisfaction
4 Advertising and	14 Signal	29 Well-being
promotion	15 Reassurance	30 Recognition/respect
5 Country of origin	16 Character of fragrance	31 Security
6 Designer fragrance	17 Functional performance	32 Harmony
7 Bottle design	of fragrance	33 Sense of individualism
8 Price	18 Inner security	34 Concern for the
9 Place of distribution	19 Special	environment
10 Other influences	20 Quality	35 Quality of life
	21 Value/price	
	22 Influence on behaviour	
	23 Acceptability as a gift	
	24 Pleasing	
	25 Environment concerns	

aggregation becomes difficult. Reynolds and Gutman (1988) provide guidance on this matter by asserting that, 'It is the relationships between the elements that are the focus of interest, not the elements themselves.' This resonates with the opening section of this chapter concerned with meaning, that understanding meaning comes from seeing the context in which things are situated. The interconnecting lines of psychological movement thus become the prime interest.

For purposes of demonstrating this exemplar, the output of the categorization process (the summary content codes) is listed in Table 12.5 for the UK interviews only.

These summary content codes then serve the function of master codes and each element of the respondents' ladders is identified with a master code. A total of 64 ladders was recorded for the UK respondents (with a mean length of 5.33), with a total of 72 for the German respondents (with a mean length of 6).

To summarize, across the countries, 136 ladders were recorded. The longest ladder recorded consisted of nine steps and the shortest consisted of two steps. This analysis of ladder length vindicates the decision not to use the paper and pencil method to elicit the raw data (where typically space for a maximum of three responses – or steps – only is provided).

The implication matrix

The next stage in the research process is to enter the data into an implication matrix which displays the number of times each element leads to each other element. Two types of relations are represented: direct and indirect relations. Direct relations are those in which one element leads to another with no other elements intervening (relations between attributes are not recorded) and indirect elements are those in which there are intervening elements. An example of the technique is highlighted below:

makes you feel good (29) – value

|

feel more confident (18) – consequence

|

nice and refreshing (11) – consequence

|

not musky or spicy (1) – attribute

|

sweet, like flowers (1) – attribute

|

flowery (1) – attribute

(UK perfume respondent 9)

The (1)–(1) relations are not recorded as they concern attribute to attribute relationships. The other relationships are recorded: (1)–(11) is a direct one, as are (11)–(18) and (18)–(29). There are usually many more indirect relations than direct relations and these are also examined. In this example, (1)–(18), (1)–(29) and (11)–(29) are indirect relations.

The matrix is drawn up, with numbers expressed in fractional form, with direct relations to the left of the decimal point and indirect relations to the right. Appendix A shows the summary implication matrix for the English perfume sample. Thus, 'Nature of the fragrance' (element 1) leads to 'Self-expression' (element 12) four times directly and twice indirectly, etc.

Constructing a hierarchical value map

The implication matrix provides the 'blueprint' for drawing up a hierarchical value map (hvm). Mapping provides a meaningful way of representing subjective data; its main benefit can be summed up in the old adage that 'a picture paints a thousand words'. This graphic device can be used to record and communicate information and can, furthermore, act as a tool to facilitate decision-making, problem-solving and negotiation (Huff, 1990).

Hvms are created by reconstructing chains from the aggregate data. (Chains are sequences of elements that emerge from the aggregate implication matrix, whereas ladders are the sequences of elements for each individual respondent.) In this way the consensual nature of the data is determined, that is, it becomes possible to see how individuals may share a more or less common point of view: 'Part of any consumer's thinking will be idiosyncratic, but part will also present a common way of thinking' (Calder and Tybout, 1987).

Considerable ingenuity is required to build up an hvm as the guidelines are that 'one should try at all times to avoid crossing lines' (Reynolds and Gutman, 1988). In addition, the criterion for evaluating the ability of the map to represent the data is to assess the percentage of all relations among elements accounted for by the mapped elements. The hypothetical case shown by Reynolds and Gutman (1988) uses 94.5% of all relations. Aiming at this figure is a hard task and some comfort can be derived from the fact that other researchers do not divulge their percentages or report results below this figure (77% in the case of Jolly et al., 1988). As an example, the number of relations used as a percentage of the total recorded is given for the UK hvm in Appendix B. The actual number was 55.0% in the case of the UK data and 73.86% in the case of the German data.

An arbitrary decision is made about the cut-off level and having selected a level (say two direct or indirect relations), relations are then plotted by working through each row. Significant values are identified and then followed through the matrix, creating a chain that can be graphically represented. This forms the start of the hvm. The aggregated map (where data across the two countries are plotted) was drawn up using a cut-off level of four.

In drawing up the hvm, cut-off levels become more of a guideline as the key is to get the best fit of data. On occasion, certain relationships falling below the adopted cut-off level were plotted where the relationship was proving to be meaningful in terms of the numbers of direct and indirect relations. This is permitted by Reynolds and Gutman (1988), who, in their paper, describe the various sorts of relations that should be plotted.

Having plotted all relations, it is desirable to look at all elements in the map in terms of the numbers of direct and indirect relations they have with other elements.

Determining dominant perceptual orientations

Once a hierarchical value map is constructed, one typically considers any pathway from bottom to top as a potential chain representing a perceptual orientation. To fully understand the strength of the chains, Reynolds and Gutman (1988) describe a technique for evaluating intra-chain relations. Essentially, the data on direct and indirect relations for the dominant chains in the map are summarized and presented in a format that is easier to read than the implication matrix. (These data are presented in aggregated form in Appendix C.) The output of the table (the aggregated dominant perceptual orientation) is shown below:

value	– Well-being
consequences	– Signal
	Self-expression
	Character of the fragrance
attribute	– Nature of the fragrance

Reading a hierarchical value map

The 'vertical axis' is divided into three parts – attributes, consequences and values – while the 'horizontal axis' sets out the summary content codes. Effectively, these are 'layered', like a cake, with the summary content codes listing the attributes positioned beneath those listing the consequences, which are in turn positioned beneath those listing the values. The lines running between the summary content codes represent the linkages. Generally, maps reflect a pyramid-like shape, with fewer values depicted than attributes and consequences.

The aggregated or combined map for both UK and German respondents shown in Figure 12.7 illustrates the dominance of the elements (1) 'Nature of the fragrance' → (12) 'Self-expression' → (29) 'Well-being'.

Other key consequences are (14) 'Signal' and (16) 'Character of the fragrance'. This dominant chain is reflected in the German map (Figure 12.8), where the consequences (16) 'Character of the fragrance' and (24) 'Pleasing' are also of significance. In the UK map (Figure 12.9), the dominant chain is recorded as (1) 'Nature of the fragrance' → (11) 'Personal hygiene' → (29) 'Well-being', perhaps reflecting an emphasis on the physical benefits of perfume ('it makes you smell pleasant'), which in turn 'make you feel good' (because your odour does not offend). Amongst German respondents a different orientation was recorded since perfume is used as a means to self-expression that, in turn, confers a feeling of well-being (*'man fühlt sich dabei wohl'* – one feels good about it). Interestingly, the consequence (11) 'Personal hygiene' is of minor significance in the German map.

A major difference in the two maps is the role of (3) 'Packaging'. In the German map this is linked to (25) 'Environmental concerns', which is, in turn, linked to (29) 'Well-being'.

As this study shows, one of the major advantages of using means–end analysis is that the cognitions of consumers within different geographical markets can be compared immediately for differences and similarities. In this international context, the model offers a potent tool for market segmentation as groups of consumers sharing common personal values can be identified and, hence, the market can be segmented. The resulting segments may well cut across the more traditional bases for segmentation, such as demographic or socio-economic variables, but the likelihood is that the production of marketing strategies based on enhancing consumers' relevant, personal values is more likely to be successful.

Not all segments identified will be of commercial interest to the organization but pursuing a values-based marketing strategy in those niche markets that have the potential for profitability will go some considerable way to fulfilling the key marketing task of enhancing customer value.

As an example of this, with perfume, a marketer with responsibility for the German and UK markets would be able to ascertain from the study that the issue of packaging would need different treatment in each country. The attribute 'Packaging' linked in to 'Acceptability as a gift' among UK consumers, but was linked to 'Environmental concerns' among German respondents. In the UK, the more packaging, the better suited the product is to a market that is

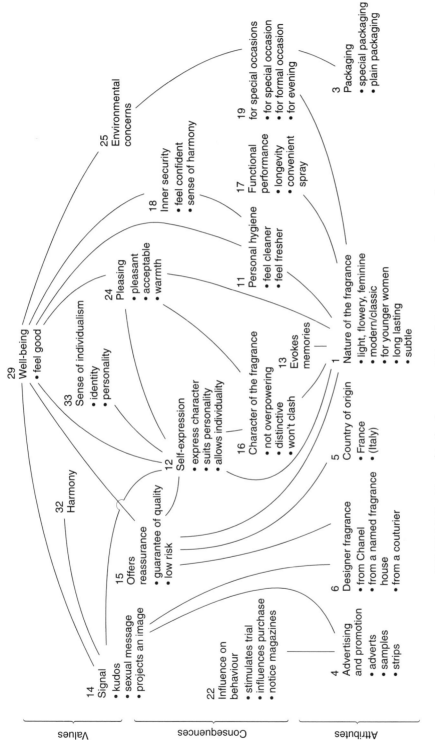

FIGURE 12.7 *Hierarchical value map – UK and German respondents combined*

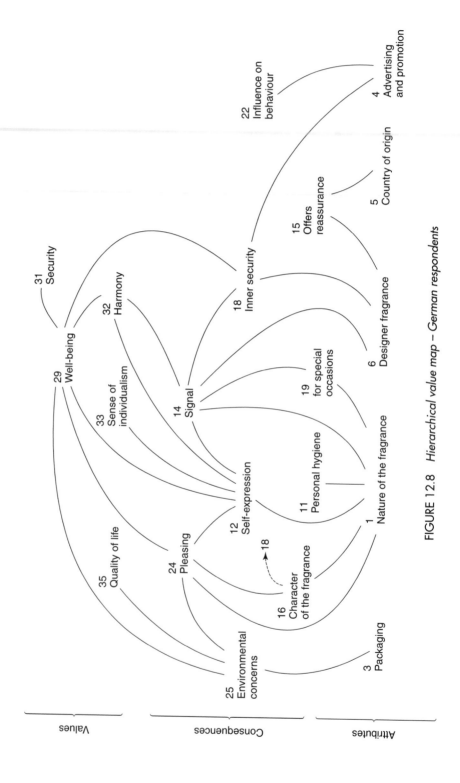

FIGURE 12.8   *Hierarchical value map – German respondents*

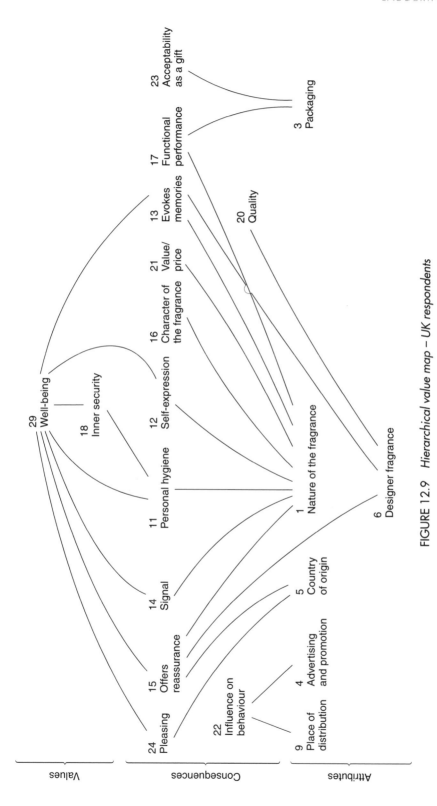

FIGURE 12.9   *Hierarchical value map – UK respondents*

made up of a substantial proportion of gift sales, while a minimalist approach would be more appropriate for the German market where consumer behaviour is influenced more by 'green' (or environmentalist) concerns, embodied in the 1991 *Verpackungsverordnung*.

Furthermore, perfume marketing is about communicating a 'message in the bottle' and, as an example, the importance of the product attribute 'Designer fragrance' has been used to spearhead the advertising campaign for Parfums Cartier with the slogan *'tout Cartier dans un parfum'*, suggesting consumers will find all of the design style, prestige and appeal of the Cartier (designer) name in the perfume itself. The message is both reassuring (in terms of risk reduction) and aspirational and works explicitly at the attribute → consequence level, with the consequence → value level implied.

Thus, the salient attributes of the product, as revealed through means–end analysis, can be used by the practitioner in deciding on positioning, while the detail provided by the dominant perceptual orientations of aggregated maps can be used to provide even more focus. With multinational means–end research a comparison of salient attributes can assist in finding common ground for a pan-European campaign, thereby helping build a pan-European brand. For example, with the perfume data, the dominant elements 'Nature of the fragrance' → 'Self-expression' → 'Well-being' could be used as an acceptable positioning platform in both markets.

Observations on laddering technique

1 All respondents quickly understood triadic sorting and many seemed amazed at how much they 'knew' about various brands. This was exemplified by a couple of interviews where the subjects seemed more grateful for the interview experience than the researcher herself!

   However, a major drawback of the initial interview technique is the tendency for some responses to be utterly valueless in terms of the type of information being sought. These were typified by the 'I like those two; I don't like that one' sort of response. The task of the interviewer then becomes one of trying to 'enable' the respondent to better articulate an answer. This in itself can make the technique seem like more of a test that some respondents find off-putting.

2 Attempting to convert laddering data into an hvm is reminiscent of trying to squeeze a quart into the proverbial pint pot. Somewhere along the line, it is inevitable that data will be lost. It is disappointing only to be able to utilize about 55–74% of responses in drawing up the hvm. However, this is a consequence of the aggregation process whereby richness is lost. This occurs at each of the categorization processes, particularly that outlined in the section on data reduction above. At this stage the researcher was reasonably satisfied that the data were not too constrained by categorization, but had they been reduced rather more, it is conceivable that it would have been possible to utilize a greater percentage of relations in drawing up the hvms. The literature does not state where it is more appropriate to lose the richness.

It is conceivable that paper and pencil techniques may assist in avoiding this problem, although they can be seen also as merely restricting the richness of data to begin with.

In addition, there are no formulas given for deciding which cut-off levels to use and this becomes a process of trial and error whereby one must decide with what percentage of the total relations available one is satisfied in drawing up the hvms. The cut-off levels used were arrived at after an iterative process and appear to offer the most efficient use of the available data.

3 It is very difficult to avoid crossing lines. This echoes the view of Butt (1995), who commented that difficulties in laddering procedure 'frequently produce snakes as well as ladders, going both up and down the system in a looping and circular fashion'. Thus it would seem that lines of possible psychological movement may not always be free of bisections.

However, a device for assisting in making connections that would otherwise involve crossing lines has been introduced. Where absolutely necessary, it has been indicated with dotted lines (— — →) where one element should be connected to another at some mid point in the body of the map (see Figure 12.8). This also obviated the need for lines to be crossed. Where necessary, one line was crossed with another using the device (—⌒→)(see Figure 12.9). Both these devices, again, aid readability and preserve a clarity of style.

4 Laddering procedure is costly in terms of money and time. It is a manually intensive research process; organizing and covering fieldwork costs, transcriptions and managing the coding/categorization processes make significant demands on the researcher. All of these aspects need to be taken into account when planning for studies using the means–end method.

5 Using laddering in international research: from the outset, this research study was designed to take place in two markets. Such a research environment makes additional demands on the models adopted and some of these issues are discussed below in reference to use of the technique.

A key problem in international laddering research is to ascertain whether different attributes, consequences and values are relevant in different countries and whether they carry the same meaning. Any cross-cultural comparison of data raises questions of validity, particularly where respondents' use of their vernacular is central to the methodology. Newmark (1988) posits that there are three functions of language: expressive, informative and vocative (directive or persuasive), and in translating a text, the translator must adopt either a semantic or a communicative approach. A semantic translation leans more towards word-for-word and literal approaches and has a strong source-language emphasis. A communicative translation, on the other hand, has a stronger target-language emphasis and adopts a free, idiomatic approach, where the sense and not the words are deemed to be of most importance. Thus, there are assumptions to be accepted or challenged in the theory of translation, and researchers must familiarize themselves with these and be explicit about the approach they adopt to cope with the issues raised in attempting to transfer meaning.

CONCLUSION

This chapter has introduced laddering technique as a research tool for making sense of personal meaning by anchoring it in the literature, exploring ontological and epistemological perspectives and highlighting the essential authors who chart the pathway between Personal Construct Theory, laddering and means–end analysis. Moreover, a practical example of the operationalization of the means–end model from the field of marketing graphically illustrates the saliency of the approach, providing readers with an exemplar that should enable them to effectively design and carry out their own laddering study.

Study questions

1 Consider how laddering technique could be used in your research design. List the benefits and drawbacks.
2 Is the means–end model applicable to your research design? If so, in what way?
3 Does your research design offer an opportunity to advance the means–end model or apply laddering technique in a hitherto unreported situation?

Recommended further reading

Fransella, F. and Bannister, D. (1977) *A Manual for Repertory Grid Technique*. London: Academic Press. (The authoritative guide to repertory grid technique and essential reading for anyone planning to use this approach)
Peter, J.P., Olson, J.C. and Grunert, K.G. (1999) *Consumer Behaviour and Marketing Strategy* (European Edition). London: McGraw-Hill. (A comprehensive textbook which authoritatively covers the subject of understanding consumer buyer behaviour and demonstrates, through numerous case examples, how this best links with marketing strategy)
Pope, M.L. and Keen, T.R. (1981) *Personal Construct Psychology and Education*. London: Academic Press. (A useful guide to personal construct psychology to broaden and deepen your reading in this area)

Note

1 Affect can be distinguished from cognition largely by thinking about affective states as something that people *are* ('I am happy, she is sad') while, on the other hand, one *has* cognitions ('I believe Coke is the best cola drink, he knows where the superstore is').

References

Adams-Webber, J.R. (1979) *Personal Construct Theory*. Chichester: Wiley.
Agle, B.R. and Caldwell, C.B. (1999) 'Understanding Research on Values in Business', *Business and Society*, 38 (3), pp. 326–87.

Bannister, D. and Mair, J.M.M. (1968) *The Evaluation of Personal Constructs*. London: Academic Press.

Blaikie, N. (1993) *Approaches to Social Enquiry*. Cambridge: Polity Press.

Butt, T. (1995) 'Ordinal Relationships Between Constructs', *Journal of Constructivist Psychology*, 8, pp. 227–37.

Calder, B.J. and Tybout, A.M. (1987) 'What Consumer Research Is', *Journal of Consumer Research*, 14 (1), pp. 136–40.

Gengler, C.E. and Reynolds, T.J. (1989) 'Means–end Structural Analysis: Computer Generated Hierarchical Value Maps', paper presented at EIASM Workshop on Consumer Behaviour: Extending the Cognitive Structure Perspective, Brussels, Belgium.

Gordon, W. (1999) *Goodthinking, A Guide to Qualitative Research*. Henley on Thames: Admap.

Gutman, J. (1982) 'A Means–End Chain Model Based on Consumer Categorization Processes', *Journal of Marketing*, 46 (2), pp. 60–72.

Holman, R.H. (1984) 'A Values and Lifestyles Perspective on Human Behavior', in R.E. Pitts and A.G. Woodside (eds), *Personal Values and Consumer Psychology*. Lexington, MA: Lexington Books, pp. 35–53.

Huff, A. (1990) 'Mapping Strategic Thought' in A. Huff (ed.), *Mapping Strategic Thought*, Chichester: Wiley, pp. 11–49.

Jolly, J.P., Reynolds, T.J. and Slocum, J.W. (1988) 'Application of the Means–End Theoretic for Understanding the Cognitive Bases of Performance Appraisal', *Organizational Behavior and Human Decision Processes*, 41 (2), pp. 153–79.

Kahle, L.R. and Kennedy, P. (1988) 'Using the List of Values (LOV) to Understand Consumers', *The Journal of Services Marketing*, 2 (4), pp. 49–56.

Kahle, L.R., Beatty, S.E. and Homer, P. (1986) 'Alternative Measurement Approaches to Consumer Values: The List of Values (LOV) and Values and Life Styles (VALS)', *Journal of Consumer Research*, 13 (3), pp. 405–9.

Kelly, G.A. (1955) *The Psychology of Personal Constructs*. New York: W.W. Norton.

Morgan, G. (1993) *Imaginization: The Art of Creative Management*. Newbury Park, CA: Sage.

Newmark, P. (1988) *A Textbook of Translation*. Hemel Hempstead: Prentice Hall.

Peter, J.P. and Olson, J.C. (1990) *Consumer Behavior and Marketing Strategy*. Homewood, IL: Irwin.

Reynolds, T.J. and Gutman, J. (1984) 'Laddering: Extending the Repertory Grid Methodology to Construct Attribute–Consequence–Value Hierarchies', in R.E. Pitts and A.G. Woodside (eds), *Personal Values and Consumer Psychology*. Lexington, MA: Lexington Books, pp. 155–67.

Reynolds, T.J. and Gutman, J. (1988) 'Laddering Theory, Method, Analysis and Interpretation', *Journal of Advertising Research*, 18 (1), pp. 11–31.

Rokeach, M.J. (1973) *The Nature of Human Values*. New York: The Free Press.

Rosch, E. and Mervis, C.B. (1975) 'Family Resemblances: Studies in the Internal Structure of Categories', *Cognitive Psychology*, 7, pp. 573–605.

Rosch, E., Mervis, C.B., Gray, W.D., Johnson, D.M. and Boyes-Braem, P. (1976) 'Basic Objects in Natural Categories', *Cognitive Psychology*, 8, pp. 382–439.

Vinson, D.E., Scott, J.E. and Lamont, M. (1977) 'The Role of Personal Values in Marketing and Consumer Behaviour', *Journal of Marketing*, 41 (2), pp. 44–50.

Wright, K.J.J. (1970) 'Exploring the Uniqueness of Common Complaints', *British Journal of Medical Psychology*, 43, pp. 221–32.

Young, S. and Feigin, B. (1975) 'Using the Benefit Chain for Improved Strategy Formulation', *Journal of Marketing*, 39 (3), pp. 72–4.

Appendices

APPENDIX A: SUMMARY IMPLICATION MATRIX – UK PERFUME

From ↓ to →	11	12	13	14	15	16	17	18	19	20	21	22
1 Nature of the fragrance	8.2	4.2	4.0	3.0	2.1	4.0	4.1	0.4			2.0	
2 Brand name					0.1	1.0			1.0			0.1
3 Packaging												
4 Advertising and promotion							2.0				1.0	
5 Country of origin		0.1		1.1	0.1						1.0	5.1
6 Designer/fragrance house					0.3	0.1	0.1	0.1				
7 Bottle design			2.0	1.0	2.1		1.0		0.1	0.1		
8 Price										1.1	1.0	1.0
9 Place of distribution		1.0			1.0						1.0	
10 Other influences			1.0					0.1				2.0
11 Personal hygiene								1.1				1.0
12 Self-expression	1.0							3.0				
13 Evokes memories				1.0		1.0						
14 Signal (image and sense)		1.0										
15 Reassurance		1.0		1.0				1.0	1.0	1.0		

APPENDIX **B**: SUMMARY OF DIRECT AND INDIRECT RELATIONS FOR
EACH ELEMENT
HIERARCHICAL VALUE MAP – **UK** PERFUME

No.	To	From	
1	—	31.18	
2	—	—	
3	—	4.1	
4	—	5.1	
5	—	5.1	
6	—	5.5	
7	—	—	
8	—	—	
9	—	2.0	
10	—	—	
11	8.2	7.0	
12	4.2	1.1	
13	6.0	2.0	
14	3.0	1.1	55.0% of relations
15	7.2	1.2	plotted (99/180) cut-
16	4.0	—	off level = 2 relations
17	6.1	—	
18	3.4	3.0	
19	—	—	
20	1.1	—	
21	2.0	—	
22	7.1	—	
23	2.1	—	
24	2.0	2.0	
25	—	—	
26	—	—	
27	—	—	
28	—	—	
29	14.16	—	

APPENDIX **C**: DETERMINING DOMINANT PERCEPTUAL ORIENTATIONS
COMBINED PERFUME

	1	16	12	14	29	
1	—	15.1	14.11	6.6	0.20	35.38
16	—	—	4.3	2.0	0.4	6.7
12	—	1.0	—	4.0	5.4	10.4
14	—	1.0	3.0	—	2.3	6.3
29	—	—	—	—	—	—
						58.78

1 = Nature of the fragrance
16 = Character of the fragrance
12 = Self-expression
14 = Signal
29 = Well-being

13

Action Research

Colin Eden and Chris Huxham

OVERVIEW

In common with other forms of qualitative research (Denzin and Lincoln, 1994; Gummesson, 1991; Miles and Huberman, 1984; Strauss and Corbin, 1990), action research has become increasingly prominent among researchers involved in the study of organizations as an espoused paradigm used to justify the validity of a range of research outputs. The term is sometimes used rather loosely to cover a variety of approaches. In this chapter we shall use the term to embody an approach for researching organizations and management which, broadly, results from an involvement by the researcher with members of an organization over a matter that is of genuine concern to them and in which there is an intent by the organization members to take action based on the intervention.

Interventions of this kind will necessarily be 'one-offs', so action research has frequently been criticized for its lack of repeatability and, hence, lack of rigour. These criticisms are countered by the argument that the involvement with practitioners over things that actually matter to them provides a richness of insight which could not be gained in other ways (Reason and Rowan, 1981; Whyte, 1991). This is a valid and important argument to which we shall return. However, in this chapter a major concern is to identify the range of approaches over which the argument may apply. For example, we would not consider any organizational intervention project to be necessarily action research, unless it satisfies characteristics which make it *rigorous research*. Similarly, we would not consider any piece of research within an organization to be necessarily action research, unless it satisfies characteristics to make it *action oriented*.

Aguinis (1993) argues that action research has much in common with traditional scientific method. Our own view, however, is that good action research will be good science, though not in a way that depends necessarily upon meeting all the tenets of traditional scientific method. But this requires a clear understanding of what is needed to achieve 'good quality research' *in this type of setting*. Criticism of action research as poor social science is often made without understanding the (albeit often unrealized) *potential* for rigour. Nevertheless, the label 'action research' *is* unfortunately often used as an excuse for sloppy research.

The main thrust of this chapter is thus an exploration of the nature and boundaries of good action research in the context of the study of organizations. We are not an attempting to argue, in general, for action research as against other types of research. We do not intend to formulate a definition of action research because we do not believe this would be helpful or productive. To do so is likely to narrow its application as well as encourage wasteful definitional debate. We believe that action research is better captured through an interlocking set of characteristics than a definition. Inevitably, many of the characteristics of good action research apply to any good research, but we see those identified in this chapter as particularly pertinent for those undertaking action research. In relation to action research these characteristics are often ignored, because they are either seen as not relevant or taken to be not attainable.

We indicated, in the first paragraph of the chapter, our starting point for an exploration of the nature and boundaries of action research, where we asserted that: *action research involves the researcher in working with members of an organization over a matter which is of genuine concern to them and in which there is an intent by the organization members to take action based on the intervention.* The underlying argument of the chapter will be that while the above attributes are clearly important to action research, they do not alone give sufficient guidance about its nature. The chapter will thus both narrow down this initial description and elaborate on the detail of it.

ACTION RESEARCH CHARACTERIZED

We have divided our discussion of the characteristics of action research into three groups. In this preliminary section we will discuss just one characteristic: the key feature which distinguishes action research from other forms of management research. The following sections focus first on action research *outcomes* and secondly on action research *processes*. The broad issues that we regard as particularly important are: the action focus of action research; generality; theory development; the type of theory development appropriate for action research; the pragmatic focus of action research; designing action research; and the validity of action research.

We are seeking to identify a set of characteristics that can inform practically the research process. The final list of fifteen characteristics can be used as a checklist to guide thinking about the design and validity of action research. However, we wish to make clear that the discussion leading to the derivation of each characteristic is crucial to a proper understanding of its use in this way.

The action focus of action research

Our first characteristic is almost, but not, definitional:

> (1) action research demands an integral involvement by the researcher in an intent to change the organization. This intent may not succeed – no change may take place as a result of the intervention – and the change may not be as intended.

This is saying that action research must be concerned with intervening in action; it is not enough for the researcher simply to study the action of others. While the latter can be a valid alternative form of management research, it is not action research. Action research thus carries a particular set of concerns along with it which the remaining characteristics seek to encapsulate.

THE CHARACTERISTICS OF ACTION RESEARCH *OUTCOMES*

Generality

In common with Lewin, many authors on action research stress the importance of the work being useful to the client. For example, Reason (1988) quotes Torbert as arguing that action research must be: 'useful to the practitioner *at the moment of action* rather than a reflective science about action' (emphasis added), and Elden and Levin (1991) argue that action research should be a way of *empowering* participants. Although these two outcomes are related – because empowering demands use at the moment of action – empowering goes significantly further by demanding a change in the power relationships within the organization. Other authors stress that the development of 'local theory' – theory which applies in the specific context of the research – is a central feature of the approach (Elden, 1979).

While these comments support the role of action research for enhancing action (characteristic 1 above), they tend to ignore the role of research for a wider audience. They also ignore the role of reflection to the practitioner as a part of changing their future behaviour (as with action learning). For the practitioner there will be benefits that go beyond the moment of action towards some generality that is related to their expectation of implications for future situations. This circumstance provides the opportunity for collaborative or participatory research. For other practitioners, and researchers, the generality will go even beyond this by having something to say about other contexts than that within which this specific practitioner operates.

Many critics of action research reasonably take from the above authors the view that results can only be bounded tightly by context. We, however, see action research as an approach that can build and extend theory of more general use than implied above. We are not, of course, arguing for a level of generality which is devoid of context. Rather, we are arguing that the general theory derived from action research must be applicable significantly beyond the specific situation.

Following from this, our second characteristic is that:

(2) action research must have some *implications beyond those required for action or generation of knowledge in the domain of the project*. It must be possible to envisage talking about the theories developed in relation to other situations. Thus it must be clear that the results *could* inform other contexts, at least in the sense of suggesting areas for consideration.

This means that the outcomes must be capable of being couched in other than situation-specific terms.

Thus, 'the name you choose [for a category] . . . must be a more abstract concept than the one it denotes' (Strauss and Corbin, 1990). It is important to be careful, of course, to avoid the danger that the abstractness is meaningless, generates more unnecessary jargon and obfuscates the power of the research. The ability of the researcher to characterize or conceptualize the particular experience in ways that make the research *meaningful to others* is crucial. This usually means that the reported research must be translated so that different circumstances can be envisaged by others. It is this that may promote interest from other practitioners in how to understand situations they expect to find themselves in, and from researchers by informing their own theory development.

Theory development

It is the careful *characterization and conceptualization* of experiences which amount to the theory that is carefully drawn out of action research. This leads to our third characteristic, that:

> (3) as well as being usable in everyday life, action research demands *valuing theory*, with theory elaboration and development as an explicit concern of the research process.

This may appear to suggest a dichotomy between research aims and intervention aims (Friedlander and Brown, 1974). There is, however, no reason why the two need to be seen as mutually exclusive. It is possible to fulfil the requirements of the client and at the same time consider the more theoretical implications, though it should be recognized that addressing these dual aims often means that more effort has to be put into achieving research results than would be the case with more conventional research paradigms. Research output can often be the direct converse of what is required for a client, where situation-specific terminology may be key to gaining ownership of the results.

The research output will also tend to be different from the immediate concerns of professional interventionists (that is, consultants) even though the latter may have an interest in generally transferable aspects of their interventions in order to enhance their professional adequacy. Our fourth characteristic, below, relies on exploring this point further.

Professional interventionists are sometimes engaged by immediate and incremental development of practice – 'How will I do better, work more effectively and efficiently, on my next project?'. Among other things, they will be interested in a transfer of tools, techniques, models and methods from one specific situation to another. This does demand the need to generalize from the specific, but this is most likely to be an incremental transfer from one specific context to another specific context. By contrast, observations about the specific situation will, *for the researcher*, raise broader questions that are of interest to a wider community who will work in a wider variety of contexts.

Researchers *qua* interventionists, as distinct from interventionists *qua* researchers, address themselves to a different primary audience. The 'interventionist as researcher' seeks to uncover general principles with implications for practice that can be shared between practitioners. The 'researcher as interventionist' seeks to talk to other researchers, and, in addition, to other interventionists. Notably both reflect a practical orientation and both are focusing on the generality of the ideas expressed (that is, they are extending them beyond the setting in which they were designed) but they are meeting different needs and (in the first instance) satisfying different audiences. There is a distinction here between concern with direct practice and the concern of action research to *develop theory to inform a more reliable and robust development of practice*. Lewin's much quoted, 'there's nothing so practical as a good theory' should perhaps become the action researcher's motto.

Despite this, we emphasize the importance of the development of tools, techniques, models, or methods as possible expressions of the outcome of action research. These can be an excellent outcome of action research, providing they embody a clear expression of theory. Unfortunately, often the embodiment is implicit, if it exists at all. Action research demands that the research output explain the link between the specific experience of the intervention and the design of the tool or method – it is this *explanation which is a part of theory generation*. Thus:

(4) if the generality drawn out of the action research is to be expressed through the design of tools, techniques, models and methods then this, alone, is not enough – the basis for their design must be explicit and shown to be related to the theories which inform the design and which, in turn, are supported or developed through action research.

The type of theory development appropriate for action research

What kind of theory then is an appropriate output of action research? The notion of *drawing out* theory is important for action research and suggests an approach to theory development which recognizes that while the researcher always brings a pre-understanding (Gummesson, 1991) – a starting theoretical position – to the situation, it is important to defer serious reflection on the role of this until the later stages of the project. This contrasts with other research approaches which are committed to setting out in advance the biases of the researcher.

In action research the researcher needs to be committed to *opening up the frame* within which the research situation and data related to it are explored. To do so requires the researcher to have a commitment to the temporary suppression of pre-understanding. This decreases the likelihood of the researcher's theoretical stance closing off new and alternative ways of understanding the data and so extending theory. In addition, suppression of pre-understanding encourages generation of a holistic and complex body of theory, concepts and experience. By contrast, being explicit about pre-understanding tends to result in a neatly bounded and 'chunked' list of biases which inevitably, even if unintentionally, takes on the form of separable propositions.

Thus, for action research it is important to move towards reflecting upon the role of pre-understanding only as theories begin to emerge, rather than in advance of the research. This is a matter of emphasis and timing not a question about whether the researcher's own theoretical stance is influential and needs to be made explicit. This *is* influential and it *must* be made explicit, but its influence will be less constraining if made explicit later rather than earlier. It is important to note that this is neither the position taken by Glaser (1992), who argues for the complete suppression of pre-understanding, or, at the other extreme, of the emphases within the collection of papers in the *Journal of Applied Behavioral Science* (Alderfer, 1993), which seem to assume a hypothesis-testing approach for action research.

By its very nature, action research does not lend itself to repeatable experimentation; each intervention will be different from the last. Over time, it is possible to try out theories over and over again, but each context will be slightly different, so each time it will be necessary to adjust the interpretation of the theory to the circumstances. Action research is therefore not a good vehicle for rigorous and detailed theory *testing* (at least in the traditional sense where explicit awareness of a theoretical pre-understanding is crucial).

On the other hand, interventions in organizations provide ideal opportunities for experimentation in the sense that they provide opportunities to try out complex theoretical *frameworks* that cannot be pulled apart for controlled evaluation of individual theories. This is important in organization studies research where it is often the systemic nature of a uniquely interlocking set of theories from many disciplines that makes the body of theory powerful and useful. Action research is, at its best, therefore, importantly concerned with such *systemic relationships*, rather than with single theories – the aim is to understand conceptual and theoretical *frameworks* where each theory must be understood in the context of other related theories.

Intervention settings can also provide rich data about what people do and say – and what theories are used and usable – when faced with a genuine need to take action. These settings are thus likely to provide both new and often unexpected insights. They are settings that are much more amenable to theory generation and development than theory testing.

It would be unusual for action research to deliver fundamentally new theories. Rather, the research insights are likely to link with, and so elaborate, the work of others. The areas in which action researchers choose to work will often be influenced by their interest in the kinds of theory that already exist (or do not exist) in the area. So each intervention provides an opportunity to revisit theory and develop it further (Diesing, 1972). The overall process of theory development is a *continuous cyclic process* in which the combination of the developing theory from the research and implicit pre-understanding informs action, and reflection upon the action informs the theory development. There will be a close interconnection between what may emerge from the data (and indeed what data are used), and what will emerge from the implicit, and explicit, use of theory for driving the intervention (Figure 13.1).

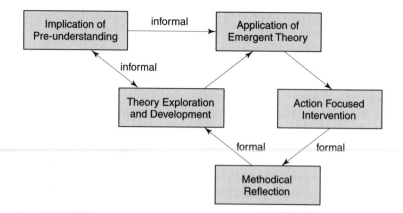

FIGURE 13.1   *The cyclical process of action research*

Thus:

(5) action research will be concerned with a system of *emergent theory*, in which the theory develops from a synthesis of that which emerges from the data and that which emerges from the use in practice of the body of theory which informed the intervention and research intent.

And:

(6) theory-building, as a result of action research, will be incremental, moving through a cycle of developing theory-to-action-to-reflection-to-developing theory from the particular to the general in small steps.

This contrasts with Lewin's argument for hypotheses to be empirically testable. The very richness of the insights that action research should produce and the relative complexity of the theoretical frameworks suggest that it will usually be difficult – even logically impossible – to design experimental situations in which we could be clear about confirmation or disconfirmation (Eden, 1995; Sandford, 1981).

The value of action research can therefore be seen to be in *developing and elaborating theory from practice*. As an aside, developing 'grounded theory' (Glaser, 1992; Glaser and Strauss, 1967; Strauss and Corbin, 1990) is a well-recognized example (but only one of many) of emergent theory-building.

The pragmatic focus of action research

Most of the often referred to writers on action research, including Lewin, demand that it be pragmatic. This is not a criterion which distinguishes action research from consultancy, but one which justifies the use and value of action research rather than other forms of research.

If the practicality criterion is taken seriously, this might be interpreted as suggesting that prescriptive theory is more appropriate than descriptive theory. This is a false dichotomy. Descriptive theory can, and does, seriously influence the actions of the consumer of the research because it does (not necessarily intentionally) highlight the important factors the consumer should be concerned about. For example, descriptive insights about why things go wrong are suggestive of actions that might be taken to avoid problems in similar situations. By implication, descriptive theory also draws attention away from those aspects of the situation that are not included in the description. It is thus, by implication, prescribing one way of accounting for a situation rather than another (Allison, 1971). But if descriptive theory is to be the output of action research it is important that its practical implications be recognized, even if these are presented implicitly. This means that the researcher must recognize that the language, metaphors and value orientation used to present the theory will seriously influence the understanding of the theory in relation to the future thinking and actions of the consumer of the research.

Thus our seventh characteristic is that:

(7) what is important for action research is not a (false) dichotomy between prescription and description, but a recognition that description will be prescription, even if implicitly so. Thus presenters of action research should be clear about what they expect the consumer to take from it and present it with a form and style appropriate to this aim.

THE CHARACTERISTICS OF ACTION RESEARCH *PROCESSES*

Designing action research

In order to be effective in the sort of action research we are concerned with, it is clearly important to be credible as an interventionist. A researcher thus needs to pay a great deal of attention to developing a competent intervention style and process. However, while consultancy skills are an important part of the action research toolkit, they do not, in themselves, justify the activity as *research*. Much more fundamental is *the need to be aware of what must be included in the process of consulting to achieve the research aims*. This, of course, implies being aware of the research aims themselves.

This is not intended to imply that the researcher should have a precise idea – or pre-understanding – of the nature of the research outcome of any intervention at the start, but rather, a strategic intent for the research project. Indeed, since action research will almost always be inductive theory-building research, the really valuable insights are often those that emerge from the consultancy process in ways that cannot be foreseen. Whilst it is legitimate for an action researcher to enter a consultancy interaction with no expectation about what the specific research output will be, it is crucial that an *appropriate degree of reflection* by the researcher is built into the process. This process must include some means of recording both the reflection itself and the method for reflecting.

Action research therefore demands a high degree of *self-awareness* in knitting together the role of the consultant with that of researcher. In addition, researchers must recognize that they not only have the roles of researcher and interventionist, but – because of their role as interventionists – are also a part of the situation that is being researched.

It is also important to consider the role that the client or other participants play in the generation of theory. There are many different levels at which they may be involved, ranging from 'pure subjects' whose aim is to get the benefits of the intervention but have no involvement with the research, to 'full collaborating partners' in the research (Rowan, 1981). Exactly how the roles of the action researcher and the practitioners are played out at any level of involvement can vary, but they need to be thought about and understood.

Designed into any action research programme should thus be a consciousness of the roles to be played by the researcher and the participants and a process of reflection and data collection which is a separate activity – though often connected – to the intervention itself (Figure 13.1). At the least, this demands that extensive amounts of time away from the intervention setting and the 'hands-on' problems be devoted to reflecting about process and data in relation to research issues. The exact nature of the reflection is relatively immaterial – though we may debate the validity of any particular one; what is crucial is that the process exists explicitly. Glaser and Strauss (1967) suggest an appropriate approach to this process of methodical reflection, and Richardson (1994: 526) builds on this approach, suggesting that the time away from the intervention setting is used to record observation notes, methodological notes, theoretical notes and personal notes which are a journal recording of feelings about the research.

Thus our eighth characteristic is that:

(8) for good quality action research a high degree of systematic method and orderliness is required in reflecting about, and holding on to, the research data and the emergent theoretical outcomes of each episode or cycle of involvement in the organization.

Furthermore, and our ninth characteristic,

(9) for action research, the processes of exploration of the data – rather than collection of the data – in the detecting of emergent theories and development of existing theories, must either be replicable or, at least, capable of being explained to others.

Thus, the outcome of data exploration cannot be defended by the role of intuitive understanding alone – any intuition must be informed by a *method of exploration*. In essence this means that compared to 'everyman' as researcher, professional researchers need to be professional.

Towards the closing stages of a project, the design of action research must also acknowledge an important extension of the cycle depicted in Figure 13.1. This is concerned with the process of explication about pre-understanding and the role of writing about research outcomes in a formal manner for theory development (see Figure 13.2). Writing about research outcomes is a 'way of

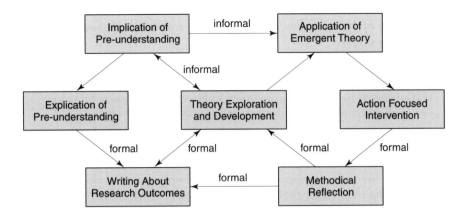

FIGURE 13.2   *The latter stages of an action research project*

"knowing" – a method of discovery and analysis' (Richardson, 1994: 516). It is a *formal process* of integrating the records of methodical reflection, prior theory development and the explication of pre-understanding. At this stage the use of pre-understanding is more formal than the reciprocal influence between the – deliberately suppressed – implicit pre-understanding, and theory exploration and development which has been occurring throughout the project (Figure 13.1). This writing process continues to inform theory exploration and implicit pre-understanding. Also, in this way, action researchers use this cycle to acknowledge to themselves and the consumers of the research that the research process and outcomes were influenced by the researcher's particular pre-understanding.

> (10) The full process of action research involves a series of intercon- nected cycles, where writing about research outcomes at the latter stages of an action research project is an important aspect of theory explo- ration and development, combining the processes of explicating pre-understanding and methodical reflection to explore and develop theory formally.

The validity of action research

We have argued above that action research as intervention does not lend itself to repeatable experimentation; indeed, its distinctive role is played when such experiments are inappropriate. The results of action research lie open to criticism if their validity is judged *solely* by the traditional criteria of positivist social science. Under these circumstances, we would agree with Susman and Evered (1978) that it is likely to fail.

Action researchers therefore need to be keenly aware of the key issues in the validity of action research and that a designed action research process must address these. In this section, we consider what we see as the most important of these.

The validity of action research: adhering to action research as a coherent paradigm

First and foremost, we consider:

(11) adhering to the ten characteristics above is a necessary *but not suffi-cient* condition for the validity of action research.

Without attention to each of these characteristics, an intervention cannot be considered as research at all. These characteristics may thus be thought of as concerned with the *internal validity* of the research *as action research*. By contrast, the remaining topics that we discuss are concerned with *external validity*. That is, they are concerned with the degree to which the results may both be justified as representative of the situation in which they were generated and have claims to generality.

The validity of action research: theory in use

Our second point then stresses the need to be aware that much of action research's validity comes from the theory developed not simply being 'grounded in the data' in Glaser and Strauss' (1967) sense, but being *grounded in action* (cf. characteristic 1). One of the most persuasive reasons for using action research is that when subjects do not have to commit to real action and to creating a future which they will inhabit, any data gained from them is inherently unreliable (Eden, 1995). This is because it is impossible to test whether what people say they would do is what they actually would do if it 'came to the crunch'.

The role of the past, of history, and of the significance of established patterns of social relationships in determining organizational behaviour cannot be overestimated (Vickers, 1983). Reliable data, and hence theories, about both past and future aspects that influence the way in which people change a situation are much more likely to emerge from a research process that is geared to action than from more traditional approaches. This is because it is possible to track what participants actually say and do *in circumstances that really matter to them*, as compared with what they might say hypothetically, or do in controlled circumstances (as for example in the use of students as research subjects acting as if participants in an organization). Using Argyris and Schon's (1974) terms, an action research setting increases the chances of getting at participants' 'theory-in use' rather than their 'espoused theory'. It is in this way that action research can be regarded as action science. The change process provides a forum in which the articulation of complex or normally hidden factors is likely to emerge as well as an incentive to participants for spending time in articulating.

However, in the action research setting there will be forces pushing against, as well as in favour of, the articulation of theories-in-use. Most obviously, it is important to recognize that the intervention will result in organizational change and will challenge the status quo. Inevitably some people will anticipate being disadvantaged by the proposed changes and it is unlikely that the interventionist will gain full trust from all parties (Argyris and Schon, 1991). *The politics of organizational change are thus a force acting against getting fully reliable data from all concerned.*

Yet there are other arguments, not directly linked to the reliability issue, in favour of the action orientation. One important one is the notion that the best way of learning about an organization is by attempting to change it. The very process of change is likely to reveal factors that would not have been unearthed in a stable environment. *The process of change forces a dialectic – a contrast – which helps articulation.* For example, Fineman's (1983) research on unemployed executives probably provided more useful data about the nature of *em*ployment than it did about *un*employment. It was the dialectical experience of unemployment which enabled an understanding and so articulation about the role employment played in the lives of the research subjects.

In summary, we are arguing that while there may be some forces acting against easily getting reliable data through action research, *the method is likely to produce insights that cannot be gleaned in any other way.* This means – as with any kind of research – that it is important to consider explicitly where the kinds of weaknesses and strengths discussed above are likely occur in any particular research situation. But it also means that:

> (12) it is difficult to justify the use of action research when the same aims can be satisfied using approaches (such as controlled experimentation or surveys) that can demonstrate the link between data and outcomes more transparently. Thus, in action research, the reflection and data collection process – and hence the emergent theories – are most valuably focused on the aspects that cannot be captured by other approaches.

This, in turn, suggests that having the knowledge about, and skills to apply, method and analysis procedures for collecting and exploring rich data is essential. A detailed introduction to methods for the analysis of rich data is beyond the scope of this chapter, and has, in any case, been covered in a much more appropriate level of detail by others. The kinds of approaches suggested by Cassell and Symon (1994), Glaser (1992), Miles and Huberman (1984) and Strauss and Corbin (1990) fulfil most of the requirements for a systematic and methodical exploration of data. In addition a form of 'cognitive mapping' along with associated computer software (Decision Explorer) provides an extremely powerful method for 'playing' with the *structure*, as well as content, of qualitative research data (Cropper et al., 1990; Eden and Ackermann, 1998a; Eden et al., 1992). The added advantage of using computer software of this sort is that it can provide a continuous record of the process of play and exploration and so of the emerging theory development.

None of these methods is easy to use; all require a great deal of skill both in applying the analysis to the data and, more significantly, in moving from analysis of the data itself to the more valuable insights and conceptualization that result from discussion of and reflection on the data. The analysis of action research data thus requires craft skills, which take time for an individual researcher to develop, as well as knowledge about specific methods of data analysis.

The validity of action research: triangulation

In the course of the preceding discussion, we have highlighted some concerns about getting at particular 'truths' of situations, rather than 'the truth'. Argyris, Putnam and Smith (1985) also emphasize the difficulty of ensuring that the theories identified by the research process are thoroughly developed or the only theories that could have been developed. Our third topic therefore focuses on *triangulation*.

Triangulation of research data refers to the method of checking its validity by approaching the research question from as many different angles as possible and employing redundancy in data collection (Denzin, 1989). The principle is that if different research approaches lead to the same conclusions our faith in the validity of those conclusions is increased. The analogy with the triangulation process surveyors use to check a sequence of measurements from one point to another is clear. Triangulation is always important in understanding uncertainty in interpretation or measurement.

In part, this is an argument for a multi-method approach to research; Denzin (1978a, 1978b) provides a comprehensive argument for the use of multiple studies where each study acts as a cross-check on others, and so the process of developing reliable conclusions is enhanced. Denzin also argues for triangulation to be applied in five aspects of the research: methodological, data, investigator, theoretical and multiple triangulation.

Triangulation to check the validity of data is as important in action research as in other forms of research. However, action research provides *also* a uniquely different interpretation of the concept of triangulation. Exceptionally, action research provides an opportunity to seek out triangulation between (i) *observation* of events and social processes, (ii) the *accounts* each participant offers and (iii) the changes in these accounts and interpretation of events *as time passes* (Haré and Secord, 1976). From *these* three perspectives *the data are not expected to triangulate* (agree). Indeed, we may be more surprised if they do agree than if they do not given the deliberate attempts at discovering multiple views. This procedure 'underlines the possibilities of multiple, competing perspectives on how organizations are and might be' (Jones, 1987: 45). Importantly a lack of triangulation acts as an effective dialectic for the generation of new concepts. The focus is therefore on what could be rather than what is (Elden and Chisholm, 1993).

Thus triangulation has a different significance for action research compared with using triangulation only as a cross-checking method. Similarly, action research provides the opportunity for *cyclical* data collection through exploiting more continuous and varied opportunities than is occasioned by more controlled research. The chaos and the changing pace and focus of action research are used as a virtue. Thus:

(13) in action research, the opportunities for triangulation that do not offer themselves with other methods should be exploited fully and reported. They should be used as a dialectical device which powerfully facilitates the incremental development of theory.

The validity of action research: the role of history and context

The previous two topics have been largely about external validity in the specific project context. The fourth topic focuses on the problems of generalizing beyond that. It concerns the need to understand and project the role of history and context in deriving research outcomes (Pettigrew, 1985, 1990). Given that action research generally deals with a one-off case study (and hence incurs all the issues inherent in case study research – Yin, 1984):

(14) the history and context for the intervention must be taken as critical to the interpretation of the likely range of validity and applicability of the results of action research.

Identification of the crucial variables that determine the particularity of the context is non-trivial and it is likely that individuals with different experiences and aims would focus in different areas. Discovering history and its relevance is, in any case, more problematic than Pettigrew implies. History, and context, are differently defined by different actors in the situation and by different observers – historians have always recognized the contribution of bias, selectivity and interpretation. Nevertheless, even given these difficulties, *a concern* to understand *the role of* context, and the different interpretations of it, is a most important requirement of action research. Indeed working with *the selective nature of different accounts* of a history of the organization, of the individuals and their relationships with one another and of the wider context within which the research took place, is as important as paying attention to their role.

Exposing action research

So far we have addressed issues in doing action research. Disseminating to the world beyond where the research was undertaken, however, raises a number of additional issues. For example, the seventh characteristic raises an issue about the style of presentation (recognizing the prescriptive aspects of action research). Also the fourteenth characteristic suggests that it is important to consider the possible interpretation of results in the light of history and context. Each of these have specific implications for the style of dissemination of action research. In this section we shall discuss some of the difficulties inherent in writing about action research. Our final characteristic is:

(15) action research requires that the theory development which is of general value is disseminated in such a way as to be of interest to an audience wider than those integrally involved with the action and/or with the research.

The demands we have set out, in the first fourteen characteristics, mean that it is unlikely that action research can be written about fully in anything shorter than a book-type format. Relative to 'straightforward' positivist research, there will always be more to say about the incremental nature of the theory development, about the research method in overall terms as well as the detail of data exploration method, about history and context, and the implications of theory for practice. This is more material than can be contained easily within the confines of an article. An article always leaves many important questions about the status of the research unanswered.

In writing this chapter we have been particularly interested in the difficulty we have had in finding written exemplars of action research that have been explicitly acknowledged by the author to be action research. Most action research sees the light of day through a variety of indirect methods. Clearly, some explanation for this phenomenon can be derived from the circumstances discussed in the above paragraph.

However, we do find many written examples of the outcome of action research. In these instances, we believe – because we have had the opportunity to discuss, in depth, the research process with the authors – that the action research satisfies the majority of our first fourteen characteristics. These examples have in a sense cheated the action research paradigm by disseminating research outcomes in a way that hides the method in a variety of forms of presentation.

Thus one example is the promulgation of action research through the discussion of a methodology for organizational intervention. Here the theoretical framework is explicated as the *raison d'être* for the design of a method, technique, or tool for intervention. In most examples of this way of exposing the outcomes of action research, the authors make no explicit mention of action research as the research paradigm for theory exploration, but exemplify the relationship between theory and practice through technique and tool (our fourth characteristic). It is clear that their technique and tool has been developed in parallel with *theory development through its application* in long sequences of action settings which have been fully researched following an action research procedure. In the United States, Nutt and Backoff (1992) and Bryson (1995) build theory and practice from undeclared action research. In the UK, Checkland (Checkland, 1981; Checkland and Scholes, 1991) and Eden (Eden and Ackermann, 1998b; Eden et al., 1983) follow the 'cycle of developing theory-to-action-to-reflection-to-developing theory from the particular to the general in small steps' (our sixth characteristic).

A second example is where researchers use action research to provide a rich source of examples and *stories to illustrate theory*. For example, Mangham (1979, 1986) has used many projects where he was involved as an organization development consultant as the action research basis for his development and elaboration of 'symbolic interactionism' into a coherent dramaturgical theory. The theory has been more persuasive and more practical because of the rich examples within the text. But nowhere is there acknowledgement of the role played by action research, conducted in a manner that would meet most of the standards established here, in the written outcome.

CONCLUSION

The standards we have set for action research to be considered as *research* (pulled together in Table 13.1), are undoubtedly hard to achieve.

TABLE 13.1   *The 15 characteristics of action research*

(1)   Action research demands an integral involvement by the researcher in an intent to change the organization. This intent may not succeed – no change may take place as a result of the intervention – and the change may not be as intended.

(2)   Action research must have some *implications beyond those required for action or generation of knowledge in the domain of the project*. It must be possible to envisage talking about the theories developed in relation to other situations. Thus it must be clear that the results *could* inform other contexts, at least in the sense of suggesting areas for consideration.

(3)   As well as being usable in everyday life, action research demands *valuing theory*, with theory elaboration and development as an explicit concern of the research process.

(4)   If the generality drawn out of the action research is to be expressed through the design of tools, techniques, models and methods then this, alone, is not enough – the basis for their design must be explicit and shown to be related to the theories which inform the design and which, in turn, are supported or developed through action research.

(5)   Action research will be concerned with a system of *emergent theory*, in which the theory develops from a synthesis of that which emerges from the data and that which emerges from the use in practice of the body of theory which informed the intervention and research intent.

(6)   Theory-building, as a result of action research, will be incremental, moving through a cycle of developing theory-to-action-to-reflection-to-developing theory from the particular to the general in small steps.

(7)   What is important for action research is not a (false) dichotomy between prescription and description, but a recognition that description will be prescription, even if implicitly so. Thus presenters of action research should be clear about what they expect the consumer to take from it and present it with a form and style appropriate to this aim.

(8)   For good quality action research a high degree of systematic method and orderliness is required in reflecting about, and holding on to, the research data and the emergent theoretical outcomes of each episode or cycle of involvement in the organization.

(9)   For action research, the processes of exploration of the data – rather than collection of the data – in the detecting of emergent theories and development of existing theories, must either be replicable or, at least, capable of being explained to others.

(10)   The full process of action research involves a series of interconnected cycles, where writing about research outcomes at the latter stages of an action research project is an important aspect of theory exploration and development, combining the processes of explicating pre-understanding and methodical reflection to explore and develop theory formally.

(11)   Adhering to the ten characteristics above is a necessary *but not sufficient* condition for the validity of action research.

(12)   It is difficult to justify the use of action research when the same aims can be satisfied using approaches (such as controlled experimentation or surveys) that can demonstrate the link between data and outcomes more transparently. Thus in action research, the reflection and data collection process – and hence the emergent theories – are most valuably focused on the aspects that cannot be captured by other approaches.

(13)   In action research, the opportunities for triangulation that do not offer themselves with other methods should be exploited fully and reported. They should be used as a dialectical device which powerfully facilitates the incremental development of theory.

(14)   The history and context for the intervention must be taken as critical to the interpretation of the likely range of validity and applicability of the results of action research.

(15)   Action research requires that the theory development which is of general value is disseminated in such a way as to be of interest to an audience wider than those integrally involved with the action and/or with the research.

Understanding the methodological issues involved in action research in practice is difficult and must be expected to take time and experience – action research is an imprecise, uncertain and sometimes unstable activity compared to many other approaches to research. Enacting the standards in practice demands holistic attention to all the issues. Given the complexity and pressure of the real world action research setting, this provides a major challenge. Indeed, it is probably not an achievable challenge, though this should neither deter researchers from trying to achieve the standards nor, worse perhaps, from using action research at all. For ourselves we are not convinced that our own research has fully satisfied the standards we have set. However, what is important is having a sense of the standards that make for good action research and evaluating the research in relation to them.

Action research is also challenging for two further reasons: first, the uncertainty and lack of control create anxiety for anyone other than confident and experienced researchers; and secondly, doing *action* in action research demands experience and understanding of methods for consultancy and intervention. This second challenge suggests the need to face up to conceptual issues about the nature of problems in organizations and the concomitant demands for change, the nature of a client-centred activity, the issues involved in building and sustaining a consultant–client relationship, and so the nature of power and politics in the context of intervention.

Study questions

1 Take a recent 'research' project (or an MBA project, or undergraduate final project) and score yourself against each of the 15 characteristics of action research identified in the chapter (see Table 13.1). Then reflect on the relationship between the characteristics of your research and those of action research.
2 Take a piece of published research that is clearly positivist in nature and then explore the contributions that might have arisen if the work had been undertaken from an action research perspective. Also consider the disadvantages of so doing.
3 Identify a 'consultancy' project and consider what would have needed to be done for the project to be a high quality action research project.

Recommended further reading

Eden, C. and Huxham, C. (1996) 'Action research for the study of organizations', in S. Clegg, C. Hardy and W. Nord (eds), *Handbook of Organization Studies*. Beverly Hills, CA: Sage (see esp. the section entitled 'A Contextual Perspective'). (It is important to note that the current chapter represents a distinctly different view of action research than that represented by many other authors. This section places our view of action research within the context of history, alternative interpretations and related concepts)

Huxham, C. (2001) 'The New Public Management: An Action Research Approach', in K. McLaughlin, S. Osborne and E. Ferlie (eds), *The New Public Management: Current Trends and Future Prospects*. London: Routledge. (A case study of action research which demonstrates one approach to intervention, data collection and theory-building)

Checkland, P. and Holwell, S. (1998) 'Action Research: Its Nature and Validity', *Systems Practice*, 11 (1), pp. 9–21. (Another related perspective that emphasizes the concept of 'recoverability' of the research for application to other areas)

Eisenhardt, K. (1989) 'Building Theories from Case Study Research', *Academy of Management Review*, 14 (4), pp. 532–50. (Not action research, but Eisenhardt elucidates a process for building emergent theory)

Note

Abridged from C. Eden and C. Huxham (1996) 'Action Research for the Study of Organizations', in S. Clegg, C. Hardy and W. Nord (eds), *Handbook of Organization Studies*. Beverly Hills, CA: Sage.

References

Aguinis, H. (1993) 'Action Research and Scientific Method: Presumed Discrepancies and Actual Similarities', *Journal of Applied Behavioral Science*, 29, pp. 416–31.

Alderfer, C.P. (1993) 'Emerging Developments in Action Research', *Journal of Applied Behavioral Science*, Special Issue, 29 (4).

Allison, G.T. (1971) *Essence of Decision: Explaining the Cuban Missile Crisis*. Boston, MA: Little, Brown and Co.

Argyris, C. and Schon, D.A. (1974) *Theories in Practice*. San Francisco: Jossey–Bass.

Argyris, C. and Schon, D.A. (1991) 'Participatory Action Research and Action Science Compared: A Commentary', in W.F. Whyte (ed.), *Participatory Action Research*. London: Sage, pp. 85–96.

Argyris, C., Putnam, R. and Smith, D.M. (1985) *Action Science*. San Francisco: Jossey–Bass.

Bryson, J. (1995) *Strategic Planning for Public and Nonprofit Organizations*, rev. edn. San Francisco: Jossey–Bass.

Cassell, C. and Symon, G. (1994) *Qualitative Methods in Organisational Research: A Practical Guide*. London: Sage.

Checkland, P. (1981) *Systems Thinking, Systems Practice*. London: Wiley.

Checkland, P. and Scholes, J. (1991) *Soft Systems Methodology in Action*. New York: Wiley.

Cropper, S., Eden, C. and Ackermann, F. (1990) 'Keeping Sense of Accounts Using Computer-based Cognitive Maps', *Social Science Computer Review*, 8, pp. 345–66.

Denzin, N.K. (1978a) *The Research Act: A Theoretical Introduction to Sociological Methods*, 2nd edn. New York: McGraw–Hill.

Denzin, N.K. (1978b) *Sociological Methods: A Sourcebook*, 2nd edn. New York: McGraw–Hill.

Denzin, N.K. (1989) *The Research Act*, 3rd edn. Englewood Cliffs, NJ: Prentice Hall.

Denzin, N.K. and Lincoln, Y.S. (eds) (1994) *Handbook of Qualitative Research*. Thousand Oaks, CA: Sage.

Diesing, P. (1972) *Patterns of Discovery in the Social Sciences*. London: Routledge & Kegan Paul.

Eden, C. (1995) 'On the Evaluation of "Wide-Band" GDSS's', *European Journal of Operational Research*, 81, pp. 302–11.

Eden, C. and Ackermann, F. (1998a) 'Analysing and Comparing Idiographic Cause Maps', in C. Eden and J.C. Spender (eds), *Managerial and Organizational Cognition*. London: Sage, pp. 192–209.

Eden, C. and Ackermann, F. (1998b) *Making Strategy: The Journey of Strategic Management*. London: Sage.

Eden, C., Ackermann, F. and Cropper, S. (1992) 'The Analysis of Cause Maps', *Journal of Management Studies*, 29, pp. 309–24.

Eden, C., Jones, S. and Sims, D. (1983) *Messing About in Problems*. Pergamon: Oxford.

Elden, M. (1979) 'Three Generations of Work Democracy Experiments in Norway', in C. Cooper and E. Mumford (eds), *The Quality of Work in Eastern and Western Europe*. London: Associated Business Press.

Elden, M. and Chisholm, R.F. (1993) 'Emergent Varieties of Action Research: Introduction to the Special Issue', *Human Relations*, 46, 121–42.

Elden, M. and Levin, M. (1991) 'Cogenerative Learning: Bringing Participation into Action Research', in W.F. Whyte (ed.), *Participatory Action Research*. London: Sage, pp. 127–42.

Fineman, S. (1983) *White Collar Unemployment: Impact and Stress*. London: Wiley.

Friedlander, F. and Brown, D. (1974) 'Organization Development', *Annual Review of Psychology*, 25, pp. 313–41.

Glaser, B.G. (1992) *Basics of Grounded Theory*. Mill Valley, CA: Sociology Press.

Glaser, B.G. and Strauss, A.L. (1967) *The Discovery of Grounded Theory*. Chicago: Aldine.

Gummesson, E. (1991) *Qualitative Methods in Management Research*. London: Sage.

Haré, R. and Secord, P.F. (1976) *The Explanation of Social Behaviour*. Oxford: Blackwell.

Jones, S. (1987) 'Choosing Action Research', in I.L. Mangham (ed.), *Organisation Analysis and Development: A Social Construction of Organisational Behaviour*. London: Wiley.

Lewin, K. (1946) 'Action Research and Minority Problems', *Journal of Social Issues*, 2, pp. 34–46.

Lewin, K. (1947) 'Frontiers in Group Dynamics: Channel of Group Life: Social Planning and Action Research', *Human Relations*, 1, pp. 143–53.

Mangham, I.L (1979) *The Politics of Organizational Change*. London: Associated Business Press.

Mangham, I.L. (1986) *Power and Performance in Organizations*. Oxford: Blackwell.

Miles, M.B. and Huberman, A.M. (1984) *Qualitative Data Analysis: A Sourcebook of New Methods*. London: Sage.

Nutt, P. and Backoff, R. (1992) *Strategic Management of Public and Third Sector Organizations*. San Francisco: Jossey–Bass.

Pettigrew, A.M. (1985) *The Awakening Giant*. Oxford: Blackwell.

Pettigrew, A.M. (1990). 'Longitudinal Field Research on Change Theory and Practice', *Organisation Science*, 1, pp. 267–92.

Reason, P. (ed.) (1988) *Human Inquiry in Action*. London: Sage.

Reason, P. and Rowan, J. (eds) (1981) *Human Inquiry. A Sourcebook of New Paradigm Research*. Chichester: Wiley.

Richardson, L. (1994) 'Writing: A Method of Inquiry', in N.K. Denzin and Y.S. Lincoln (eds), *Handbook of Qualitative Research*. Thousand Oaks, CA: Sage.

Rowan, J. (1981) 'A Dialectical Paradigm for Research', in P. Reason and J. Rowan (eds), *Human Inquiry. A Sourcebook of New Paradigm Research*. Chichester: Wiley, pp. 93–112.

Sandford, N. (1981) 'A Model for Action Research', in P. Reason and J. Rowan (eds), *Human Inquiry. A Sourcebook of New Paradigm Research*. Chichester: Wiley, pp. 173–82.

Strauss, A. and Corbin, J. (1990) *Basics of Qualitative Research*. London: Sage.

Susman, G.I. and Evered, R.D. (1978) 'An Assessment of the Scientific Merits of Action Research', *Administrative Science Quarterly*, 23, pp. 582–603.

Vickers, G. (1983) *The Art of Judgement*. London: Harper and Row.

Whyte, W.F. (ed.) (1991) *Participatory Action Research*. London: Sage.

Yin, R. (1984) *Case Study Research: Design and Methods*. Thousand Oaks, CA: Sage.

Index

Index compiled by Indexing Specialists